Radical Botany

Radical Botany

Plants and Speculative Fiction

Natania Meeker and Antónia Szabari

FORDHAM UNIVERSITY PRESS

New York 2020

Fordham University Press gratefully acknowledges financial assistance and support provided for the publication of this book by the University of Southern California.

Copyright © 2020 Fordham University Press

All rights reserved. No part of this publication may be reproduced, stored in a retrieval system, or transmitted in any form or by any means—electronic, mechanical, photocopy, recording, or any other—except for brief quotations in printed reviews, without the prior permission of the publisher.

Fordham University Press has no responsibility for the persistence or accuracy of URLs for external or third-party Internet websites referred to in this publication and does not guarantee that any content on such websites is, or will remain, accurate or appropriate.

Fordham University Press also publishes its books in a variety of electronic formats. Some content that appears in print may not be available in electronic books.

Visit us online at www.fordhampress.com.

Library of Congress Cataloging-in-Publication Data available online at https://catalog.loc.gov.

Printed in the United States of America

22 21 20   5 4 3 2 1

First edition

CONTENTS

Preface vii

1. Radical Botany: An Introduction 1
2. Libertine Botany and Vegetal Modernity 28
3. Plant Societies and Enlightened Vegetality 56
4. The Inorganic Plant in the Romantic Garden 86
5. The End of the World by Other Means 114
6. Plant Horror: Love Your Own Pod 144
7. Becoming Plant Nonetheless 171

Acknowledgments 203
Notes 205
Works Cited 253
Index 269

PREFACE

Radical Botany is the story of a series of imagined allegiances between plants and humans—a speculative form of collaboration across and within modes of being. This book was born out of a collaborative practice that is not the norm in U.S. scholarship in the humanities today, although it is more common in other fields and places. As coauthors, we began to explore together the uneasy alliances and ambivalent attachments that plants make with humans, and humans with plants, at the same time that we embarked on the process of working together. Collaborative thinking, writing, and reading shaped the production of this book just as collaborative acts have shaped its many subjects.

With our book, we affirm that there is a vegetal dimension to the practice of collaboration. While experimenting concretely with that practice, we were forced to accept that our work process and its outcome were no longer tied to an individual sense of self, nor did they affirm our limits or boundaries as individual scholars. An emphasis on collaboration—which poses a challenge to individuated modes of thinking and being—is also present in some of the key moments in the development of radical botany as a way of relating to plant life. Most notable in the contemporary context is perhaps Gilles Deleuze and Félix Guattari's work on the rhizome, a radical botanical figure if there ever was one.

Commenting on their 1972 book *Anti-Oedipus*, Deleuze writes: "We no longer knew who had written what."[1] Elsewhere, he elaborates: "We were more like two streams coming together to make a third stream, which I suppose was us."[2] We can attest to the kind of confluence that collaborative writing allows; there are precious few sentences or ideas in this book that have not been produced jointly, and practically all of its elements have been jostled back and forth between us in the process of writing. Deleuze and Guattari protest eloquently against the idea that intellectual creation happens in the inner sanctum of one mind, or necessarily takes the shape of a unified system of thought. They jettison this neo-Platonist conception of the creative process in favor of a more fluid model of dynamic intermingling. At the same time, the image of the stream or flow elides some of the discontinuities and discomfort that working together can entail, as was the case for Deleuze and Guattari, too, the metaphor of confluence notwithstanding.[3] For our part, we would like to pause to consider the pragmatic dimensions of the collaborative process, noting that cowriting is a way of putting to work many differences, including in writing and thinking styles, backgrounds, institutional positions, gendered identities, constraints on time, and teaching schedules.

Collaborative work and play occur regularly, perhaps more often than we realize, in daily life, among friends and family, as well as in the biological world where different living (and nonliving) entities can and do join forces. Because it entails the pooling of resources and forging of allegiances to make things happen, collaboration is sometimes the best way to realize a project that perhaps could not come about otherwise. This condition certainly applies to this book. In our case, the collaborative work takes the place of the single-minded effort of the individual, who no longer realizes a vision for which she alone bears responsibility and over which she alone has ownership (although such visions are themselves made possible by the support of many others). But this act of conjoining entails a quotidian effort to work through differences and dissimilarities. The final piece of writing may resemble a continuous flow in which distinctions among voices and positions all but disappear, but the writers themselves never merge. Generating the text entails coping with this multiplicity, which is at the same time its most important source of inspiration.

Collaboration is often born out of necessity. It also introduces the possibility of noncompetitive work in an institutional space increasingly defined by quantification, scarcity of resources for humanistic research, and intense competition for those resources that remain. The structures of the modern university all too often do not protect those who inhabit them from exploitation; on the contrary, they regularly enable it. Yet, collaboration does not put an end to inequity. In geobiologist Hope Jahren's literary memoir, *Lab Girl*, one of the books that inspired *Radical Botany*, the author, a tenured professor, describes in detail her collaboration with her lab manager Bill Hagopian (who for the most part does not enjoy the privilege of stable employment). Jahren eloquently outlines the need for shared work in a time of scarce funding for scientific research, time-consuming application processes, increasing reliance on contingent and exploited academic labor, and gender discrimination. She also shows how such collaboration is inevitably affected by structural inequality. Outside and within the institutional context, Jahren speaks to the impact of seemingly personal circumstances, including disability, on scholarship and institutional positions. While our academic status is a highly privileged one—we are both tenured professors—we nonetheless count ourselves lucky to have found a space of relative equity in this project.

As two women working on a collaborative endeavor that engages with the richness, diversity, and importance of plant life, both materially and theoretically, we are also conscious of the long history of women's particular relationship to botany and the attachments they have forged with the vegetal world. Women have long collaborated with plants in ways that were regularly unacknowledged or underrecognized. In eighteenth-century Europe, women often worked with men to produce botanical scholarship, although just as often they were not credited in their roles as illustrators, researchers, and technicians. At the same time, the history of botanical writing involves many notable women who, in their contacts with plants, revealed the vastness and power of the seemingly mute—and often small—beings to which they devoted a life's work. In this context, women such as Maria Sibylla Merian (1647–1717), Madeleine Françoise Basseporte (1701–1780), Katherine Esau (1898–1997), and Barbara McClintock (1902–1992), among many others, are inspirations to us, in their fascination with and dedication to plants and plant life.

As our work progressed, we discovered how the process of collaboration between humans might resonate with the process of crafting alliances between plants and people that *Radical Botany* charts. The emergent field of critical plant studies abounds with examples of this resonance, including in the writing of Hope Jahren, Donna Haraway, Carla Hustak and Natasha Myers, and Luce Irigaray and Michael Marder.

Yet we began thinking about the ideas in this book before critical plant studies had taken shape, at a moment when the plant was only beginning to become an academic object of interest. Since that time, the importance of ecocritique in its many variants, and of reckoning with climate crisis, has become ever more clear. The plant has moved front and center in a particular critical discourse, and has even become an object of academic fashion. The slow genesis of this project has helped us examine this "plant turn" from a certain distance, as has our training as early modernists. The plant has a presence in human life that obviously predates critical plant studies; it has often been a figure to which humans have had recourse. Still, we argue in this book that modernity itself gives rise to and invokes a particularly ambivalent (albeit productive) relation to the plant.

We thus strive in *Radical Botany* to think genealogically about the relationship of early modern botany, among other areas of human endeavor, to the present. Conversely, we remain interested in the plant not just as a philosophical concept, or even as a political one, but as part of a lived experience that is variegated and poetic and often strange, and that has changed over time. Our collaboration has helped us follow both of these strands of inquiry through a longer timeline than either of us would have been able to take on alone. We test Deleuze and Guattari's famous motto—"follow the plants"—and their even more famous concept of the rhizome, born out of 1968 and left-wing protest. But we do so by showing that there is an extensive history to what could otherwise seem to be a particularly trippy political slogan. We argue for their rootedness in a materialist tradition in which plants have been regularly used as figures for thinking about, and critiquing, social and political ideals.

In the present-day context of decentralization and deregulation of market forces—their deterritorialization, in other words—we can say that Deleuze and Guattari's rhizome not only responds to the past but anticipates a future in which the kind of resistance that was the hallmark of their work and writing becomes all but impossible, "a world," as Adam Shatz puts it, "which neither of them would have wanted to live in."[4] In what way are plants still our allies, as many of the radical botanists we study suggest? How can they be engaged as such? We want to explore what the many human attachments to plants have given rise to, in terms of thought and works of art, but we also want to think about the points of resistance and reluctance, the moments in which plants refuse to respond. These moments are also life-changing, for us as well as for our vegetal interlocutors.

The experience of plants as not only objects of study, contemplation, and classification but as living beings, with all their quirks and stubbornness, is perhaps a familiar one for both scientists and gardeners, who regularly come up against the unwillingness of plants to fit into the spaces and categories they make for them, even as they work to mold them into particular shapes and meanings. For theorists of the plant, as we are, it can be harder to keep in mind this vegetal recalcitrance. But we want here not only to foreground the plant in the way it does *not* meet or bend to our expectations but to honor this resistance as a necessary element of truly generative collaboration. In this sense, our own collaboration—with its stops and starts, hesitations and forward movement—serves as a daily if not hourly reminder of the positive effects of difference, even or especially when this difference refuses to be resolved into a seamless unity.

As other critics before us have emphasized, plants provide us with a mode of being that is neither individuated nor autonomous but collective, swarming, multiple. Our attachments to plants and our relationships with them challenge our notions of self and other, subject and object, activity and passivity—often in ways that we ourselves find disturbing and troubling. But, just as often, in ways that are joyful, enlivening, transformative.

Radical Botany

CHAPTER 1

Radical Botany: An Introduction

Do Plants Speculate?

Plants are alive, yet they do not present us with the same impression of life that animals do. Are we, as the victims of plant blindness, simply unable to notice their liveliness, or are they so different from us that we have to invent new ways of seeing and apprehending them?[1] *Radical Botany* uncovers a long speculative tradition that conjures up new languages to grasp the life of plants in all its specificity and vigor. In this book, we study the invention and dissemination of forms of mediation that bring plant sciences into relation with the arts in order to posit plants as the model for all animate life. Their way of being is material and nonanthropomorphic, yet profoundly generative for human thought and practice.

Radical Botany begins in seventeenth-century France with the gradual development of a botanically oriented thought that accords power and vitality to vegetal life in ways that trouble orthodox modes of classification. At the same time, this corpus recognizes the withdrawal of plants and their animated materiality from human society and ethics. Offshoots of this tradition wend their way into the twenty-first century, moving through different historical periods and cultural frameworks and gradually taking on global significance. In a context where modernity is often equated with the exploitation and brutalization of nature, the authors, critics, filmmakers, and theorists whose works we study here present us with an understanding of vegetality as driving the production of technology, scientific knowledge, and new media forms. This is radical botany, in which plants are not just objects of manipulation but participants in the effort to imagine new worlds and to envision new futures.

Classically, the botanical sciences that develop over the course of the long eighteenth century function as a project for ordering, visualizing, labeling, and classifying life.[2] In *Radical Botany*, we unearth an alternative set of engagements with the plant as a life-form—a tradition that conceives of vegetal life as resisting representability even as it participates in the production of new representational modes, including the novel, early cinema, and contemporary virtual reality, and new affects,[3] including queer desires, feminist affinities, and ecological solidarities. These texts and images do not or *do not just* anthropomorphize or zoomorphize plants in order to explore their ways of living otherwise. Even as the past four centuries of scientific research have enhanced our knowledge of vegetal physiology and biology, it is difficult for us to experience plants as fully alive. While animals (including human ones) are regularly portrayed by us moderns as full of hidden worlds, plants do not so much appear to hide an interiorized subjectivity as they compel us to imagine an ingeniously animated and animating matter that we are never able to observe in all its operations. Within this framework, the plant becomes capable of unleashing speculative energies for envisioning and indeed participating in the world as other than it may appear to us. At the same time, plant life does not somehow remain outside of modernity or inherently in opposition to the forces that structure it. Plants do not represent an opportunity for escape from exploitation or a direct or unproblematic outlet for utopian fantasy. Rather, they oblige us to come to terms with our own vulnerability in the face of processes of ecological, social, political, and intellectual change, and, often, with our profound, complex dependence on the very forms of life that we are least inclined (or simply unable) to acknowledge.

Radical Botany begins in early modernity and concludes with our contemporary period, which we are calling here late modern, in part to underscore the connection to what has come before. In seventeenth-century France, an eclectic materialist thought, inspired by Epicurean atomism, corpuscularianism, and alchemy, seizes upon the plant as a technology for animating bodies and for creating pleasures in the encounter with vegetality. Libertine botanists such as Guy de La Brosse (1586–1641) and libertine authors such as Savinien Cyrano de Bergerac (1619–1655) find an opening to the cosmos in the humble garden plant, which becomes a device for mediating the animatedness of matter, including the human body, to human observers who struggle to see or otherwise sense it adequately. As part of his dream of a new kind of garden, La Brosse invokes the plant as a percipient, desiring, and mobile being. Some years later, in the process of crafting his otherworldly fictions, Cyrano invents the tongue-in-cheek image of "speculative" plants. In so doing, he not only pokes fun at Scholastic theologians who arrogate the position of active speculation to human beings but also contributes to a mode of thought that is both materially constituted and materialist, visually productive yet at odds with human capacities for sight and rationality. This kind of speculation does not prioritize intellection as the power to grasp higher metaphysical entities; instead, it highlights ingenious ways that we might imaginatively encounter what remains beyond our direct apprehension.

In the seventeenth and eighteenth centuries, the investigation of plant life serves to generate hypotheses about the nature of matter and, by extension, the order of the cosmos. Vegetal bodies become a kind of experimental laboratory through which atoms, corpuscles, "cylinders," and other invisible particles in motion might be imagined, studied, and perhaps understood. The works we have chosen to analyze here allow us to trace a genealogy of radical botany in which it is the animated materiality of the plant that first enables speculation about its mode of being, which in turn allows new experiences of embodiment to arise from the encounter with vegetal matter. The plant body is an active presence in this early modern materialist tradition, and its peculiar vitality continues to inform modern and late modern literature, cinema, art, and the twenty-first century's various virtual realities. It circulates transatlantically and transnationally.

The philosophically oriented corpus from the seventeenth and eighteenth centuries with which our book begins provides a persistent source of inspiration for speculative and botanically inclined thought. We investigate the extensive, ongoing connections among science, literature, and art that this tradition generates. The writings and other artworks that we analyze are rarely studied as a group but are nonetheless linked together in a common project that takes seriously the effects of plants, and their specific life, on the social, cultural, and political world of humans. By highlighting a current in French materialist thought that cuts across the domains of philosophy, literature, art, and film, influencing other national and cultural contexts in the process, we also engage in an examination of how this radical botany differs from a prominent tradition of botanizing that is more tightly linked to Anglophone and Germanophone textual production. In this vein, we turn away from some of the central assumptions of a Romantic tradition that combines an interest in species-specific traits of plants with a desire to find in plants a mode of being that is responsive to human ethical or social investments and thus stresses the close affinity of humans and plants. Romanticism, with a double emphasis on the alterity of plants on the one hand and their possible inclusion in human visions and endeavors on the other, has served as a frequent and highly productive point of reference for those who wish to think about the rise of contemporary theories of the environment, even as the Romantic attitude has received strong criticism for reifying nature as "a mirror of our mind," as Timothy Morton puts it.[4] This is particularly true of a strand of British Romanticism that finds in the plant an intensely vibrant and capacious figure for exploring the interface between humans and the natural world. The contemporary critical thought that might be called "new Romantic" continues to dream of a fusional relation to the plant as a counter to the violence done by modern economic systems, politics, and culture; the plant's radical lack of zoomorphic qualities, its resistance to anthropomorphic analogies, and its lack of interiority all paradoxically incite a desire to include it in the human world.[5] Under this lens, through the call for greater attention to vegetal life, the plant seems to become our companion, an ethical and sympathetic interlocutor that is not only worthy of consideration in our worldly calculations but that may indeed outlive us.[6]

Radical Botany reaches back to the pre-Romantic era to show how plants, rather than being systematically excluded from human deliberation, have, in fact, participated in what we call modernity, of which the aims even come to imitate those of the plant in certain respects. The French authors with whom our work begins approach plants as instantiations of a materiality that includes humans but does not prioritize them; they turn to plants as a way to think through the problems and paradoxes that face all forms of life considered first as matter. Within this framework, plants are ascribed an agency and vitality that might otherwise seem foreign to them, but they are also envisioned in their radical impassivity vis-à-vis human demands and concerns, as beings that resist incorporation into human contexts and thus oblige humans to confront their own status as both vulnerable and powerful components of an expanding universe. The radical botanical works we explore not only prioritize plants as active participants in "their" world but suggest that the apparent passivity of plants can function as a powerful, destabilizing force in its own right.

During the Romantic era, radical botanists respond to intensifying efforts to establish the interconnectedness of all life-forms by positing the idea of a plant life that remains fully indifferent to human reason and ethics yet also profoundly imbricated in human experience. For them, the plant has not been waiting to be included in or domesticated by human projects but rather has generated and continues to produce effects in humans that oblige us to call into question our own distinctiveness and authority. The plant invades and saturates human consciousness—even as it remains wholly unconcerned with its effects on us. We follow the (sometimes subterranean) movement of a radical botanical tradition through western Europe in the eighteenth century and eventually into North America in the nineteenth, when Edgar Allan Poe is inspired by the idea of a "sentience of all vegetable things" that is based on Enlightenment analogies and speculations even as it threatens to undo these modes of thought. While in certain cases the authors and artists we discuss are directly inspired by one another, we are not tracing a genetic inheritance or direct lines of influence, nor are we identifying a dynamics of intertextual imitation and rivalry. Instead, we excavate an assemblage of literary and cinematic narratives that lends primacy to vegetality as a mode of being and that continues to generate new iterations in what are now global contexts. We trace a history that is halting and reluctant but remains vital nonetheless in its capacity to be reactivated at different times and places.

Historians have emphasized the importance of botany in western Europe, from about the sixteenth century through the eighteenth, as a means of subjecting plant life to a visual regime of classification and categorization, thereby making plants into what Michel Foucault has called a limpid object of knowledge.[7] Within this framework, Romantic vitalism is thought to intervene in the ongoing transformation of plants into passive objects of observation, classification, and aesthetic manipulation by stressing their vigorous and specific life. In the nineteenth century, the discovery of photosynthesis in the sciences works in tandem with the personification of plants in poetry in order to attribute new forms of agency to plant life now perceived as strangely unlike animal life. *Radical Botany*, however, traces a different trajectory in which the exceptional activity—and power—of plants is assumed at the outset in a speculative process in which plants are coparticipants. Their vitality is not the product of a particular scientific (human) understanding of the plant. Our turn to the plant is thus a return to a materialist poetics and philosophy with specific (but by no means exclusive) ties to Francophone works of science (early modern and modern), fiction, theory, and film that give pride of place to plants in their efforts to define life under modernity. This corpus imagines plants as animate, animated, or animating matter and gives shape to a series of speculative experiments that seek to understand plants as participating in our mediated worlds and our modes of self-determination. It suggests that both vegetal liveliness and vegetal impassivity have profound effects on human life, and it foregrounds the exposure of humans to the vegetal and material forces that often overwhelm them. Radical botany puts plants at the forefront of its theories of life and living; it suggests options for survival but does not guarantee them. As a fictional, cinematic, or otherwise mediatized production of vegetal life, one in which plants themselves emerge as the medium in which subjects take shape, it embraces a view of modernity as both disastrous and generative in the new kinds of contingency that it permits. In its approach to the plant as a figure for the animation of matter in general, radical botany allows us to think the calamity (for us) of human insignificance together with the intensity of our desire for recognition and the dream of multispecies attachments and solidarities.

In the nineteenth century, radical botany confronts the Romantic desiring plant with a percipient vegetal life that is powerful, disturbing, and ultimately indifferent to humans. In the early twentieth century, the speculative energies unleashed by the plant are reanimated once again with the use of time-lapse photography. Modern cinema, especially the minor genre we call "plant horror," envisions the posthuman future as profoundly vegetal. In the twenty-first century, feminist, new materialist, and environmentalist authors continue to venture into encounters with mediated vegetal identities to highlight the material and historical underpinnings of gendered subjectivities that are both virtual and deeply felt and to conjure a possible future for life in crisis. Once again, a speculative tradition with its emphasis on newly vibrant materialities and bodies makes it possible to think how becoming plant can disassemble and reassemble us. Taken together, these modes of speculation are not "just" another form of fiction—or the anthropomorphic projection of human and animal qualities onto the plant. Instead, we read these radical botanical narratives as the result of the gap between our perceived world and that of plants.

We show how plants have inspired materialist thought that prioritizes plant life in both its indifference to humans and its fascinating animacy[8] and situates plants not just on the receiving end of technologies but also as agents that can inspire technological change. These projects are part of the development of a *vegetal* modernity, one whose figures might include seeds that model animate matter, the "electric plants" of time-lapse film and photography, and transgenic and interspecies life. In making these claims, we do not implicitly endorse practices of logging, deforestation, genetic modification, or the production of immersive CGI (computer-generated imagery) that promise that technology can provide remedies for the very harm it does. Instead, we argue that it is only by acknowledging plants' participation in the modern period (from early to late) that we can open up speculative possibilities to reject their mere instrumentalization. We examine a tradition in which plants (and the technologies that both reveal them to us and are engendered with and by them) are granted, albeit playfully and in fiction, the power of resistance to the objectification and instrumentalization to which all forms of life are increasingly subjected. But this resistance is not necessarily a source of emancipation or renewed vitality for the humans who encounter it. Plants are troubling in their seeming passivity, and in their indifference to our needs and ends. As beings that cannot fully be incorporated into our frameworks for understanding or recognizing life, agency, and subjectivity, they oscillate between soliciting our interest and refusing to ratify our concerns. Nonetheless, plants have power, at least within the speculative fictions that invoke them and in the scientific thought that remains in conversation with these fictions. Their peculiar way of being inspires new media for entering into contact with them and new forms of enjoyment and terror, often both at once. *Radical Botany* explores the contradictions and tensions that emerge from a prioritization of plant life by and for humans; our focus on the vegetal presence in modernity underscores the latter's development as a jagged and discontinuous line of speculative possibilities. Plants make available to our imagination a life that continues without humans or renders the human unidentifiable to itself. Throughout, vegetality becomes a propulsive force, as humans are moved by anxiety about our own survival, a desire for companionship, and both delight in and horror at our own insignificance.

If we extend our genealogy beyond early modernity, it is because the pre-Romantic materialist fascination with the plant continues to cut through and reshape the attitudes that dominate the vegetal imaginary of the nineteenth, twentieth, and twenty-first centuries. In this sense, we diverge from the argument made by T. S. Miller that the various forms of plant horror, which become commonplace in the twentieth century, express a fear of the enmeshment of human and vegetal life as a response to Darwinian theories of evolution and common descent.[9] Instead, we see the problem of what will become, in our current theoretical era, lively matter or transcorporeality (to use Stacy Alaimo's term[10]) posed at the beginning of the modern period in a way that both critiques and enables the development of this modernity. Speculative plant fiction and film show us how what has been called new materialism finds affinities with an older materialist tradition that takes the plant as its key animating figure. The corpus we explore stresses the limitations of a model of plant-human interaction based on desire or language or indeed any recognizably human qualities to suggest both that we are not the only agents of this encounter and that we ourselves may be vegetal, in the sense that our desiring subjectivity may be an illusion or a contingent historical artifact.[11]

Plant Studies and Thinking with Plants

In posing the question of how to encounter and acknowledge plants in their difference from us, we find ourselves squarely within the double bind that, as Dominique Brancher has shown, already characterizes the early modern relationship to vegetality. Either the plant is regarded as primarily an object of knowledge and thus objectified remains inaccessible in its alterity, or the plant is granted the capacities that are shared by animals and humans, which results in a kind of misrecognition of its "true" nature, destined to be formulated in human terms that are foreign to it.[12] How is it possible to understand the plant without deliberately or inadvertently likening it to humans and thereby missing the point altogether? If we deny this likeness, how are we to prevent the figure of the plant from retreating into obscurity, from remaining the mysterious, inaccessible other to an increasingly active, loquacious, and manipulative humanity? This tension, which regularly inflects efforts to account for the specificity of vegetal life, appears in early modernity, increases with the gradual development of a modern botany that highlights the unique structures and functions of plants, and stays with us today as a continued source of speculative energy that animates artistic and scholarly production. Here, too, we are struck by the ability of vegetality to oscillate between two modes of being that are seemingly diametrically opposed to each other: the plant is *both* an object in persistent withdrawal from us *and* a subject with its own unique mode of life, one that brings into sharp relief the limitations of human capacities and faculties. Speculative fiction and art take up and inhabit the space of this oscillation.

But artists have not been alone in their investigations of the surprising effects of plants on human assumptions about life and liveliness. Modern plant biologists, especially those engaged in writing popular science books for the greater public, have also affirmed the need to enhance institutionalized scientific knowledge with a seemingly more personal and subjective consideration of plant life as an autonomous animation of matter. The French botanist Francis Hallé—who specializes in the study of tropical rain forests—is an eloquent advocate for a greater awareness of plants' needs and unique way of being alive. He has also written extensively about their physiological and biological alterity. Hallé contends that animal properties such as interiority, desire, mortality, and individuality are largely meaningless for understanding plant life.[13] In addition to creating traditional line drawings of plants, Hallé deploys digital imaging, film, and poetry to make vegetality available to human perception and speculates about technologies that can transform "a weed into a marvel."[14] In *Lab Girl*, American geobiologist Hope Jahren uses the memoir genre not only to describe her work and its vegetal objects but to create experimental links between plants and human experiences such as being a woman in science, living with a disability, and working as a nontenured academic or contingent researcher.[15] Even as Hallé and Jahren anthropomorphize plants on occasion, their focus is on the tension between the objectification of plants in science and the recognition of shared need as an ethical problem concerning both plants and humans, especially in times of capitalist exploitation of environments, global heating, the accelerating annihilation of wildlife, the destruction of ecosystems, and, in Jahren's case, the neoliberalization of scientific research that renders human lives and research more precarious. Despite and because of plants' undeniable difference from us, scientific knowledge about plants calls for a visual and embodied mediation of plant being—through human imagination and imaging technologies—that goes beyond the production and practices of scientific objectivity, as both Hallé and Jahren allow us to see.

At the same time, the difficulty in assimilating plants to human or animal models of life means that plants regularly elude our ways of worldmaking. They often fail to confirm the desires and attributes we project onto them. Plants are undeniably lively and animate—they move, nourish themselves, reproduce, engage in marvelously complex chemical signaling, sense, relate to an external world, and even, as some claim, display intelligence—yet they cannot be said to possess a point of view or a consciousness that we recognize and that recognizes us in return. Contemporary science confirms plants' apparent lack of interiority—their inability, unlike animals, to mirror back our concerns. Without faces, they cannot look at us or register our gaze. Lorraine Daston and Gregg Mitman, in their 2005 collection titled *Thinking with Animals*, suggest that our failure to recognize ourselves in plants leads to an epistemological impasse.[16] As they put it: "Plants are beautiful, endlessly varied, and marvels of organic adaptation. Yet they radiate none of the magnetism animals do for humans. Even the most enthusiastic fancier of orchids or ferns rarely tries to think with them, in either sense of the phrase."[17] If plants thwart our attempts to identify with them, does that indeed make thinking with them out of the question?

In the past decade or so, the controversial notion of "plant intelligence," based on the idea that intelligent behavior is possible even in the absence of a central nervous system, has achieved a certain visibility, particularly in popular science writing. Discussions of plant intelligence are once again symptomatic of the challenge that plants represent to anthropocentric notions of life; they also show clearly how this challenge functions as a spur to speculation. Plant biologist Stefano Mancuso and journalist Alessandra Viola argue that it is cultural prejudice rather than scientific evidence that keeps us from attributing intelligence to plants.[18] They propose a notion of plant intelligence as networked and distributed over multiple data-processing centers rather than centralized—akin to the swarm intelligence observed in certain animals (including insects and human crowds). This paradigm remains not only highly speculative but the object of intense criticism from within the field of plant biology. Mancuso and Viola are arguably attempting, with the notion of plant intelligence, to move plants "closer" to us—to recreate them as human surrogates (albeit ones with very special abilities!). But the notion of an intelligent plant also exerts pressure in the other direction, on the idea of intellection or consciousness itself as a defining human or animal characteristic.

Theories of consciousness have, of course, been long debated, with some philosophers and cognitive scientists questioning its existence altogether, while others have understood consciousness as a fundamental or even universal trait of all animate life. Contemporary neurobiologist Antonio Damasio defines consciousness as a constant sense of self that is the product of the brain stem's map of the body.[19] In contrast, the French Enlightenment philosopher Denis Diderot (1713–1784) ascribed a certain degree of consciousness to molecules. According to other definitions, including those of Renaissance writer Michel de Montaigne (1533–1592), human perceptions are constantly in flux, and our sense of self is not "naturally" coherent or even materially consistent but held together by acts of writing or memory (in which plants do not participate). Of course, natural history and science in general are loath to attribute any kind of consciousness to plants, which not only lack a brain stem but do not seem to have access to the kinds of mnemonic techniques—or curative therapies—that stabilize human selves even contingently. Montaigne's hypotheses continue to resonate with those of much later philosophers, who think about plant life without attributing consciousness to it. Indeed, the difficulty of ascribing consciousness and concern (for us) to plants forces us to think otherwise, even as we think *with* them, and it has done so since at least the first half of the seventeenth century. Contemporary critic and media theorist N. Katherine Hayles has claimed that "we can no longer simply assume that consciousness guarantees the existence of the self. In this sense, the posthuman subject is also a postconscious subject."[20] Perhaps it is, or can be, or has long been, also a vegetal one?[21] *Radical Botany* traces the emergence of such a vegetal subject, one whose persistent presence in narratives of modernity has so far been overlooked.

By approaching the question of subjectivity through the purchase plants gain on it in speculative fiction, our book engages with the contemporary scholarly field in formation that we will be referring to as "plant studies." We seek to situate the appearance of plant studies within a much longer debate over the role of plants in the modern period. *Radical Botany* makes its own philosophical investments in plant studies, foregrounding the importance of materialist strands of botany; the relation of plants to modernity; the affective, animated, and animating power of plants as they are mediated to us; and the significance of plants for posthumanist theories and feminist and queer ecologies. We excavate a tradition that moves alongside but does not always intersect with a philosophical conversation that appears to denigrate and deride plants, one that has been subject to eloquent deconstruction by some of today's most prominent plant theorists. Philosopher Michael Marder's seminal work *Plant-Thinking: A Philosophy of Vegetal Life*, published in 2013 (the same year that the author founded a series called Critical Plant Studies for Rodopi Press), issues an eloquent challenge to the presentation of the plant in Western metaphysics as devoid of agency, subjectivity, and abstraction (among other qualities). At the same time, Marder affirms that the plant is characterized by "non-conscious intentionality"[22] and a relentless turning toward the environment. In Marder and Anaïs Tondeur's collaborative book *The Chernobyl Herbarium*,[23] Tondeur's photograms of plants grown by scientists in radioactive soil taken from the zone of contamination around the former nuclear power plant of Chernobyl (destroyed in the April 26, 1986, disaster) represent this "exploded consciousness" of plants.[24] The book stresses plants' heightened vulnerability to the totalizing techniques and effects that suffuse bodies and environments in technological modernity, of which radiation represents the most brutal and extreme degree. "For the plant, the ongoing monitoring of environmental conditions in the place of its growth is a run-of-the-mill operation; for us, who are accustomed to thinking of plants as passive beings devoid of consciousness or as persisting in a state of torpor at best, it is extraordinary," Marder affirms.[25] Marder makes this constant monitoring of an "outside" into the model of modern subjectivity, one that is thoroughly fragmented and traumatized, and argues that the life of the plant coincides with that of the modern subject, incessantly and absolutely exposed to its environment. Marder turns the postmetaphysical plant into a figure of resistance to the destructive forces of technology and of capitalism—both of which, Marder believes, work to extend a logic that subordinates and instrumentalizes matter and material bodies. Marder's fecund work has made vegetal ontology, the concept of plants' unique being, accessible in academia and beyond. However, his writing also suggests that access to this unique ontology requires a set of contemporary critical investments and tends to obscure a longer, predominantly materialist, and aesthetic tradition of representing and thinking with plants.

Marder's willingness to cultivate our sympathy for plants, so that they seem to reflect back to us the ethical and political selves we wish to become, is an example of one tendency within plant studies to assume that plant life exists in tension with and thus might provide a resolution to the problems of modernity, since plants remain excluded from it in their guise as its victims.[26] Of course, we always have a mediated experience of plants, but Marder seems to suggest that some forms of mediation bring us closer to plants than others. He writes, "More often than not, the cultural modes of routing growth rely on violent impositions that fail to respect the inherent tendencies of the plants themselves. The notion of economic growth is oblivious to the limits, within which quantitative increase may unfold."[27] Marder thus claims an unprecedented critical role for plants within the framework of his postmetaphysical ontology, ethics, politics, and art. Plants alone can bestow meaning on a broken world destroyed by our violent technoculture, but only as its outside. Although Marder admits that leaving this context is not an option for us, the plant still becomes a guide for us at a moment when we have lost the possibility of living in our natural environment. Thus, plants always evoke loss, fragmentation (revalorized as such), and, ultimately, access to a past that we cannot recapture. We can trace the origins of this kind of critique back at least to the work of Jean-Jacques Rousseau (1712–1778), who in his attachment to plants found a means of pushing back against some of the imperatives of modernity in its cultural and philosophical modes (to which he retained a deeply ambivalent relationship). For

Rousseau, communing with nature, and engaging with plants and botany in particular, was also a means of practicing self-examination.[28]

Theorist Jeffrey T. Nealon takes issue with Marder's aim, as outlined in *Plant-Thinking*, to make of the plant a marginalized subject that in turn might inspire an ethical program. In a review of Marder's book, Nealon writes: "But the more 'positive' account of vegetal life is, I think, where the book falters. This is primarily because Marder's plants teach us lessons that seem strangely familiar: 'The positive dimension of plant-being, as the outcome of a critique of metaphysics, will spell out an inversion of traditional valuations, valorizing the other over the self, surface over depth, and so on.'"[29] In this sense, as Nealon suggests, Marder's plants join the ranks, after animals, of the marginalized and the powerless, who become prioritized as such within certain strands of ethical and political philosophy. Instead, Nealon proposes a biopolitics that does not exclude any form of life and argues that what Marder sees as the defective plant of metaphysics has had a much more positive function, particularly within the domain of continental philosophy, despite the extent to which vegetal life may appear to be occulted and occluded there. Nealon's *Plant Theory: Biopower and Vegetable Life*, published in 2016, intervenes in discussions of animal studies and biopolitics by emphasizing the importance of plants and other photosynthesizing organisms for these debates. Nealon follows Foucault in arguing that one of the defining characteristics of modernity is the sovereignty of an animal model of the subject—one in which agency is structured by desire, appetite, movement, expansion, domination, and consumption. Nealon contends that this sovereignty is nonetheless being called into question today by plants. He thus proposes a break from the predominantly animal logic of modernity, a break that he sees foreshadowed, if only minimally and marginally,[30] by various moments in the history of philosophy that, although they fail to prioritize plants, also attribute positive qualities to them. These include Aristotle's claim that plants are "atelic," that is, that their proper purpose, or entelechy, is growth, which is limitless and lacks an aim or telos.[31] Nealon considers this "uncontrolled growth, without any kind of obvious analogy to the higher functions of the human—to mind, reason, appetite, and so on"—to be manifested in philosophy from Aristotle's plant *psūchē* to Jacques Derrida's worldless plants and Gilles Deleuze and Félix Guattari's inorganic life and rhizome; it is a positive trait of plants (*contra* Marder, who sees it as a form of privation).[32] By evoking Timothy Morton's "mesh" and Richard Doyle's "plant superpower," figures of strong or "dense" interconnectedness that destroy any notion of a contained world, Nealon firmly places this "atelic" plant back into modernity, not just as a conceptual tool that operates within theoretical debates but as a rhizomatic agency that we share "territory" with.[33]

Perhaps Nealon's most provocative claim is that the status of animals (including humans) is not the most urgent biopolitical question facing us today. Instead, in an era characterized by the "subsumption of life" under capitalism,[34] when life is manipulated in its everyday rhythms and on the molecular level, and when a climate crisis and other anthropogenic causes have put countless species on the course of extinction, plants become the paradigmatic biopolitical subjects. They are accordingly worth particular consideration—that is, "[p]lants . . . are quickly becoming the new animals."[35] With this statement, Nealon does not mean that plants are literally becoming animals (i.e., individuated beings who can assume a subject position and lay claim to the capacity for autonomous ethical decision-making, or at least silently demand ethical consideration from humans). Instead, he sees plants as particularly vulnerable to biopolitical control (e.g., through their atelic life that renders them available to genetic modification), even as they also resist individuation, one of the signature elements of the reterritorialization of subjectivity by late capitalism.

Nealon revises Marder's emphasis on the plant as the next model of ethical and political subjectivity by contending that thinking with plants does not simply involve extending an ethical status to vegetal "others." Instead, plants, with their very existence, trouble human ethical and political models. Plants may be the new animals, but they are, in fact, not animals at all; this is the far-reaching argument of Nealon's book. Moreover, Nealon contends that the ambiguous status of plants in Western philosophy—not animals, without telos, and even on occasion inorganic—forces us to come to terms with our own unwilled enmeshment in structures of domination: we cannot simply decide to abstain from eating plants. Thinking about plants thus reveals to us the very impossibility of making a fully ethical choice, thereby calling into question the paradigm of animal or human sovereignty. Confronting plants in ethics, we become more plantlike. Or, at the very least, we are forced to think *with* plants, long and hard. We have to face the fact that we must make decisions about which lives we save or protect, decisions that do not easily affirm our human agency or moral autonomy.[36]

Marder and Nealon represent two distinct theoretical responses to the specificity of plant life and its position vis-à-vis philosophy. These contemporary theorists interpret plants' lack of interiority, and their differences from animals, as the basis for new political and ethical paradigms. They each take seriously the threat of climate emergency as it compels us to reconsider the problem of our shared future, yet their arguments, and their investment in plants in both their material and conceptual dimensions, are more than just symptoms of human vulnerability. Instead, Marder and Nealon engage a certain speculative energy, seeming to hold out some hope for a new world, or at least a revision of our world, which plants will either usher in or help us create. In this sense, in plant studies, plants remain our partners in modernity, even as we both, plants and humans, find ourselves under threat by forces that vastly outstrip our abilities to master, grasp, or model them.

Speculative Fiction and the Mediated Plant

At its core, *Radical Botany* concerns speculation, in particular the speculative excess that is generated by our recognition that plants do not share or respond to our world-making desires, even as they retain the ability to contribute in significant ways to human life on earth, and kindle our admiration, fascination, and ethical concern. Our attraction to them notwithstanding, plants are not concerned with the world we are building. In the tradition that we trace, this simultaneous presence and absence of plants leads to an oscillation of the plant between two relational modes—the double bind described by Dominique Brancher. On the one hand, the plant appears to withdraw from a human economy of desire and hovers at the limits of our affective identification. But it also produces profound effects on us, including setting in motion our imagination. This oscillation is not only a defining characteristic of vegetality but functions as a key trait of speculative literature, giving this genre a power and agency that is inherently linked to the vibrancy of plant matter.

Literary fiction, with its long-standing commitment to the construction of proxies of consciousness and points of view, often seems inextricably bound to the categories of experience that organize human (and animal) life, including mortality, subjective emotions, individuality, and interpersonal recognition. Yet, literary narrative displays a renewed interest in plants at about the same time as botany, the organized and increasingly institutionalized practice of studying plants, becomes a field of natural philosophical and (later) scientific inquiry in the seventeenth century. Of course, imagination can easily turn plants into plant-shaped animals of sorts—anthropomorphic and zoomorphic plants traverse ancient and modern narrative traditions, from Ovidian myth to Disney cartoons. In sharp contrast, the narratives that we gather here take up a different challenge—that of imagining plants as both vibrantly alive and fully material—which is to say without a hidden or transcendent animating principle (e.g., anima, spirit, personality, will, or desire). Our book traces the intersections of botanical observation, philosophy, nonrealist modes of literary production, and the cinematic use of the imaging technologies of time-lapse photography to expose the liveliness of plants. These fictions and imaging techniques, while they animate plants, do not loop back to anthropomorphizing them—that is, to the realist mode of world creation.

From the perspective of radical botany, plants confront us with a mode of life that is entirely immanent yet still active and difficult to capture. This embodied, affective relation to plants is in many cases represented as a kind of "dance," which is to say a series of movements and encounters in which the interdependency of bodies acquires shape and form. In this sense, radical botanical texts are not only closely tied to materialist philosophies of life in general but also force us to reckon with our own experience and condition as deeply, inexorably material. The texts we explore are in conversation with an empirical tradition of botanical observation and research, although they do not form an integral part of it. Rather, they extend their reach beyond observable facts, and even provable hypothesis, to make speculation about the plant the vehicle of speculation about human social and political life. Here the primacy given to the plant reflects back upon human existence in sometimes troubling ways. Human desire ceases to become the means for understanding vegetal nature; the plant, lacking a percipience in which we can recognize our own, nonetheless takes priority in the conceptualization of life as matter. This shift in perspective requires—and produces—new fictions. Radical botanists develop ways of describing and investigating the unique life of plants even as this life resists incorporation into human categories; the study of plants becomes, in this context, an engine of social critique and speculation about possible futures. More specifically, the appearance of plant surrogates in fiction enables a materialist reading of human social life that denaturalizes human experience. From the outset, these literary narratives are in conversation with the natural sciences as another zone of defamiliarization, in which the strange and alien qualities of plants likewise incite curiosity and interest.

"Speculative fiction" is a category used in contemporary discussions of literary genre as an umbrella term for all types of nonrealist writing (including fantasy, sci-fi, horror, and weird fiction).[37] These are the forms of writing in which we find a concerted effort to imagine a vegetality that remains inaccessible to realism. The fact that our relationship to plants is of necessity highly mediated (even as they remain coparticipants with us in the assemblages of life) and that our attempts to understand them as analogous to us are regularly unsuccessful means that plants inspire speculative activity in our efforts to think with them. "Speculation" is, of course, also a term drawn from philosophy, used by Immanuel Kant (1724–1804) to designate a realm that cannot be experienced but nonetheless can be thought. We do not, however, need to wait for the advent of Kantian philosophy for this term to give us purchase on the activity of poetic writing in its efforts to pass beyond the limit of the visible or phenomenological world. We can find this speculative impetus already in Lucretius, to whom early modern thinkers of science (and of plants) often owe a debt, even when they are not systematically Epicurean in their commitments. The *De rerum natura*, Lucretius's influential poem, lushly describes the way in which the mind moves beyond "the flaming ramparts of the world" in an action that might well be termed "speculative."[38]

We note that speculation is rooted in the Latin *specere* ("to look," "to watch," "to observe") and thus evokes both a process of visualization as well as the limits of the human vision. Radical botanists accordingly have a complex and nuanced approach to the plant as a visible object. On the one hand, they are suspicious of regimes of visibility that seek to fix and stabilize the plant body. While human beings are dependent on their limited sensory capacities in order to perceive the world, radical botanists wonder if plants perhaps possess other senses unknown to us. On the other hand, they turn to technologies of visualization to enhance and enrich the encounter with plant-being. The plant, with its resistance to our attempts to fully "see" it, seems to invite us to imagine new ways to come into contact with it. We thus retain an emphasis on speculation in this work despite the more recent Deleuzean coinage of the term "fabulation" as part of a transcendental empiricism that is resolutely non-Kantian.[39] While radical botanists are engaged in fabulations of their own, they remain attentive to the relationship of the plant to human practices of visualization in which they seek to intervene. Moreover, our usage of speculation is meant to evoke the importance of the plant to a history of financial as well as philosophical speculation; plants are privileged bodies, for better and most often for worse, within the decentralizing mechanisms of capitalism. We note that, historically, plants have been at the forefront of financial speculation, from the key example of "tulipomania" in the seventeenth-century Dutch Republic to the contemporary example of the agricultural futures market. Today, plants are massively subject to biotechnological manipulation, and, if they have thus lost some or even most of their botanical integrity, they have emerged as paradigmatic biopolitical subjects under late capitalism, as Nealon has argued.

We thus use speculation in two senses. First, the term denotes for us any nonrealist form of narration that spills over into cinema and the arts. Second, we intend a more specific reference to the fact that plant life, while it has been a privileged object of scientific disciplines from botany to physiology and microbiology, and attendant techniques for creating regimes of objectivity and visibility, maintains an intimate relation to the visual field. Plants in the speculative fictions we study are not limpid objects of knowledge as eighteenth-century botany seems to claim but instead help generate experimental epistemologies and narratives. The texts and artists we examine sometimes reject and other times seize upon the ambiguities of scientific regimes of visibility. For example, early modern libertine botanists often rely on literary or textual figures rather than on the visual images that are regularly deployed in botanical works; their plants first appear not as illustrations, but as tropes. One reason for this may be the fact that libertine works were often clandestinely written and circulated, and did not benefit from the kind of institutional support that more orthodox forms of botanical science could increasingly muster. On the other hand, this ambivalence around the status of visibility does not prevent the photographic image of the plant from generating new speculative potential with the advent of cinema. The avant-garde "electric plant" of the early twentieth century makes provocative use of the nonrealist dimensions of scientific imaging of the plant in black and white. "Plant horror," which adopts visual images of the plant in order to both terrify and fascinate, continues to occupy this margin between the objective and the otherworldly visualization of the plant body.

Plant speculative fiction and art thus differ fundamentally from traditional botany as a predominantly visual and objectifying mode of knowledge, tightly linked to practices of taxonomy and classification. In the context we delineate, plants tend to frustrate human attempts to consign them to a particular place on a hierarchy of being. The diverse texts that we have chosen for this study are distinguished by their willingness to hypothesize about a hitherto invisible, ignored, or intangible world in which plants play a crucial role; these fictions prioritize contingency and transgress the regulatory principles that tend to govern classificatory schemata. The worlds that plants inspire remain open to change precisely because plant-becoming eludes observation while enabling affective and corporeal mediation and the technologies that enhance it.

Very recently, speculative fiction has gained new traction in the context of a critical practice that draws not only on Deleuzean materialism but on the fields of science studies, anthropology, and ethnography. Contemporary authors such as Donna Haraway[40] and Bruno Latour develop what might be called a critical organicism, a mode of thought through which human bodies (among others) are shown to be fragmented by and interconnected with both organic and inorganic things. Both of these thinkers take seriously the interpenetration of scientific and speculative modes of description. In a passage drawn from his work *Aramis, or the Love of Technology*, Bruno Latour has written that "the hybrid genre that I have designed for a hybrid task is what I call *scientifiction*,"[41] while Haraway is herself profoundly influenced by "sci-phi" (the Deleuzoguattarian version of philosophically inspired science fiction or fabulation).[42] In her most recent work, *Staying with the Trouble*, Haraway cultivates a passionate mode of storytelling in order to create possible futures, thus making narrative an integral part of the practice of theory in the humanities and the social sciences. Her writing emphasizes the participation of all kinds of bodies in networks and assemblages that include not only plants and humans (among others) but the fictions and artifacts created by both.[43] In an argument that resonates profoundly with Haraway's work and practice, theorist and cultural critic Stacy Alaimo suggests transcorporeality as a principle of solidarity that acknowledges both our immersion and our fragility in a world in which boundaries between and among beings are rarely if ever stable. Anthropologist Anna Tsing describes forms of "collaborative survival" involving cooperation among mushrooms, trees, and human beings (to name only a few). While these accounts have something in common with Marder's insistence on the need for plant-thinking, the vision of nature and the natural world that they conjure up is in no way separate from human (or machinic) activities and agents. Instead, beings (and worlds) permeate one another. Alaimo, Haraway, and Tsing—along with many others, including Jane Bennett[44]—make it clear that we only have a future in our connections to other bodies, alive or not in the traditional sense. These bodies all have stories to tell.

Anthropologist of science Natasha Myers has been developing, in conversation with these thinkers, a new materialist approach to science studies in which plants in particular play a specific and powerful role, one that extends beyond their ubiquitous participation in assemblages. Although she is not an author of fiction, Myers is attentive to the role of storytelling and narrative in human engagements with the plant world. Myers treats plants as distinct and different from human beings (and animals, presumably) at the same time as she recognizes their rich and fundamental aliveness, their "demands" and "desires."[45] Myers asserts that "[w]e must get to know plants intimately and on their terms. And so we need a *planthropology* to document the affective ecologies taking shape between plants and people, to learn to listen to their demands for unpaved land and for a time outside of the rhythms of capitalist extraction. We need to tap into their desire for forms of life that are not for us."[46] Myers directly evokes here capitalism's push for objectifying plants as resources and offers as an alternative a strategic anthropomorphism, a form of fabulation that she critically explores in her work, especially in her studies of scientific descriptions of molecular organisms and plants. Her focus on scientists' discursive habits reveals their own struggle with the constraints of impersonal and nonanthropomorphic description. Throughout, Myers's research emphasizes the qualities of living matter that tend to evade the mechanistic models of knowledge production imposed on them.[47] Her work thus directly exposes the discrepancy between practices of producing objectivity in the empirical sciences and a speculative dimension of experience in which organic bodies mediate affects for one another. Myers is committed to investigating how desire and emotion cross not only species boundaries but also the boundaries between the (human) observer and the object in the lab (be it molecule or plant).

In a blog post titled "Photosynthesis," Myers addresses the scientific debates around the role of trees in the production of Earth's atmosphere to promote a strategic intervention in the scientific discourse around climate change. She makes a forceful argument for the existence of a plant-made geology and a plant-human entanglement (of, as she puts it, "cosmic") proportions that she names "Phytocene" (to replace the term "Anthropocene"). As she states:

> These green beings have made this planet livable and breathable for animals like us. We thrive on plants' wily aptitude for chemical synthesis. All cultures and political economies, local and global, turn around plants' metabolic rhythms. Plants make the energy-dense sugars that fuel and nourish us, the potent substances that heal, dope, and adorn us, and the resilient fibers that clothe and shelter us. What are fossil fuels and plastics but the petrified bodies of once-living photosynthetic creatures? We have thrived and we will die, burning their energetic accretions. And so it is not an overstatement to say that *we are only because they are*. The thickness of this relation teaches us the full meaning of the word *interimplication*.[48]

While science does not allow us to decide, given the affective component of such a choice, if plants are strictly speaking "allies" or "enemies" in the current climate crisis, Myers advocates for seeing them as the former. This is a strategic speculation that counters deterritorialization and reterritorialization as a result of capitalism and scientific objectification, to reference Nealon following Deleuze. The deliberately anthropomorphizing language deployed by Myers aims to build a political world in which we involve ourselves (affectively and scientifically, aesthetically and ethnographically) in plant life in order to create a new political world *with plants*, even as we cannot be certain what is proper to them.[49] At the same time, her emphasis on affective alliances presumes at least a minimal optimism regarding what plants might "want." Myers imagines life as a territory, and she offers concrete scenarios of sharing this territory that suggest that affective sympathies may function to hold certain assemblages together (while revealing others as the product of violence and alienation). From this perspective, we need to adapt our desires to the needs and demands of these vegetal others, now under the pressures of extraordinary environmental change. The outcome of this process would not be beautiful or architectonic gardens but new, messier spaces, the products of plant-human mutuality, "conspiracies" and "alliances." This hopefulness is fueled in part by speculative storytelling (as we explore at more length in Chapter 7). At times enlisting the plant's uncertain properties to subvert global capitalism from within, at others asserting that plants stand outside the logic of the capitalist system that exploits them, Myers and her interlocutors probe the possibilities for a resistance that emerges from an effort to think with and alongside plants—to speculate about them in other words and other worlds.

In *Radical Botany*, we propose "staying with the trouble"[50] that plants introduce into these and other long-standing debates around the nature of life, human life not excepted, and the regimes that represent it. Moreover, we argue that this "trouble" has its own history, one that has had an influence on the development of human thought and practice under modernity. Plants are not just now opening up new possibilities for thinking speculative futures. We trace a longer history of such mixed affective and objective involvements with plants and the socially and politically productive forms of narrative speculation that ensue from this involvement. We thus work in this book to uncover a series of interlinked texts in which plants are at the center rather than at the margins of a discussion of life. The authors that form our corpus tend to see modernity as linked to an awareness of human contingency in the face of a vegetal potential (or perhaps a becoming plant) that succeeds where humans fail. We trace a genealogy of works in which the vegetal becomes a model for life as such, impelling developments in technology and changes in human culture, in part by bringing us into contact with its own materiality.

Even so, our experience of plants through fiction, film, and immersive or interactive media reminds us that we live in increasingly mediated environments that instrumentalize plants even as they appear to bring us into contact with them. Michael Marder has been a forceful critic of the exploitative use of plants in these environments. He writes, "What appears to be meaningless and obscure to us becomes meaningful as soon as we try to imagine, at the edge of our imaginary capacity, the perspectives of those beings that live unconcerned with symbolic meanings."[51] Marder is suspicious of all imposition of human interest or "meaning" on plants (from using them as raw material, to scientific study and time-lapse photography), yet art and philosophy become within his approach a privileged site for revealing plant-thinking as an imaginative activity that makes our own thought more plantlike. Marder is less troubled by the idea that the plant-thinking his philosophy proposes and activates relies precisely on those symbolic activities—including ethical imperatives as such—that he critiques as the source of our often violent manipulation of plants. The art that Marder analyzes, including the work of Tondeur, which we discussed previously in this chapter, is assumed to be operating at the limit of human and plant-being, infusing with meaning the senseless aggression inflicted on bodies by and in the name of metaphysics, human representational regimes, and technology. Marder's fecund work consistently reminds us of the narrow margins we have to find (existential and ontological) meaning in plants. Yet his own authorial voice affirms that it hovers precisely at this narrow limit.

While media may saturate our experience more completely under late modernity than in earlier periods, *Radical Botany* shows that it has consistently been an indispensable part of our attempts to access plant life. We aim at broadening the margins of meaningful interactions with plants, even at the risk of including among these interactions mediated encounters that Marder considers violent. The literary and visual narratives that we examine in this book, stretching from the seventeenth to the twenty-first centuries, foreground plants with world-altering consequences. These narratives use an array of representational or animating modes, from personification, analogy, time-lapse photography, and the visual imaging of plants in movement, to the projection of plants into human subject positions with the help of visual art or experimental fiction. In each case, giving plants priority in shaping narrative reveals the contingency of the human condition and of the world.

In our era of anthropogenic global heating and ecological breakdown, we have discovered that our own world-building poses an existential threat not just to us but to other species. Despite having learned to think of ourselves as postmodern, we nonetheless find ourselves having to face the increasingly dire effects of modernity. At this moment, it is tempting to turn to the plant as not just a figure of thought but a living "thing" with which to connect. This need for connection is both an instance of our dependence on vegetal life and an effect of our desire for recognition. Radical botanical fictions that stress the incommensurability of human desire with atelic plant growth double back to show that there is no outside for us to the territory we share with plants. Because of our enmeshment with them and because they block our attempts to render them analogous to us, they call into question our assertions of our own autonomy and priority. In our shared territory with plants, we are always already outside the closed worlds that we project for ourselves. This kind of simultaneity—in which plants move us beyond ourselves but also reveal that we were there all along—is yet another dimension of the oscillation that plants enable and provoke.

In calling for an extended attention to plants that does not presume their affinities with our interests or concerns but stresses their active presence in the worlds that we seem to make for ourselves, we are inspired by Nealon's careful reconstruction of a plant theory excavated from within a philosophical tradition that can appear to ignore vegetal life. Nealon reveals both how the concept of the animal comes to dominate modern thought and how the plant might serve as a particularly generative figure for thinking life today. We argue here for the ongoing (yet occluded) significance of plants—and in particular theories and representations of vegetal being—to the rise of modernity in Western contexts. From our vantage, the current critical investment in the plant is part of a much longer history beginning in the early modern period—one in which the plant is deeply implicated in human attempts to understand the limitations of our own perceptions (including of plant life) and our vulnerability in the face of social, political, and environmental change. Plants regularly exceed and challenge the selves and the worlds we construct, and in doing so propel us toward speculative futures. As we trace a genealogy of speculative narrative and thought about plants, our aim is both to allow a macrohistory of radical botany to emerge in its outlines and to anchor each chapter, arranged in chronological order, in a small number of texts and artifacts. At times, we highlight the affiliations among texts in ways that allow us to complicate the more straight-forward linearity of our main narrative. This book prioritizes not the steady accumulation of knowledge about plants but the speculative drive to bring plant life into relation with human experience. In this way, early modern technologies of animating plants, we hope, can be just as inspiring and relevant as contemporary ones. With this book, we do not so much wish to promote a vision of progress in the botanical sciences—indeed, there is an argument to be made that botany has never again attained the prominence it achieved in the eighteenth and nineteenth centuries[52]—as encourage finding affiliations and connections between, for example, science and the arts, early and late modernity, and visual and textual forms of mediation and speculation.

The first Western plant fiction appears with the waning of the Renaissance (and may be considered one of the earliest forms of science fiction more generally). While the Aristotelian endorsement of vegetal ensoulment gradually falls out of favor as a natural philosophical approach to plants, we show that the autonomous liveliness of the plant inherent in the Aristotelian notion of vegetative *psūchē* is reawakened from its Scholastic slumber by two authors, the aforementioned Guy de La Brosse and Cyrano de Bergerac, both belonging to a circle of *libertins érudits*. We investigate how the botanically oriented texts of La Brosse and Cyrano generate an eclectic combination of proto-scientific ideas, borrowed from traditions spanning atomism to alchemy, to significantly increase the animatedness of the plant. "Freed" from the confines of metaphysics by scientific thought, the plant penetrates into the domain of literature. The plant is thus not only present but takes pride of place at one of the points of origin of science fiction.

The materialist tales of Cyrano and the botanical writings of La Brosse speculate about a vegetality that is bursting with life, percipient, and libidinal, to an extent that humans may struggle even to comprehend. In the second chapter, we examine the origins of a radical libertine botany that gives primacy to plants, not just in order to think their being but to postulate an emergence into modernity—a break with the past that predates the Cartesian denunciation of Scholastic orthodoxy. We discuss how these two writers, in different ways, prioritize the plant as an instantiation of a material flexibility that is responsive to stimulation. They show how plants not only contain their own modes of apprehension and their own technologies of generation but also retreat from human economies of desire and social and political orders, even as they set these economies in motion. The libertine plant thus enables other forms of mediation—writing notable among them—which La Brosse and Cyrano use to generate new encounters and new allegiances.

Our third chapter takes on the emergence, in the form of an enlightened plant, of utopian theories of vegetal sociability in the eighteenth century, at a time that witnesses the proliferation of schemes for botanical classification and physiological inquiries into plant life. These theories both herald and resist the development of classificatory systems and a biopolitics modeled on vegetal life. Authors Ludvig Holberg (1684–1754) and Charles-François Tiphaigne de La Roche (1722–1774) create new narratives of liberal and rationally governed societies by peopling them with plants. Yet, these utopian visions are not only hopeful but also bring into view a plant that troubles the very concept of society by existing in a state of utter indifference to need and human desire. Thus, we see in these works, too, the possibility of an alternate conception of modernity in which the plant delivers a powerful critique of enlightenment itself.

In the fourth chapter, we move into the era of Romanticism, during which representations of nature are so often inspired by scientific vitalism. We approach Romantic aesthetics through the fiction of Edgar Allan Poe (1809–1849), an author who had an ambivalent relationship to both vitalism and Romanticism more generally, and study the way in which his arabesque vegetality travels into the work of later writers, including Charlotte Perkins Gilman (1860–1935). We explore the migration of eighteenth-century scientific theories of vegetal sentience, originally based on analogical models, into Poe's work, especially in his short story "The Fall of the House of Usher." Poe's foregrounding of the eighteenth-century idea of "the sentience of all vegetable things" in "Usher" represents an important turning point in the tradition we present because it both responds to and undermines Romantic ideas about human affinities with plants. Poe follows the Enlightenment analogy of human to plant to its logical conclusion in order to expose its aporias; for him, vegetal sentience cannot be contained within any hierarchy of being. At the same time, Poe destroys the Romantic fusional model—in which humans and plants commune within a shared physical world—by focusing on the destructive, indeed rapacious, qualities of the vegetal. The transcendental ideas of beauty and the sublime, which allow for nature to be tamed and aestheticized, give way in Poe to a vegetality that invades human consciousness. He suggests that we might be horrified, rather than delighted, by the calamity that a vegetal modernity represents, even though (and perhaps because) we have no alternative to it. The consciousness infiltrated by the vegetal produces, in "Usher," a weird art in which the plant does not function as an instance of the beautiful but as the expression of a process of contamination and as a medium for amplifying affect. Poe's vegetal horror takes us into symbolism, and from there to French avant-garde cinema of the early twentieth century. It also inflects a feminist reflection on plant life as dismantling and destroying patriarchal models of the family. Poe reunites a tradition of speculative fiction with modes of scientific speculation drawn from an earlier era; he thus allows for the passage of radical botany into the art and thought of the future.

The fifth and sixth chapters examine the twentieth-century cinema boom that invents the "electric plant," first in French experimental cinema inspired by time-lapse images of plant movement, then in the form of monstrous plants as a medium for engendering desires—a double of cinema itself. The astonishing fascination with time-lapse images of plants, which show them in motion and indeed alive, and the fright that these images evoke, had to do not so much with the ability of these films to turn plants into animals but with the deployment of the plant as a medium in which human experience is expanded, destabilized, and reanchored. As we move from the early decades of the twentieth century to late modernity, it becomes clear that humans, like plants, may also have flat or atelic lives. The plant turn of the early twentieth century, in film, allows for a transfiguration, defamiliarization, and ultimately reanimation of human experience along vegetal lines. In the fifth chapter, we return to the French context to investigate the way in which early avant-garde film takes up the very forms of vegetal sentience and plant-inspired calamity that so terrified Poe, rewriting the plant once again as an opening onto new worlds. Here the "inorganic" function of vegetality—as linked to and inspiring new forms of technology and new means of sociability—returns in the visual domain, generating an "electric plant" that retains its utopian dimensions *and* its power to deprioritize the human.

In the sixth chapter, we move into the world of plant horror to explore the ways in which the plant becomes a figure for both cinema itself and for life under global capitalism, inspiring fear and desire all at once. The B movies that we examine in this chapter posit vegetality as the experience of *all* beings under capitalism. They visualize the dark side of a global modernity that is vegetal in essence yet still stimulates our interest and even fascination. This critique of capitalism is coupled with an attempt to project a view of a purely material reality—that is, the reality of the plant on film. Such a projection represents not just a horrifying loss of human authenticity—after all, this loss already occurred 150 years ago, in the work of Poe!—but a pleasurable cinematic experience that foreshadows a new materialist approach to the interpenetration of bodies. Finally, in the seventh chapter, we read the work of twentieth- and twenty-first-century authors and visual artists who seek to move with us into a vegetal future. What might it mean to think speculatively with plants today? Can we *become* plants in order to become critically postconscious, posthuman, feminist or queer subjects? If so, this process takes place through assemblages with fiction and other technologies of embodiment. Here we take up the plant as an engine of speculation that helps us negotiate our relationship to a late modernity that seems always on the verge of ending—a constant calamity that might nonetheless still enable a new way of living and being.

CHAPTER 2

Libertine Botany and Vegetal Modernity

The Botanical Cosmos

In an ever-expanding universe, it is enough to look at the ground to see the stars. In seventeenth-century Europe, as the ancient distinction between the sublunar and the supralunar realms fades, the Copernican turn and subsequent astronomical discoveries open up the physical world to scientific inquiry and technological manipulation.[1] In a cosmos conceived according to mechanistic, mathematical, and chemical principles, plants shed their lowly status on the bottom of a hierarchy of being and take on a role—one not shared by animals, humans, or angels—as the emissaries to a physical world that lies beyond direct human perception and reach. Seventeenth-century libertine botany, our focus in this chapter, finds in the apotheosis of the local—the plant—a mobile agent that moves over the earth, in part due to the efforts of explorers and colonizers. In certain scientific and literary works, the plant even becomes an interplanetary traveler. While Aristotelian philosophy accorded plants only a minimal (and distinctly nonanimal) form of life, during this period plants emerge as the instantiation of a material universe; they navigate the divide between animal and mineral kingdoms and bridge the distance between the living and the inanimate. Libertine botany actively negotiates the Aristotelian inheritance of the "vegetative soul," which provided a rationale for the taxonomical distinctiveness of plants, even as Aristotelianism itself comes under increasing attack by Cartesian and other forms of mechanism. Plant life, a sign of the astonishing vigor and liveliness of matter, thus becomes a key figure in a materialist rethinking of the relationship between humans and other modes of being. In their withdrawal from human and animal models of subjectivity, consciousness, and perception, plants represent a challenge to an orthodoxy that places humans at the center of the cosmos and even to human thought as such.

In *Quand l'esprit vient aux plantes*, Dominique Brancher eloquently recounts how the ascription to plants of sensitivity, and even intellection, in the works of libertine authors helps to destabilize conventional hierarchies of being.[2] The plant functions, she shows, as a significant player in the libertine critique of anthropocentrism. In this chapter, we argue that the plant not only works as a tool with which to undermine anthropocentric narratives but as a key figure for the material life of the universe and the nature of matter itself. We explore the ways in which two *libertins érudits*, Guy de La Brosse and Cyrano de Bergerac,[3] not only question and undo scientific and other orthodoxies but offer an image of the plant as an autonomous material being in possession of technologies for animating itself and others. La Brosse and Cyrano both affirm an enlivening, fiery libido that pervades and animates plants in particular (as well as other kinds of beings on occasion). With this fire drawn from the medieval alchemical tradition, they paradoxically lend strength to the Aristotelian notion of a distinct plant soul, even as they also partake in a radical critique of the Aristotelian hierarchy of being. La Brosse and Cyrano strive to establish vegetal specificity as a new model for life in general, conceived in a material sense.

The Aristotelian tripartite system of ensoulment designated plants as a specific form of life. Aristotle defined life by function and created a hierarchy comprised of the vegetable *psūchē* (capable of nutrition, growth, and reproduction), the animal *psūchē* (capable of sensation, appetite, and movement), and the rational *psūchē* (capable of reasoning).[4] In Aristotle's world, rationality thoroughly informs matter as purpose rather than taking up residence in a separate realm as in Plato.[5] While in Aristotelian philosophy the plant is certainly not endowed with the multiple capacities that define the animal and the human, the plant-as-being nonetheless continues to express an aim that is uniquely its own. This special purpose, rather than its lack of "higher" attributes, defines it. In *De anima*, Aristotle writes: "For this is the most natural of the functions of such living creatures as are complete and not mutilated and do not have spontaneous generation, namely to make another thing like themselves, an animal an animal, a plant a plant, so that in the way that they can they may partake in the eternal and the divine. For all creatures desire this and for the sake of this do whatever they do in accordance with their nature."[6] As this passage makes clear, reproduction is a particularly important element of "completion," and it is their reproductive capacities that make plants complete. Here plants are portrayed as having their own desires—and their own relationship to divinity—even as they lack desire understood as appetite, imagination, movement, and action. While from the metaphysical point of view plants may be said to lack that which humans and animals possess,[7] in Aristotle's ontology and in his disciple Theophrastus's botany, they also contain their own principle that organizes and drives their participation in a cosmic order. Plant "entelechy," or aiming toward a purpose, then, is both stripped down (in comparison to the complex sensitive and intellectual life of humans) and highly specific, in that plants retain a kind of ontological uniqueness that makes it possible for them to act "in accordance with a nature that is their own and not that of another. We may thus speak of plants, animals and humans as all ensouled, insofar as the soul is that which gives the body its reason for being (and, in effect, causes this body to be)."[8] Indeed, in certain respects, plants in Aristotle's natural philosophy are more successful than humans in this project—particularly where reproduction is concerned. They are what we might call super-reproductive: thoroughly and successfully dedicated to their all-consuming tasks of growth and the production of new members of the species.

As Brancher shows, the nested structure of Aristotle's ontology was gradually replaced in the Scholastic tradition with the one-soul doctrine (originally proposed by the fourth- and fifth-century Christian theologian Augustine of Hippo), according to which only human beings possess an immortal and divine soul. All other souls are material and corruptible.[9] It is this Scholastic "denaturalization" of plants that solidifies a hierarchy of beings in which plants (and to a lesser degree animals) are defined as inferior. While La Brosse and Cyrano are engaged in an active critique of the Aristotelian orthodoxy of their time, they also expand upon an Aristotelian interest in the specific powers and ontological attributes that plants possess. If, in the Aristotelian system, plants are defined by their immanent mode of being (growth and reproduction), La Brosse and Cyrano extend this vegetal immanence to the world. Their rereading of the plant soul thus resonates with some contemporary materialist reconsiderations of the Aristotelian paradigm. Mel Chen, for instance, has recently emphasized the materiality of Aristotle's notion of the soul alongside the Aristotelian critique of the Platonic immaterial soul. According to Chen, "We might therefore say, if we took Aristotle to one end point, that it is possible to conceive of something like the 'affect' of a vegetable, wherein both the vegetable's receptivity to other affects and its ability to affect outside of itself, as well as its own animating principle, its capacity to animate itself, become viable considerations."[10] La Brosse and Cyrano make good on the promise that lies dormant or occluded in the Aristotelian model by parsing the vegetative soul through both alchemical and Epicurean filters.[11] Their plants possess the ability to be affected and the means of affecting others, attributes that La Brosse and Cyrano imitate in their writings, thus intervening in the "animacy hierarchy" implicit in Aristotelianism as well as in some forms of mechanist botany.[12] At the same time, for both authors, the specificity of the plant guarantees its resistance to human economies of desire. In a time when the French garden, on country estates and under royal patronage, is well on its way to symbolizing social prestige, order, and national power, La Brosse and Cyrano seize upon the garden plant in order to show the withdrawal of a cosmic material world from the social and political realm of human beings. Simultaneously, they imagine this plant as the source of formal flexibility, uniquely vibrant materiality, and hitherto unforeseen technologies—a newly vital mode of vegetal life. Their libertine botany is a productive site of epistemological oscillation in which plants both stimulate humans and retreat from their grasp.

In 1626, Guy de La Brosse (1586–1641), King Louis XIII's personal physician, founded the Jardin du Roi, with the Académie royale des sciences one of the two most important scientific institutions of seventeenth-century France. His project for the garden was extraordinarily ambitious, conceived and developed in opposition to the committed Galenists of the Faculté de médecine de Paris at a time when botany was still considered a crucial branch of medical knowledge. With the Jardin, La Brosse aimed to promote the study and knowledge of plants from all over the world; he advocated on behalf of an experimental practice that involved not just observing or describing plants but analyzing their chemical composition, and he hoped that the Jardin would become a place where those too poor to pay for other remedies could come to find plant-based medicines free of charge. René Pintard compares La Brosse's commitment to experimental methods (rather than reliance on textual authority, as was the practice of the Sorbonne) and his condemnation of all orthodoxies unbuttressed by

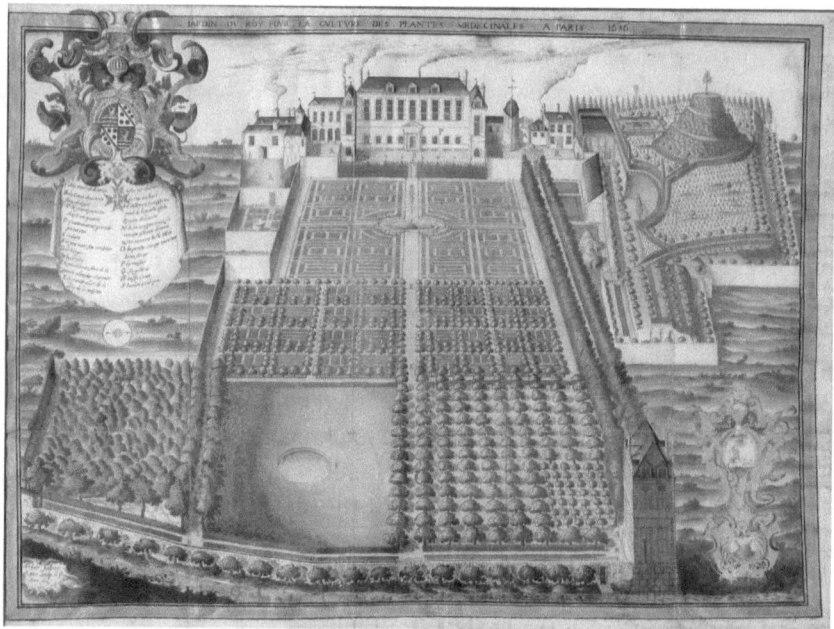

Figure 1. *Jardin du roy pour la culture des plantes médicinales*, signed by Federic Scalberge, Paris (1636). Bibliothèque nationale de France.

reason to the positions more famously (and arguably less boldly) taken up by Descartes some years later.[13]

For Pintard, La Brosse performs an "audacious synthesis" of disparate libertine ideas.[14] While botany might seem an unlikely place for such audacity to realize itself, the libertine dimensions of La Brosse's latent materialism make themselves acutely felt in his relationship to plant life.[15] La Brosse's plants become the locus for studying an animated materiality that serves as a point of contact linking heavens to earth, even as La Brosse uses plants to articulate an understanding of terrestrial life as infinitely diverse, variously animated, and vibrantly ensouled. This vision is both poetic in its recourse to analogy and scientific in its reference to (and endorsement of) experimental practice and observation. It is also heterodox and forward-looking. For La Brosse, it is the Jardin du Roi that will eventually serve as the instantiation of his intellectual approach. The garden is meant to make visible and material the (alchemical) philosophy of plant life that he outlines, and allow the public at large to enjoy the powers and proximity of plants.[16]

Savinien Cyrano de Bergerac (1619–1655), despite and perhaps even because of Edmond Rostand's play[17] loosely based on his life, is an enigmatic figure, like La Brosse, associated with the libertine milieus of his time. Part of Pierre Gassendi's circle, he was a brilliant but also dangerous disciple of the master.[18] Cyrano's philosophical positions are eclectic and unsystematic, libertine (particularly in their insistence on the animating force of sexuality) and difficult, if not impossible, to classify. Yet for Cyrano, as for La Brosse, plants—more specifically, the forms of life of which plants are capable—play a key role in the development of a theory and poetics of materiality in which humans are not given precedence. Where La Brosse dreams of a garden that will make the curative powers of plant life accessible to a broader public, Cyrano animates his plants primarily in fiction. His novels make of the literary work a space for experimenting with, and feeling the effects of, the deprioritization of human beings in a marvelous cosmos that teems with creatures, real, fictional, and mythical. While Cyrano was not a practicing botanist like La Brosse, plants appear at key points in his narratives, not just as an index of human contingency but as crucial interlocutors for humans on a journey through a new spatiotemporal continuum.

In the works of La Brosse and Cyrano, a realization settles in: plants are both familiar and strange, part of our most mundane reality and key actors in a physical reality that surpasses us. This realization had also been harbored, in different contexts, by medieval alchemists and the French essayist Michel de Montaigne, and thus is not entirely without precedent.[19] But the way in which La Brosse and Cyrano prioritize vegetal matter and plant bodies as a model for animate life in general is new. The libertine botany practiced by La Brosse, wherein plants, in their multiplicity, specificity, wondrousness, and curative force, compel human attention and care, has a deep kinship with the libertine materialism expressed in the fantastic tales of Cyrano de Bergerac, wherein humans seek a new relationship to a cosmos that far exceeds them. Reading La Brosse's botanical work and Cyrano's fiction side by side allows us to avoid positioning these syncretic writers within rigidly defined conceptual frames (whether atomistic or alchemical in the case of Cyrano, or Paracelsian or medical for La Brosse) and to concentrate on their eclectic ways of describing and interacting with the natural world, in particular by according a privileged place to plants. By juxtaposing these two authors, who approach an infinite universe through the intermediary of a radical botany, we can locate the emergence of a vegetal modernity in the first half of the seventeenth century. These libertine plants are the carriers of a form of life that moves in ways that are never fully apparent—or indeed fully accessible—to humans but that nonetheless seems to enable new modes of relationality, new affects, and eventually new practices of sociability to come into being.

Guy de La Brosse's Garden of Particularized Plants

In his important botanical text *De la nature, vertu et utilité des plantes*[20] (1628), La Brosse undertakes a systematic investigation of plant life that begins with a rejection of ancient forms of knowledge in favor of an emphasis on the examination of living bodies.[21] Yet, *De la nature* is committed to a vision of plant life that retains the notion of the soul as an animating force. As Rio Howard has argued, La Brosse's interest in the particularity and variability of individual forms of plant life is in tension with his attempts to establish a botanical system for the consideration of the plant as such. In the end, he is more committed to describing the specificity of each and every plant as it is available to experience and experiment than to the unchanging plant soul, an entity that he considers to be ultimately unknowable. La Brosse's work thus becomes a remarkable and sometimes disorienting concatenation of different strands of late sixteenth-century and early seventeenth-century thought, including Baconian empiricism, Paracelsianism, and hermeticism, each of which is mobilized to serve the purpose of describing how individual plants grow and (literally) behave. But it is in La Brosse's acknowledgment of the amazing suppleness and richness of each plant as a singular being that the plant becomes a figure for life and materiality more generally.

Indeed, perhaps the most astonishing feature of La Brosse's botanical speculation is that he lends to each plant an "incorruptible" soul that is "individual and indivisible," and that lasts as long as the earth does. "We have shown that they are individuals," he writes, "and that, if they live on, they do so individually, and as result we understand that they are incorruptible, and that they will only perish with the earth."[22] The life of plants is both tied to the soil and to the earth considered as a planet (since "*terre*" also has both meanings in French), but Earth itself is on the way to becoming a self-animating garden, no longer in need of supralunar governance or the transcendental or divine breath of life. While La Brosse's position is not a materialist one—in that it preserves an emphasis on the soul as the vital force that gives form to each individual plant—he ties the soul so intimately to the body in its specificity (each plant retains its own soul, and souls are not shared across beings, or across categories of being, although souls have properties in common) as to generate almost a materialism *à demi-mot*, as Didier Kahn has put it.[23] Moreover, the ascription of a soul to each individual plant motivates the close observation and examination of *every* plant, considered in the fullness of its own being. The reader can find in La Brosse's vegetal ontology a move toward a radical botany that will place the plant at the center of investigations of a universe that engenders both human awe and desire for mastery.

La Brosse's insights into the souls of plants come from direct observation in the botanical garden, an empirical engagement that is nonetheless augmented by poetic descriptions and alchemical speculation. He writes, "So one should not enter into [the study of nature] with arms crossed and hands tucked into one's armpits, both arms and hands should be used to search the ground for metals, to tear out and dig up plants, and to eviscerate animals, then to examine the whole with fire, for this is how one acquires real wisdom."[24] Here minerals, plants, and animals become the focus of a scientific practice that violently searches out, excavates, and even disembowels its objects. All creatures are made to be submitted to the alchemist's fire. Yet, the violence of this image belies the extent to which La Brosse, in the work that follows, not only ascribes to the plant faculties more commonly accorded animals but elevates the plant to the level of the stars. Human access to life is violent and interventionist, but this violence is exceeded by the marvel of the life that it uncovers. In La Brosse's cosmic garden, matter is not only a passive object or a mere reflection of the agency of the human mind but is also active like the human being who observes, manipulates, and experiences wonder in it. La Brosse describes the "excellence of plants" in his first chapter:

> The innumerable and various forms of beauty that we see in plants can reasonably persuade us, through their silent mouths, that these first daughters of the earth are not produced by wise nature as a frivolous ornament of the countryside, and that, surpassing in quantity and in bounty the stars of the firmament, they have another purpose entirely. For this fine language, written in so many vibrantly [*au vif*] beautiful colors, tastes, odors, and figures, is not less understandable than that of mouths that speak openly: the latter can deceive, but the former, carrying their heart on their lips, oblige us to believe them. The favors that they have received in appearing first among the living things on the face of the earth, even before the stars that embellish the sky, and in feeling first the effect of divine benediction, are a certain proof of their worth.[25]

La Brosse's plants are in conversation with the cosmos, while also calling into question the hierarchy of a closed system in which the sublunar realm corresponds to and is governed by the supralunar one. Plants are not regulated by the movements of the stars but by souls (and accompanying properties) that are specific to each one. If La Brosse invokes a divine rationality for being, he does so in order to give plants priority over all other forms of life. Plants speak—and they always tell the truth. He goes on to argue on behalf of "the diminished utility of minerals and animals in comparison to plants,"[26] and to claim that there are no humans on Earth who have succeeded in living without them.

The likening of plants to stars promotes plants to one of the primary mysteries of nature and gives them a cosmic significance that they would otherwise lack; this elevation of the plant is coupled with the emphasis on close observation (and dissection) of actual plants to create a mixture of hermeticism and the new post-Baconian science.[27] La Brosse's initial goal in *De la nature* is to identify in plants a richness and diversity of life that the Scholastic tradition denies them. According to La Brosse's definition: "[T]he plant is an animate and living body, halfway between mineral and animal, and attached to the earth, its womb and nursemaid, without which it would be able neither to live on its own nor to reproduce. This definition, more extensive than that of our predecessors, is also more obvious."[28] Here La Brosse follows Montaigne in affirming that the connection of plants to the mineral earth does not prevent them from being alive and animate. La Brosse's notion of the soul is both specific to any given being— "all subjects of nature have individual souls"[29]—and common to all beings without hierarchical distinction: "[O]f all the souls that inhabit the universe, as forms that give being to things, some are not more ensouled than others, just as the life that results is not more lively in one subject than in another."[30] By way of contrast, Francis Bacon, La Brosse's contemporary, did not privilege the specificity of plants but described plants as having less animacy than other beings. In his *Sylva sylvarum*, Bacon claims that plants lack the "cell or seat" of life (the heart in animals), and that their souls hold less heat ("flame") than animal souls. Moreover, he depicts plants as immobile, incapable of selective nutrition, lacking sense and voluntary motion, and defined by internal simplicity as opposed to the complexity of animals.[31]

As La Brosse points out, not only does a close observation of plant life and plant functions make it difficult categorically to deny them capacities for movement and even feeling (including affects such as joy and sadness), but animal life, too, has variants that are so restricted in their mobility or sensations as to functionally resemble plants (at least as they are described by Aristotle, reduced to nutritive and reproductive capacities). However, La Brosse's granting of animal qualities to plants does not simply make them analogous to animals. Here we diverge from Brancher's reading of La Brosse's plants as fully animalized,[32] since in La Brosse the analogy is never completely developed, merely intimated, and is ultimately abandoned in favor of a more vivid interest in animated matter that is shared across different life-forms, along the lines of alchemical conceptions of precreational matter as vegetal and Montaigne's animated plants. With La Brosse, we see that uncovering the libidinal, emotional, and sensitive properties of plants does more than blur the distinctions between the two orders of being by reclassifying plants as lesser animals. La Brosse charts the incredible specificity of plants by widening the scope of meaningful observation to include the capacities for sleep and wakefulness, but he also uses the example of plant life to argue on behalf of an ensoulment that both traverses all beings and varies (potentially infinitely) according to the capacities of each individual. His model for this project is not the animal—or the human—but instead the "fine language" of plants. The ensouled, animated plant acquires an extraordinary degree of integrity and liveliness, one that far exceeds the liveliness attributed to plants by Aristotle. Contra the Aristotelian position, La Brosse claims that the equality of animal and plant life manifests itself through equivalent actions carried out by both plants and animals; he thus also revives a pre-Aristotelian ascription of desire, feeling, and movement to plants while retaining an emphasis on vegetal ensoulment.[33] In this way, La Brosse deprioritizes the human and animal soul, so that plants take on the capacities normally associated with "higher" forms of life. At the same time, La Brosse suggests that our habitual denigration of plants as beings of minimal life or lowly status is a sign not of defects in their nature (as in the Aristotelian and Scholastic paradigms) but in ours. If we do not perceive the diversity and variety of plant life, it is because our observational skills are lacking; our inability to distinguish among plants is comparable to the inability of a dog to distinguish finely among human beings using only his nose. La Brosse's methods of observation and description serve to take us beyond the limits of our own senses and to suggest that the knowledge of plant life requires humans to reorient themselves vis-à-vis a physical world that is more profoundly marvelous than they have ever suspected.

La Brosse writes eloquently of the way in which plants "choose" their food and "have their seasons when they fall in love,"[34] of their reactions to touch and of their expressions of pleasure and displeasure. The animating function of La Brosse's botany is not just applied to the plant as an object. In *De la nature*, plants also index a form of materiality that is animated in ways that we might not even perceive. In his affirmative response to the question "Do Plants have several senses?"[35] La Brosse writes, "And then we do not know all the senses in nature; she provides various means for perceiving objects to her subjects, means that we know nothing of, since it is impossible for us to penetrate all the way to the causes that nature gives. The ancients only envisioned five in man, even though there are seven in fact; perhaps at some other time more will be found."[36] We can observe many instances of plant sensitivity, but there may be others to which we do not as yet have access. The complexity and richness of plant life is an incitement to humans to know more, as well as a sign of the diversity of the natural world, of which humans constitute only a part.

Plants certainly also serve La Brosse as objects of knowledge to be manipulated, distilled, and exploited. The establishment of the Jardin du Roi brings the animated plant out of the context of botanical theory and under the control of the gardeners, scientists, and natural philosophers who will occupy and manage this new institutional space. Yet even within the garden, plants continue to serve an active, mediating function. The garden works to harness their power on behalf of humans but also to establish the proximity between humans and the plants they cultivate. (La Brosse repeatedly remarks that the reason that plants are so useful for medicine is that their nature is closer to that of humans than is the nature of minerals.) After outlining a long list of doctors and natural philosophers who have prized plants for their medicinal properties, La Brosse explains: "For, having noticed that our bodies have connections and relations to everything that this terrestrial globe contains, they have observed that these bodies were more violently or imperceptibly affected through the use of minerals than they were of vegetables, the former being more distant from the animal kingdom, while the latter are in between the two."[37] Plants are animate on their own terms, but they also serve to reanimate and rehabilitate human bodies in ways that confirm their kinship with us. They remain both mysterious to us and powerful over us.

La Brosse's science is not just a description or observation of plants in motion and in action; it also aims to function as a technique of animation in its own right, in this perhaps imitating plants themselves as animated and animating matter, and making use of the inherent mobility of plants to imagine new technologies of representation. In the sixth chapter of *De la nature*, on the incorruptibility of the plant soul, La Brosse describes an extraordinary scene of plant "resurrection" (as Brancher puts it[38]):

A certain Polish doctor, according to Joseph du Chesne, knew how to enclose the ghosts of plants in vials, so that as often and as many times as he wished he could make a plant appear in an empty vial; each vessel contained its own plant; at the base of it appeared a bit of earth like ashes; it was sealed with the seal of Hermes; when he wanted to expose the plant to our sight, he heated up the bottom of the vessel; the heat, penetrating the container, caused to rise up out of the bosom of the matter within a stalk, some branches, then leaves and flowers according to the nature of the plant in question, whose soul he had enclosed; everything remained for a while before the eyes of the spectators, as long as the heat remained; the latter ceasing, this plant withdrew into its matter and back into a state of repose.[39]

This experiment with palingenesis (first described by the French Paracelsian Joseph du Chesne in 1604[40]) is used by La Brosse as an example of plant immortality. Yet, if this scene looks back to a tradition originating in alchemy, it also looks forward to techniques of animation three hundred years in the making—the time-lapse films of late nineteenth-century science and early cinema that animate the plant in an electric form. The unnamed Polish scientist here mobilizes the plant, albeit with a technique that is difficult to repeat (much to La Brosse's chagrin). These resurrected plants appear before viewers in a simulated model of actual plant growth, whereby stalks and branches precede the appearance of leaves, flowers, and presumably fruits. With this magical scene, La Brosse not only enters into the realm of animation as representation—what is exposed to the eyes of observers is in a sense the image of the materializable plant soul, rather than the soul itself—but prefigures the rise of imaging techniques as a means to plumb the "secrets" of the enigmatic plant. He also conjures up vegetal copies, images, and ghosts. At the same time, the scientific experiment described here operates as an allegory for his arguably much more successful attempts to animate plants by means of the descriptions of *De la nature*. La Brosse invokes the visual representation of plants through the reanimation of the spectral plant, but he does not privilege visibility as such. La Brosse's ghostly plants work together with his project for the garden in order to generate a new scientific and poetic epoch—one in which vegetal materiality provides the model for a universe in motion where human beings are not the only agents. As we move toward the texts of Cyrano de Bergerac, we see how this materiality can become the key to a new kind of fiction, one in which the plant, a being in which natural philosophy, poetry, and legend commingle and commune, functions as the carrier of a materialist message across the cosmos.

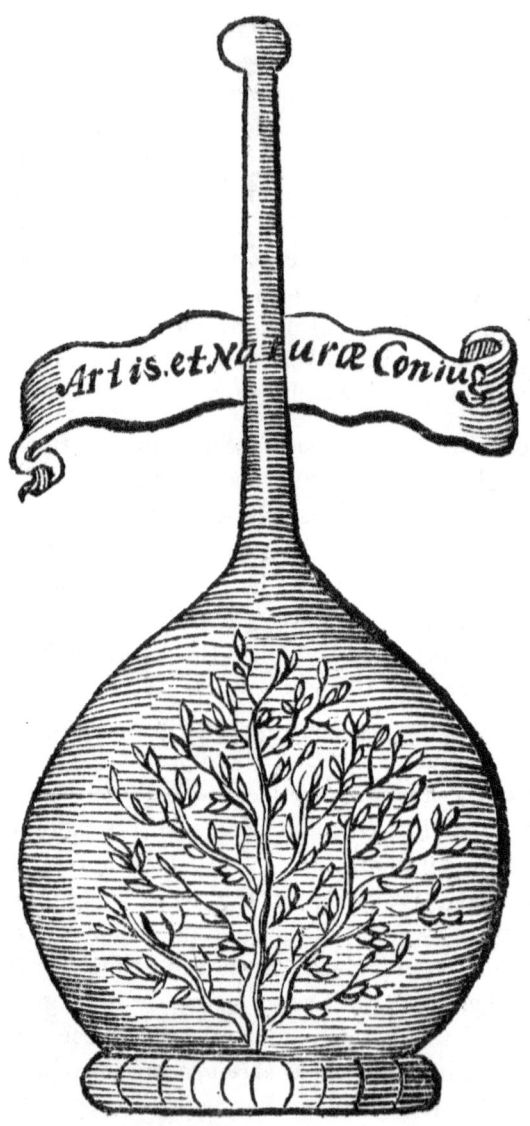

Figure 2. Palingenesis, or the rising of a plant from its burned ashes. Athanasius Kircher, *Mundus subterraneus* (vol. 2, book 12, p. 414), apud J. Janssonium and E. Weyerstraten, 1665. The Huntington Library, San Marino, California.

Cyrano de Bergerac's Marvelous Vegetables

Cyrano de Bergerac's fantastic tales *Les États et Empires de la Lune* (*The States and Empires of the Moon*) and *Les États et Empires du Soleil* (*The States and Empires of the Sun*),[41] first published separately after his premature death in 1655 and commonly referred to as *L'Autre monde* (*The Other World*), are hybrid works in both form and content. Neither romances nor "*récits de voyages*," neither "*contes*" nor fables but "philosophical fictions,"[42] mixing references to actual philosophers, the Bible, Greco-Roman mythology, and literary characters, these two works narrate the adventures of a man (eventually given the name "Dyrcona," a modified anagram of Cyrano) who journeys first to the moon and then to the sun in vehicles he builds with his own hands. If the tales convey some of the most salient philosophical and scientific thought of the period, they do so through a variety of perspectives with which they experiment and play. Italian philosopher Tommaso Campanella, the great alchemist and hermeticist of the early seventeenth century, appears as a friend of the rationalist Descartes. Socrates's demon, a mobile (yet material) spirit whom Dyrcona first encounters on the moon, recounts the tale of having visited La Brosse (as well as the Renaissance mathematician Gerolamo Cardano, the occult philosopher Cornelius Agrippa von Nettesheim, the fictional Doctor Faust, Campanella, and fellow French libertine thinkers François de la Mothe le Vayer and Gassendi[43]) during a journey to Earth. Renaissance and medieval alchemy and the doctrine of sympathetic resemblances take their place alongside a neo-Epicurean atomism and an emphasis on the transformative power of the imagination. Libertine materialism, in which sexual pleasure plays such an important role, exists in tandem with an emphasis on rational scientific inquiry into the physical world.[44] Scientific and philosophical syncretism, which is defiantly naturalist but also accommodates marvel, characterizes Cyrano's fiction and resonates with La Brosse's willingness to adapt Paracelsian principles to his practice of observation.

While Cyrano is no botanist, plants feature prominently in his tales of voyages to the moon and sun, and participate in an exemplary way in the wondrous variability of the natural world. Animated plants not only render the mechanics of matter increasingly visible but also allow an affective relation to form between human subjects and this newly conceived infinite nature. Cyrano's narrator reacts to his explorations of diverse modes of being mostly with pleasure and interest; he is stimulated by travels in which his own humanity is repeatedly called into question. His initial encounters with plants—both familiar material beings and privileged examples of the movement of matter—allow for a passage toward a cosmos in which conventional hierarchies (plant/animal, small/large, inanimate/animate) are overturned and assumptions about the status of individual life-forms are repeatedly called into question. As it is described in both journeys, space travel implies these reversals of perspective—from the vantage point of the moon, the earth is a moon to the moon that has become an earthly paradise—and puts seemingly commonsensical and ordinary ideas, including the belief that plant life is passive and without feeling, into question. However, Cyrano's botanical images are most lively, most spirited and witty, when his writing seizes upon vegetal shapes, such as that of the cypress tree, which he humorously describes in a letter: "I wanted to send you the description of a Cypress tree, but I did not get beyond drafting it, for it is so pointy that my spirit was not able to settle on it. Its color and shape remind me of an upside-down lizard, spearing the sky while biting the earth."[45]

Cyrano is inspired by seventeenth-century interpretations of ancient atomism, including the work of Gassendi,[46] that move from an investment in the atomic structure of material bodies toward a mechanistic view of the universe. As Jean-Charles Darmon has expertly shown, Cyrano takes the central questions of the new mechanistic philosophy—the material constitution of reality, the relationship between atoms and the void, the place of humanity in the hierarchy of beings—and transforms them into experimental and speculative fiction.[47] Alexandra Torero-Ibad has suggested that the various worldviews presented in the *L'Autre monde* converge in a sense of matter as self-organizing and a universe that is thoroughly material, where the miraculous gives place to the marvelous.[48] The Spaniard whom the narrator meets on the moon dismantles Aristotelian notions of matter; the second lunar professor outlines the main tenets of Epicurean atomism but also emphasizes the significance of fire in a distinctly non-Epicurean manner; Campanella, the philosopher whose soul appears on the sun, outlines a Cartesian mechanism devoid of its transcendental dimensions; and, finally, the narrator espouses a form of materialist vitalism in his description of the "little men" who inhabit the sun. The goal is thus not to present a coherent theory of matter or the cosmos but to suspend the common perception of the world that is ratified by received authorities (especially the Catholic Church and Scholastic philosophy) while also representing for the reader a diversity of material forms that engender and organize themselves.[49] It is in this latter capacity that the plant—and the seed in particular—plays a crucial role.

Libertine Botany and Vegetal Modernity 43

Conceptually, the seed has a powerful resonance for this period; as a figure and an organizing idea, it wends its way through Stoic, Epicurean, and, later on, Paracelsian doctrine, as Hiro Hirai shows.[50] Cyrano makes a typically eclectic use of the image, in a way that mobilizes both atomist and alchemical traditions. At the same time, though, seeds in Cyrano take on a strong vegetal element; they are the seeds of real, material plants in addition to serving as a metaphor for the constituent parts of the universe, or for the energy that animates this universe. In this sense, where Cyrano draws on the image of the seed culled from various schools of thought in order to tie together multiple and potentially contradictory philosophical approaches to the question of matter and its operations, his most important contribution may be that he also *vegetalizes* these approaches—making them over in the image of the plant itself even as he brings back this image to its roots in living beings. Cyrano's fiction concretizes and materializes the metaphor by stressing the connection between seed and plant.

Seeds in various episodes—including in the narrator's speech to the governor of New France, the demon's description of a rational cabbage, the dancing pomegranate seeds, and the oak trees that travel as acorns from the earth to the sun—constitute a self-replenishing world of beings. Cyrano's seeds generate their power and motion not mechanically but from the fire that they contain. (Of course, a mechanistic universe does not need fire or any other special substance to keep it moving; the emphasis on inner fire makes for another departure from any dogmatic Epicureanism.) Cyrano's expansively mobilized seeds work as both a concrete instantiation of an abstract concept and as a poetic device. Indeed, Cyrano's fiction precedes mechanist inquiries into the physiology of the plant and cannot be assimilated into a proto-empiricist orientation that seeks to identify or calculate the mechanisms of vegetal function.[51] For Cyrano, fiction is a technology of animation that functions similarly to alchemy in La Brosse, for whom fire also plays a key role; it "resurrects" and vivifies its objects. As atoms (for Lucretius) resemble letters, the book itself takes on a motion all its own—one of the first images of the narrative is that of a self-moving book—and communicates this motion to the reader. Cyrano's literal rendering of "the seeds of things" thereby takes on a double trajectory. On the one hand, the seeds of plants, animated by fire and fiction, lead us out into an expansive cosmos in order to make visible the inherent mobility of the physical world; on the other hand, the plant itself acquires previously unheard of capacities to figure movement and engage humans. Cyrano's fictional plants actively solicit our interest—affective, libidinal, and intellectual.[52]

The vegetal seed appears in the text even before the narrator succeeds in making his lunar voyage, in the episode in which he arrives in New France (today's Canada) in a failed attempt to reach the moon.[53] In a conversation with the governor of New France, the narrator explains his view of a heliocentric universe by means of a comparison linking plant seeds, the genitals of animals, and the sun: "[I]t is common sense to believe that the Sun has taken up its place in the centre of the universe, since all the bodies in nature need this radical fire, which dwells in the heart of the kingdom just so that it may promptly satisfy their needs and so that the cause and origin of all generation may be placed equidistant from the bodies on which it acts, just as nature in her wisdom has placed the genitals in the middle of man, the seeds in the centre of apples, and kernels in the heart of fruit."[54] This early passage affirms that the seed (in the heart of the fruit), the genitals, and the sun all contain fire.[55] The significance of this "radical fire" or heat reappears as an element of the modified atomism of the second lunar professor whom the narrator encounters on the moon. The second lunar philosopher first describes the universe as made up entirely of atoms but then characteristically diverges from the teachings of Epicurus and his followers to speculate that fire is made up of a combination of pyramidal and round atoms that allow it to flicker forever and penetrate all matter as a material source of perpetual movement. In this way, fire becomes a figure for the infinite motion of atoms themselves. Thus, while the lunar philosopher distinguishes fire as its own special kind of matter, "which both builds up and breaks down the universe in its parts and as a whole . . . [and] has pushed and gathered into an oak all the shapes necessary to make up that oak,"[56] he also makes fire both the cause and the vivid image of the animatedness of all matter in an atomist universe. Fire makes up the sun itself and later becomes the material ground for the marvelous experiences of the sun-bound narrator. As Torero-Ibad argues, fire is a form of material soul, one that circulates from one being to the other. As the demon suggests: "Do you not see that an apple tree, by the heat of its germ, as if through a mouth, sucks and digests the grass that surrounds it?"[57]

The vegetal example of this material soul, the apple tree that ingests and digests the meadow around it, is a recurrent theme in Cyrano's tale. Cyrano attributes an animating material soul to plants that guarantees both their transmutability and the transmutability of all matter. The theory of fire as a galvanizing force explains why the seed as the reproductive part warms and fructifies the rest of the vegetal body—both building and, ultimately, destroying the plant—just as the sun warms the earth and the genitals enliven the human body, thereby activating the process of generation. This explanation posits an equivalence among beings normally considered entirely distinct from one another. The fire-induced process of generation also implies the eventual degeneration of all bodies, except for fire itself, which continues to circulate. The souls of human beings fly up to the sun and merge with it, with the exception of philosophers' souls, which continue an individual existence on the sun (thereby allowing Dyrcona to encounter Campanella and Descartes there). The soul of all beings consists of fire, says the second lunar philosopher, and this soul behaves according to the capacities of the organs that are attached to it.[58] Thus, the difference between animals and vegetables does not reside in the material soul but in the other atoms that form organs around it. Plants in these tales will act according to their outward shape and function, mostly as seeds, branches, and fruit that appear in fantastic combinations, but these shapes are prone to transformations due to the fire within. Cyrano does not lend to plants an individual vegetal soul, as La Brosse does; instead, he privileges the vegetal as a prime example of the mutability that informs the cosmos as a whole, even as he populates this cosmos with vegetal characters. At the same time, his emphasis on plant forms attributes specific functions and capacities to plants in an otherwise materially continuous universe. Plants thus retain an alterity within a fiction that stresses their particular shape and formal properties and turns these shapes into the concretization of speculative possibilities inherent in matter in movement.

The narrator lands on top of an apple tree when he first arrives on the moon. He finds himself among the broken branches, his face spattered with the apples that he has squashed. He soon discovers that he has landed in earthly paradise, albeit transported to the moon, and on top of the Tree of Life (in a parody of the biblical text). As the narrator surveys the scene, he describes colossal oak trees that seem not so much to be supported by the earth as holding it up with their enormous roots. In this marvelous garden, flowers do not require the assistance of a gardener to bloom and fill the air with their fragrance. This garden is self-generating and self-maintaining, unlike the biblical Eden, created by God. Next to the grove of oak trees, the narrator sees two meadows, where "flowers toss in the breeze . . . [and] seem to be chasing after each other to escape the wind's caress."[59] The plant world appears to be animate and to participate in an erotic game—a vision that will take on a more definite and material shape at the end of *Les États et Empires du Soleil*—while the fiction gives concrete life to what is here described as an impression or a mental image: a garden composed of and by sensitive and animated plants not unlike those invoked by La Brosse. What is more, just by gazing at the garden, the narrator feels himself revitalized and rejuvenated by a good fourteen years. This is a moment where material finitude (in the form of aging) is affirmed alongside the marvelous infinity of movement and life as nonanimal animation. Throughout the narratives, plants make visible to us, in fiction, the principles about which philosophers have hitherto only speculated.[60]

Toward the end of his voyage to the moon, the narrator meets a group of philosophers, one of whom refuses to consume plants that have not died a natural death because of his conviction that plants, like humans and animals, can feel pain. This proposition is usually read as a burlesque parody of received theological ideas, but since Cyrano's fiction affirms the equivalence of vegetal and animal souls, it can be seen as more than just mockery of authority. Instead, it ultimately gives plants priority as a mode of life, one that encompasses human ideals (of rationality and generosity) but also invites speculation to "descend" to the ground level. Socrates's demon explains:

> This cabbage you mentioned is surely as much a creature of God as you are? Do not both of you have God and Privation as your father and mother? Has God's intellect not been occupied for all eternity with the birth of the cabbage as much as with yours? Indeed it seems that he has more necessarily provided for the birth of the vegetable than for that of the reasonable creature, since he has placed the generation of a man at the whim of his father who could, as his pleasure decreed, either beget him or not, and yet he refused to treat the cabbage with the same severity; instead of placing it in the father's discretion whether or not to engender his son, God, as if more fearful that the race of cabbages might perish than that of men, constrains them to give themselves to each other whether they are willing or not, quite unlike men, who at best can engender in their whole lives only a score or so, while cabbages can produce four hundred thousand of their kind per head.[61]

With this statement, the demon places the cabbage outside of any economy governed by the pursuit of rationality, or self-interest. Where human beings are at the mercy of paternal caprice for their very existence, plant reproductive life is neither beholden to nor constrained by such an arbitrary authority.[62] The cabbage signals its animate and animating power (as well as its affective grip on the philosopher who refuses to eat it) by its capacity to reproduce itself *à l'infini*. The cabbage is its own hypereffective reproductive engine, in need of no paternal authority *and* no partner. The vegetal sexuality that is depicted here is unorthodox and without parallel in human society yet astonishingly productive. Although inassimilable to human models, it nonetheless exerts a power on the human observer who contemplates it and speculates about it.

The passage also calls into question, as Bruno Roche has shown, Christian ideas of the superiority of men.[63] God and metaphysical entities (e.g., generosity) are evoked systematically only to be brought "down" to earth, that is, to the cabbage and the material world. This is the purpose of the syllogism Socrates's demon resorts to by making the hyperbolic claim that the sin of killing a cabbage may be greater than that of murdering a fellow human, since the cabbage lacks an immortal soul (and thus has no afterlife to look forward to), "if cabbages were not given the inheritance of immortality with us."[64] Since the equality of cabbage and man is claimed by the demon, and since cabbages are mortal, the mortality of human beings is implied. As Roche's close reading reveals, the philosopher's subsequent words call into question, in a cryptic fashion typical of libertine writing, any transcendental attributes pertaining to both cabbage and human.[65] Here, too, Aristotelian hierarchies are "diverted" in order to affirm a materialism that pays particular attention to vegetal life. Once again, the garden, including the humble *potager* or domestic vegetable garden, is made into a site of cosmic significance.[66]

The demon, moreover, activates the image of the cabbage "head" (both a figure of speech and a reference to the portion of the plant that is usually consumed) by attributing to it rectitude and even saintliness. The demon defines the cabbage as the more obedient species, for it follows the divine command to reproduce and engages in a generous self-sacrifice by offering itself to the gardener. Yet, perhaps, he surmises, the cabbage has received other advantages from God to make up for the brevity of its existence. Might not cabbages, in their muteness, be concealing a supremely powerful intellect?[67] The demon continues, "[P]erhaps you will ask me which of their great thoughts they have ever communicated to us? But tell me, have angels ever taught us more than cabbages have?"[68] What may at first seem to be a gesture serving to anthropomorphize the vegetable is soon deployed to deny the existence of the transcendental categories on which the category of the human depends. The philosopher places the cabbage among the angels in order to destabilize our sense of our own (metaphysically guaranteed) superiority over other life-forms. Angelic cabbages, the demon postulates, are able to contemplate timeless entities: "[T]hat wise Maker ... gave them instead other organs, more ingeniously shaped, stronger and more numerous, which enable them to indulge in their speculative conversations."[69] Cabbages "speculate," according to the demon, by means of growing and reproducing in the garden. With the transcendental thus voided from the vegetable patch (and the universe), the demon's words celebrate the material cabbage, which is able to reproduce and engender itself and even hypothesize about and animate infinite worlds. The cabbage head thus leads us into a world that is in motion and self-generating but has no anthropomorphic direction or governance. In a hyperbolic image that collapses the superproductivity of the garden into that of language itself (through the play on the word "head"), vegetal generation again reveals the workings of a material yet marvelously vibrant universe, whose mechanisms are concealed by social conventions on earth.

Thus the plant is made of the same particles as other things, but it becomes functionally distinct and formally prolific in Cyrano's fiction. Reproduction was one of the specific purposes of plants in Aristotle's philosophy, their entelechy, so that anyone or anything reproducing had to have a vegetal *psūchē*. Cyrano materializes this Aristotelian vegetal aim, which is no longer embedded within transcendent rationalities (animal, human, divine) but characteristic of the sheer self-generation of matter, pleasure, and contingency, accompanied by a subversion of social norms and all activated in fiction. The demon underscores the difference between the Aristotelian ontology of embedded souls, in which the vegetable *psūchē* is contained in all other, more noble living organisms, and a libertine botany that sees in the plant a distinct and particular body, one that is not fully incorporated into human society and economy but remains capable of exerting a destabilizing force on these latter forms of organization with the mediating help of fiction.[70] Indeed, as evinced by the philosopher in the grip of the cabbage's affective force, the plant wields its own "technology" that allows it to exert its power over the human observer. What we trace in this book as speculative fiction—narratives of life and sociability that go beyond anthropocentric and anthropomorphic limits—owes a large part of its genealogy to Cyrano's humble cabbage.

At the same time that Cyrano's tale asserts the incommensurability of the garden vegetable with human reason, the plant is also being recuperated for an alternative economy of pleasure and desire—one that might eventually enfold the humans who are willing to acknowledge it. Thus, the demon's vegetal universe reveals itself as infinite and (eventually) capable of generating distinct types of pleasures.[71] The cabbage signals its difference from humans by its capacity to reproduce itself without limitations, as if to people infinite worlds with beings that, in their specificity, invite us to engage with them and discover alternatives to our own social identities. Finally, this moment in the text may be said to gesture in enigmatic ways to a homoerotic or queer sexuality as another nonnormative mode of action made possible by (or disclosed within) the lunar and solar voyages. Cyrano's material cabbage might thus find its place within the libertine garden populated by La Brosse's sensitive, individualized plants, animated by autonomous movement and desire.[72]

The alterity of the vegetable on the moon opens up a space for social and erotic encounters with the vibrant matter of plants in the *Les États et Empires du Soleil*. On the sun, where matter is particularly refined and changeable, the narrator finds out that beings can morph from one into the next in the blink of an eye. Shortly after landing on the sun, Dyrcona meets a being that takes on the form of a plant, at least temporarily. Falling asleep in a desolate landscape, he finds himself upon awakening under a very tall tree, which is a tree only in its form and that of its parts: its bark is made of gold, branches of silver, leaves of emerald, and its fruits (similar to pomegranates) made up of a "swarm" ("essaim") of large rubies.[73] To complete the uncannily bucolic arrangement, on top of the tree, a nightingale sits and sings. As one fruit detaches itself from this marvelous plant and gradually acquires a humanlike body, this "little man," who calls himself king of what turns out to be a society of atomlike particles, evokes the admiration of the narrator: "I must admit that when I saw this rational pomegranate, this little dwarf no larger than my thumb yet powerful enough to create himself, walk so proudly in front of me, I was seized by respect."[74] But here too, as in the vegetable garden, human form is deceptive. The tree itself falls apart only to recompose itself as "seeing, feeling, and walking" little men dancing festively around Dyrcona. Mineral, plant, and animal all resemble one another; all are animated by the imagination of the "little man," a sort of materialist homunculus, a figure of the sovereignty of matter. The anthropomorphic, albeit dwarfish, pomegranate-king commands respect as self-animating matter, rather than as a human being, and becomes his own organizing principle. In this regard, he elicits respect and wonder from Dyrcona, who, as we have discussed, sometimes has to rely on the marvelously revitalizing force of plants on his journeys to keep his youth or replenish his energy, and who is often powerless in his own (human) society, where he is the victim of uncurious, dogmatic authorities.

The dance of the parts of the tree creates a kind of vortex or "*tourbillon*" (possibly of Cartesian inspiration) that is "agitated" by the observer

Dyrcona as it also agitates him, constituting an interaction or exchange among bodies that is pleasurable to all parties, almost certainly erotically so. Dyrcona describes:

> I am wondering if, by restraining the inner springs of the will, he excited some movement outside himself, which led to what you will hear, but immediately afterwards, all the fruits, flowers, leaves, branches, and, finally, the whole tree fell apart into little men, seeing, feeling, walking, who then began dancing around me. As soon as these little men began to dance, I seemed to feel their excitement and movement in me, and my excitement and movement in them. I was not able to look at this dance without feeling that all parts of my body were pulled from my place, as if by a vortex moved by its own vibration and by the excitement of each and every one, and I felt the same joy spreading over my face that was spread over theirs by the same movement.[75]

This image of the vortex[76] evokes both the capacity of matter to communicate forms through contact and the idea of a sympathetic animation of which the principles will be recounted later in the text. As we witness here, it turns out to be possible to incite and transmit affect through the adoption of particular postures—or the mimicry of specific forms, including vegetal forms (themselves particularly changeable). Thus, the arboreal ballet that the narrator observes brings to him the kind of delight that is characteristic of the *"petits hommes"* who make up the elements of the tree itself. All matter is swept into the same vibration or shaking ("branle," a term with erotic connotations and the name of a dance from the period), and the plants turn out not only to be able to revitalize Dyrcona, as the Tree of Life does on the moon, but to engender in him a sympathetic feeling of delight. In their animation, they animate him in return. Dyrcona and the little men share in a collective pleasure that is immanent to matter.

This principle receives a more expansive explanation in the encounter with a solar philosopher who will be revealed to be Campanella. Dyrcona is surprised to discover that Campanella is able to read his mind, but the philosopher soon discloses his secret, saying: "Please know that, in order to know what is inside you, I arranged all the parts of my body in an order resembling yours, for, when all my parts are positioned like yours, I excite in me the same disposition of matter and the same thought that this disposition of matter excites in you. . . . It is impossible that the same vibration of matter not cause in both of us the same movement of the spirit."[77] The shaking or agitation of various bodies—including that of the pomegranate tree and, later, those of Dyrcona and Campanella—transmits not just specific postures but specific sensations, emotions, even thoughts. On the one hand, this vision of how bodies, ideas, and feelings come about relies on a mechanical or formal relation between particles, opening everything, including human bodies and minds, up to manipulation (a possibility that eighteenth-century authors such as Charles-François Tiphaigne de La Roche, whom we discuss in Chapter 3, will expand on). The vegetal form of this tree, capable of "humanizing"[78] itself in multiple ways as well as of "caressing"[79] the narrator, is what first draws him in and renders him curious. Vegetal postures and dispositions relay sensations to the human observer and interlocutor. The tree, the seed, the branch, the flower, and the fruit are productive, albeit mutable, vegetable forms activating Dyrcona's feelings and desires. On the other hand, this scene suggests the supreme malleability of bodies, events, and customs. Everything that exists—from relations, sentiments, and ideas, to politics, society, and sexuality—depends on an arrangement of parts. In this conjunction, fiction, which is also a disposition of material letters, words, sounds, characters, images, and thoughts, itself comes to serve as an activating force and as a conduit for the adoption of new attitudes and ideas, new political and social modes. The dispositional quality of matter is shared by writing and the garden, among all other things, and may be one of the reasons (besides the problem of censorship) why libertine botany's preferred medium is the written word rather than drawings and illustrations. Fiction is able to perpetuate the process of putting bodies in pleasurable communication by ensuring the passage of "a movement of the spirit" from one body (that of the book) to many others.

In the example of the pomegranate tree, the "unformed" flexibility of the plant, capable of taking on multiple shapes and attitudes—is recuperated by Cyrano for a materialist position.[80] Where the cabbage is sealed off from human contact—even as it gives itself to the human who will eat it—the tree actively solicits human desires and pleasures. The description of the tree, of course, suggests the continuity across matter of different sensations—even thoughts—but it also retains a specificity for form as such, in that distinct feelings are shown to be capable of being transmitted across different bodies that take on the same shape.[81] The dance of the elements of the tree, then, opens the possibility of a libertine pleasure that is communicated from plant to human. This is not to say that the plant is somehow reabsorbed back into the economy of human desire, but that vegetal difference—envisaged again as one of form rather than essence—might itself be the source of new and stimulating sensations (and the thoughts that accompany them) for humans.

If the head of cabbage and the pomegranate tree made up of little men suggest that the formal flexibility of plants can engender a kind of libidinal communication across diverse bodies that take on each other's positions, a vegetal mode of being initially inaccessible to humans returns in the oak trees that Dyrcona eventually encounters on the sun. It is at this point in the tale that the narrator evokes the creative power of human imagination, which, although weaker than that of the solar "animals," has nonetheless contributed to the multiplication and diversity of animate beings, particularly in myths and stories.[82] Various "demons" link the lunar and solar landscapes to the earth throughout the two journeys, but the oaks that appear toward the end of *Les États et Empires du Soleil* further enrich and complicate this connection.[83] On the sun, the narrator finds a forest of talking trees that turn out to be descended from the legendary oaks of Dodona of Greek antiquity. In the form of a talking oak grove, the plant as vegetal voyager speaks intimately with the human visitor to the sun and shares with him a knowledge that is at once earthly and otherworldly. As the oaks explain to Dyrcona, they were brought to the sun in the belly of an eagle, who swallowed acorns from the original grove in Greece and vomited them up when he arrived at his destination.[84] They tell Dyrcona that, while they are the only trees that speak Greek (which their ancestors learned in order to be understood by the human beings for whom they served as oracles), all plants are capable of language. Indeed, "the birch tree does not speak the same language as the maple tree, nor the beech tree the same as the cherry tree."[85] Here we might recall the "fine language" of plants ("*beau langage*") cited by La Brosse, which has become more than a banal metaphor; Cyrano imagines this language as a material possibility. As the solar descendants of the original groves, the oaks on the sun tell Dyrcona tales of love and metamorphosis inspired by Virgil and Ovid, in which men love other men, women love women, fathers love daughters, women love animals, and men love plants (among many possibilities). They explain that all sorts of mythological couplings—Pasiphae and the bull, Cinyras and Mirra, Iphis and Ianthe—are due to the consumption of apples from the trees that grew out of the ground upon which the true friends Orestes and Pylades expired. "Finally, these blessed lovers brought forth apples, but magic apples which produced even more miracles than their fathers. As soon as a person ate from Orestes's apples, he or she fell violently in love with the person who ate from Pylades's apples."[86] The oaks describe a world in which plants engender erotic experiences of astonishing diversity, running the gamut from the perverse to the normalized. In this encounter, the outlandish oak trees create a link between plant agency, sexuality, and enduring fictions drawn from or inspired by Greek mythology. And, in so doing, they once again implicate plants in the production of human imagination, speculation, and pleasure. The plants that we consume affect us in mysterious yet often delightful ways that introduce into our human sociability a vegetal element.

The oaks of Dodona speak to Dyrcona not only of human sexuality but also of the erotic life of trees, in a fashion similar to the modes of generation described by La Brosse (by whom Cyrano may have been inspired in this example) in *De la nature*.[87] They introduce explicitly erotic delight, no longer characteristic of the corruptible earthly realm, into the ethereal productivity of the solar landscape. Thus, while the lunar encounter with the idea of the celestial cabbage debunks earthly pretensions to patriarchal authority, the solar plants, both pomegranate tree and oaks, bring Dyrcona himself into the realm of unrestrained productivity. Initially, they elicit horror in Dyrcona, as he attempts to decipher who is speaking to him. However, they turn out to be beings with a role to play in human history, culture, and social life, even as they cultivate a vegetal communication of their own that withdraws from the human world. With the appearance of the oaks, Cyrano holds up the plant as the origin of (unorthodox) connections among humans. Moreover, these plants serve to defy the wishes of parents "who allow themselves to be governed by nothing but interest"[88] and thus set out to destroy the source of the apples, the better to be in charge of their children's desires.

Yet, these quasi-Ovidian tales that speak of the movable and permeable boundaries among minerals, plants, animals, and humans in general—and between plants and humans in particular—do not serve the sole purpose of "humanizing" plants. Trees speak Greek, but they also speak their own languages, for their own purposes. They retreat from human knowledge even as they affect and shape this knowledge. Like the Trees of Life and Knowledge in the first tale, they provide a material (and materialist) basis for a set of utopian possibilities. Plants allow for human pleasure in an infinite world without, however, requiring a human center for this world. The plant, throughout Cyrano's tales, works as a sign of both familiarity and difference, as a source of wonder and esteem, and finally as an interlocutor, a sort of extraterrestrial diplomat who gives a purchase for human interest and even serves as a conduit for human culture.[89] But the plant is not finally fully recuperable within that culture. Ultimately, in Cyrano's two narratives, plants provide us with insights that are valid both on the cosmic scale and on the human one. But they also engender in us a sense of the limits of our perceptions and our faculties. They inspire in us a respect for their power and vitality, and they oblige us to come to terms with the constraints that govern our experience. Plants inject joy into the otherwise dehumanized world of atoms, a joy unbounded by the norms that Cyrano thinks define the human realm. Plants and human beings might take on each other's shapes, but plants do reproduction better; they inspire respect and physical attraction; and they are even miraculously carriers of culture, as they transmit Greek language and classical sources to the sun all while preserving for themselves a language that we cannot speak.

Cyrano de Bergerac uses fiction as a site for exploring a world in which the animated plant is the messenger for a materialism that aims to transform our sense of the universe and of our place within it. His plants are rich in figural detail and intertextual references; at the same time, they reflect and intervene in philosophical debates around the nature of vegetal being. By comparison, Guy de La Brosse's empirically observed plants may seem much more concretely anchored in a scientific practice that takes the natural world as its object. Yet, La Brosse, too, approaches the plant as the example of a newly significant, autonomously animate mode of being that both eludes human knowledge and inspires in us curiosity and a desire to live in its affecting (and effective) presence. By locating the plant as a privileged figure for making sense of a post-Copernican universe, La Brosse and Cyrano stand at the origin point of a tradition of representation that reunites modernity and early modernity, and posits vegetal life as an interlocutor for a humankind coming to terms with its own removal from the center of things.

The plant, by virtue of its liminal status in the hierarchy of beings and its crucial role in inspiring social criticism and utopian speculation, signals both the tensions and potential joys of an emergent modernity. Plants serve as objects of study and as active participants in the world, vessels of speculative activity and the generative engines of production and reproduction. They oscillate between activating human desire and signaling the limits of the human way of apprehending the world. Moreover, La Brosse and Cyrano do not simply describe these vegetal beings but aim to imitate their technologies for receiving and producing affect with their writings. In both of these texts, then, plants stand out as the figures of a nascently modern world in which they play an ambivalent but important role. Plants' nonanimal animacy inspires new practices of writing and, at least in fiction, new ways of interacting. In the eighteenth-century texts that we analyze in the next chapter, a new form of vegetal sociability will be consolidated in narratives that seek to make of the plant a mechanism for the transformation of human society. But, here, too, the vegetal can never be fully recuperated into the human models that mobilize it in the name of a better life. The plant is thus a tool for sizing up worlds that are not quite on a human scale, although these worlds remain within the realm of speculation.

CHAPTER 3

Plant Societies and Enlightened Vegetality

Plant-Human Analogies in the Eighteenth Century

Theories of vegetality serve to propel a new form of social and political speculation in the eighteenth century, one that departs from long-standing pastoral and botanical models in which the plant primarily served as an "object of knowledge and poetry,"[1] and instead experiments with the intermingling of science and fiction, thus continuing the literary and epistemological project begun by Cyrano de Bergerac. In the imaginary vegetal societies of the eighteenth century, readers encounter a new kind of sociability, in which humans and nonhumans form various alliances, and allegiances among beings shift and migrate. Here the plant is once again prioritized, as in the work of Cyrano and La Brosse, for its specific vigor and growth, continuing the reworking of the Aristotelian qualities that are given a positive reading in the materialist critiques of the seventeenth century. These eighteenth-century fictions are more explicitly utopian than those generated by their precursors—that is, they use plant life as a basis for imagining a better human existence. Ultimately, alongside the gradual birth of biopolitical theories of government based in the management of populations and resources, vegetal vitality emerges as a mode of biopower that is autonomous and self-organizing, and thus becomes a model for the proper administration of human affairs despite its potential for exceeding or overturning all forms of political control. This chapter examines the ways in which the utopian plant, animate both physically and epistemologically, is put to work as part of an Enlightenment project of social and cultural reform.[2]

Plant life in this speculative context functions as both a privileged object of exploitation and a technology in and of itself. François Delaporte argues in *Nature's Second Kingdom* that in eighteenth-century botany, "[n]either the inner nor the outer structure of the plant lends itself to comparison with the artifacts of technology ... in large part because of what Jussieu calls 'the singularity of their structure.'"[3] Bernard de Jussieu (1699–1777),[4] along with other prominent botanists and classifiers of his period, moves away from the mechanical view of vegetal life by recognizing the unique organs that make up plant physiology. Conversely, in the fictions we examine, the technological "artifacts" to which Delaporte refers nonetheless remain in intimate relation with the vegetal world, for the especially complex and particular life of the plant suggests the need for a technology that will enable its apprehension. This linkage between organic and inorganic realms represents an ambivalent affirmation of human weakness rather than strength, in that it is based on the idea of a limited human perception that cannot grasp the plant in the fullness of its nature. Vegetal reticence—coupled with vegetal autonomy—inspires imagination in a way that extends to the production of fantastical technological forms.

The narratives that we examine here explore the analogy between plants and animals—so crucial to plant science during the period—as the basis for social and political thought. While these plant fictions may begin in a playful effort to extend to the "inferior" forms of vegetal life a "superior" organization typical of humans (in order to have anthropomorphic plants figure in human stories of perfection), they do not consistently remain in this anthropomorphizing stance. Delaporte argues that, for eighteenth-century botany, the analogy linking the structures and functions of animal life to those of the plant kingdom serves as a dominant epistemological and ontological paradigm. Yet, this analogy is mobilized to call into question the seemingly self-evident hierarchical relationship between humans and plants in at least some of the marginal works that use plants to think through the management of all life, including human social and political life. Thus, Ludvig Holberg (1684–1754) and Charles-François Tiphaigne de La Roche (1722–1774), authors of two examples of speculative plant fiction whose work we will discuss here, deploy the human-plant analogy to anticipate the move that Delaporte will claim as more typical of nineteenth-century plant physiology, for which "the lower forms of life were to shed light on the higher."[5] In doing this, they upend and unsettle human assumptions about who wields power, and how. For them, a vibrant but also unsettling plant life serves as both an exemplary mode of social reason and the end point or limit of reason as such.

Holberg and Tiphaigne are part of a sustained Enlightenment debate around the place of plants in a hierarchy of being that is itself often represented as a nested series of analogies. As Delaporte emphasizes, in this series, the animal term is often privileged. Botany as a systematic discipline of studying plants perhaps never enjoyed as much social prestige as in the eighteenth century, but its primary mode was most often to justify the instrumentalization of plants for "higher" human social ends. The management of populations also entailed feeding them, and agricultural and forest lands were limited resources; moreover, the demand to heat forges and glass kilns and to feed horses competed with the human need for food. The late eighteenth century was, in fact, a time of crisis in western European forestry, resulting from two and a half centuries of deforestation, which ultimately produced the first "energy shock"—the doubling of the price of wood in France between 1770 and 1790.[6] In this context, the question of how best to put plants to use for humans is literally a matter of life and death on both sides; the analogical connection between plant life and human life is no "mere" figure of speech.

This period also witnesses the development of a radical materialism that attacks ontological distinctions among life-forms as contested matters of belief rather than accepted truth. For instance, French materialist Denis Diderot (1713–1784) intervenes in debates about the status of animal versus vegetal life to question accepted hierarchies. In the article "Animal," from the *Encylopédie*—written in the form of an extended dialogue with passages drawn from Georges-Louis Leclerc, Comte de Buffon's *Histoire naturelle, générale et particulière* (1749–1788)—Diderot comments on the difficulty of establishing an absolute distinction between animals and vegetables. Diderot notes, in response to Buffon's remark, that the difference between animal and vegetable cannot be established "based on the means by which they nourish themselves": "This may be true, all the more so because this air of spontaneity that strikes us in animal movement, either when they seek out their prey or on other occasions, and that we do not see in plants, is perhaps a prejudice, an illusion of our senses that have been deceived by the variety of animal movements, movements that could be a hundred times more various than they are without being more free for all that."[7] Here Diderot elaborates suggestively on Buffon's own description of vegetal movement—a movement that is visible only if we pay close attention to root structure and action. As Buffon describes this activity: "We will soon recognize that plants make use of external organs in order to ingest food: we will see that roots avoid an obstacle or a bit of bad soil to go search out the good; even that these roots divide, multiply, and go so far as to change form in order to procure nourishment for the plant."[8] Diderot highlights the possibility of vegetal self-determination in this passage in order to question easy assumptions of human superiority—and even of human agency. While Buffon offers up a vision of roots actively seeking out an environment that might be propitious for them, Diderot gives us a picture of animals with all the spontaneity of vegetables—that is to say, entirely constrained (albeit variously so). Our inability to see in vegetables what we seem to see in animals may be nothing but a human prejudice, suggests Diderot. (Similarly, our tendency to find in animals what we do not find in plants—namely, freedom—may be an illusion of a different kind.) In this exchange, the conventional boundaries separating different modes of being are increasingly destabilized; the human tendency to privilege free will and autonomy of movement as sources of superiority is reconfigured by Diderot as a symptom of our inability to ascribe value to life-forms that do not resemble us.

Diderot's provocative revision of Buffon is in line with a radical philosophical materialism that fully levels ontological divisions among beings and was by no means a conventional (or risk-free) stance to assume.[9] Yet, visions of animallike vegetables and vegetablelike animals proliferate across the eighteenth century, both as an extension of earlier research into representations of vegetal life and as a response to period-specific discoveries including perhaps most famously that of Abraham Trembley's polyp, a freshwater "zoophyte" originally classified as a plant by Antonie van Leeuwenhoek in 1703.[10] Close examination of and experimentation with the polyp led Trembley to make a case for its animality, an account first published in his 1744 *Mémoires pour servir à l'histoire d'un genre de polypes d'eau douce, à bras en forme de cornes*.[11] The polyp, with its ability to regenerate itself when divided into pieces and its seemingly animal sensibility in a body that lacked recognizably animal organs, appeared to blur the distinctions between the two kingdoms and gave rise not only to vigorous scientific and philosophical debate but to provocative representations of "human polyps," including those populating Julien Offray de La Mettrie's 1748 treatise *L'Homme-plante* (*Man a Plant*). In these discussions, as in Diderot's response to Buffon, we see how eighteenth-century scientific materialism, like some of its earlier instantiations, emphasizes both the diversity and interconnectedness of living beings and works to counter and complicate the idea of the passive and transparent plant body, impervious to sensation. At the same time, as we will see, plants also remain troublingly indifferent to efforts to know them. They thus remain figures capable of oscillating between seemingly contradictory or opposing epistemological and ontological positions.

Yet, in key ways a response to the polyp such as that appearing in *L'Homme-plante*, published anonymously in Potsdam and attributed to La Mettrie, also departs from the libertine botany of earlier authors, such as Cyrano and La Brosse. Where La Brosse and Cyrano arguably establish vegetality in its fundamental difference from the human as the foundation for a newly lively vegetal materiality, La Mettrie's analogy between human and plant life-forms draws out multiple physiological similarities between humans and plants but ultimately refuses movement, desire, and, perhaps most significantly, needs to plants.[12] With La Mettrie, the ascription of need to humans (and not to plants) preserves for the human a place of epistemological superiority. In fact, desire—and a refined experience of pleasure of which plants are not capable—is what makes life interesting for La Mettrie in the first place. The networking of life that is characteristic of certain versions of eighteenth-century materialism does not *necessarily* involve a more positive assessment of the specific faculties of plants, although it may in certain instances.

La Mettrie writes, "Plants are rooted in the earth which nourishes them. They have no needs. They fertilize themselves. Lastly, plants are immobile. In sum, plants have been seen as immobile animals that lack intelligence and even feeling."[13] Here La Mettrie ratifies the plant/animal divide even as he vegetalizes key human functions—including, most notably, reproduction—and animalizes specific plant structures according to a hydraulic and mechanical model of the animate body. He continues, "Air seems to produce the same effects in plants that are rightly attributed to the subtle spirits in the nerves of man, spirits whose existence is proved by a thousand experiments."[14] La Mettrie sees plants as analogous to animals and animals as analogous to plants, yet by denying plants access to animal forms of movement, freedom, and need, he reinscribes the primacy of the animal model of life into his analogical system, with its fine gradations among beings. For example, structures such as the amnios, the chorion, the womb, and the umbilical cord are shared by plants and humans, as La Mettrie points out. Conversely, while in human birth the embryo emerges from the "material prison" of the mother's body by its own efforts, plant birth consists of a passive falling away from the mother plant.[15] While La Mettrie's vegetal physiology does tend to consider plants in their specificity—by identifying structures that are particular to them—it also threatens to erase this specificity by making them animals of a lower kind.

Moreover, La Mettrie affirms that intelligence, in organized bodies, is linked and proportionate to need. Lacking needs, plants also lack intellect. Vegetal structures and capacities might be understood as analogous to those of the human body, but plants remain at the same time, for La Mettrie, deprived of that which is properly human, specifically human sociability and social life: "The superior quality and ability of the human soul, its overabundance of illumination, that obviously result from man's constitution, make man the king of the animals, the only animal suitable for society, the only one to produce language, the only one with the wisdom to establish laws and morality."[16] The human soul may here be a result of material, physiological organization rather than divine creation, but it is no less distinct and exceptional for all that. It also retains sovereignty over nature in and through its ability to organize its own life socially. Even so, plant and human are not entirely detached from one another: "If chance has placed us at the top of the ladder, just remember that a trifle more or less in the brain . . . could immediately throw us to the bottom."[17] La Mettrie both sets up a distinction between human beings and plants based on need, and renders this difference a matter of degree rather than essence, thereby granting humans a form of fragile sovereignty that is vulnerable to being lost. His argument also implies that humans may in certain cases be cultivated like plants.

A striking image of the possible transformation of the human into a plant is given in La Mettrie's evocation of the army of the Prussian ruler Frederick the Great (1712–1786) as a "forest of fine men who cover Prussia."[18] "Moreover," La Mettrie asks, "do we not prune men like trees?"[19] The idea of forests of human beings (growing like trees), in which practices of cultivation and acculturation merge, evokes a dream of sovereign power over raw materials and populations for which Frederick serves as a model. The old topos of cultivation as metaphor for acculturation here is taken a step further to become a mode of sovereignty over life, and the fundamental passivity said to be characteristic of plants enables them to serve as model subjects for new forms of management. Indeed, the cultivation of people as if they were plants—a set of discourses and practices whose rise throughout the eighteenth and nineteenth centuries Michel Foucault famously identifies as the birth of biopolitical control—provides an alternative to the much more contentious social management of power through the negotiation of competing interests.[20] La Mettrie hints at—but does not develop—the idea that it is plants' unparalleled capacity for growth, strength, and uniformity of reproduction that renders them a privileged example not only of instrumentalized objects but also of subjects acting in the world. Within the image of cultivating men like trees, a new kind of vegetal sovereignty arises—one in which plants come back to haunt the human as the very origin of power over life. La Mettrie's description of the plant as a being without needs thus not only confirms the status of the plant as a lesser form of life, available for manipulation and exploitation, but also makes of it a double of the human.

The authors who will concern us in what follows, Holberg and Tiphaigne de La Roche, strengthen the ties between human society and vegetal life. Their utopias (or dystopias, depending on our perspective) appeal to a form of alternative reason generated by the plant in order to make this specifically vegetal rationality the organizing principle of human society. Up to a point, the plant serves as an exemplary model for human political control at the same time as it eludes humans' attempts at mastery when the analogy is pushed to its limits. The unique ways of being of plants—their slowness, their muteness, even their resistance to human modes of perception—also generate in these fictions a logic that can never be fully integrated into human society and politics. Thus emerge utopias within utopias that pivot around the alterity of the plant. Holberg and Tiphaigne de La Roche deploy the analogy between plant and animal life to upend assumptions of animal superiority and to imagine a world without desire.

We trace here a marginalized but resonant mode of thought, scientific yet imaginative and speculative, that affirms many of the aspects we associate with the unfurling of modernity, including an emphasis on the power of technology and scientific knowledge, on the importance of social reform and a (better) management of life and the living. These utopian plant worlds draw inspiration from a life-form that is typically externalized and instrumentalized by modernity, thereby providing a kind of counter to the latter's logic. Enlightened vegetal utopias can neither be fully separated from an emergent modernity, conceived in biopolitical terms, nor fully realized as an alternate reality that redeems or corrects modernity's errors. In these narratives, plants, instead of providing a foundation or origin point from which the human must extract itself, help to formulate the goal or end of human existence, so that vegetality provides the example of what life should and must be, if it is to reach its full potential. Yet, this ideal is ultimately inhuman in its transcendence—and erasure—of human institutions, themselves very much informed by human passions. Here Cyrano's angelic cabbage has become a whole society of vegetal angels, who have no need for culture. The deep (pastoral) connection between cultivation and acculturation, when pushed to its limit, breaks down.

Holberg's Enlightened Trees: Biopolitics *and* Ataraxia

Cyrano's *L'Autre monde* serves as a direct source of inspiration for the Dano-Norwegian Ludvig Holberg, who writes the tale of a society composed entirely of trees. While the text itself is not well known to present-day readers, Holberg's utopia had an influence on the work of Edgar Allan Poe[21] and might be considered the precursor to the fantasies of arboreal and vegetal societies that reappear throughout more contemporary works of fantasy and science fiction writing and film, including J. R. R. Tolkien's Ents; Italo Calvino's *The Baron in the Trees*, a historical novel set in the eighteenth century;[22] Ursula K. Le Guin's story "Vaster Than Empires and More Slow" (discussed in Chapter 7); James Cameron's *Avatar*, in which humanoid creatures commune with the forest landscape they inhabit; and Margaret Atwood's MaddAddam trilogy, a dystopian tale in which human society, driven into a crisis by unbound capitalism, is restarted with the help of a genetically engineered species, a docile, mildly plantlike, and herbivorous new human race called Crakers.[23] These works collectively consider alternatives to modern society, thereby sustaining and extending a broader eighteenth-century tendency to envision botany and plant life as sources of utopian social thought and reform. A return to Holberg's plant fiction, however, shows that plants also manage human life by dehumanizing it. The power of vegetality lies not just in its ability to be put to use by humans but in its capacity to undercut the human qualities of society itself.

Holberg's *The Journey of Niels Klim to the World Underground*, first published in Latin in 1741, follows the travels of a human to a subterranean world within our world, where he first lands upon a planet entirely inhabited by intelligent, rational trees.[24] The book's young narrator, Niels Klim, is a penniless Norwegian student who returns from his studies in the arts and sciences at the University of Copenhagen and goes to explore a deep cave, "in order to clear up by experience some points of natural philosophy."[25] As he begins his descent into the cavern, his rope breaks and he falls into a seemingly bottomless abyss only to find himself caught in the orbit of another planet inside the earth. Transformed from a speleologist into a celestial body in his own right (he calls himself "a new constellation"[26]), he is attacked by an eagle or griffin, who ends up pulling him down to the surface of the subterranean planet Nazar after Klim wounds him with the iron hook he was using to climb into the cavern. Having returned to the ground, Klim falls into a deep sleep, only to awaken when the attack of a bull drives him to take refuge in a tree. From here he makes an amazing discovery. Perching among the branches, he is struck by a blow that sends him back to the ground again. "Having opened my eyes, I beheld all about me a whole grove of trees, all in motion, all animated, and the plain overspread with trees and shrubs, though just before there were not above six or seven."[27] As Klim learns, the trees of this place, called Potu, are mobile and rational creatures, although he does not understand their language at first. Where La Mettrie's plants are denied language and sociability, the Potuan trees are possessed of both. Still, Klim has doubts: "For although these trees seemed to me to be sociable creatures, to enjoy the benefit of language, and to be endowed with a certain degree or portion of reason, insomuch that they had a right to be inserted in the class of rational animals, yet I much doubted whether they could be compared to men; I could not bring myself to think that justice, mercy, and the other moral virtues had any residence among them."[28] His sense of human superiority to other life-forms dies hard.

The tree Klim had attempted to climb turns out to be the wife of the principal magistrate of the nearby city—a discovery that provides the impetus for a series of reflections on government and gender equality. The Potuan society of animated trees is an enlightened one. The inhabitants are naturally good and treat Klim with a humanity that surpasses that of humankind itself. Yet, Potu is not a state of nature, unmediated or self-regulating, but a society whose laws ensure that everyone acts in the interest of the common good. The tree sheriff is shocked when he hears from Klim how trees are treated on "our Earth": "But it kindled his blushes when I told him of the trees of our globe, which were lifeless, immovable, and fastened by the roots to the ground; nay, he beheld me with some resentment when I attested that our trees were cut down for fuel to heat our furnaces and dress our provisions."[29] On Potu, the animal/vegetable hierarchy is inverted: vegetal society appears here as a kind of enlightened utopianism, where each member is compensated according to his or her merit, where women are not excluded from public functions based on their gender, and where everyone works diligently to ensure the prosperity of all. The inversion on which the fiction is based, that trees are not passive objects of exploitation but active subjects who wield sovereign power, does

Figure 3. Niels Klim in the land of Potu, Johan Frederik Clemens's illustration, based on drawings by Nicolai Abraham Abildgrad, in *Niels Klims underjordiske reise, oversat efter den latinske original af Jens Baggesen*, 1789. Cotsen Children's Library, Department of Rare Books and Special Collections. Princeton University Library.

not so much liberate all plants from being used as food or raw material (for the Potuans still practice agriculture and build houses like their human counterparts), as it doubles the role of plants as both exploited "things" *and* agents who deploy technology (including but not limited to agricultural techniques) and political power (in the form of an enlightened monarchy). For all its seemingly pastoral trappings, the world of trees is a modern one that parallels human society imagined in the utopian mode. While Klim notes quaintly that "[t]he art of printing, of which the Europeans and Chinese boast themselves to be inventors, was of far greater antiquity among the Potuans,"[30] the latter's most developed technology involves their careful biopolitical management of their own society, including promoting reproduction, sustaining and nurturing life, disciplining and "pruning" the body, and administering death.

Holberg's tale is marked throughout by the characteristically human hubris of the narrator, who first introduces himself as a notable graduate of the University of Copenhagen ("dignified indeed with various marks of honour from the gentlemen of the several faculties, but in my fortunes quite impoverished"[31]). While in the beginning of the tale the narrator's self-regard appears to be the characteristic immaturity of a recent graduate—he even shows his university testimonial to the griffin that attacks him in his plunge to the subterranean world—by the end this arrogance is revealed as typical of his species: "[W]hat, I say, could redound more to my glory than to have asserted that dominion which Nature gave mankind over the animal creation?"[32] This human presumption is consistently shown up as not only absurd—a refusal to acknowledge the evidence that he has before him—but as a source of the tribulations that beset Klim throughout his adventures and that end with him being sucked back out of the interior of the hollow earth and deposited at the mouth of the cave into which he had disappeared many years before. It is at this moment, lying in the mountains, "almost destitute of sense,"[33] that the narrator compares himself directly to a plant: "But a few days ago glory, hope, victory, and success attended my steps, and now care and misery, tears and lamentation are all my companions. In short, I resembled those summer plants which suddenly spring up and as suddenly die away."[34] If he is chastened enough, at this moment, to stress his similarity to a plant—when over the course of the novel he insists despite all evidence to the contrary on his innate superiority to the rational trees and intelligent animals he meets—this image of the summer plant serves to bring him down from his high horse of human superiority and thus bolster the narrative of inversion, in which trees rather than human beings represent rationality. With this lament, Klim paradoxically applies the perspective of the Potuans to himself, with respect to whose constancy and endurance he is indeed nothing but a short-lived and fickle being. At the same time, the comparison highlights the existence of a kind of plant that is unlike the arboreal members of the Potuan society, since it is vulnerable and without purpose outside its brief existence. While the strength of the Potuan trees indicates the presence of virtues to which humans could conceivably aspire (up to a point, as we shall see), thus ultimately furthering the utopian aim of improving human society, the image of the summer plant reveals the weakness of humanity. Holberg here signals a second dimension within the narrative of vegetality. We are not simply in the space of a philosophical lesson in which every fictional element can be retranslated as rational argument, but in the realm of a speculative fiction that enables multiple trajectories through a world that it both constitutes and illuminates.

Klim's initial disdain for the trees—who move slowly and deliberately in all things—is countered by their disdain for animal life. The latter, unlike the former, is more than justified by the available evidence. When Klim deplores the fact that he has been assigned the lowly position of King's Messenger due to his "swiftness of foot,"[35] the trees remind him that his relative speed is, in fact, his one redeeming characteristic. "'If Nature had not made you amends for the defects of your mind by some one excellence of body, all would behold you as an unprofitable load upon the earth; for that very quickness of parts permits you only to see the surface of things, and not the substance, and since you have but two branches, you are inferior to the Subterraneans in everything that depends upon the hands.'"[36] Holberg's rational trees do mammalian things but have a disdain for animals, who are too hasty. Their society collapses the distinction—between the raising of humans and the cultivation and harvesting of plants—that works in the human world to sustain a modern division between knowing subjects and objects of knowledge, between life-forms worthy of recognition and those destined for exploitation. At the same time, Holberg stresses the proximity of vegetal life to a rational ideal. The plant functions both as a satirical device (since it is ironic for a lowly being to embody the highest ideals of reason) and as a utopian figure for exemplary social organization, while humans are mocked for being less suited than plants to a rational order of things. From a twenty-first-century perspective, such ill-suitedness might be for the better, in that it allows humans the potential to evade or elude biopolitical control, an alternative narrative of vegetal enlightenment that will be activated in other, later contexts.[37] For Holberg, however, the ability of the trees to seamlessly instantiate a rational social order remains an ideal rather than an object of critique.

Potuan social life is tied to the nature of plant motion: the trees move very slowly compared to the earthly visitor, and this slowness confers upon them a moral and intellectual advantage over Klim, who appears prone to "too forward and unsettled judgment."[38] The justice of the Potuan trees is both absolute and passionless. At the same time, relentless measures ensure that no obstacle interferes with the power of law. The Potuans enjoy an impressive number of freedoms, including the freedom to abrogate existing customs and propose laws, but those who make such proposals must accept the risk of capital punishment if the new law is deemed by the Senate to be counter to the common good. At the same time, Potuan society is without ranks and titles: the subjects of the Potuan prince enjoy equality of standing. "You see here no different ranks and titles of honour. Inferiors obey their superiors, and the younger the elder, and this is all."[39] The Potuans also respect inherent virtue, as in the example of a distinguished teacher who is named preceptor of the royal children not because of his qualifications for the post but because he has proven his patience and good character by having put up with the fate of being cuckolded by his wife for a long period of time. Power operates here without gap or flaw: "The power of the Potuan monarchs, although subject to no laws, is yet rather a paternal than a regal power. For being naturally lovers of justice, power, and liberty, things totally incompatible elsewhere do here go hand in hand."[40] Public and private happiness are identical to each other; form and sentiment are in perfect harmony. Indeed, after his arrival on Potu, Klim has artificial branches fitted to his body by the trees, who cultivate him in body as well as in mind.

Thus, many elements of human society are excluded from Potu, even as the Potuan government is presented as fully humane in the ideals it upholds and the structures it employs. Ambition is largely eliminated, as is idleness; public posts are distributed on the basis of suitability and merit—what Klim calls "dexterity."[41] The Potuans unanimously worship one god; commentary on the sacred books is prohibited. In the Potuan academies, "genius alone is regarded without any respect to sex and condition."[42] Klim's "hastiness" and his "unsettled judgment"[43] render him a figure of mockery for the otherwise patient, benevolent trees, although they make use of his particular talents by appointing him King's Messenger; Klim is accepted into their fold as a curiosity who is valued only insofar as he is useful to them. In other words, in Potu, the vegetal is privileged and the animal is excluded, ridiculed, punished, or reshaped into the form of a plant. The Potuans are without horses (and they do not even grow oats), while the humanoid monkeys who live in the forests and seem to recognize themselves in Klim are objects of derision. "We were something [sic] infested by the monkeys from the woods, which rambling up and down, and from an affinity in my shape imagining I was of their race, were continually teasing me with their approaches and touches. I could scarce suppress my rage when I perceived that this was a perfect comedy to some of the trees."[44] Klim ends up using his harpoon, the relic of his fall to Nazar, to keep the monkeys at bay.

The Potuans have created a society governed by a social logic that nonetheless functions with the smoothness, reliability, and ruthlessness of a mechanism. In their privileging of natural and biological processes as objects of social control, including their use of bloodletting to determine moral character and their strong endorsement of breastfeeding, their society is nascently biopolitical. The primary form of status in their society, besides the hereditary title of the monarch, is based on the number of branches that grow on each Potuan. Vegetal life thus serves as a model for a sovereign power that exerts itself without obstacle across the social body. The fictional sovereign power exercised by the Potuans is part of a utopian vision in which the smooth rationality of the trees optimizes the management of life and society (but only up to a point, as we shall see). Moreover, in Potu itself, two modes of plant life exist: the first is rational, ordered, and more or less anthropomorphized, while the second is without consciousness and available for exploitation. The Potuans have an excellent knowledge of natural history and they value agricultural labor above all other professions. The plants they grow to feed themselves do not possess the sovereign rationality the social trees do. Some forms of vegetal life retain their instrumental function even as vegetal modalities of being (slowness, interconnectedness with the natural world, benevolence) are lauded for their specific affinities with reason.

As it proceeds, Holberg's narrative expands on the initial ironic reversal of human and plant ways of being, in which the trees embody human ideals while humans are betrayed by their own animalistic qualities. Although their anthropomorphic characteristics are emphasized by the illustrations accompanying the work, Potuan society retains a vegetal quality that cannot be fully "humanized." The collapse of culture and cultivation into each other—so that the nature of the trees becomes a perfect embodiment of the rational principles governing the social order as a whole—tends toward its own limit case, in which reason entirely outstrips the passions and the plant is revealed as a perfectly generative and generous body—in other words, as a quasi-divine being, detached from human cares and concerns in its ineffable self-sufficiency. Holberg's text thus recalls La Mettrie's privative definition of the plant as a being without needs, but in Holberg's case, the lack of needs raises the status of the plant rather than reduces it.[45] Plants' withdrawal from the context of human passions both sets them up as a model for humans to strive toward (albeit never attain) and renders them something other than human in their specific nature.

This oscillation of the plant between seemingly irreconcilable modes of being becomes more pronounced during Klim's travels around Nazar—a journey on the course of which he encounters many different kinds of vegetal societies, both incredibly various and strikingly homogenous. In his capacity as royal messenger on a voyage of discovery, he remarks that "the inhabitants of the whole planet, though wonderfully different in their manners, yet all spoke the same tongue."[46] The Potuans themselves travel only with difficulty, and thus the planet as a whole comprises a vast "variety of inhabitants, and even opposite natures and tempers," whose differences mirror those inherent in the land itself. At the same time, the inhabitants all conform in certain respects to the laws of arboreal nature—including a uniformity of "sense and judgment."[47] The putative malleability of the plant, its availability for pruning and culling, enables it to function (as in La Mettrie's description of the young Prussian men) as an example of the efficiency of a program of social engineering that hews close to nature in its operations. The Potuans embody many of the rational ideals of Enlightenment social thought, and in this way, they, too, prove themselves to be the instruments of a higher reason, not unlike the crops they cultivate. Yet, the plant as a figure does not remain entirely within this program. Instead, it unsettles or destabilizes the very utopian model that it grounds, by adhering all too perfectly to the rationality that distinguishes it.

One of the societies Klim encounters, in Spalank, or the Country of Innocence, is entirely without laws. It is a utopia within a utopia. The trees who inhabit this land are "all beeches, and esteemed the happiest of the whole creation. They are subject to no passions and affections, and consequently free from all vices."[48] Laws are unnecessary here because virtue is entirely innate for the beeches; they are not disposed to vice in any way and thus have no need for a regulatory principle external to them. Without vices, however, this society is also without sociability: "But with the vices there were also many things wanting which adorn the human species and seem to distinguish them from brutes."[49] This passage sets up a connection between vices—springing from the passions—and those qualities that separate humans from beasts, yet it does so in the context of a society populated entirely by trees, in which neither humans nor beasts appear (with the obvious exception of Klim himself, who is, on Nazar at least, poised uneasily on the border between man and animal). Klim has an ambivalent reaction to this perfectly virtuous country yet ultimately decides that "an uncultivated creature was however better than a vicious creature and that, though they had no arts, they had also no thefts, murders, and other atrocious crimes which destroy both body and soul, [and] I could not help pronouncing them happy."[50] In Spalank, the only management required is a zero degree of agriculture—a means of sustaining growth. Klim remarks, "To say the truth, I seemed here to be rather in a forest of real trees than in a rational society."[51] Yet, this is in its own way a distinction without a difference. The existence of the Spalankians seems to make the point that the "forest of real trees" is the closest approximation to a rational society available, albeit not to humans, who struggle against their own worst (and best) impulses. This is a world that paradoxically remains closed to the humans who dream it up as ideal, even as it is at the same time open to visitors as a place of perfect hospitality. It is also a space in which the ability of the vegetal to intervene in other bodies—including the human body—makes itself felt.

Klim's only sustained encounter with one of the Spalankians occurs when he strikes his leg against a stone and is unable to walk. "An honest countryman" sees him and applies an herb to the wound, thereby relieving both the swelling and the pain. It turns out that, even without cultivated forms of knowledge, the Spalankians are masters of the art of healing. Klim is so impressed by the generosity and simplicity of his benefactor that he "had really some apprehensions it was an angel in the shape of a tree."[52] Here the comparison of trees to divine beings might remind us once again of Cyrano's angelic cabbage. Of course, Cyrano mocks the idea of the plant as eminently rational—the cabbage is among other things ridiculous—as a way not just of satirizing the authority of rationalism (and the idealism that it brings with it) but also of evoking the extrahuman or inhuman function of reason itself, so that reason's sovereign power is exercised *on* rather than *through* human bodies. In Holberg, while the Potuans function as a satirical contrast to human corruption and irrationality, the Spalankian example transforms humans into the beneficiaries of a vegetal benevolence that derives from plants' specific healing powers. The capacity of the plant to recede from human control and thereby suggest the impotence and vulnerability of humans in the face of a reason that exceeds (and

Figure 4. A Spalankian offering, Johan Frederik Clemens's illustration, based on drawings by Nicolai Abraham Abildgrad, in *Niels Klims underjordiske reise, oversat efter den latinske original af Jens Baggesen*, 1789. Cotsen Children's Library, Department of Rare Books and Special Collections. Princeton University Library.

does not need) them is developed in the form of a vegetal utopia that doubles itself.

Klim goes on to compare the impassive benevolence of his tree doctor to the Epicurean ideal of inner peace generated in the absence of desire (*ataraxia*): "that calm philosophy of some men who neither wish nor grieve, are neither angry nor pleased, who divest themselves of all the impetuous passions of the soul, and whom we therefore accuse of leading a life of indolence and softness."[53] The tree acts out the therapeutic management of the passions characteristic of ancient materialisms. This is not to say that Holberg himself had materialist leanings. But we find in the perfect innocence of the Spalankian tree doctor a reminder of the proximity of vegetality to the realm of the materialist philosophers, who, like Cyrano and La Brosse, subscribed to a philosophical ideal in which pleasure (the "life of indolence and softness" evoked by Holberg) might be cultivated in both dynamic and more tranquil forms. The society of Spalankian trees is the Epicurean Garden made literal.

In Holberg, though, the Spalankian ideal represents a limit point for the text rather than a model to be implemented. The Spalankians operate outside of the analogy comparing humans to plant life; their society cannot be made to "work" in human terms, and Klim leaves it behind relatively quickly. This is because the Epicurean logic of vegetal life—which operates to eliminate pain—is not a social power in the sense of allowing for laws and reforms to ameliorate society. Instead, it is the Potuans who serve as the most prominent chastening example for the narrator; they provide the example of a reformed sociability in which improved laws and technologies of governance produce a better community. The trees of the Kingdom of Spalank put into practice an absolute justice, one that human physiology (and, it is suggested, human morphology) prevents us from achieving. Yet, they have no recognizable institutions—no social order as such. Conversely, the Potuans retain enough proximity to human modes of life to have a need for institutional structures—including academies of learning, courts, and government. Through the example of the Potuans, Holberg's vision validates authority in what he sees as its most rational forms—the paternalistic monarch, the institutional power of the law, the commitment to a social good—and is thus far from Cyrano's anti-orthodox and frankly libertine bent. Yet, as in both Cyrano and La Brosse, too, the vegetal "nature" of particular plants is linked to the production of a more modern and potentially just social order. Holberg's tale endorses, in the name of plants, a rational, legalistic, egalitarian (within limits), and technologically advanced material prosperity that is both profoundly humane and potentially inhuman. But the existence of the Spalankians suggests that the logic of the Potuans, carried to its conclusion, is unassimilable to human society. From a twenty-first-century vantage, Potuan reason carries with it its own forms of violence, while the Spalankians expose this reason as nonhuman in essence. The subterranean world containing Nazar and other planets,[54] a world that can only be plumbed by an accident brought about by all-too-human curiosity, suggests that undergirding the drive for enlightenment lies a vegetal reason that cannot be assimilated into human life, even as it exerts power over human beings. The image of a sovereign plant haunts these and other eighteenth-century fantasies of a better world.

Tiphaigne de La Roche and Vegetal Materiality

Holberg's model of a vegetal utopia stresses the distinctions separating reasonable, technologically advanced plants from fickle, distractible humans, even as these same plants often seem to have taken from humans their most recognizably human characteristics. He imagines the plant as the bearer of a sovereign rationality that initially governs through principles that produce ideal human societies but eventually, in the case of the Spalankians, who have perfectly internalized the law and thus need no formal politics, places itself beyond government and human reason. In his plant fictions, medical doctor, philosopher, and fantasist Tiphaigne de La Roche returns to the question of the continuities cutting across the plant/human divide—as if to readjudicate the concerns troubling La Mettrie's plant-man. Unlike La Mettrie, however, Tiphaigne specifically prioritizes the plant in his hypotheses concerning the nature of materiality. As in Holberg's *Niels Klim*, we find with Tiphaigne a turn to the plant in the context of speculative and philosophically informed fiction. Plants and humans accompany one another in their journeys through the cosmos, but the fundamental structure of animate bodies is based on a vegetal (rather than an animal) model. As we will see, Tiphaigne's speculative notion of the "tubules végétables" that provide the building blocks for all animate beings renders plants the engine of growth, production, and reproduction. The very structure of matter becomes, with Tiphaigne, a vegetal one.[55]

In his *Questions relatives à l'agriculture et à la nature des plantes* (1759), Tiphaigne exhorts the reader: "Let us thus view plants as beings in possession of sensation and regard those of their number that surround us as our contemporaries and compatriots. It will only render nature, now animate through and through, more interesting."[56] This remarkable text is, like La Mettrie's *L'Homme-plante*, invested in the analogy between plant and animal as a way of questioning the boundaries that appear to separate the two kingdoms. While Tiphaigne is not a materialist, he contends that there is no "essence" (as he puts it) of animal life—"There is perhaps in animals no part that constitutes their animality"[57]—and that plants and animals may simply be different arrangements of the same fibers: "Soon we will conclude that, essentially, plants are the same as animals, for like animals, plants are composed of corresponding fibers, but they differ from them in form."[58] His insistence that "[a] bundle of fibers placed in the hands of nature can form the body of a human or a plant"[59] echoes La Mettrie's affirmation that the uniformity of matter establishes all life-forms as interrelated—different arrangements of the same basic substance (although, unlike La Mettrie, Tiphaigne holds firm to his belief in an immaterial soul and, unlike mechanist materialists, doubles down on the distinction between organic and inorganic matter).

In his ascription of sensations, including those of pleasure and pain, and even something like a brain, to plants, Tiphaigne permits himself moments of speculation in which he uses the plant to suggest the limits, rather than the superiority, of human intelligence and perception. This reevaluation of the plant at first involves a shift in emphasis from the relative status of particular faculties or capacities—plants that move less than humans are still for all that animate—to the enmeshment of the plant in its environment. While plants, in their relative immobility, may seem less developed than humans or other mobile creatures, from another vantage their seeming inability to move may be understood as an adaptive response to their surroundings. Unlike humans, they have no need for motion, since their desires are met in place. The fact that they are sessile represents, then, a form of "perfection" rather than a defect:

> I have always regarded local or partial movement as a perfection accorded to certain organic beings and refused to others. I have perhaps been wrong. In reality, both types of movement could be viewed as proceeding from an attention paid by nature to provide for specific needs.... There exist organic bodies that . . . have the advantage of finding in water and liquids in their environment enough nourishment, and that are in addition always ready to seize it. These beings have no need either for local movement or for partial movement, as is the case for plants. Does this prove that plants lack certain perfections? Does not it rather prove that they lack certain needs?[60]

The plant becomes in this comparison a body not lacking key faculties but ideally suited for its environment. Its inability to move is not a sign of diminished capacity but of self-sufficiency. Tiphaigne thus, like Holberg, calls into question the inferiority that La Mettrie ascribes to plants. He also shows a willingness to imagine different sorts of possible lives in different sorts of environments. With this gesture, he opens up the analogical thought of Enlightenment natural history and natural philosophy to the possibility of thinking life (and plant life in particular) otherwise.

As he proceeds through the essay, Tiphaigne develops this theme of a putative vegetal superiority, which becomes in his work the subject of a pattern of questioning. In an echo of La Brosse's suggestion that plants may reveal to us the ways in which our knowledge of the world is constrained and in certain cases impoverished, Tiphaigne writes: "I know that one cannot see without eyes, but I do not know if sight is the only sensation that light can provoke. I do not know if there is in nature some other organ upon which light can act. If this was the case, plants could perceive objects just as well as we, albeit in a different manner. They could enjoy the spectacle of nature, but for them this spectacle would be completely different from the one we perceive, so that we cannot form any idea about it."[61] This statement, anticipating the development of plant physiology and microbiology, is, however, even more notable for its investment in the possibility of plant sensation and apprehension of an outside world that remains outside the reach of human perception. If plants do sense light, as Tiphaigne rightly suspects, their mode of doing so is completely different from our own and in this sense inaccessible to us other than through the mediation of instruments not yet created. This plant matter that is hypothetically capable of sensation turns out even to constitute us as animate bodies, yet it is only speculation—fictional or philosophical—that might partially uncover its operations.

How might we begin to apprehend the "spectacle" to which plants have privileged (and perhaps unique) access? In the preface to the *Questions relatives*,[62] we read a confirmation of the idea that the faculties of plants can only be considered in speculative fashion. "[O]ne tries to find faculties in them that perhaps never existed," the preface continues, skeptically.[63] The essence of plants remains indeterminate because it cannot be submitted to the trials of experience. It is Tiphaigne's fiction, then, that opens vegetal life up to a wide range of imaginative possibilities, even as his scientific writings on "the nature of plants" posit their astonishing vigor (and even superiority). As is the case for Holberg, this vision is in many respects a modern one; its concerns are social, biopolitical, and technological. It does not represent a return to some arcane and mysteriously hidden vegetality or the revival of a pastoral ethos. And in the end, the "spectacle de la Nature" in which plants partake demands that we experiment with media that might be capable of making it fully tangible to us, its products.[64]

For Tiphaigne, the vitality of the vegetal being, coupled with its indifference to both the constraints and incentives that serve to mobilize human beings, coexists with the capacity of the plant to submit to government—to let itself be grafted, transplanted, sorted, identified, and classified. Whereas La Mettrie defines this vitality as availability for domination by reestablishing the hierarchy of living beings, Tiphaigne speculates in his fiction that vegetality, in the form of "cylinders" or "tubules," might become the key to all growth and, ultimately, the source of the very forms of knowledge and sociability to which growth eventually gives rise. He envisions the plant as providing the deep structure for life itself—as well as the model for how this life might be managed, cultivated, and culled. As in Holberg's work, Tiphaigne's prioritization of the plant reveals the doubleness (rather than the mere passivity) of vegetal "nature." It is all around us, and yet it recedes from our world of rational and emotional decision-making, even as it threatens to take control of us. It might provide the model for a new form of human society, yet in its fundamental (material) form it exceeds and unsettles the institutions that are meant to contain it.

Tiphaigne's satirical and speculative narrative *Amilec ou la graine d'hommes* (1753) opens with mockery of the pedantry and defective reasoning of those who call themselves "a physicist, a naturalist, a physician, a philosopher."[65] The hero shuts himself away in his study to read "a rather ample volume in which there was a discussion of generation."[66] But in perusing the book he soon becomes frustrated with its contents and throws the work aside. He addresses humankind: "'[Y]ou take yourself for a guide and you lead every child astray; you claim to be enabling us to see the truth, but you show us nothing but chimeras.'"[67] Like Cyrano's hero, Tiphaigne's narrator soon lapses into sleep, and in his dream he meets a man "who had something more than human in his physiognomy."[68] This is Amilec, a mysterious personage who will reveal to the narrator that human reproduction mirrors perfectly the generation of plants. While Tiphaigne draws playfully here on the analogy between human and vegetal "seed,"[69] he does more than just manipulate the comparison between human and plant to satirize the vagaries of human social life.[70] Tiphaigne instead develops a concept of vegetality as undergirding the reproduction of all animate bodies: plants, animals, and humans alike. Where Holberg tends to vegetalize qualities and capacities that seem paradigmatically human, Tiphaigne vegetalizes animate matter itself.

As Amilec leads the hero on a journey through the heavens, we learn the secrets of both plant and human reproduction. Amilec reveals that human types may be cultivated from seeds. "'Thus, when one knows how the generation of plants is carried out, one [also] knows approximately how that of animals and humans takes place. In general, plants come from seeds; humans and animals must do so too.'"[71] Reproduction, for both plants and humans, may take two forms; the seeds in both cases emerge either from "particular reservoirs" (flowers in the case of plants; the reproductive organs in the case of humans) or "'little cavities, tiny voids'"[72] located on the surface of the bark or skin. It is this second mode that allows for the satirical intervention of the genies, of which Amilec is one. As Amilec explains, "'We are, in regard to you, what you are in regard to plants. You humans sow, cultivate and gather fruit; we genies sow, cultivate and gather human seeds.'"[73] Here the genies become the cultivators and harvesters of particular varietals of humans, thereby both materializing and literalizing the metaphor deployed by La Mettrie with his forest of young men.

Of course, the resemblance to La Mettrie's text is not accidental. While Holberg's narrative contains no references to the contemporary understanding of plants and their physiology, Tiphaigne's fiction is clearly informed by his interest in the questions and knowledge generated around plants—their classification and physiology—during this period. He thus evokes both the eighteenth-century scientific tradition that explores similarities between animals and plants, and the satiric genres that depend upon anthropomorphization as their governing trope. As in *L'Homme-plante*, the analogy between human beings and plants that the satire is based on is not mere anthropological fiction, since Tiphaigne argues in the *Questions relatives* that plant seeds are analogous to eggs in animals.[74] He writes, "Just as you do among animals, you will find males, females, and hermaphrodites in plants. You will find mixtures, inseminations, and shoots (*germes*) that will result from them. Moreover, you will find that a seed contains the rudiments of an individual resembling its progenitor; in plants, this is the egg."[75] Yet, Tiphaigne's insistence on the structural similarities linking animals and plants is coupled with an equally forceful commitment to the inherent mystery of the mechanical processes involved in the work of reproduction: it is a "labyrinth where nature labors in absolute secret."[76] It is this mystery that the narrator's dream resolves in the form of a fiction that draws on the desire to penetrate the secrets of nature and thereby master its processes (as Amilec does). The genie's presentation of the work of the human harvesters, who only collect "'human seeds furnished by men and women of the most distinguished merit,'"[77] takes on a eugenicist tinge, although "merit" here is defined in reference to social caste or position and not biology or physiology. Tiphaigne's speculative dive into the mysteries of generation foreshadows modern biotechnologies such as gene-splicing or editing that intervene in life on the microscopic and molecular level, and he valorizes the vegetal for its availability to such mastery while also gesturing to a vegetal autonomy that thwarts any attempts at control. The human beings cultivated by the genies display a kind of vegetal sexuality, one governed not by internally generated desire as much as by the external authorities (the genies themselves) who manipulate and spark attraction.[78]

Tiphaigne's fiction thus takes on the contours of another kind of biopolitical vision, one in which the uncorrupted seeds of people from all walks of life are separated from the corrupted ones. In Holberg, it is the trees themselves, in their proximity to a benevolent and well-regulated nature, that manage the social hierarchies they uphold and represent; natural and political reason coincide. In Tiphaigne's satire, these hierarchies require a mechanism that is both mystical (in the form of the genies) and bureaucratic (in the form of their vast office or warehouse) in order to emerge. Tiphaigne's narrative includes an inventory of techniques and tools that recall those of both eighteenth-century natural science and *ancien régime* bureaucracy. Amilec describes the warehouse in which his harvester genies perform their work: "Imagine a vast apartment, the walls covered with shelves and labeled boxes and the middle occupied by a huge table, laden with little bags, packets and twists of paper, with workers busy on every side, urgently winnowing, sifting, sorting and packing, and that is the interior of Amilec's warehouse. . . . You've just seen how much discernment, attention and patience is required to collect human seed; you can see by the activity of the genies laboring in this warehouse."[79] In the face of the inscrutability of the origins of life, Tiphaigne produces here a fantasy of an enlightened and superhuman agency, an office that is in possession of the knowledge it takes to produce life out of seeds. This space is furnished with the technology for evaluating the seeds and with a cadre of envoys who perform the functions of farmers, bureaucrats, and space travelers all at once. Jacques Marx suggests that Tiphaigne's vision implies a certain pessimism about nature: the seeds themselves are easily corrupted and the human is small and vulnerable, in biological as well as moral terms. This pessimism propels a desire for mastery that is typically associated with modernity and that enables the dissemination of seeds across different planets and multiple worlds; the efforts of a massive network of genies to populate the cosmos reveal the potential plants hold in regularizing the management of life.

But the pessimism underscored by Marx needs to be contrasted with the power of vegetal matter in *Amilec*, where vegetal bodies and structures generate both living beings and the cosmos as a whole. Amilec describes the planets of the solar system as apples on a tree, which ripen according to their distance from the Sun. "'Those different Earths are like as many large apples, which, although attached to the same tree, don't all ripen at the same time.'"[80] Thus, Mercury, Venus, and Earth—the planets closest to the Sun—have already ripened and been populated while the others are waiting to receive their inhabitants, with Mars next in line. Moreover, the entirety of the universe was once contained in a seed. "'Would you believe,' Amilec resumed, 'that the whole of this innumerable multitude of Suns and habitable Earths that comprise this vast universe was once—no, you'll never believe it—was once all contained in a seed scarcely as large as a pea.'"[81] Worlds gradually grow, develop, and ripen like so many fruits, or like the shoots of plants: "'There are many worlds that one could compare to young plants that have, so to speak, barely begun to germinate.'"[82] Here both the cosmos and the individual bodies that it contains are generated in a delirious movement of seeds.

Tiphaigne creates a world governed by a strong authority, although his fiction also exposes this authority to critique. He imagines political power as a material "attractive force," by means of which other seeds are kept swirling around the sovereign in a kind of whirlwind (an image, like Cyrano's "tourbillons," perhaps inspired by Descartes's vortices). But the vegetal productivity of the universe engenders diverse modes of existence, themselves no longer based on a singular center and principle of cohesion. On the moon, under the charge of one of Amilec's lieutenants, Zamar, the hierarchy of the terrestrial order is reversed. Here inhabitants have been rendered sterile by "certain contagious corpuscles,"[83] but the planet itself is very fertile, thanks to "seeds of all kinds" that have drifted up from Earth and germinated in a process characterized by a high degree of spontaneity. Because of the fertility of seeds that travel from Earth to the moon, in an image that Philippe Vincent has described as operating a kind of transition between preformationist and epigenetic models of generation, children grow on the moon "like mushrooms" and are harvested, then distributed, to adoptive parents depending on the latter's competence and the total number of children available. Life may be weakly productive in its lunar version—in that life spans are short and humans there lack a certain vigor—but it is still surprisingly plentiful. Zamar remarks, "'It is strange to see the tender attachment that these fathers have for children that are not theirs, who come to them from they know not where—but that is a feature of Providence, of which you have enough examples on Earth.'"[84] Here the vitality of the plant is integrated into the project of building a society and produces a social order that is the mirror image of the one available to us on Earth—an anti-utopia that hearkens back to the traditional portrayal of the moon as a space of inversion and reversal.

Perhaps the most idyllic and harmonious vision of social cohesion promoted by the genies is found in the "dance of the seeds," described by Amilec in the first part of the narrative. Amilec possesses a violin "'tuned to the passions. Each note corresponds to a passion, in such a way that when some principle of passion puts a seed in harmony with a certain note, that seed, by virtue of a physical necessity, will vibrate when the note is played.'"[85] Playing the violin produces a dance; plucking each string makes different seeds move to the tune of emotions like avarice, jealousy, and pride. This dance is, of course, a satirical way of rendering human society, but it also underscores the role of affect in mobilizing bodies. Yves Citton, looking ahead toward late modernity, affirms that Tiphaigne envisions an "economy of passions" as an alternative to the predominance of regimes of quantification in modernity. Citton underscores the wealth of passions in Tiphaigne's imaginary worlds.[86]

This economy is both liberating and disturbing—with its vision of the all-penetrating nature of political power, since, if we follow Citton's activating reading, we also need to acknowledge the biopolitical uses of affect in the political sphere.[87] Tiphaigne's planetary monarchies do not depend on the contingent abilities of a monarch but find their own sovereign power in a much richer and more penetrating vegetal logic of cultivation. "'You have before your eyes . . . ,'" remarks Amilec, "'an image of human society. The harmony of the tune you're playing is sustained by the relationship of the notes composing it; in the same way, society, which is represented by the methodical dance of the seeds, is sustained by the different passions that agitate humans.'"[88] Where the dance of the pomegranate tree in Cyrano materialized the movement of atoms in their production of diverse individual bodies, the dance of the seeds materializes the movement of the social body as a whole. At this moment in the tale, a hierarchy and order emerge from the seeds. Tiphaigne's tale stresses the insight that populations can be governed by affective manipulation, and that affects can be produced in "tune" with an instrument designed to mobilize material bodies. Unlike Cyrano's use of the figure of the vortex, here nature authorizes a mode of political control, exercised by certain beings over others, that can take not only rational but also affective form.

Yet, the prioritization given to human rationality and affect formatted into patterns of movement (here centrally and harmoniously arranged as if by an instrument) is called into question precisely by the ambiguity surrounding the operations of generation itself—an ambiguity that threatens to expose the worst of human proclivities (for dissension, pedantry, and dogmatism). Tiphaigne's seeds, like Holberg's, are capable of exceeding (if not bypassing) the models that initially seem to contain them. Plants not only create visible worlds (to be populated by humans who are carried there in the form of plants) but inspire speculation around the nature of invisible worlds as well. They are microcosmically and macrocosmically active. The original hierarchy laid out in the genie's opening remarks is first doubled by the work of the genies themselves, who vegetalize humans by cultivating them as humans do plants. It is then resituated within a context in which the basic structure of all animate bodies is given as a form of vegetality.

After his tour through the warehouse, the narrator is struck by the contingency and smallness of human life. With some perplexity, he refers to man as "'[o]ne seed rescued from oblivion among millions of others.'"[89] At this point, Amilec promises to reveal to him the remaining secrets regarding the multiplication and propagation of human seeds; these secrets turn out to involve materiality in its most fundamental dimensions, including the smallest particles of which animate matter may be formed, which themselves have a vegetal structure. Here Amilec develops his theory of the "little vegetable cylinders"—tiny invisible tubes that, slotting together, generate the bodies of all animate beings. "'Sometimes the cylinders have been mistaken for the rudiments of plants and animals, sometimes for worms; recently, they have been mistaken for organic molecules—but in truth, they are merely vegetable cylinders.'"[90] These cylinders explain and engender the extraordinary growth of plants and their wondrous animation: "'That shape, those openings and the proportionate distances are so disposed in the tubules of plants that no obstacle is anywhere offered capable of impeding continual development and growth. If no internal corruption were to manifest itself, a seed placed anywhere on your globe could develop, grow, extend, and eventually form a tree capable of giving shade to half the world.'"[91] The idea of the enormous tree covering half of Earth seems to be a symbol of the terrifying yet also marvelous vigor that plants carry with them. As it turns out, however, and fortunately for the planet, plants like humans are vulnerable to age and the "corruption" that comes with it. Nonetheless, plants remain notable here (as in Aristotle) for their amazing growth, since they are at least theoretically capable, in Tiphaigne, of overwhelming the world. Unlike Aristotle, however, Tiphaigne makes the vegetal cylinders the principle of *all* growth and development in the world as we know it. Amilec concludes his explanation of the "tubules" with a remarkable endorsement of the generative productivity of these structures, at the origin of all life: "'Who will dare to count those instruments of propagation and impose calculation on the treasures of Nature? A plant, a tree, an animal, a human being, is nothing but an immense mass of tubules, each one of which can reproduce a complete vegetable or animal. O simplicity! O variety! O wealth of Nature! O eternal wisdom of the Creator!'"[92] Here the simplicity and variety of nature as a whole—and indeed of the divine reason that provides the ordering principle of this world—is figured as a form of vegetality. Tiphaigne marries his earlier emphasis on microcosmic and macroscosmic structures to speculation around the building blocks of matter itself, thereby producing a kind of vegetal atomism in which all reality, seen through the lens proffered in the dream (itself a kind of becoming-vegetable of the human), appears in a form borrowed from the plant world. The tubules recall the principles of sameness and differentiation that characterize the atom; they combine according to regular and determined principles but are at the same time susceptible to infinite variation. But they also bring with them an immense and unrestrained energy—a powerful force for growth—perhaps more reminiscent of the molecule. Tiphaigne's tubules appear to couple a nascent vitalism with what Gilles Deleuze and Félix Guattari will much later refer to as the "inorganic life of things."[93]

In a sense, Amilec's remarkable exegesis of the function of the cylinders seems to have little in common with the relatively conventional social satire with which the work begins (and continues). But we might see in this narrative, as in Holberg, a kind of oscillation between two notions of vegetality, both with their utopian (and dystopian) dimensions. On the one hand, the susceptibility of humans to cultivation enables a kind of biopolitical control on the part of the genies; it is not only vegetal vitality but vegetal passivity (the muteness, slowness, and transparency of the plant body) that are at issue here, and that are transferred in part to the humans subject to manipulation and propagation. As in Holberg, cultivation and acculturation merge. Yet, Tiphaigne's vision of the plant as both the technology of and subject to sovereign power is doubled and in a sense overtaken by the image of the cylinder as the vegetal structure that gives all life both its order and its variability at the most basic level. This vitality is not governable in its essence. At the same time, its existence opens up the possibility of a scientific—and technological—intervention in the life of plants, the possibility of knowing their way of apprehending the world. Fiction becomes the space of this possibility in its most fantastic, and speculative, modes; it is the zone where the promise of speculation is made good. Plants make not only other worlds but *our* world, which has been opened up to a vitality that exceeds human reason and experience. In their indifference and strangeness—and in their fascinating vigor—they suggest techniques of world-building that humans have yet to deploy or even imagine. It is perhaps no accident that Tiphaigne's and Cyrano's texts both begin with a scene of sleep, in which the human narrator resembles most closely a plant (at least according to the Aristotelian doctrine of plants being analogous to sleeping animals). Perhaps it is in sleep that a new kind of consciousness opens up, a consciousness that awaits the technology that might make it fully accessible to us.

Even as enlightened modernity subjects plants to sovereign power, it also endows them with autonomy, a nonhuman and ultimately asocial vitality that nonetheless inspires utopian fantasy. La Mettrie, Holberg, and even Tiphaigne clearly think of the plant as a model for society—ensuring in part the stability of populations—with a cosmic and interplanetary dimension (that often takes the form of colonies). The vegetal model of government, based on the cultivation of plants proposed by Holberg and Tiphaigne, recognizes that life is open to manipulation; it is not a fixed object but subject to growth, cultivation, increase, and forms of control exercised not over but in and through the living beings who function as political subjects. This recognition enables the production of new social ideals, but it also allows for new forms of violence and domination (imposed on human as well as vegetal bodies) to emerge.

In the Enlightenment, the inclusion of plants in the design of human social worlds begins a project that is both utopian and dystopian; vegetality is present at the onset of a biopolitical regime in which every improvement comes at the cost of subjecting living matter to techniques of control, whether through the management of populations or in the dream of cultivating tall and strong young men like trees. But plants also regularly evade the modes of control they make imaginable. Later, we find plants both enabling and troubling human intervention in their tissues and basic molecular structure (an increasingly salient part of the world of "late late capitalism,"[94] as Christopher S. Nealon has described it).[95] Plant specificity, which can never be fully assimilated into the human order, opens up these fictions of improved societies to critique and revision, even as it seems to permit and engender new ways of regulating and managing life. This is what we understand to be the enlightened plant's ability to allow us to envision a continuation of the project of vegetal modernity begun by La Brosse and Cyrano in the previous century. The eighteenth-century production of vegetal societies, which both ratify and destroy the human world, informs *and* counters what will become Romantic conceptions of the continuity of living beings—models in which desire (ultimately) flows back and forth between humans and vegetables as the boundary between the two orders breaks down.

CHAPTER 4

The Inorganic Plant in the Romantic Garden

Radical Botany in a Romantic Age

Even as they prefigure the vitalist turn in the life sciences, the seventeenth- and eighteenth-century narratives of botanical speculation that we analyzed in the previous two chapters also suggest the sustained proximity of plants to modes of animation and vitality unrelated to and undefined by organisms and the life that they embody.[1] This is the kind of life to which Gilles Deleuze and Félix Guattari will eventually turn in their deployment of the rhizome, a twentieth-century instantiation of radical botany. As we have shown, eighteenth-century visions of utopian plants are influenced at least in part by mechanist and materialist paradigms that find their origins in antiquity, dominate the sciences of the seventeenth century, and remain in conversation with the emergent vitalist models of the eighteenth century. This influence often takes the form of a literary debt—as in both Holberg's and Tiphaigne's nods to Cyrano—rather than an explicitly philosophical one. The botanical utopias of the Enlightenment revisit seventeenth-century materialist speculations about plant vitality as an impetus for fictional world-making.

Our goal in this chapter is to show the subterranean roots that an earlier tradition of speculative botanical writing extends amid the triumph of organicist and vitalist conceptions of the plant in nineteenth-century botany and the ascension of a Romantic aesthetics of mutuality.[2] The authors we examine here—including U.S. writers Edgar Allan Poe (1809–1849) and Charlotte Perkins Gilman (1860–1935)—continue to build upon a legacy of both fictional and scientific speculation that rejects or revises some of the primary assumptions of Romantic vitalism, especially the latter's concern with the affinities binding plants to humans. At the same time, for both of these authors, the vegetal ornament or arabesque represents a specific inspiration.[3] Poe and Gilman either criticize or downright reject the Romantic idea that the garden can serve as the model of a political community, and they remain hostile to the bourgeois and patriarchal ideals this model serves, even in the reformed and progressive guise championed by many of the European Romantics. Consequently, Poe and Gilman—and their intertexts—also generate an important critique of notions of familial lineage and descent, both as scientific ideas and as kinship structures. Poe, who will be our primary focus here, specifically reaches back to a corpus that was constitutive of an earlier alchemical and analogical approach to life. In his short story "The Fall of the House of Usher" (first published in 1839), he treats the elements of this corpus as forbidden, or at least forgotten, texts not only unreadable from within but also anathema to the organicist-vitalist paradigm. Gilman will later incorporate a notion of vegetality inspired in part by Poe into her critique of women's mental and physical subjugation.

If we proceed, in this chapter, by way of a detour through a North American tradition of speculative botany, it is because Poe's texts in particular will be of inspiration to French symbolism (including the poetic arabesques of Charles Baudelaire) and, through this line of transmission, early avant-garde French cinema. Later, in a more popular mode, the plant horror films of the mid-twentieth century will reactivate a vision of vegetality as fascinating, even in its rapacious indifference to human life, thereby expanding, however surreptitiously, on the preoccupations animating the turn to the plant by the French avant-garde. Gilman's influence in the Francophone context is less explicit, but her use of vegetal life-forms as part of a feminist critique represents a key development in the deployment of plant life to destabilize or undo patriarchal modes of subjectivity. In the present day, as we discuss in the final chapter of this book, an emergent genre of feminist, queer, and ecologically oriented speculative fiction will embrace the plant as a model of a becoming that fully disengages from the patriarchal family (as in the writings of Belgian author Anne Richter) and from imperialist epistemologies and techno-capitalist modes of identity formation (as in the work of Ursula K. Le Guin, Han Kang, and Jeff VanderMeer). In this global vegetal turn, we can still recognize the influence of the ideas and figures animating earlier instances of radical botany.

Poe's preoccupation with vegetal life emerges out of his ambivalent engagement with the organicism of his day, itself influenced by the vitalist turn of the previous century. Poe transforms what we will call the Romantic plant from within by turning back to one of its points of origin in the eighteenth century. In so doing, he also intervenes in a seemingly idyllic mutuality that strands of Romanticism posit as shared in by plants and humans alike. While Poe's figure of vegetable sentience will have far-reaching effects on the modernity that follows him, he is not the origin point for the radical botanical tradition that we identify as working through him. He reactivates this tradition, which foregrounds plants as a source of power and inorganic agency, even as he continues to inhabit the context of Romanticism, thereby eventually generating a "plant horror" that envisions a powerful vegetality as *the* defining attribute of life itself.

Early Romantic vitalism continues to prioritize continuities across the various orders of living beings, even as it allows the plant to take on certain animal characteristics (albeit often in a muted form). In recent scholarship that returns to the plant in our own, posthuman context, the figure of the Romantic plant has drawn considerable critical attention.[4] Mid-to-late eighteenth-century botanists, including, among many others, authors such as Jean-Jacques Rousseau (1712–1778), Erasmus Darwin (1731–1802), Jacques-Henri Bernardin de Saint-Pierre (1737–1814), and Johann Wolfgang von Goethe (1749–1832),[5] participate in the construction of a plant life that is vibrant on its own terms yet exquisitely responsive to human interests and preoccupations. In this model, plants become equated with a somewhat less intricately organized but nonetheless fully organic matter. The qualities that botanically inclined philosophers and scientists discover in plants may initially seem to set them apart from humans and animals, but under the gaze of Romanticism, plants themselves come to be viewed through a primarily animal lens, even when their difference from humans is increasingly acknowledged. In other words, from this vantage, plants are conceived as unlike us in their structures and functions yet operating according to a logic recognizable (and sympathetic) to us.

For Rousseau, for example,[6] plant life is worthy of prolonged and appreciative consideration. The plants that he encounters on his herborizing journeys are imbued with a rich sentimental resonance that puts humans in touch with the natural world in its most intimate, local, and immediate dimensions. This world is aesthetically and affectively vibrant and materially rich. The contemplation of botanical specimens brought back from his travels helps him assuage the pain caused by "the persecutions of men, their hatred, their contempt, their insults, and all the evils with which they have repaid my tender and sincere attachment to them."[7] Rousseau describes plants as a refuge from the scourge of human passions; they are proffered by god to humans as a kind of invitation to the study of the marvels of nature. At the same time, they can be intimately appreciated by humans because they inhabit modes of being that can be hard to sustain in human society. Rousseau reanimates La Brosse's comparison of plants to stars but he does so in order to emphasize the accessibility and proximity of the vegetal world to humans. He writes, "Drawn in by the delightful objects that surround me, I consider them, I contemplate them, I compare them, I finally learn to classify them."[8] But it is in their "natural" complicity with human emotion, attention, and appreciation, not in their resistance to or rearticulation of our modes of apprehension, that plants acquire their most profound interest for Rousseau. Similarly, for Bernardin de Saint-Pierre, in many senses Rousseau's disciple, plants, animals, and places are bound together in a system of natural harmonies that guarantees affinities among life-forms and allows for intensive consideration of plants as crucial elements of a natural order that nevertheless surpasses them. For all the wonders that plants make manifest, plant life remains subordinate to animal life (and animals to humans) in Bernardin's system, as in Rousseau's.[9]

But it is perhaps the English polymath Erasmus Darwin (grandfather of Charles) who develops the most persuasive Romantic account of a mutualism in which plants play a central role. His presentation of the natural world domesticates and reorients an earlier libertine materialist tradition that ascribes desire to plants. At the end of the eighteenth century, Darwin published his two-part poem *The Botanic Garden* (1789–1791), written at least in part for women, in which he argues that botanical knowledge should be available to all. His adoption of the Linnaean classificatory system, which the poem fleshes out in great erotic detail, shapes Darwin's sexual politics in the poem, so that for him vegetal sexuality parallels human sexual life and can be translated into a liberal but still patriarchal political agenda. In parsing the poem and its paratexts, including the copious scholarly notes that Darwin appended to its lyrical descriptions of vegetal life, Darwin's ambivalent positioning between an older, libertine model of plant being, which highlights vegetal specificity, and a newer, vitalist model, which promotes an animalized version of plant life, becomes clear.

On the one hand, Darwin's poetry represents an extension of the Lucretian project in which poetry makes an invisible world come into being. Darwin sees nature, and plants in particular, as artful and generative beings with a close relationship to mediatic devices including poetry, which he also compares to the camera obscura. On the other hand, Darwin's plants transmit and embody a patriarchal and anthropocentric notion of the function and structure of erotic desire. Recent scholarship has stressed Darwin's significance for Romantic writers such as William Wordsworth (1770–1850) and Percy Bysshe Shelley (1792–1822) in England[10]; Devin Griffiths, who reads Darwin's cosmology, embryology, and botany as imbued with seminal vitalism, has pointed to Darwin's profound influence on Goethe in Germany.[11] Darwin's notion of sexual elective affinity, elaborated on in his late work *Phytologia* (1803), is based on a model of heterosexual generation extended as an organizing concept for matter itself. (As Griffiths points out, this point is subsequently illustrated by the plot of Goethe's novel *Die Wahlverwandtschaften* (1809), perhaps inspired by Darwin's concept). Darwin thus both evokes in his botany the libidinal vitality of matter, its auto-affective and self-moving qualities, and tames this animation for a Romantic view of life according to which human affects and values can be projected onto the physical world. *The Botanic Garden* signals the importance of women's role in botanical pursuits and suggests the significance, for botany, of women's apprehension of and connection to nature.[12] At the same time, it attempts to reorganize a libidinal and libertine vegetality along heteronormative lines, thereby reasserting the power of human models of sexual difference and the social regime that upholds them.[13]

Romanticism has classically been understood as in part a reaction to disenchanted models of matter as a passive and fully reified object: the triumph of the sensitive and sensible molecule over the coldly mechanistic atom.[14] As Romantic theorists of vegetal life, Rousseau, Bernardin, Erasmus Darwin, and Goethe all lend to the plants they consider a vital energy, just as they find in botany an intense form of pleasure and emotional satisfaction. The affective power of their plants often lies in those traits that distinguish them from animals—their small size, their capacity to escape our notice, their beauty, the wonders of their relationships with one another, the ways in which they embody a sense of place—yet their ascription of an extraordinary vitality to the vegetal world does not overturn the hierarchy that places animal life above that of plants. More often, it makes of plants themselves a kind of offering to humans, or renders the plant body a sort of animalcule, or reinscribes human cultural and social institutions in the context of vegetality. Romantic botanists fantasize about a mutuality linking humans to plants, but this possibility tends to be defined in animal and human terms.[15]

The Romantic plant allows humans to project onto it a dream of intimacy, the flip side of which is the nightmarish fantasy of an appetitive and monstrous vegetable that seeks to devour humans. In either case, plants are understood as acting according to an interiorized desire that activates human sympathy and concern. Plants thus come to provide the Romantics with a model for experiencing our interconnectedness with other lifeforms, at the same time as they serve as evidence for the way in which the ebbs and flows of desire appear to structure the cosmos as a whole, its harmonies and discontinuities. The privileged Romantic site for bridging or negating the difference between plants and humans remains the garden, understood as a place where reciprocal relations among plants and humans bear witness to an exchange between vegetal and human desires, even as this garden is still capable of containing (and perhaps taming) a certain wildness of being.[16] Here the plant is valorized primarily for its connection to human concerns, not, as in the speculative approaches we have considered so far, for its strange and often quasi-machinic power over them.

Yet, the radical botany of the seventeenth and eighteenth centuries is still remembered in the nineteenth. Poe brings together his interest in speculative fiction and science with a reflection on plant-human ecologies that do not fit the Romantic mold. He intervenes in Romantic vitalism both by extending an earlier scientific tradition that uses the plant-human analogy against itself to deconstruct the divide between vegetal and animal kingdoms and by refusing the Romantic ascription of human desire to plants. At the same time, he still acknowledges the possibility of a mutuality that binds vegetal and animal forms of life to one another, albeit to the detriment of humans. In *Ariel's Ecology*, Monique Allewaert eloquently shows how Poe's resistance to a dominant imperial biopolitics of race becomes part of his efforts to dissolve sedimented social hierarchies and creolize American literature.[17] Where Allewaert is able to trace, through Poe, a minor tradition within canonical American literature that "dissolves majoritarian cultures into a cross-cultural aesthetics,"[18] we point to the power of Poe's literary project also to extend a transnational conversation that is centered around the figure of the plant and that includes both fiction and natural philosophy. We argue for the importance of Poe's return to "the sentience of all vegetable things" in the development of an antipatriarchal mode of speculative critique, which is made explicit in the writings of Gilman (herself a reader of Poe), as well as in the symbolist recuperation of the vegetal figure of the arabesque. This double lineage, wherein Poe's sentient vegetables inspire a dismantling of the bourgeois family and a materialization of botanical metaphors and figures, reappears in the twentieth- and twenty-first-century tradition of speculative fiction and cinema that we trace in the second half of this book. Through Poe, the radical botanical plant, which shapes eighteenth-century science and literature in sometimes obscure but nonetheless significant ways, makes its way forward into the twentieth and, eventually, twenty-first centuries. The figure of a percipient vegetable, inherited from the eighteenth century, allows Poe to imagine a world that is simultaneously horrifying, rich in intertextuality, and deeply, resonantly alluring for humans. His reawakening of eighteenth-century theories of plant sentience in the context of a nineteenth-century hylozoism eventually makes a place for new technologies of representation such as cinema to inhabit, thanks to its persistent contact with earlier modes of speculation and imaginative botanical fictions.

In the U.S. context, it is transcendentalist authors such as Henry David Thoreau (1817–1862) and Ralph Waldo Emerson (1803–1882) who expand upon a European Romanticism that is the site of particularly intense expressions of bio-, eco-, or phytophilia, in which plants, in all their singularity and difference from humans, become coparticipants with humans in the active creation of a transpecial atmospherics of desire. Poe's relationship to the Romantic plant is at times dismissive (he refers on occasion to the transcendentalists as the "Frogpondians"), at times openly conflictual, and at still other times grudgingly admiring. Poe was also not afraid to borrow from other authors even while subjecting them to harsh criticism. In this sense, he rereads a vegetal Romanticism from within rather than rejecting its presuppositions outright. Poe's critique of the Romantic relationship to the animated and vital plant is important not just for the way in which it builds on earlier nonanalogical models of plant, human, and animal interrelations but for its generative effects later in the century, across visual and textual media.

Plant-Human Mutuality and Romantic Desire

"Plants are no longer these beings whose organization once seemed so simple" declares Jean Senebier in 1787 in his introduction to the works of natural scientist Lazzaro Spallanzani (1729–1799).[19] Senebier's own realization that plants need carbon dioxide in order to produce oxygen, first published in 1782, provided one of the many clues that led to the discovery of photosynthesis. (Others stemmed from the work of Stephen Hales, Joseph Priestley, Jan Ingenhousz, Erasmus Darwin, and Nicolas-Théodore de Saussure.) Insights into plant physiology from the later eighteenth and early nineteenth centuries rendered plant life increasingly specific and complex, invalidating the analogical models that reigned earlier. As research into plant structures showed, plants engage in sexual reproduction and interact with their environment by emitting "vapors" that are gradually defined as oxygen and carbon dioxide. Yet, the specificity of plant life generated different philosophical and aesthetic responses. At its extreme, in Hegel's dialectical system, for example, plants are pushed to the outside of what defines human civilization, to which they become antithetical. Hegel affirms in his discussion of natural religion in the *Phenomenology of Spirit* that the plant is essentially passive. This "innocent" and "indifferent" plant life needs to be overcome by the violence of the spirit.[20] Thus, Hegel qualifies the vitality of the plant, increasingly revealed by physiology, as essentially alien to history. If plants are somehow an excess of nature, they can never be subsumed under the enlivening principle of the spirit. Conversely, as a kind of failed or never achieved life, their contingent processes serve as the very animating ground of that which overcomes them.[21] Hegel echoes and magnifies not only earlier metaphysical ideas that plant growth is infinite and always incomplete but also eighteenth-century scientific ideas about plants as lacking needs and intelligence.[22]

Hegelian botanophobia is matched if not outstripped by a Romantic botanophilia that lends not only complexity (and mystery) to plant life but the capacity for a kind of affinity with human desires and concerns. The counterpart of the plant that is utterly excluded from human care—incapable of meaningful contact or exchange with animal or human life—becomes the sensitive and desiring plant, whose existence not only enriches but reflects and illuminates human experience. Percy Bysshe Shelley's poem "The Sensitive-Plant" (1820) is a paradigmatic example of the Romantic ideal of plant-human mutuality. In three parts and a conclusion, the poem describes the life of a garden from spring through winter. In the first part, the growth of the flowers within is encouraged by the winds, sunlight, and "warm rain" as well as by their "[s]hared joy in the light of the gentle sun."[23] The flowers are like "lovers" "interpenetrated" by sunlight and each other's emanations, and thereby "wrapped and filled by their mutual atmosphere."[24] This is especially true for the Sensitive Plant, the first to sprout in the spring, which bears no fruit or flower yet is moved by joy. In the second part of the poem, the gardener, "a Lady" who "had no companion of mortal race,"[25] is described as lovingly taking care of the garden. She treads "with airy footstep," pities the grass crushed underfoot, waters the plants "faint with the sunny beam,"[26] props up those who are fading, and removes harmful insects while sparing beneficial ones such as bees and moths. The third part of the work describes the death and burial of the Lady, the Sensitive Plant's sorrow, the passing of summer into autumn, and the transformation of the garden, "cold and foul/Like the corpse of her who had been its soul."[27] The Sensitive Plant weeps, attacked by a "venomous blight,"[28] then sheds its leaves, as do the other plants at the approach of winter. In the cold, when even the moles and the dormice under the Sensitive Plant's roots die, it becomes a "leafless wreck" in a dead garden in which only "mandrakes, and toadstools, and docks, and darnels" thrive.[29] The poem concludes with the poet's uncertainty about the survival of either the Sensitive Plant's or the Lady's spirit. Not able to confirm any immaterial soul amid the material decay announced by the poem, the text resorts to stressing the survival of "love, and beauty, and delight" as the immanent but enduring values of poetry, art, and gardening in a mortal world.

In his book *Experimental Life*, Robert Mitchell emphasizes the figure of "mutual atmosphere" in Shelley's poem and the fragile yet happy reciprocity of the flow of desire in the garden. Mitchell suggests that it is essentially the human perception of the "alien" way of living of plants that calls for their "domestication" in Romantic poetry.[30] The "deep time" and the "proto-drives" of trees appear to human beings (when they are noticed at all) as "dark, explosive generativity," an indifference to everything that animal desire grasps.[31] Mitchell shows that Shelley's garden plants tame this troubling notion of indifferent life by making human desire "mimic the life of the plants by moving closer to the elements."[32] In other words, when we desire the fragrance, transitory beauty, and pleasant air of a garden, we exchange our animal appetite for a tamed, dampened one that is closer to vegetality, all while expecting plants to meet us halfway. Plant and human desire move in proximity to each other, in order to achieve a kind of sympathetic affinity. In the botanophilic turn to the plant, plants reveal to us an aim that is ultimately compatible with our appreciation of them. Thus, in "The Sensitive-Plant," Mitchell finds a shared atmosphere created by the plants and the gardener, wherein the former's "striving" for sunlight and the latter's desire for beauty meet and interpenetrate.[33] Of course, Shelley's garden is organized according to a gendered logic, for it is a feminized form of human desire that enables a sympathetic alliance with (some of the) plants. The garden only exists in a symbiosis with the human (female) gardener. Thus, for Shelley, as for Erasmus Darwin and Goethe, affinities in and with the material world follow the pattern of human heterosexuality.

Shelley's rendering of plant-human mutuality is nonetheless fragile, as the third part of the poem reveals, since the death of the gardener brings about the decay of the garden. The winds free the seeds of weeds; the weeds grow and "stifle the air." Fungi, mildew, and mold proliferate in the decaying garden, which leads to the emergence of a new "life" or at least to another form of animation:

> And agarics, and fungi, with mildew and mould
> Started like mist from the wet ground cold;
> Pale, fleshy, as if the decaying dead
> With a spirit of growth had been animated![34]

The domesticated plants thus have their wild double in the gloomy vitality of weeds, fungi, molds, and elements, which collectively serve as a reminder of the transitory nature of the mutual bliss that the first parts of the poem describe. Indeed, the Romantic framing of the flower as an aesthetic object of consumption is informed by the depiction of this disturbing counterpart that Shelley harnesses as part of a reflection on vulnerability. Human-plant mutuality ideally provides a kind of bulwark against extinction, but one that is not guaranteed. An exclamation point reveals the poet's astonishment at the sight of lively, animated weeds, which mark the end of the domesticated plant and produce an emotional response in both poet and reader. What returns here is the plant's strange animacy (shared by the fungi and other microorganisms that invade the garden). In a manner reminiscent of Hegel, this other vitality remains fully alien to human concerns and, Shelley agrees, cannot be domesticated.[35]

It is with this excess life that Poe is concerned in "The Fall of the House of Usher." Instead of seeing it as the necessary limit point of Romantic mutuality and thereby the manifestation of evil, Poe reaches back to eighteenth-century vitalist analogies to discover there a plant that is sentient but without a moral sense (good or evil), indifferent yet not separable from the human consciousness or spirit (pace Hegel), and thus the figure of a matter that fully penetrates and threatens human social structures and the very category of the human itself (mostly to the author's horror). Poe was an admirer of Shelley generally, and of "The Sensitive-Plant" in particular, which he commented on in the *Southern Literary Messenger*.[36] Poe's representation of vegetality intervenes at the moment when the affinities between plant and human described by Shelley threaten to break down or collapse, precisely in the emergence of a vegetal sentience that cannot be either tamed or fully distanced from human life. Shelley establishes the undomesticated weed or fungus as the "outside" to the Romantic plant (and to its double, the human being), but Poe, relying on the instability of the botanical analogies of the eighteenth century, brings this outside in—or, more precisely, destroys the distinction separating plant from human by once again prioritizing the animated, alien vitality of the vegetable.

Poe's Vegetal Sentience and Natural History

Poe's corpus reveals a passionate engagement with organicist vitalism, what critic John Limon has called "an interest in life, and in life within life."[37] As early as in his "Sonnet—To Science" (1829), Poe rejects Baconian empiricism and taxonomy in favor of a vision of the world as abundantly filled with life, although this abundance is not necessarily cause for celebration: his vitalism often takes a disturbingly prolific, indeed excessive, form.[38] In this context, Poe is in step with the great preoccupations of the period— the turn to life as what Amanda Jo Goldstein has called the "distinctive problem" of the nineteenth century.[39] Limon, for his part, reads Poe's gloomy "picture of the vital universe" as under the influence both of Okenian *Naturphilosophie* and the theories of disease and contagion generated by American Puritans such as Cotton Mather. The astonishing proliferation of life across and within the cosmos gives rise in Poe at first to horror at this "swarming universe"[40] and, finally, to a kind of joyously macrocosmic yet apocalyptic hylozoism in the 1848 prose poem *Eureka*. In many of his short stories, Poe persistently explores the interrelationship of human and nonhuman forms of life, and even the construction of human life out of inorganic forms (e.g., in "The Man That Was Used Up" [1839]).[41] Often in Poe, human bodies themselves are disordered, disorganized, or disaggregated by the forces of matter—exposing their own tendency to dissolve or collapse in the face of a dynamic materiality. Limon's focus is on Poe's emphasis on the animalcule—he affirms that in Poe's science, "we are animalcules inhabited by animalcules"[42]—but the figure of the plant has an especially significant function within Poe's aesthetic vision, including in the latter's embrace of the arabesque or vegetal line.[43]

The image of vegetal vitality takes a particularly compelling form in Poe's "The Fall of the House of Usher," although it remains present, in a less developed way, in some of his other stories.[44] Herbert F. Smith[45] (and later, in much more detail and complexity, Limon) argue powerfully for Poe's horror at the vast and swarming liveliness of small life-forms—a world in which matter is more or less animated all the way through. Yet, they do not account for the particular status of the plant in this horror. Other recent critics, including Matthew Taylor and Sara Crosby, have emphasized the extent to which Poe can be said to provide a "dark reinvention of environmental narrative," in Crosby's words.[46] Taylor reads Poe's texts as providing a "negative ethics" that moves beyond both ecophobia and ecophilia (even while engaging them) in order to "expose the inextricability of dependency."[47] This is an "uncertain" yet intimate relationality from which human beings have nothing to gain, unlike ecophilic efforts to find or lose oneself in nature in order to acquire a greater control over both self and world.[48] Taylor, like Crosby, positions Poe at the center of discussions about materiality and ecology, and stresses the way in which he functions as an outsider within the dominant discursive contexts of his time, one who reveals the aporia of Romanticism as a mode of thought or indeed of apprehending and representing the environment.

In the context of his particular brand of ecohorror and in relationship to his preoccupation with the arabesque, Poe's special emphasis on vegetal sentience in "Usher" is not just a cipher for a broad-based vitalism. It takes on a particular importance for the way in which the problem of animated plant matter, as Poe represents it, forces an engagement with a Romantic tradition that articulates itself primarily as a mode of botanophilia—one that, as Poe shows, conceals (even from itself) its own phobic relationship to the plant in particular. In other words, Poe reveals the plant both as a particularly compelling figure of mutuality and, precisely for this reason, as the primal scene of the horrifying return of an indifferent life. Paradoxically, this indifference is both unmarked by desire and profoundly powerful. In the end, despite (or indeed because of) its immanence—and its resistance to sublation in human terms—the plant becomes the source of a new mode of aesthetic production even as it provides a model for the (re)vitalized materiality that will loom large in Poe's corpus. While it is tempting to read Poe as the flip side of the Romantic vision of mutuality, his work opens up a vegetal ontology that no longer privileges a human model of subjectivity but transforms its contours. Where the opposition of "wild" to "domestic" retains a trace of anthropocentrism, Poe refuses this distinction to narrate the emergence of an aesthetics (and a science, however speculative) based on the interpenetration of plant and human, a dynamic in which the plant retains priority and assumes the dominant position. The discovery of a terrifying affinity with the plant, not insofar as it desires but insofar as it does not, allows for a human passage into the world of vital materiality (a passage that is also an act of consumption and dissolution) and the horrifying discovery of the contingency and fragility of human life—its indistinctness—when confronted with vegetal animation. The plant that is no longer outside but within us lays the foundation for a new aesthetic and affective mode—plant horror—as well as for materiality as such. Poe rewrites the radical botanies of an early period in a gloomy minor key and prepares their reception by later generations of artists, writers, and eventually filmmakers. Poe's work thus serves as a kind of hinge between early modern and modern speculations that foreground plant life.

In "The Fall of the House of Usher," a man comes to visit an old friend, Roderick Usher, who lives with his mysteriously sick sister, Madeline, in a decaying mansion with "bleak walls," "vacant eye-like windows" surrounded by "a few sedges," and "white trunks of decayed trees."[49] The house and the landscape around it, including the "black and lurid tarn that lay in unruffled lustre by the dwelling," are ascribed agency of their own. The narrator attributes "the power of thus affecting us," in this case with sorrow and fear, to the "combination of very simple natural objects" that appear before him, without his being able to fully grasp what he apprehends.[50] Later in the story, Roderick confirms the premonition of the narrator about the mysterious vitality of Usher's environment by relating an "opinion" or "belief" he has about the house. As the narrator explains:

> The opinion, in its general form, was that of the sentience of all vegetable things. But, in his disordered fancy, the idea had assumed a more daring character, and trespassed, under certain conditions, upon the kingdom of inorganization.... The belief, however, was connected (as I have previously hinted) with the grey stones of the home of his forefathers. The conditions of sentience had been there, he imagined, fulfilled in the method of collocation of these stones—in the order of their arrangement, as well as in that of the many *fungi* which overspread them, and of the decayed trees which stood around—above all, in the long undisturbed endurance of this arrangement, and in its reduplication in the still waters of the tarn. Its evidence—the evidence of sentience—was to be seen, he said, (and I here stared as he spoke,) in the gradual yet certain condensation of an atmosphere of their own about the waters and the walls. The result was discoverable, he added, in that silent, yet importunate and terrible influence which for centuries had molded the destinies of his family, and which made *him* what I now saw him—what he was.[51]

Usher's notion of vegetal sentience (which is not in itself novel, as the narrator underscores) is remarkable, especially because he extends it to inorganic matter, "the kingdom of inorganization." The double figure of the plants and the mineral elements of the stone walls—linked to the institution or social structure of the family via the metonymy of Usher's "house"—becomes an uncanny precursor to Deleuze and Guattari's rhizomes as concatenations of seemingly incompatible elements that mutually transform one another. The inorganic power of the plant modifies the very substance of the human family so that something conceived as organic and whole acquires a new life as an assemblage of nonorganic or inorganic elements. As Deleuze and Guattari put it: "Becoming is a rhizome, not a classificatory or genealogical tree."[52] The narrator's uneasy description of the house, with the specific "collocation" of the stones—fungi "spread over" them and dead trees standing around—itself evokes the attributes of an assemblage, complete with an agency that is both living and not organic. In this sense, Poe's story immediately takes us outside the kind of mutualism that Shelley and the "Frogpondians," among others, so powerfully champion.

The mention of "all vegetable things" follows on the heels of Usher's poem "The Haunted Palace," which he sings to the tune of his guitar. The precise moment of the turn to vegetal sentience—as Usher's most prominent *idée fixe*—is highlighted within the text itself by the insertion of a footnote (added to the second edition of the story by Poe), in which the sources that influence Usher are outlined. The footnote outlines a series of references: "Watson, Dr. Percival, Spallanzani, and especially the Bishop of Landaff.—See 'Chemical Essays,' vol. v." This list reveals that vegetal sentience is tightly linked to the destabilization of natural historical taxonomies via the plant-human analogy. Richard Watson's *Chemical Essays* (1785–1787), like the other works cited by Poe, is an exemplary instance of the Enlightenment reliance on analogical comparisons between plants and humans to describe and explain plant life. Conversely, Watson's work also speaks to an increasingly widespread vitalist tendency within eighteenth-century natural philosophy, a tendency that provides a bridge from eighteenth-century empiricism (with its materialist underpinnings) into a Romanticism that cultivates a transcendental bent. Poe is returning here to an analogical tradition that holds within it the possibility of a prioritization of the plant vis-à-vis the human, even as these analogies ultimately move toward a recentering of human subjectivity. He reveals how the plant-human comparison might be used not to shore up human claims to superiority over other life-forms (e.g., as we saw in the previous chapter in the example of Julien Offray de La Mettrie) but to question the distinctiveness and power of the human vis-à-vis vegetal modes of being that are no longer muted (e.g., as is the case for Tiphaigne). Gradually, Poe connects his ontological vision of a vegetalized matter, derived from this earlier moment in vitalism, to a vegetal aesthetic with powerful and ongoing effects. He also reasserts the importance of speculative fiction within this aesthetic, in another nod to his eighteenth-century forebears, including Ludvig Holberg.

Watson was professor of chemistry at Cambridge University prior to his appointment as Bishop of Llandaff. The fifth volume of his *Chemical Essays* includes a reprint of his privately printed "An Essay on the Subjects of Chemistry, and Their General Division" (first circulated in 1771), with the addition of a seven-page preface that cites several of the authors listed by Poe in the footnote, including Spallanzani and Percival.[53] With these references, Poe in one sense is committing to an anachronism, since by the 1830s the philosophy of science had definitively moved on from the kinds of analogies that deeply inform both Percival and Watson in their attempts to argue on behalf of a percipient vegetable. But Poe is anachronistic with a purpose. As we have seen, the dominant epistemological frameworks in the late eighteenth and early nineteenth centuries ultimately reestablish the hierarchy initially troubled by the discovery of qualities shared by plants and animals. Poe returns to the plant-human analogy to reveal the way in which it opens out onto a disturbing monism, in which plants (in his model) overtake all other life-forms. In other words, he allows us to imagine a "minor" vitalism whose governing logic is vegetal rather than animal.

Rather than making the plant a participant in vitality more generally—one animated instance among a myriad of others—"Usher" makes of vegetality the model for materiality as such. And a disturbing model it is. The vitalism of Spallanzani, Percival, and Watson was, for the most part, an optimistic one. In the *Chemical Essays*, Watson, given particular prominence by Poe, is careful to justify his critique of the customary divisions between minerals, vegetables, and animals on the grounds of a general increase in happiness that results from the extension of percipience to additional life-forms (e.g., plants). For Watson, the boundaries separating plants from animals and minerals are open to speculation and critique. He mobilizes a curious argument that engages both the empirical sciences—the more we subject plants to scrutiny, the more we discover that the structures and functions that characterize them have their analogies in the animal kingdom—and metaphysics. As he contends, plant perception, should it exist, would serve to increase the sum total of happiness in the world. Thus, assuming a benevolent creator, there is no reason not to presume the existence of percipient plants. This is the case even though plants are clearly subject to the voracious appetites of animals (who also eat one another). Nonetheless, since animals eat animals and animals eat plants, the massive consumption of plants by animals is no reason to refuse the faculty of perception to the former.[54] On the one hand (and counter to Poe's emphasis), Watson is not interested in denying the superiority of humans, but he ultimately marshals for his anthropocentrism an argument from theology, rather than from chemistry. In this sense, Watson's metaphysical commitments rescue his chemical ones from a wholesale investment in a radical vegetality. His is a hopeful world—since we humans can be assured that God has our interests in mind—that Poe successfully mines for potential horror, given that percipient beings are here infinitely available for consumption by their fellows. The insertion of the plant into the schema of percipience might oblige us to look again at the violence that characterizes the natural world. Watson forecloses the disturbing aspects of this violence with his turn to the divine, but Poe most emphatically does not.

The authors whom Poe cites in "Usher" are, like Watson, all interested in the interstices between the three kingdoms (vegetable, animal, mineral) and the way in which divisions among forms of being both open up and foreclose a consideration of the marginal life-forms that seem to fall between the cracks. On the one hand, the limit cases become more interesting by virtue of their failure to conform to a schema. On the other, systems of classification tend to operate as if they were common sense, blinding us to continuities that might otherwise be visible. As Watson puts it, "This preprossession in favour of systematic arrangements, operates more forcibly upon us as the ideas to which it is usually annexed become the more abstracted. The strongest analogies are overlooked, the plainest reasonings thought fallacious, and decisive experiments inconclusive, when their tendency is to subvert a distinction, of which we had wrongly supposed Nature herself the author. Every one thinks that he knows what an animal is, and how it is contradistinguished from a vegetable, and would be offended at having his knowledge questioned thereupon."[55] In Watson, the inquiry into chemical principles of "internal constitution" becomes the engine for a dissolution or disfiguring of seemingly obvious external principles of differentiation. He writes, "But when the whole external appearance of a plant, or an animal, is taken into consideration, it is far easier to refer it to a particular class, than from a chemical enquiry into its internal constitution."[56] Chemistry resists sublation.

Watson, by raising the possibility of a percipient plant life that is infinitely subject to exploitation and indeed destruction by humans, produces a vision of plant-human mutuality with a deeply macabre aspect, which he nevertheless seems content to ignore. While it might be easy to dismiss Poe's citation of Watson and other authors of his moment as a kind of faux erudition, a close reading of Watson's argument in the context of "Usher" suggests that Poe was, in fact, sensitive to the Gothic and disturbing elements of Watson's seemingly optimistic extension of percipience to even the lowest forms of animated life. Vegetal life, for Poe as for Watson and the other authors cited by Poe, takes on a particularly prominent status in a context where the differences among beings are subject to flux and reconsideration. While, as the privileged object of Linnaean taxonomy, the plant seemed to lend itself transparently to classification (thanks to its apparent lack of an interior life, as Foucault describes it), Poe finds at the heart of eighteenth-century vitalism a vegetal awareness that fully destabilizes the very order that the taxonomical plant is meant to passively and gracefully uphold.

The consequences of this move toward the sentient vegetable—active in its relations with humankind—are very different for Poe than they are for writers such as Shelley, or, on the other side of the Atlantic, Thoreau and even Emerson. Where his counterparts emphasize the reciprocity of plant-human relations (the atmospheric mixing that is underwritten and enabled by internal and external continuities, including a shared environment and sensitivity), Poe envisions the undoing of the human by the vegetal that invades it. Horror functions as the aesthetic medium in which sentient beings—human and plant—lose themselves. Here we find, as Limon argues, the plunge from taxonomy into the world of the microbe that infects and inhabits every kind of body, without discrimination, but we also find the plant as the agent rather than the object of this transition. The plant actively tears down taxonomic boundaries in the very specificity of its mode of being. And it does so more violently than other forms of life precisely because Poe is so keenly aware of an earlier speculative botanical tradition that stages the plant against the human even while positing their interpenetration. If there is a reciprocity here, it is one defined in and by the destruction of the human from within.

But Poe, unlike, for instance, Tiphaigne, also moves the matter of the plant closer to an inorganic vitalism in which vegetality penetrates both animate and inanimate bodies, thereby blurring the divide between them. Both "Usher" and Watson's treatise emphasize the role of the plant as the mediator between two different categories of being: the living and the nonliving (Poe's "kingdom of inorganization"). The plant represents once again an intermediate order, thereby undoing distinctions that serve to organize human knowledge and human selves. For Watson, the mediation performed by vegetality leads to the possibility of an enlivened mineralogy—and to a comforting turn to a belief in the increase in percipience as corresponding to an increase in happiness (via the intervention of God). Poe's affective relationship to the intermediary function of the plant is very different, as are the outcomes of the function itself. In "Usher," we are treated to the "trespassing" of the plant on the realm of the inorganic in a manner that Herbert Smith describes as "colonial organicism."[57] These invasive attributes are all the more marked since some of Poe's plants are, in fact, fungi (which were initially classified as plants). The chemical, subterranean mode of reproduction (in need of no sunlight) of the "[m]inute fungi" that "overspread the whole exterior" of the house thus works as an extension of the vegetal sentience capable of invading the mansion's very stones; this joint process of contamination results in the mysterious atmosphere of the landscape, including a strange odor, the zigzag-shaped "fissure" that marks the house's facade, and Roderick's and Madeline's physical and mental suffering—all elements in the narrative that sustain and intensify the gloominess of the Gothic story. The liveliness of the plant not only points to the possible liveliness of the mineral world; the plant actively infects the matter of the house with its undead potency. It "implants" itself within the minerals, causing them to emit a strange electric glow.

In the place of the fragile mutuality of the Romantic human subject, communing with the flowers cultivated in the garden, Poe envisions in "Usher" an unwilled participation in the undomesticated vitality of plants, a force that serves as a structuring principle (both inchoate and powerful) for bodies more generally. Poe's return to an eighteenth-century vitalist science allows him to steer clear of the Hegelian botanophobic current of the Romantic movement, a context in which the animated plant is placed on the outside or at the limits of the human world. Of course, the Romantic consideration of the plant as possessed of its own particular physiology (and biology) represents a partial recognition of vegetal alterity, an alterity that becomes the basis for a positive human relationship to the plant world. Yet, Poe, in his specific interest in the question of vegetal animation, does not focus on this relatively modern sense of what the plant is and what it can do (including newly discovered capacities such as photosynthesis). Instead, "Usher" is built around the question or problem of an experience of vegetal sentience as a mechanism through which the plant paradoxically resists incorporation into or assimilation with human paradigms of desire, consciousness, or intention. These seemingly superior modes of apprehension, however, do not disappear altogether but are effectively "remixed" within the medium generated by vegetable percipience—an alien sensibility, a grasp of the world that is altogether indifferent to the human but retains a powerful hold over it. At the same time that its indifference to humans is made horrifyingly manifest, the plant remains powerfully alive and even conscious, gradually becoming capable of generating a new mode of aesthetic experience as it overtakes and consumes the human protagonist. In "Usher," the plant serves as a model for inhuman forms of perception as such, and it puts the lie to the human fiction of the universality of desire.

Vegetal sentience, which begins to infect Usher himself even as it retains its independence from human forms of cognition, is linked by the narrator both to biological modes of decay and to figures of inorganic liveliness such as luminosity or form. (The zigzag-shaped fissure in the house is thus a way in which the very stones come alive.) Usher himself appears to the narrator to be "terribly altered," with a face both "cadaverous" and "luminous beyond comparison."[58] The narrator asserts, "I could not, even with effort, connect its Arabesque expression with any idea of simple humanity." At this moment, Poe expands upon the orientalist and Gothic genealogy of the arabesque line to link this style of ornament back to natural history and the ontological question of life. If "simple" humanity signifies humanity without any supplements, Usher is no longer solely human; he, too, has joined "the kingdom of inorganization."[59] The art produced by Usher also undergoes a mysterious change that strongly evokes the vegetal in the Hegelian sense of a zone of utter indifference, even as it overwhelms and denaturalizes the Romantic image of the evil plant. As the narrator remarks, Usher's creations vie with and seem to outdo Henry Fuseli's (1741–1825) nightmarish paintings. (Strikingly, the reference to Fuseli in this context represents another botanical connection, since he was one of the illustrators of *The Botanic Garden*.) The "ghastly and inappropriate splendor" that appears in one of Usher's works has its own vegetal elements, if not chemical ones; it is described as without directionality, not unlike the arabesque line itself.

The light that comes from the gasses produced by the atmosphere reappears in and infuses Usher's painting. Thus, gazing at Usher's art is like gazing at the tarn: both are material atmospheres that also function as media. The light in the tunnel featured in Usher's painting is ghastly perhaps because it does not originate in the sun (which is, of course, an important figure both for Shelley's poem and in Hegel's work, where it becomes an emblem of Spirit). In the narrator's description, this nonphotosynthetic atmosphere extends from the visual realm into the olfactory one: "I had worked upon my imagination as really to believe that about the whole mansion and domain there hung an atmosphere peculiar to themselves and their immediate vicinity—an atmosphere which had no affinity with the air of heaven, but which had reeked up from the decayed trees, and the grey wall, and the silent tarn—a pestilent and mystic vapour, dull, sluggish, faintly discernible, and leaden hued."[60] If Poe's story seems on the one hand to embrace the indifference of the Hegelian plant, Poe, unlike Hegel, presents this "ghastly" plant life as highly productive—of an aesthetic, of an affect, of a smell shared across bodies, of a contagion, and perhaps of a perverse fascination fueled by fear, even as it operates inside the human, reshaping it from within. Vegetal sentience transforms human perceptions, although it does not originate with them.

This dismantling of the traditional taxonomic separation of beings thus corresponds to a vegetalization of the world, humans and minerals included.[61] Poe's plant life, rather than being a passive life-form consumed by all others, takes on the active capacity for violence that Watson registers in the natural world more generally (and which he hopes to eradicate through a recourse to divine logic).[62] This agentive vegetality emerges as a result of the cross-pollination of science, albeit an anachronistic science, with a new aesthetics of horror that likewise finds its inspiration in an earlier period. In addition to reactivation of eighteenth-century speculations on the nature of plant being, Poe contributes to and extends a long-standing tradition of speculative fiction. The books in Usher's possession that are "in strict keeping with this character of phantasm"[63] include Niccolò Machiavelli's anti-marriage novella *Belfagor* (published in 1549 but written some time before his death in 1527), Tommaso Campanella's *The City of the Sun* (first published in 1623 but written some twenty years earlier), and Holberg's *The Journey of Niels Klim to the World Underground*—references that collectively open up a cosmographic dimension within the stuffy Gothic mansion. Of course, Holberg's narrative not only contains the image of a planet inhabited by plants but the figure of a hollow earth—championed by John Cleves Symmes (1742–1814) and dear to Poe, who often resorted to it. The tarn into which the mansion eventually collapses suggests a subterranean world into which the vegetal invites the reader even as Usher is ultimately consumed by it.

In fact, subterranean images or forces, including the whirlpools in "MS. Found in a Bottle" (1833) and the maelstrom in "A Descent into the Maelström" (1841), are not rare in Poe's fiction. In the 1833 story, the narrator, who has descended into a cavity under the surface of the ocean, finds himself on a strange ship manned by an ancient and remarkably infirm crew who remain unaware of his presence. The ship's timbers are distinguished by their "extreme *porousness*" even as they are "distended by any unnatural means." In his description of the composition of the ship, the narrator recalls an "apothegm" from "an old weather-beaten Dutch navigator": "It is as sure . . . as sure as there is a sea where the ship itself will grow in bulk like the living body of the seaman."[64] This saying, meant as a marker of veracity, associates the strange, enormous ship, made of porous timber yet still growing, with the living matter of the human body. In the story, the dead wood seems to come alive but without the attribution of sentience that it acquires in "Usher." At the same time, the ship, along with its sailors, remains profoundly indifferent to the narrator. The unexplained dilation of the ship to ten times its original size, "like the living body of the seaman,"[65] also changes the scale of the world in which the narrator finds himself. Matthew Taylor argues that, in these and other narratives, Poe fashions "heterodox literary cosmographies" containing disturbing reversals of the Cartesian universe that keeps active rational minds and inert objects separate. For Taylor, these cosmographies allow us to envision "alternative pasts, presents, and futures of the self-world imaginary."[66] Yet, the sailors of the ship are not simply uninterested by the narrator; they do not even notice him. Like Usher, they appear to possess an awareness of their circumstances, muttering strangely to themselves, revealing concern, anxiety even, but they remain ultimately out of the narrator's reach. In this, they not only evoke Usher's disconnected consciousness and artistic sensibility but also prefigure the facial and bodily gestures that are transmitted on the cinematic screen, proximate yet out of reach. Perhaps they, too, are becoming plant?

In "Usher," we remain in close proximity to the transformation of human subjectivity as the latter becomes vegetal. While this process entails a partial disintegration of the human in the face of vegetal indifference,[67] it also opens up new, posthuman perspectives in which an altered consciousness might be imagined to live on as a speculative possibility. Poe's story produces continuities among modes of being rather than breaks between them, so that the world, the thought, and the life of Usher and his sister hover between the inorganic and the organic realms. In this way, too, their sentience is vegetalized. While the narrator does not share their fate, his lingering presence throughout the narrative suggests that he is also vulnerable to invasion. On the one hand, the narrative voice manages to maintain a certain distance from the nonphotosynthetic atmosphere that is specific to the mansion, the decaying trees, and the tarn, even though this distance is menaced and nearly collapses, not unlike the house itself, by the end of the story. On the other hand, Usher's own consciousness, with its vegetal aspect, does not consistently recognize this outside; it is eventually fully penetrated by that which fascinates it, "the grim phantasm, FEAR."[68] Just as Shelley's gardener cultivates the beauty she sees with her mind's eye while tending to the flowers of the garden, Usher is terrified of the "opinion" that he has formed about vegetal sentience. In a manner typical of Poe's stories, we become privy to a consciousness able to reflect on its own dissolution, in which it simultaneously participates.

Usher's vegetal hypersensibility and the horrific image reflected in the tarn refer us to various media that might take us toward a sentience indifferent to human desire by allowing for the partial representability of this sentience. The tarn is not so much a seat of organic matter in water as a reflection, not unlike a screen, which is a medium for fear itself, as the narrator reveals in his account. Vegetal sensibility is a surrogate but alien form of quasi-consciousness, for which the human does not exist; it does not attack it from the outside but inhabits it, while the human comes to exist in an assemblage with the vegetal sentience that alters it. This sensibility opens onto a world that is not given to human consciousness and is not "for us" without the mediation of writing and, later, cinema. Fear is thus not a dead end in Poe's writing.

The horror that marks the encounter with the plant as arabesque or inorganic arrangement does not so much produce a nostalgia for a lost affinity with the domesticated plant as it gives way to a new aesthetics. Can there be a consciousness invaded by vegetal sentience that moves toward the life that the Hegelian spirit has to violently reject, thereby precluding this violence in its embrace of interpenetration? As experimental French filmmaker Jean Epstein (1897–1953) notes, for Poe, fear was the "imp of perversion," driving an exploration of its own origins and causes, even as it amplifies itself as an affect that becomes the screen or medium of a new type of experience.[69] Epstein found in Poe's writing the suggestion that even seemingly negative modes of affect can draw us toward those forms of being that we experience as alien and threatening to our identity and, in the process, can transform us. Critics have often treated Usher's *idée fixe* as something of an embarrassment; it is regularly passed over in readings that highlight the more traditionally Gothic elements of the story (whereas, as we have shown, Poe strives to outdo the existing Romantic conceptions of horror and the Gothic that continue to privilege the integrity of the human). Via his filmic interpretations of Poe, informed by symbolism,

Epstein will zoom in on the motif of vegetal sentience in order to translate inorganic plant life into a figure for the animation of all matter, brought to human perception by the cinematic technology of the camera.

Poe's interest in scientific theories of vitalism and in the vitality of inanimate things points to a contentious engagement with nineteenth-century vitalist science, one in which the organic and the inorganic slide into each other. The same ambiguity characterizes his embrace of the Hegelian plant, or of the arabesque, which in Poe is materialized and becomes a kind of writing that cannot be read, whose "meaning" is material and thus not for the spirit to grasp. Via late eighteenth- and early nineteenth-century chemistry, and scientific investigations that blurred the boundaries not only between humans and plants but also between organic and inorganic states of being, Poe explores the minerality of the vegetal that is noted by Aristotle and will ultimately be extended by Deleuze to all life.[70] Still, Poe thinks of this life as sensitive and sensing, and thus his vegetal arrangements always maintain a contentious hold on the living and organic world while remaining in contact with the mineral and inorganic one. We see a tendency today to push plants toward the animal definition of life—for example, in Michael Marder's work, which resonates with a Romantic assertion of plant-human affinity. But Poe, via a critical interpretation of Hegelian vegetal indifference, might be said to inherit Aristotle's realization that plants are sites where inorganic matter transforms itself into something productive but atelic. This legacy, too, connects him to the satirical revisions of Aristotelianism that mark the origins of radical botany in the seventeenth century.

Poe, Gilman, and the End of the Family Romance

Poe's story suggests a vegetalization not only of particular minds but of the family as a social and biological category. Familial relationships as they are conceived in "Usher" are originally structured according to the conventional taxonomic model of a tree, albeit a stunted one. The narrator remarks, "I learned, too, the very remarkable fact, that the stem of the Usher race, all time-honored as it was, had put forth, at no period, any enduring branch; in other words, that the entire family lay in the direct line of descent, and had always, with very trifling and very temporary variation, so lain."[71] Roderick and Madeline's relationship, with its strong hints of incestuous passion, suggests the collapse of the family line upon itself. At the same time, the figural family tree turns horrifyingly literal through the evocation of the vegetal sentience that gradually colonizes the house, itself an increasingly vegetalized structure, and its inhabitants. Human genealogy, with its social power, is no longer fully separable from material things, "natural objects," and the life of matter. Indeed, the first trees to appear in the narrative are those dead and decaying ones that mark the landscape as the narrator makes his way through the "singularly dreary" countryside. Unlike much Gothic fiction, the villain here is not paternal authority turned cruel and terrifying but a force or mode of life that dissolves this authority altogether. In the process, vegetality is revealed as the agent of the disintegration of genealogies that should otherwise preserve distinctions according to a familial logic.

With "Usher," Poe also takes up the Romantic notion of elective affinities or, as Poe's narrator puts it, "sympathies of a scarcely intelligible nature." The "striking similarity" between Roderick and his twin sister Madeline can also be represented as a vegetal bond. Their sexual and individual difference from each other, conventionally maintained within the family through exogamy, is increasingly elided as the narrative proceeds. Madeline is both sister and companion to Roderick; they are the sole surviving descendants of the family line and live together in isolation. Even their features are similar. Roderick displays a heightened and increasingly "vegetal" sensibility, while Madeline is portrayed as a kind of plant herself: "cataleptical," located between life and death, ultimately shut in a casket but still alive, sister but also proximate to the role of wife. Vegetal sentience thus marks a place where individual human life comes to an end even as it remains neither traceable back to an origin nor reducible to a genealogy. It is in this plantlike sense that Madeline is Roderick's double or twin rather than in her role as a descendant from the same father. In this context, the entombment of Madeline after her apparent death is not only yet another symptom of the patriarchal exclusion of women from public life and agency in general, although Poe does inherit this particular theme from Gothic fiction, but the "burying" of an inorganic vegetal life that is generated via doubling, in arabesque lines that run through and divide the house (as in the zigzag crack in the facade), the face of Roderick himself, and the family. As one might expect, this shutting away of Madeline's body causes her to reanimate, but in a new (and quite terrible) form.

In his film version of "Usher," Epstein transforms the relationship between Madeline and Roderick into a marriage, thereby both highlighting the incestuous potential of the original story and eliding it. Before Epstein, symbolist poet Charles Baudelaire (1821–1867), who helps disseminate the works of Poe in France, turns specifically to "Usher," using a fragment from Roderick's composition "The Haunted Palace" in the concluding allusion of "Héautontimorouménos" ("The One Who Strikes Himself," *Fleurs du mal*, 1857). In Baudelaire's poem, we experience the crisis of a consciousness divided against itself, so that Roderick's musical poem becomes an allegory not so much of the house itself as of the relationship between the siblings as constituent parts, masculine and feminine, of a fractured self. In "Héautontimorouménos," the self-tormenter seems to direct his violence at a female counterpart who is both internal and external to him, yet in Poe's story it is Madeline who issues the final blow. Throughout the story, she appears to serve the role of Roderick's faithful echo, but in the end, rising from the tomb, she strikes him dead. The wild atmosphere (low-hanging clouds without any sight of moon or stars) that surrounds and presses down on the mansion at the time when Madeline, previously entombed, reveals herself to be alive—or, at least, undead—is also strangely connected to her. Madeline's death and bizarre resurrection enable a confrontation with vegetality as a challenge to patriarchal models of the family and patriarchal authority generally; the inaccessibility of the plant to human norms becomes an engine for the reshaping of human social bonds. Thus, the sentient vegetable holds within it a certain political potential, even though it does not coincide with human political models; indeed, its power might perhaps derive precisely from this noncoincidence.

Still, in Poe's story, the threat to human precedence of the horrifyingly yet vitally alive plant does not open out onto a more just or better social world. Only later will speculative fiction mine the potential of Poe's plants for a specifically antipatriarchal and eventually feminist critique, thus reconfiguring an early modern interest in vegetality as the source of an unorthodox epistemology. Alongside the symbolist transmission of Poe's vegetal life, we can locate a corpus of feminist narrative that reworks Poe's vegetal attack on the human family—one in which Roderick and Madeline undo the specificity of human sexual difference in favor of a more plant-like proliferation of "copies"—into a critique of patriarchal models of gender and sexuality (i.e., a vision of the haunted house and its occupants presented from Madeline's point of view). In their analysis of the feminist legacy of "Usher," critics Dennis R. Perry and Carl H. Sederholm read Charlotte Perkins Gilman as specifically taking up and animating the feminist possibilities inherent in "Usher." They explore "The Yellow Wallpaper" as a revision of Poe's Gothic tale from the point of view of the women who are entombed within patriarchal culture, as Madeline arguably is.[72] Their reading thus insists on discerning the outlines of a patriarchal system in the decrepit mansion, which, as we have argued, ultimately undoes and vitiates both natural and familial taxonomies. But the connection between Poe and Gilman is not just one of genre—through the medium of the Gothic story or the haunted house narrative—but one of joint animation of vegetal models.

Charlotte Perkins Gilman may be best known for "The Yellow Wallpaper," now a canonical narrative of feminist protest, but she is also the author of the short story "The Giant Wistaria," first published in 1891 (a year before the publication of "The Yellow Wallpaper" in the same journal, *The New England Magazine*). Gilman appears to have been reading Poe during this period, and in "The Giant Wistaria," as in "The Yellow Wallpaper" (with its arabesque motifs of plant life), she clearly turns to vegetality as a destabilizing influence—the source of a violence rendered in response to the dehumanization of women within patriarchy. These continuities between Poe's and Gilman's writings suggest that the materiality of the vegetal can contribute to the speculative invention of feminist topographies that do not necessarily have recourse to the privileging of female or feminine identity. Within the limits of a critique shot through with white supremacism, Gilman nonetheless suggests some of the promise Poe's vision of vegetal contamination could hold for feminism.

"The Giant Wistaria" opens with the scene of a mother tenderly cultivating a wisteria, when her daughter—who has herself just given birth, as we discover—runs up to her. The daughter is begging to see her illegitimate child, who has been taken from her in an attempt to conceal what is referred to as her "blot." The mother responds by warning her to "hush," so that her father does not hear her complaints. One hundred years later, a party of young visitors—recently married couples—discover that the wisteria vine planted by the now long-dead characters in the opening scene has grown almost to consume the house. It had "once climbed its pillars, but now the pillars were wrenched from their places and held rigid and helpless by the tightly wound and knotted arms."[73] The climax of the story comes when the visitors, who have undertaken renovations on the house, discover first the body of a baby in the old well hidden in the cellar and second the body of a woman, who is revealed to be the daughter from the opening account, lying gripped and contained by the roots of the giant plant, of which they have never seen the like. The wisteria, once ornamenting the patriarchal house, has seized the house itself in its grasp and laid hold of the corpse of the daughter. The figure of the horrific plant, both supporting and dismantling the house, suggests a feminist rewriting of Poe's "Usher," but it is important in this context to acknowledge the racist and classist aspects of Gilman's corpus, including the fact that her public critique of patriarchy remains imbued with xenophobia.

The wisteria plant that surrounds the house serves as a link between the first part of the story, which introduces the oppressively patriarchal family of English settlers, and the second part, set a hundred years later, among a seemingly reformed group of independent, well-to-do young couples. The superficially egalitarian association of young men and women is nonetheless marked by race and class. The plant is thus both the guardian of the memory of an eerie oppression in the past (that may still linger on in a much-subdued form, as indicated by some of the playful but gendered acts of the young people) and an active participant in a more equitable present in which married but childless men and women freely engage in creative and recreational pursuits. The mother's caring hands plant the vines destined to destroy the patriarchal family home that entraps the women who inhabit it, even as she cannot protect her own daughter and grandchild from the ravages of a misogynist society. In this sense, the wisteria is the symbol not just of a feminine agency that struggles against the structures that constrain it but of the power of Gilman's own writings. Ultimately, though, this agency is also shown to be reserved for those who achieve the kind of status represented by the garden, the holiday home where leisure may be pursued, and even the wisteria itself. While the modern-day characters may break away from the rigid patriarchal norms that structure the first part of the story, their prosperous whiteness is still the condition of their participation in a more egalitarian world.

However, by reading the story in the context of Poe's radical botany that inspired it, we can also highlight in it a different narrative potential, one that will only be fully actualized later on. The mother's care for the vine recognizes it as a kind of daughter in its own right, more tenderly cultivated by the mother than the human daughter herself. The care that mothers and daughters are prevented (via the figure of the father) from extending to one another is lavished on the plant, which cradles the dead daughter in its roots. The mother's solicitude for the wisteria is both a symptom of the patriarchal culture that holds all women in its grip and a remnant of the maternal care that cannot be expressed among humans; this uncanny solicitude returns from death (like Madeline) to manifest itself via the plant's arabesque embrace. The plant thus recalls an affect of care and concern that was absent on the part of the human mother, insofar as motherhood is underpinned and defined by patriarchal structures, without for all that depending on a maternal human body (or identity) to generate it. The mother disappears into the plant, and only an affect lingers. The wisteria produces both a kind of uncanny tenderness and a terrifying recognition that the plant remains outside the bounds of human subjectivity and familial relations. Later on, Gilman's mode of feminist vegetality, which stresses the ability of the plant to imbue the domestic scene with both horror and a destabilizing vitality, will reappear in sci-fi and fantasy literature of the late twentieth and early twenty-first centuries that engages with a critique of patriarchal family life under late capitalism. In this context, it becomes impossible to project any human attributes onto the vegetal other, which nonetheless retains an affective power over humans themselves.

The uncanny liveliness of the plant—whether conceived in terms of an organic (proto-) desire for or an inorganic indifference to the humans that it fascinates—opens up a space for scientific, technological, and mediatic engagement with vegetal life, not just in the possibility of knowing plants' way of apprehending the world (a world that is, after all, also our own) but in the potential for channeling and adopting their power, life, and movement. In radical botanical narratives, plants reveal their ability to make not only other worlds but to remake *our* world (and indeed ourselves). In their indifference and strangeness—and in their fascinating vigor—they also suggest techniques of world-building that, for humans, are yet to come. One of these techniques, as we shall see, is cinema. Where Poe and Gilman envision the indifferent vitality of vegetal life with horror, experimental French cinema of the early twentieth century takes the possibility of a vegetal sentience and transfigures it, suffusing it with transformative affect, to make it once again a joyous and galvanizing object. Poe and Gilman together anticipate the production of visual texts that will trace the metamorphoses of plant and human bodies to explore human subjectivity as itself profoundly vegetal. In this, they owe a debt to early modern speculations about plant vitality, as articulated in both science *and* fiction (and the moments where the two genres interpenetrate).

CHAPTER 5

The End of the World by Other Means

Imagining Vegetal Worlds

Abel Gance's (1889–1981) interwar sound film *La Fin du monde* (*The End of the World*, 1930) tells the story of a comet on a collision course with Earth. Gance's film, a commercial and critical failure, is nonetheless a spectacular exploration of the social repercussions of the impending cataclysm and of the comet's eventual impact: while the planet is miraculously spared total destruction, the comet brings devastation with it when it grazes the surface of the earth.[1] As they wait for the end of the world, scientist Martial Novalic and his idealist brother Jean take on the project of reinventing human society on the eve of the imminent catastrophe.[2] The brothers encourage the people of the world to unite in a universal republic and to leave aside an intensifying arms race and projects for financial speculation, both emblematized in the figure of the weapons supplier Schomburg. The film's deeply eurocentric idealism is inflected by an intense religiosity, even as *La Fin du monde* harkens back to an Enlightenment universalism (and faith in scientific knowledge) rooted in part in Camille Flammarion's late nineteenth-century novel *Omega* (1894),[3] on which the plot is loosely based.[4] In Gance's work, early cinema inserts itself into a space created by speculative fiction and indebted to eighteenth-century philosophy. *La Fin du monde* only features plants tangentially, first as ornamental objects and later as part of the final scene of an Edenic earth from which most human life has been erased; the film is not specifically concerned with vegetality as such. Instead, the most remarkable aspect of *La Fin du monde* is the force it attributes to cinema itself to bring about political and social change, to create a newly universalist political order out of the ruins of pre–World War II European society, and ultimately to reinvent not only religion but also the universe as spectacle or, to use Gilles Deleuze's term as inspired by Henri Bergson, the universe as metacinema.[5]

The vegetal moment in interwar French cinema, our focus in this chapter, represents an attempt both to embrace and to rethink the social project with which cinema is so clearly invested in *La Fin du monde*. While filmmakers and theorists Jean Epstein (1897–1953) and Germaine Dulac (1882–1942) turn with excitement toward vegetality, other artists, including Colette (1873–1954), reinscribe the plant into the domain of ordinary experience and human pathos. Like Gance, whom they knew, Epstein and Dulac[6] deploy their cinema, which lends a privileged place to plants, as a powerful tool for creating both a transfigured audience and a new society. In their films, vegetal life often does the work that the comet is meant to undertake in *La Fin du monde*: bringing about momentous social transformation. Thus, avant-garde vegetal cinema ties the plant once again to a tradition of speculation that extends into the production and creation of new media capable of apprehending and imitating the subtle materiality of vegetal being. The "electric plant"[7] brings to fruition the concept of cinema as a form of pure movement. The French experimental films discussed in this chapter reinvent the project of imagining vegetal worlds, this time in cinematic contexts.[8]

Interwar French cinema and film criticism[9] show a fascination with the animation of the plant in the latter's capacity to reveal to audiences something new and unfamiliar about the most fundamental components of reality—to upend the categories of space and time as humans conventionally understand them. Epstein and Dulac are thus emblematic of a broader interest in time-lapse photography of the plant and in instructional science films more generally. But these two filmmakers and authors push the engagement with plant life into new modes of cinematic theory and practice: vegetal materiality and plant movement play a crucial role in the "queered perception" Epstein and Dulac generate through their work.[10] For them, plants have a specific role to play in discussions of the power of cinema to reinvigorate and transform life under technological modernity, a function not easily fulfilled by animals. Plant motion may not be regularly accessible to the human eye, but viewed through the lens of the camera it becomes not only visible but also "life itself" (Epstein) and "pure movement" (Dulac). Thus, the relationship between the plant and the cinematic apparatus goes beyond the latter's capacity to make plant movement perceptible; the movement of the plant comes to stand for cinema's ability to show (and transmit) the liveliness of the universe, itself envisioned as perpetual, yet joyous, cataclysm. For these avant-garde filmmakers, the plant is not a passive object of representation seized upon by technology.[11] Rather, it actively participates in the creation of a new reality. In this sense, not only is the plant at work in early cinema; it provides a model for cinema's alien logic.

The experimental films of Epstein and Dulac use cinema as a medium to reinvigorate an analogical approach to the relationship between plant and animal life-forms. They thus extend and revise Poe's project of reinvesting the plant-human analogy with terrifying force. At the same time, the electric plant of the early twentieth century retains a limited anthropomorphic proximity to humans while also being resolutely strange and unlike our experience of ourselves. (This minimal anthropomorphism thus transforms the human into something other than what it is.) Epstein and Dulac endow cinema, through its affinity and relationship to the plant, with the power to generate new kinds of affect in audiences and spectators. The end of the world here does not provide redemption, as in Gance's work, or a return to universalist rationalism but an opening to perpetual motion and change. With the animated plant, the future becomes the now.[12]

La Fin du monde *and Other Cataclysms*

La Fin du monde, the last part of a trilogy about a prophet figure named Jean Novalic and his disciple Geneviève d'Arc, was famously a colossal failure.[13] While Gance had originally sought funding for the project from the League of Nations and planned to make a three-hour film (intended to be the first monumental sound feature in French), he failed to obtain the financing he needed, and the film's eventual producer, Vassili Ivanoff, insisted on cutting out some of the scenes and bringing the running time down to ninety minutes.[14] As Paul Cuff has shown, Gance viewed images not just as mimetic forms of representation but as technologies of the real. From the first scenes onward, *La Fin du monde* defines religion as a spectacle and spectacle itself as potentially transformative. Indeed, it opens by problematizing the position of the spectator, pulling back from the scene of the crucifixion to reveal a modern audience whose reactions run the gamut from deeply involved to profoundly uninterested: detached and world-weary mondains, entranced altar boys, fascinated women, distracted priests. The paradigmatic power of the crucifixion is soon to give place to another perhaps even more irresistible force, conveyed by the universe (and positivist science) to the people of Paris and later the whole planet: the comet.

As Jean declares "the necessity of a formidable cataclysm" to transform the fate of humankind, one arrives as if on cue. His astronomer brother Martial has discovered "Lexell's Comet," which is headed for a collision with Earth. The brothers declare that "the old world will come to an end" and work "to turn the cataclysm into an opportunity for transforming people's hearts." The film makes us into spectators of the comet itself, the topography of the earth (beginning with Paris but moving across different parts of the globe), and the scientific community, with its specific technologies and preoccupations. While at first few members of the public lend credence to Martial's efforts to publicize the impending impact, as the comet becomes visible in the sky, it becomes a point of attention, fascination, and terror. As the League of Nations declares the founding of a Universal Republic (together with a European Union), the camera shows images of Catholic priests and of Muslim worshippers, of terrified African villagers and of the Sphinx, of flocks of penguins and of the Sámi people. These panoramic views of the world stand in stark contrast to the economic and ontological crisis brought about by the impending arrival of the comet; we see chaos in the streets, confusion at the stock market, and ultimately an enormous orgy involving hundreds, perhaps thousands, of people in Paris, all driven to seek solace in sex and drink. As the comet draws near and a voice declares "thirty-two hours left to live," we observe a series of "extraordinary phenomena in the entire world"; nature itself seems thrown into paroxysms, just as the human society has been. In rapid succession, images of birds on the water, plants in the wind, clouds moving through the sky, deer running, and trees falling move across the screen. Finally, the domain of agriculture appears at the end of the film as the carrier of humanity across the divide of the apocalypse. Hope is placed in this orderly bucolic world as that which not only endures and survives but transmits and disseminates (human) culture across space and time. Gance's plants do not point to modernity; with its impending demise, they remain relics of a pastoral imaginary. Conversely, Epstein and Dulac take a very different approach to the representation of vegetal life, which they consider not in its agricultural or pastoral but in its physiological and microscopic dimensions. They open up what is for Gance a moment of narrative closure (the putative end of the world reasserts the pastoral order to which the narrative reverts) into a state of constant cataclysm—a situation of perpetual movement in which the plant in all of its materiality and animacy takes a key position.

The Plant as the Device of Life Itself: Jean Epstein

Epstein, who was a friend of Abel Gance and directed several scenes of *La Fin du monde*,[15] took inspiration from Gance's cinematic technique in this and earlier films, notably *The Wheel* (*La Roue*, 1923). In his essay on *photogénie*, Epstein writes in reference to *The Wheel*: "Gance—today our master, one and all."[16] However, unlike Gance, Epstein did not invest cinema with a prophetic or messianic force doomed never to be fully realized. Instead, he viewed cinema—or what he came to define after World War II as "the intelligence of a machine"—as sufficient in itself to count as a world-changing event, albeit on a much smaller scale than that envisioned by Gance. As a technology that transforms how we perceive and experience ourselves and the world, Epstein's cinema does not have a privileged object. Yet, among the beings and things in his films that take on special roles are plants (rather than animals), minerals, machines, body parts, and lifeless objects. Reflections on time-lapse images of plants crop up repeatedly and throughout his long career as a writer and theorist of cinema.

In his work as a filmmaker, Epstein's camera does not so much avoid the animal as veer away from it. Where the movements of the (human) animal are often slowed down, presented in close-ups and through techniques of slow-motion photography, to the point of losing expression and even becoming deanimated, plants, automobiles, and other machines accelerate and vibrate with a surprising inorganic vitality. Epstein's interest in the ability of cinema (and of the camera in particular) to manipulate space and time allows this medium to display the mobility of the material universe. Cinema for Epstein—and ultimately also for Dulac—is akin to a crisis that mobilizes the world but does not bring about the kind of teleological resolution that Gance imagines the cinematic spectacle will provide. The cataclysm to which Epstein cinema's "machine eye" leads us is less grandiose, since it concerns minerals, smaller living organisms, and, especially, the plant as an exemplary instance of its power. This cataclysm is ordinary, and it is modeled on the plant.

In his 1926 book *La Cinématographe vu de l'Etna* (*The Cinema Seen from Etna*), in which he develops a powerful analogy between the erupting volcano and the camera, Epstein also elevates the humble science short to quasi-mystical status. He recalls, "In front of me, at Nancy, a room with three hundred people moaned when they saw a grain of wheat germinate on screen. Suddenly, the true visage of life and death, of a terrifying love, appeared, provoking these religious outcries. What churches, if we only knew how to construct them, could accommodate a spectacle like this, where life itself is revealed? To discover unexpectedly, as if for the first time, everything from a divine perspective, with its symbolic profile and vaster sense of analogy, suffused with an aura of personal identity—that is the great joy of cinema."[17] The motion of plants, which are commonly perceived by humans as largely static, is shown by the camera to be imbued with affect and expressive of a universe animated by an inorganic life. In Epstein's film theory, moreover, the plant becomes a privileged example of the camera's ability to cast aside appearances and expose this life to the spectators' joyous apprehension. The "divine" perspective becomes that of the machine, which reveals the real and perpetual activity and affective flexibility of all matter. Not unlike religion, cinema is capable of reuniting knowledge with sensation. This quasi-mystical experience grows out of positivist science but does not remain within the latter's confines: "One of the greatest powers of cinema is its animism. On screen, nature is never inanimate. Objects take on airs. Trees gesticulate. Mountains, just like Etna, convey meanings. Every prop becomes a character. The sets are cut to pieces and each fragment assumes a distinctive expression. An astonishing pantheism is reborn in the world and fills it until it bursts. The grass in the meadow is a smiling, feminine genie. Anemones full of rhythm and personality evolve with the majesty of planets."[18] Here Epstein describes the ability of the camera to take reality apart and "fill" the world to make it "burst"; the camera has "analytic power"[19] and renders the entire universe, including nonorganic matter, as alive. In this passage, life appears in the Epicurean guise of nonteleological nature, making the cinematic experience that exposes it to spectators akin to religion. Elsewhere, in his descriptions of Etna, the volcano is not only revealed by the camera as in constant movement but also becomes its own figure for what the camera does. Epstein contends that "houses, badly protected by their holy images, exploded, making a sound like nuts cracking"; "[h]uge trees ... instantaneously burst into flames, from their roots to their tops," because of their proximity to Etna.[20] In his travels to Sicily and in the vicinity of the eruption, Epstein finds in the volcano a device like cinema (and similar to

Gance's comet), one that is able to make our stable world burst apart and open in a cataclysmic rupture.[21]

The vitality that things acquire via the intervention of the camera[22] is as disturbing as it is inspiring. What is the role of the small green plant in the largely mineral and mechanical analogies that operate in this essay, including images of the camera, the volcano, and the hall of mirrors in the staircase of Epstein's hotel? Plants also burst into movement when touched by flames or when viewed through the camera's lens. But are plants themselves devices that prefigure the operation of cinema? Do plants similarly convert matter into motion, thereby serving as a medium for the incessant cataclysm that is the universe? Answering these questions requires a consideration of the close bond between vegetal life and the invention of cinema itself. In his reflections on and representations of vegetality, Epstein builds on a tradition that takes plants as both model and inspiration for the work done by the camera. He also mines a more recent turn by scientists and plant physiologists to photography as a means of experimentation.

Experimental cinema of this period is not just indebted to an earlier tradition of narrative speculation that has links to science (as in the work of Flammarion and Poe); it also draws directly on techniques of scientific imaging. As Oliver Gaycken has shown, the connection between plants and very early cinema is especially intimate, as in the experiments and imaging techniques used by Charles and Francis Darwin in their studies of plant movement, and, a little later, in the more sophisticated time-lapse imaging of plants produced by the laboratory of Wilhelm Pfeffer and the chronophotography of the Marey Institute. Thus, "[t]he time-based visualization practices that the Darwins' research relied on were part of a culture of scientific observation from which the cinema emerged."[23] The Darwins's early experiments aimed at showing similarities between animals and plants, and Francis Darwin notes in a later article that "at least the ghosts of similar qualities" (between plants and animals) are the result of the imaging of plant movement.[24] These "phantom similarities" (Gaycken) are visible only in representations of the plant mediated by imaging techniques and, Gaycken argues, are produced by technologies that give humans access to a nonhuman temporal register. From the Darwins's attempts to make root tip trace lines on smoked glass plates to the time-lapse photography of scientific documentaries of the 1920s, these techniques create an "electric vegetable," a filmic ghost that moves and gesticulates in uncanny but compelling ways. A phantom of the cinematic apparatus is thus born, a stunning animated plant that forcefully destroys all previous conceptions of static plants, or so it seems. But when plants themselves appear in film or when cinema reveals itself to be akin to the plant, which anticipates it, do they thereby become just another version of what Akira Lippit has aptly termed the "electric animal"—the cinematic figure of animality?[25]

Filmmakers and critics, including the British documentary filmmaker F. Percy Smith, often exploit the resemblance of plant movements captured through time-lapse photography to the gestures of animals and even human beings. Smith's plants in particular become characters straight from popular narrative forms, including the detective story or the romance. Epstein's enthusiastic praise of the images of the germination of a grain of wheat, cited earlier, also celebrates this ability of the filmic medium to reveal the apparently static plant as alive and mortal—even capable of a "terrible love" and all the drama of life that we associate with animal movement and passion. The film that Epstein recalls viewing in Nancy was probably scientist Jean Comandon's "La germination d'un grain de blé," possibly made in 1922. Comandon was a medical researcher and a pioneer in microcinematography who until 1927 prepared many pedagogical films or science shorts for Pathé, then for Albert Kahn, and finally for the Institut Pasteur.[26] Comandon was in touch with a number of avant-garde filmmakers, whose meetings he frequented, including Germaine Dulac.[27]

Comandon's portrayal of plants in many ways counters the project of animating vegetables to become uncanny animals. Unlike Smith in his work for Charles Urban as part of the *Urban Sciences* series prior to World War I and after the war on the highly successful *Secrets of Nature* film series (1922–1933), Comandon did not strive to frame his time-lapse films of plants with a narrative that highlighted their similarities to animals and people.[28] Instead, his plants are photographed in an austere laboratory environment with just a few bare accessories visible, such as a flickering light denoting the laboratory equivalent of day and night or the face of a clock. The background of these films is often black. (The absence of color in the films makes their effect quite different from the brilliantly lifelike color images of plants characteristic of more recent time-lapse.) The deliberate stripping of narrative from the images of plant movement contributes to the effect that Epstein refers to as that of "life itself" (and which we can also understand as a faint echo of the Aristotelian plant *psūchē*), but it is at the same time an aesthetic choice made by Comandon. For example, his footage of a dandelion blooming and turning into a white seed head, which remains intact against all expectations, demonstrates that the vegetal movement in question comes from an internal rather than an external source.[29] The footage of the flower is followed by the hands of a clock turning with

Figure 5. Dandelion blooming. Jean Comandon, *La Croissance des végétaux*, ca. 1929 [10:04].

furious speed ("one image per 120 seconds," specifies a note). This clock is not a simple functionalist model typically used in laboratories but rather sports wrought-iron handles, an enamel face, and Roman numerals, perhaps signifying the intrusion of the domestic space into the scientific arena, as critic Philippe-Alain Michaud suggests, or, as we like to think, recalling the Gothic mansion of genre fiction.[30] Thus, like Poe, Comandon may also be aware of the reality-constructing role of plants and the disruptive effects they can have on a world conceived by human consciousness alone.

Several aspects of Comandon's choices in his time-lapse films of plants, besides the austerity of the settings and the almost total elimination of narrative or the presence of incongruous objects (i.e., the clock), interfere with the effort to compare vegetal motion to a human or animal gestural vocabulary. We see this in the moments when Comandon's interest turns to the rhythmic movement of plants, including places where this movement ends or slows. In one sequence, the tips of the honeysuckle that climb onto a blade of glass are cut off, thereby stopping the upward movement of the plant. In another, the camera captures the "sleep" of mimosas, clovers, and daisies (in order to show the mimosa, usually noted for its rela-

Figure 6. The sleep of the daisy, with older ones that no longer close up. Jean Comandon, *La Croissance des végétaux*, ca. 1929 [21:33].

tively frantic waking movements, as capable of rest). Elsewhere, the clover appears to move in a synchronized hypnotic rhythm, and older daisy flowers no longer close up at night. These films bring into focus a life that is proto-zoological and manifested as forms of diminished vibrancy: sleeping, aging, and wilting. The slow, liminal movement of these plants suggests an ambiguous state (between animate and inanimate, animal and vegetable) that has points of affinity with theories of early experimental French cinema as invoking a state of being that precedes or transcends consciousness.[31] Here plants seem to float, devoid of motive, in an unconscious torpor.

If interwar cinema is fascinated with the motion of plants on screen, then what makes the sleep of plants interesting to the scientist Comandon and the filmmaker Epstein? In his early essay "Poésie d'aujourd'hui: Un nouvel état d'intelligence" ("Contemporary Poetry: A New State of Intelligence"), first published in 1921, Epstein states that accelerated modern life takes a toll on the brain cells, causing "intellectual fatigue."[32] Epstein contends that the repetitiveness of actions in the modern workplace and the overstimulation of the sensorium have a blunting effect on the human subject; at the mercy of this repeated benumbing stimulation, emotional life, including the inner sense of being alive, becomes damned up, blocked, or dampened. As Christophe Wall-Romana puts it: "Epstein does not see fatigue as a loss or shortage of energy, but rather as a state of sensorial and affective anaesthesia."³³ Like Walter Benjamin, who identified cinema as an aesthetic medium suited to an age of highly routinized labor and automatized production, Epstein understood poetry and cinema as means to connect people with what is generally called "vegetative life" ("vie végétative")—"a deaf, silent, but active animate vitality."³⁴ According to Epstein, both poetry and cinema are able to tap into this prelinguistic sensibility or affective intensity in order to "awaken" us. For Epstein, cinema, rather than providing a representation of the body as a unified object of desire, enables a certain contact with the inner sensation of this body (coenaesthesis, in the scientific terminology that the medically trained Epstein preferred). In this configuration, vegetative life is animal life conceived as silent affect rather than as concealed interiority oriented outward. Cinema is thus no longer the experience of looking into the eyes of an animal (as described by John Berger) that offers to the human onlooker "a glimpse of subjectivity at its limit."³⁵

For Epstein, cinema takes us beyond (or simply to another place than) the moment of both self-recognition and incomprehension in the confrontation with something palpably present but unavailable. Instead, it becomes a positive, affective form of stimulation. In his career as a theorist of cinema, Epstein hesitates between an emphasis on the "deaf" animism of coanaesthesia, engendered in and revealed by vegetal movement, and consideration of plants as a kind of machinic device analogous to the camera. Perhaps it is also because of their ambiguity, their intermediary position between animals and minerals, that plants—along with lifeless or geological objects, body parts, and technological and mediating devices—occupy a central role in his cinematic universe, while animals are largely missing from it. Although animals are capable of provoking both our identification and our active noncomprehension, vegetal and mineral things, as well as some other of the objects, faces, and body parts that Epstein privileges, gradually lead us away from the "animetaphor."³⁶

Toward the end of his life, in *L'Intelligence d'une machine* (*The Intelligence of a Machine*, 1946), one of his most programmatic books on the theory of cinema, Epstein argues that cinema is an "intelligent machine" that builds and reconstitutes both time and space. The camera can, of course, slow down time and accelerate it, among other tricks. Moreover, animals, when presented in slow motion, tend to look vegetal (or mineral), while minerals and plants become animallike. The camera "rediscovers, in the movements of the torso and the neck, the active elasticity of the stem; in the undulating of hair or horse mane, the swaying of a forest; in the coiling and uncoiling of reptiles, the spiral sense of vegetal growth."[37] This passage describes the fluidity of movement that Epstein opposes to geometrical and mathematical abstractions; the animal body takes on vegetal qualities—becoming plant—thanks to slow-motion photography. Thus, cinema couples the enlivening of plants through time-lapse with the vegetalization of animal bodies. The plant body points to the yet more real aliveness of things as such. We discover in cinema *life itself*, as Epstein writes in *Le Cinématographe vu de l'Etna*, a life that is inorganic but defined by movement and transformation.[38]

The model for animation here is not an animal (or human) body with hidden desires animating it from within. In *L'Intelligence d'une machine*, Epstein defines the cinematic experience as the hybrid of two illusions or "ghosts": the first created by the camera's analytic power, the second by the human mind. The camera is able to "slice" reality into distinct parts. For Epstein, the camera's gaze is no more objective than are the images a microscope or telescope produces, and reality is something he calls "pre-material," prior to all categories of materiality (e.g., atoms or electrons) that the human understanding creates. He maintains that this discontinuity of cinematic images is a "ghost of mechanical intelligence," a positive power of the device that we can rely on.[39] When we enjoy a film as a continuous moving image, the human mind adds to this ghost the additional "ghost of human intelligence," also a positive force. The image thus created by cinema is not simply a double illusion (as Bergson described it). Rather, Epstein thought that the cinematic experience of these two "ghosts" is well worth our attention because it gives access to the very fluidity of the reality that grounds—but also often escapes—our experience.[40]

In fact, the camera represents another, alien point of view, one that becomes partially ours in this hybridization, even as it remains strange to us since it incorporates both the camera's nonhuman point of view and our eye's (and brain's) ability to produce fluidity and movement out of discontinuity. The alterity of the camera's perspective, which exceeds the realm of human phenomenology as a robot brain that can feel and think, is most evident in its relation to time, the fourth dimension. Cinema's ability to alter time's arrow and make time malleable and reversible, doing away with Cartesian causality, is apparent in techniques such as accelerated motion, time-lapse, slow motion, rapid editing, and the close-up. We are here in an experimental dimension. As Wall-Romana puts it, "It is not, Epstein suggests deftly, a matter of human subjectivity vs. mechanical objectivity, because the cinema has its own 'subjective' POV and in any case our own subjectivity has been hybridized with machines at least since the invention of the clock (according to Lewis Mumford)."[41] The ghost in this context is not so much a spectral presence (or absence) as it is a mechanism that produces a specific mode of perception. The camera and the human brain (or better, the brain-camera hybrid) resemble experimental devices (e.g., the volcano and the plant) that set reality in motion. The altered perceptions these devices can produce are more real than the "ordinary" sense of static external objects.

In this context, Epstein returns to the science short of the plant to offer an even more vivid image of the specific yet alien (to us) experience of the moving, animated vegetal life-form: "A short documentary describing, in a few minutes, twelve months of the life of a plant, from its germination to its maturity and its withering, up to the forming of seeds of the new generation, is enough to make us accomplish the most fantastic voyage, the most difficult escape, that humans have ever attempted."[42] When the camera contracts time in this scientific documentary, Epstein claims, it allows us to see "what time might feel like materially when it is fifty thousand times faster or four times slower than that in which we live."[43] Because plant movements are outside our phenomenological world, the pace of vegetal movement accelerated by the camera creates a hallucinatory experience fantastically strange to us, as if we were on a planet in the Andromeda galaxy.[44] "We feel we are presented with a new universe, a new continuum, whose movement through time is fifty thousand times faster."[45] In a new Copernican revolution, the humble science short appears to liberate us from our own world. The plant, commonly viewed as mostly static, comes to signify the changing quality of reality; plants experiment with their environment, even as they also serve as experimental subjects. "The dunes crawl: minerals flourish and reproduce; animals get bogged down in themselves and get transfixed; plants gesticulate and experiment toward the light; water sticks; clouds break."[46] Epstein attributes an agentive dimension to the plant's movement, as roots, for example, reach out to find water but may encounter a rock.[47]

Manipulation of mimosa plants in the laboratory bears out the experimental, generative potential of both the camera and the plant: "For instance, the mimosa has been trained against its habit to spread its leaves at night and curl them during the day. Vegetal movements that our gaze hardly discerns in human time are hence revealed by the gaze of the lens."[48]

The mimosa here demonstrates—with a little help from the scientists—that its time is flexible and that day and night are reversible, while the camera contracts our own sense of time to reveal the movements of the plant. Time-lapse films of plants in motion thus present a hybridization of the photosensitive plant's point of view with that of the camera. Throughout Epstein's corpus, plants seem to stand for this ability to transform time (and space) in ways that produce new spatiotemporal realities, in a reversal of the old image of (relative) vegetal immobility. Epstein does not say precisely why he is interested in the mimosa in the lab, trained to sleep during the day, but it is likely that he considers the plant capable of radically altering its perspective, just as the human-camera hybrid does. Plants and the camera not only work in tandem in Epstein's theory and films but also function analogously to the camera, which reveals to us the fundamental fluidity of time.

Plants feature in Epstein's films as well as in his criticism. They appear as objects of focus in their own right, not just in the background or as symbolic of other points of view, to show that matter writ large (and small) is animate as well as sentient. They also play an important role in mediating among various states or modes of being—including life and death, mineral and animal, domesticated and wild. They participate in Epstein's visualization of the theme of voyage or journey—not necessarily into interstellar space (as in Gance's film) but beyond the confines of the family, the home, and the structures of religious belief—toward his own "end of the world" (particularly as realized in the first of his Breton films, *Finis terrae*, made in 1928). Ultimately, plants not only stand in for the work done by cinema itself—the animation of a world always in movement—but they inspire and generate that work.

In his silent classic *La Chute de la maison Usher* (1928)—the first film Henri Langlois was to procure for the Cinémathèque française—Epstein takes up as an organizing symbol the genealogical tree of the House of Usher, "twisted as if by a tempest."[49] Set in and around a Solognais manor, the film loosely adapts and transposes two of Poe's stories, "The Fall of the House of Usher" and "The Oval Portrait" (1842). In Epstein's *La Chute*, Roderick Usher appears to bring about the death not of his sister but of his wife, Madeline (played by Abel Gance's wife Marguerite), by painting her likeness in oils. He then mourns her, until (as in Poe's "Usher") she is resurrected after being buried, a reanimation that becomes its own allegory of cinema, which mobilizes not just the formerly lifeless Madeline but an entire (natural) world. Poe and Epstein share not only the connection to symbolism (itself a key part of the evolution of impressionist film) but a mutual interest in speculative narratives in which vegetality plays a prominent role. The arabesque returns here, this time as cinematic motion.

The twisted, damaged trunk of the Usher genealogical tree is evoked early on in the images of static outlines of trees that first appear filmed from below, silhouetted against the sky, and in the desolation of the landscape through which the narrator makes his way on his journey to the house. The initial images of plants that we encounter in *La Chute* are vaguely menacing: leafless vines that wrap around a window, through which a woman peers with a horrified expression on her face as the plants that frame her threaten to cover the aperture completely; barren trees that loom over the Usher estate; the arabesque lines that surround the portrait of Madeline and appear ready to suffocate the subject they enclose. The theme of the "twisted tree trunk" reappears figuratively in the torquing and morphing of desire across and around the three protagonists: Roderick, Madeline, and the narrator (who in Epstein's version is both nearsighted and partly deaf, in contrast to Usher's heightened sensitivity and receptiveness in Poe's story). In his fascination with painting the image of his wife, Roderick seeks to render Madeline as a static form, thereby depriving her of life, while the arrival of the narrator, with his own affection for Roderick, interrupts the cultivation of the sadistic bond between husband and wife. Even before Madeline's demise, the characters seem to occupy a space between death and life; Roderick, whose movements are often rendered in slow motion, vampirishly drains Madeline of her own vital energy in order to pour it into the painting. Life flows into aesthetic expression and is arrested there. Poe's association of Usher with vegetality (and vegetal sentience in particular) is recalled in the slowed-down, even somnambulant movements of Usher himself, and in the images of trees and branches painted on the walls of the house and incorporated into the (strange and haunting) décor. (As Darragh O'Donoghue has remarked, the characters in the film "congeal into stasis," suggesting a kind of vegetalization.)[50] The house itself emerges from a blasted landscape and reproduces elements of this landscape in its interior. We also see Usher painting parts of the genealogical tree.

Epstein explores, in *La Chute*, the way in which the medium of painting does violence to Madeline, who is forced to pose, fainting, as her husband steals away her vitality. If, as Usher says of the portrait, "In truth, it is a living image" (intertitle), it is this "living image" that destroys the original. As the film continues, however, *La Chute* proposes cinema as an alternative medium, one that retains a destructive force (the film ends in a cataclysmic sequence wherein the house catches on fire as the three protagonists flee) but also, and simultaneously, vivifies. This (re)vivification is enacted by the film upon the body of Madeline, yet this process is first rendered and staged in the plant bodies that populate the film from the opening sequence. Upon Madeline's death, the plants that were previously static begin to move. Plants illustrate and initiate the transformation (and eventual conflagration) of a world that no longer "frames" the human characters but (re)animates them. The twisted trees of the beginning sequences become moving leaves and waving grasses that merge with the mist, water, and fire gradually consuming the landscape.[51]

A sequence where the mourners carry Madeline's coffin shows falling leaves and long narrow candles superimposed over images of the mourners' faces, connoting death both in the plot and in nature. But then Epstein moves the handheld camera lower to the ground, with the cameramen walking backward, thereby causing the image of the coffin to sway up and down in a manner that may make the spectator a little nauseous. This perspectival shift could be taken as an indication of what it is like to be Madeline locked in the coffin, as Wall-Romana suggests in his eloquent reading of the film.[52] As, at times, the camera turns to the surrounding barren, hibernal, and static trees, they, too, begin to appear to move, replicating what might be Madeline's perception of them from within her coffin. These trees animated by the motion of the camera reinforce the idea that matter is here in vibration, in an echo of one of Roderick's own obsessions. Objects in the film are overwhelmed by a kind of Gothic life force that eventually melds the leaves of the trees with the pages of the books that begin to tumble from the shelves in the house. The plants become vibrant in themselves, more alive than our perceived reality that the film is helping us leave behind. The presence of self-animating plants signals the transmogrification of our ordinary experience of the world as a set of enframed objects given to our senses. At this point, everything in the material world reveals itself to be alive and in movement, as in the time-lapse images produced by Comandon. (We even see images of two mating frogs in a bed of plant matter as the nails are pounded into Madeline's coffin.) The conclusion, where the three protagonists escape from the collapsing house, does not eject the humans into the "real world"—enabling them to escape from the house back into a normal frame of mind and vision—so much as into what has revealed itself on the screen as an animated ecosphere, a space that recalls Epstein's films made *en plein air*, and especially the film he turns to immediately after completing *La Chute*: *Finis terrae*.[53]

In *Finis terrae*, an island populated only by transient kelp harvesters becomes another universe; the characters who inhabit it are "separated from

Figure 7. Usher carrying Madeline's coffin: superimposition of face, tree leaves, and candles. Jean Epstein, *La Chute de la maison d'Usher*, 1928 [14:15].

the world," as the intertitle explains. The spectator is first treated to beautiful shots of a desolate island, surrounded by sea and clouds. This place is Bannec, "home" to four men who set off for the tiny, barren island during the summers to harvest large, wet bunches of *goëmon* (kelp) before returning to their homes on the larger, more hospitable island of Ouessant. The lives of these men during the harvesting season are entirely devoted to surviving in an environment that is barren. The island itself is sandy, rocky, salty, and lacking in fresh water, fertile only in the strands of kelp that they fish from the sea, which are vibrant, mobile, and lustrous. The kelp is burned to make a fertilizer that can be sold for profit, and the film, which features a conflict and subsequent reconciliation between two of the kelp harvesters, Ambroise and Jean-Marie, effectively stages a triangle between the landscape, the kelp, and the human beings who work with both. We might recall here Deleuze's insight that islands are themselves empirical signs of geological movement, in the constant shifting of the soil and the rocks that constitute them; the destabilizing possibilities of the island milieu are more visible on Bannec than on Ouessant, where patriarchal social structures, buildings, and familiar relations ossify into an exoskeleton that covers over the constant movement of matter.[54] On Bannec, plants once again become allegories of cinema. The kelp itself resembles cellu-

The End of the World by Other Means

Figure 8. Jean-Marie waves *goëmon* (kelp). Jean Epstein, *Finis terrae*, 1929.

loid strips, and when Jean-Marie waves kelp in the air, he might momentarily seem to become a crazed filmmaker, perhaps the director himself. The world of the island is vibrant despite its harshness for humans; the kelp itself seems to move and even gesticulate. Plants may not have faces or hands that move in and out of focus, but they evoke the animation of matter more generally and lend to this vital materialism of the insular world a kind of *photogénie*.

Plants are also linked, as in *La Chute*, to the reconfiguration of the desires that connect humans to one another (and to their world). The men on the island are bound to one another through their manipulation of (and struggle with) the kelp, which becomes a kind of medium for the transmission of affect (including hostility, jealousy, and envy as well as affection and even erotic longing). Wall-Romana calls our attention to the daisies that appear on the island—filmed next to the rocks and broken glass that wound Ambroise, the protagonist—as symbols of a kind of queer desire that is part of the island world but that dissipates in Ouessant, the big island that is the space of religious life, stone walls, fields of green grass, and family (including women and children). These daisies also serve as cinematic echoes of Comandon's daisies, living a sleeplike life lent them by the camera. The "other world" (evoked by Bannec) involves not just a distinct way of seeing and interacting with its elements but new experiences of desire and pleasure. The plants both heighten the solidity of certain forms such as rocks—the kelp is slippery and seemingly fungible—and tie the characters to one another, animating them (as in *La Chute*) anew.

Between the Organic and the Inorganic: Dulac's Vegetal Arabesques

Despite the publication of Tami Williams's excellent intellectual biography in 2014, Germaine Dulac remains less celebrated than some of her male counterparts, who include Epstein; she was nonetheless a pioneering force within the French avant-garde who moved from an early focus on fiction films to the production of newsreels and documentaries.[55] In contrast to both Epstein and Gance, Dulac seems less obviously committed to the theme of cataclysm or end of the (human) world, with its evident connections to the speculative fiction of writers such as Flammarion. Yet, even more than Epstein, Dulac places the animated plant at the center of her vision of an art of "pure" cinema. She was moreover fascinated by the instructional science film as the medium for transmitting a new kind of "drama" (and, as Williams eloquently suggests, a new kind of sensation) to the public of her day. We can thus speak of a Dulacian "science fiction" that takes both of these terms literally and allows for a journey to another world to unfold in the contemplation of (and vibration with) the rhythm and line of the germinating plant or the blossoming tulip. For Dulac, "Cinema expands our knowledge. It propels us out of our constraints, of our milieu, of our familiar thoughts, of our acquired knowledge, and into unknown worlds."[56] While her work, like Epstein's, is part of the development of what has been called an impressionist cinema[57] with key symbolist influences (including Poe and Baudelaire), her films also participate in a speculative tradition that embraces the science short for its world-shattering potential. As Williams points out, "for Dulac (who was inspired by pre-cinema, time-lapse scientific films, as well as by the medium's experiential approximation of duration), *cinégraphie* remained present in its most tangible forms: the visualization of life itself, in movement and rhythm."[58] The plant is a crucial participant in this project of visualization.

In her 1927 film *L'Invitation au voyage* (*Invitation to the Voyage*), an independent film made a few months prior to *La Coquille et le clergyman* (her collaboration with Artaud), the theme of the journey is parsed through Baudelaire's famous symbolist poem from which the title of the film is borrowed.[59] Williams persuasively makes the case for a queer reading of this short narrative film, in which a married woman visits a bar in order to escape her life of domestic monotony and passivity. For Williams, *L'Invitation* is "perhaps the most explicit example of a queer text in Dulac's expansive œuvre."[60] We see in this film the connection between the journey to another world—although one that remains firmly anchored in a human phenomenology—and the creation of a nonheteronormative public that might allow for the circulation and transmission of new kinds of pleasure and new attachments. Typically, Dulacian images emerge here as the heroine contemplates the dancers and musicians in the bar and then eventually joins the dance, accepting the invitation of a seductively handsome young marine (played by Raymond Dubreuil). The legs and dresses of the whirling dancers become absorbed into a flow of light; the face of the dreaming woman (Emma Gynt) is superimposed on images of clouds and the sea in motion; and the enclosed world of the bar becomes a portal (and, in fact, the heroine is shown looking through a porthole) to the open and mobile world of the elements in motion as she fantasizes about setting off to sea.

However, this is a journey in which the patriarchal structures that regulate the heroine's domestic existence—and turn out to continue to operate even within the fantasmatic space of the bar itself—reimpose themselves rather than breaking down. When the marine finds out that the object of his interest is married, he leaves her at the table and goes to dance with another woman, eventually sending her a bouquet of flowers that serves as an emblem of both his desire and its absence. The heroine leaves both the flowers and a small ship—inscribed with "invitation au voyage"—behind her as she flees the bar to return to the sphere of married domesticity. The marine then takes up the bouquet, inhales its fragrance, and lets it drop onto the banquette beside him. Once again, the flowers serve as emblems of a desire that cannot be satisfied and is ultimately withdrawn. They are all that remain of the heroine's adventure, and their presence in the film suggests the failure or nonconsummation of her illicit encounter. Do plants signal not only the flight from heterosexual marriage but an erotic life beyond heteronormativity?

Although plants in this narrative film are rendered in a (fairly conventional) symbolic mode, they regain their material specificity as human desire is deferred (or denied) and as the human characters retreat from the screen. Flowers work in *L'Invitation* as symbols of both masculine and

Figure 9. The marine leaves the flowers on the table. Germaine Dulac, *L'Invitation au voyage*, 1927 [38:41].

feminine desire to suggest a kind of equivalence between the two central characters. In her experimental films, we see Dulac (re)turn to the world of flowers (and plants more generally) to reinvigorate the drama of affect, desire, and sensation to which the heroine of *L'Invitation* is ultimately denied access. In *Étude cinématographique sur une arabesque* (*Cinematographic Study of an Arabesque*, 1929)[61] and *Thèmes et variations* (*Themes and Variations*, 1929),[62] images of plants (including time-lapse shots of germination, to which Dulac often refers in her criticism, and figures of "dancing" tulips) are juxtaposed with images of a female dancer and of machines in movement. The blurring of boundaries among bodies, which is a momentary part of the heroine's participation in the dance of *L'Invitation*, emerges as an evocation of rhythm, line, and movement. The "integral cinema" that results opens up a new kind of phenomenology in which plants play a crucial role. The static blossoms of the bouquet in *L'Invitation* take on mobility and rhythm in these abstract compositions; they suggest that the stultified desire of the heroine of *L'Invitation* might be mobilized and galvanized in the pulsation of line and form that brings together woman dancer, machine, and plant. In fact, the plant itself is the figure of this rhythm and its distillation. The experimental films take the spectator deeper into the world that is glimpsed at the bar by the heroine; they explode the image of the whirling skirts and legs of the dancers into a concatenation of organic and inorganic elements. We move away here from all narrative forms, including the moments of deferral or blockage that help to enable a queer reading elsewhere in Dulac's corpus, into the world of pure cinema.

In these experimental films, a new public (already evoked by the dancers at the bar) is interpellated not with the seductive gaze of either heroine or marine—both actors are remarkable for the limpidity and suggestiveness of their "regards"—but by the multiplication of the vegetal line—the arabesque—in motion. This is a multiplication that does not divide the organic from the inorganic—the machine is fundamentally implicated in this new world—but that uses the plant as its inspiration. The stultified heroine of *L'Invitation* becomes in the experimental films not just the emancipated body of the modern dancer—pulsing in time to the turning of gears—but the lithe, flexible, and nevertheless productive body of the germinating plant. While we do not see a cataclysm explicitly framed as such in these films, we do experience the journey into another world, albeit a world that has been with us all along. The plant, in its indifference to humans but also its remarkable vitality, is not merely the passive object of an animation by time-lapse. It is instead the principle of animation—of movement in its purest form—and thus the avatar of cinema. It is, moreover, the emblem of a modern subject who might become part of a new and potentially queer public no longer fully constrained by the heteronormative structures and conventional melodramatic narratives (with their indebtedness to earlier genres of literature and theater) that remain operative in the world prior to its transformation.[63]

For Dulac, the electric plant is not just the inspiration for but the living embodiment of a modern and modernist art form; this aesthetic is not realist, although it uses "real" objects (including, of course, the plant). Nor is it organicist strictly speaking: instead, it prioritizes the movement and line of the plant body in order to align this body with the movement and line of the (woman) dancer and the machine. The inorganic body becomes the organic body, and back again. In the 1927 typescript for the talk she gave at the conference "Les femmes et le cinéma" ("Women and Cinema"), Dulac gives the plant pride of place in her conceptualization of cinema as "a new instrument of thought, of knowledge and of art."[64] This speech, titled "Le Cinéma est un art nouveau" ("Cinema is a New Art Form"), distills a theory of cinema as a form that does not mediate between (human-generated) concepts and matter in the world but instead "captures" or "registers" life itself—in a precise and powerful gesture that is nonetheless joy-inducing.⁶⁵ Cinema is a vital art, then, without for all that being a vitalist one, at least in an organicist sense. (As she writes in the December 1931 essay "Le Sens du cinéma," which contains much of the text from the earlier talk: "By its very own technique and power, Cinema teaches Life."⁶⁶) Dulac dreams of a liberation of cinema from the constraints of conventional narrative in order to release the transformative and augmentative capacities of an art that can, "through unknown aesthetic discoveries, cause the sensibility of the public to vibrate."⁶⁷

Thus, the "artistic liberation" of which she writes is not only that of the filmmaker—who in the context of an industrialized film production has been under a generic obligation to "obey" rather than "create"—but of the medium itself. She imagines cinema as leaving behind the formulae and genres borrowed from melodramatic pulp fiction (the "roman-feuilleton") and turning to motion, form, and line as a means of transmitting meaning and indeed affect. She writes,

> What is thus the secret ideal that animates certain people? Escaping from established literary and theatrical formulas, in order to exclusively devote oneself to the movement of matter and light, to the evolution of forms, to their spirit, and to find in these elements a visual mode of expression that is analogous to that of music. Music, a coordination of sounds that lead to emotion by way of the ear. Cinema, a coordination of movements that lead to emotion by way of the eyes. Music, fugitive sounds that provoke a definitive impression through a series of impressions. Cinema, fugitive images that aim at the same goal.⁶⁸

Cinema remains in some sense an "emotive" art, but one that enables a correspondence between movement in its purest form and human affect. It is also a medium that works (like other modes of technology) to make perceptible what has been invisible to or ungraspable by humans: "While literature and the pictorial and plastic arts present to us life through a brain that describes and commentates, Cinema captures life itself in its movement, without sentences, without detours, directly, and with such subtlety that we perceive, thanks to Cinema, nuances that our eyes cannot see, and with such precision, such clarity that no transformation can disfigure the truth. Cinema captures both exactitude and the incomprehensible (*insaisissable*)."⁶⁹ In this sense, cinema makes good on its promise, in the absence of narration, to disclose a world that is otherwise imperceptible to us and to generate joy—a new kind of animation—through this disclosure.

This vitality produces new affective possibilities for humans, not just in their encounters with nonhuman objects but in their relationships with one another. Dulac, unlike Epstein who embraced melodrama, resists melodramatic forms of narration in order to preserve the flexibility and mobility of these new forms of sensation. The new worlds that the plant opens up take affective and not narrative shape; they are nonteleological because they are ever-changing. How can Dulacian cinema contribute to social change? This remains an open question. Certainly, this new art supplements our limited senses and represents a qualitative alteration in them.

In Dulac's theory of cinema, a medium that she praises for its modernity, it is the plant that emerges as the privileged example of otherworldly animation that film is paradigmatically able to capture or record. If film is able to project us into worlds that we would not have imagined existing—or even thought to look for—these worlds are often those of plants conceived in their "pure" or inorganic vitality. And, in fact, the "germination of a grain of wheat" (both the film and the natural phenomenon) functions as Dulac's most recurrent and powerful example of the work that cinema does.[70] As Prosper Hillairet puts it in the introduction to Dulac's *Écrits*: "All of Germaine Dulac's cinema is contained in this image of a grain of wheat germinating. A drama of nature, of a plant fighting to bloom, that becomes a visual drama through a cinematographic transformation of movement (the accelerated one), the vegetal rhythms becoming cinematographic rhythms like abstract lines that are deployed by the action of a force."[71] An affective narrative comes about when the invisible is made visible through the technology of cinema; the drama of the plant may be speculative, but the effects of this drama are concretely felt. The typescript for her talk reveals that Dulac planned to show films of flowers blooming and "of the life of insects,"[72] but because she was unable to get access to a projector for the occasion, she had to abandon this idea. Crossed-out sections of the typescript show her exhortations to the audience to consider the images of flowers blooming before them with a musical ear rather than a scientist's eye, thereby entering into an encounter with the rhythms and harmonics of what she refers to as "visual sensation."[73] In these vegetal images, the public will find not only life itself, in all its power, but an intermingling of thought and feeling.

Dulac claims that cinema can put us in touch with "joys" and "miseries" that are otherwise undiscernible. And these affective modes—along with the thrilling possibilities of the expressive line in motion—are especially present in the plant. She writes, "To us, a plant is no longer only a vegetal being that charms us with its appeal, its fragrance, or its beauty, but also a sentient organism that suffers or blossoms, a little living thing that gets hot, that gets cold, that needs air and sun in order to live like us, and with whose reflexes we are familiar in their precise meaning."[74] While this particular rendering of the plant has an air of anthropomorphism about it—especially in the phrase "live like us"—Dulac's goal is not so much to "humanize" this vegetal life, the "little living thing." Unlike F. Percy Smith, she does not seek to incorporate the plant into the kinds of narrative structures that convey presumably typical human experiences of, say, love, hatred, sexual desire, and sexual competition, even a longing for autonomy or an experience of collective solidarity. Nor does she project onto the plant a sense of poetry or symbolism—a capacity to signify another, mystical order of meaning or feeling that transcends the ordinariness of the world around us. Instead, it is the movement of the plant body, a mechanical movement that awakens us to the power of suggestiveness of life itself and the inherent drama of this life, that she sees as emblematic of the potential of cinema as a new art.

The movement of the plant is, in fact, *more* intrinsically cinematic than the movement of the human body: "But already the grain of wheat's sprouting appears to us to be a concept that is cinematographically more perfect, more precise, while giving the mechanical movement of logical transformation a predominant position, while creating, with its unique vision, a new drama of the mind and senses."[75] Elsewhere, in her essay "Du sentiment à la ligne" ("From Sentiment to Line"), Dulac writes of the germination of the plant seed: "[T]he vegetal being's anguish will be translated by erratic rhythms that will change the meaning of the movements, and its rhythms, already purified in their form, will have determined the emotion, the purely visual emotion."[76] The plant body is also a queer body, but not in the sense that it multiplies affective or libidinal possibilities already available to humans. Instead, it presents us with a new (nonhuman) geometry of the body, one that can then be mapped onto the human "line" with transfigurative effects. For another example of erotic vegetal transfiguration, we might look to the sketches by dancer and actress Stasia de Napierkowska, Dulac's lover, which she dedicated to "ma jeune et grande Germaine." In these images, Napierkowska labels depictions of her own body with terms drawn from the realm of vegetal life, including the word "vrille" or tendril.[77] The sketches, done in pencil, of a nude woman reclining suggest the kinship between the arabesque lines of the plant and the curves of the human form. Like Napierkowska's sketches, the "drama" that cinema is capable of producing extends beyond relationships among human beings and into relationships between humans and the nature that enfolds and shapes them. "Cinema, through its own technique in the artistic domain, has thus the ability to create new conflicts, and ceases pitting man against man, implicating him in nature."[78] Dulac shows us the plant as motion and as line, which then aligns itself with the motion and line of both the human body and the machine. This is a filmmaking of the assemblage.

Colette's Monstrous Plants and the Turn toward Plant Horror

Dulac's and Epstein's turning to the plant as an avatar of both modernity and a newly galvanizing affect is in tension with visions of vegetal life (like Gance's) that tend to emphasize the latter's connection to a pastoral (or more properly organic and hierarchical) world that in a Romantic context might counter and assuage modernity's effects. For writers and critics who approach the plant as an avatar not of cinema but of a nature that technology defaces and distorts, the electric vegetable is not a delightful alien but a monster. The "constant cataclysm" here becomes (again) an apocalypse. Like Dulac and Epstein, the author Colette[79] was an avid viewer of Comandon's work (and other instructional films with a focus on plants). Her writings on cinema (and plant life) highlight the tension between narrative and nonnarrative representations of the plant at the same time as she provides an eloquent assessment of the way in which a newly animate vegetal world might generate not just joy (as is the case for Dulac and Epstein) but anxiety and fear. Colette praises the instructional short for its capacity to fascinate and galvanize audiences even as she criticizes time-lapse representations of plants for the way in which they reveal "secrets" of vegetal life that are better off being kept. While she recognizes the extraordinary power of the instructional plant film, Colette expresses revulsion at the way in which these films seem to denaturalize the plant—removing us from the poetry of the flower (for instance) to place us in the world of a disfigured and monstrous vegetality.

Colette may still be best known for the lush botanical imagery and preoccupations of her prose fiction, but her engagement with the early science short—and in particular the time-lapse films of Comandon—has its own distinctive intensity, as Paula Amad has brilliantly shown.[80] In an essay that reveals the importance of images of flowering plants both to Colette's theories of cinema and to her writing on time and memory more generally, Amad puts Colette's work on cinematic flowers in the context of her broader appreciation for the *film documentaire*, which, as Amad points out, Colette describes as "the finest flower of cinema." Amad sees in Colette's fascination with time-lapse images of plants flowering and beans germinating—and in the audience's reception of these images—a productive interpenetration of fact and fiction capable of producing profound effects. Amad comments at length on Colette's description, in her essay "Cinéma" ("Cinema"), of children watching the germination of a bean and being suddenly compelled to imitate the bean's incredible spiraling movements with their own small bodies. Here Colette describes the children's reaction to a scene of plant movement in 1924:

> A bit later, a "fast motion" documented the germination of a bean, the birth of its tunneling radicelles, the avid yawning of its cotyledons from which sprung up, throwing its serpent's head like a spear, the first sprout. . . . At the revelation of the intentional and intelligent movement of the plant, I saw children get up, imitate the extraordinary ascent of a plant climbing in a spiral, avoiding an obstacle, groping over its trellis: "It's looking for something! It's looking!" cried a little boy, profoundly affected. He dreamed of the plant that night, and so did I. These spectacles are never forgotten and give us the thirst for further knowledge. We want, for ourselves and our children, not an indigent imagination, but the extravagance of reality, the unbridled fantasy of nature; we want the fairy tale of the germination of peas, the Arabian night's tale of the metamorphoses of a dragonfly, and the explosion, the formidable distention, of the budding lily, half-opening in long flat mandibles over a dark agitation of stamens—a gluttonous and powerful labor of flowering in front of which a little girl said, in a very low, somewhat frightened voice: "Oh! A crocodile!"[81]

In this scene, the children are physically involved in their responses to plant movement in film—an involvement that grips them in their bodies and inspires in them a desire to imitate the plants. We find both Colette and the children themselves emphasizing not the distinctively vegetal nature of this encounter but the way in which these plant bodies take on animallike qualities and the stories become fairy tales and fantasies, extraordinary versions of reality rather than a representation of nature as a reliable and familiar set of places and encounters. Amad reads in Colette's fascination with this scene something akin to Germaine Dulac's own investment in the science film (and the image of bean germination in particular) as crucial to the creation of "pure" cinema. Amad writes, "The children's mimetic style of reception (played out as they imitate the spiraling and groping ascent of the climbing plant) and the biological film's fecund structural inventiveness (displayed in techniques of temporal manipulation and microcinematography as well as formal patterns of repetition, movement, and rhythm) constituted two of the key models for avant-garde cinema discourse and practice of the twenties."[82] Following Amad, we can see Colette's vibrant description of cinematic plants as a reflection not just of her engagement with botanical imagery (and plants) more generally but as part of a collective turn toward the electric vegetable of cinema.

Colette emphasizes the ability of these documentaries to generate new narratives and to fertilize an essentially human imagination with fantastic or "extraordinary" elements. Yet, Colette's relationship to the flowering plants of Comandon and others is inflected by an ambivalence that is not present either in Epstein's or Dulac's embrace of the plant. While Colette writes eloquently and passionately of the children's reception of the animated plants—a reception that is echoed in her own fascination for the animation of the vegetal world—she is also suspicious of the alienating or dehumanizing effects of this cinematic turn on the profound affective relationship that humans have with plants, and with flowers in particular. And she tends to stress the monstrous nature of the cinematic plant—sometimes in a positive valence, sometimes less so—an emphasis that moves the blooming flower closer and closer to an animal, rather than preserving its vegetality. By contrast, Dulac's own description, in the lecture on cinema discussed earlier, of a child's reaction to a film (which remains unnamed but may have been a time-lapse scene of flowers) highlights not the strangeness or monstrosity of the image but the transformation of human perception into something equally (but joyfully) alien. She writes, "Didn't I hear one day this reflection made by a child, whose intelligence was utterly lacking in prejudice, and who cried out at the projection of a film: 'It's marvelous, you can hear with your eyes.' What more beautiful testament could be given to the originality of cinematographic expression?"[83]

The animated plant remains, for Colette, in some sense a plant whose intimate "secrets" have been too brusquely revealed and in this sense a disfigured and manipulated object. In an essay that was first published two years after "Cinéma," in 1926, she writes:

> It is now said that they have a complete sensory apparatus, a nervous system, the rudiments of eyes; one part of the scientific world probes in search of their heart, the source, the regulator of the translucid

blood that flows through them. . . . The greatest learning will once again give way to the greatest anxiety. . . . Before our very eyes the common sensitive mimosa, in order to throw off any aggressor, bends all its twiggy elbows, lowers its leafy armpits, and surrenders only one swooning trophy. The secrets of plants, their magic defenses fall one by one.[84]

Here the plant is in the process of losing not only its distinctiveness—held as a kind of secret—but its poetry. This is the case for Colette even though she privileges the instructional science short for its capacity to move (and instruct) audiences. Yet, the denaturalized and exposed plant is still enchanting, still worthy of contemplation. In the same essay, she affirms:

One day, sights such as these, which held me spell-bound in front of the screen, will, I hope, rival the toy train that falls off the bridge into the river, and the arctic debacle charged with carrying off, on its most stable floe, an overnight starlet. . . . I am easily left dumbfounded before such secrets betrayed, the secrets of huge and unrecognizable flowers. And easily do I forget them before a flower in the wild. Our crude eye, freed of overly powerful aids, recovers a traditional poetry. An almanac religion connects us to a flower, even a puny one, when it symbolizes season.[85]

We see a hierarchy emerge here that resists Epstein's effort to find in the science film a kind of pure poetry. Colette retains in this essay a vision of nature that is heavily invested with human affect and valuable for the extent to which it can serve as a register of human emotion and human memory. The cinematic flower is both gripping and "unrecognizable." She embraces, momentarily, the project of *cinéma pur* but ultimately finds its aesthetics not fully inhabitable for the human subject. At the same time as Colette contends that these images could serve audiences better than the action-driven narrative films of contemporary cinema, which are insipid and repetitious, she also tends to react with horror at the idea of a temporal and spatial order that exceeds human categories and human understanding (rather than decorously receding from them). Yet, the monstrosity that she finds in the enlarged time-lapse image of the flower emerges not just from the plant itself—looming fascinatingly above us—but from the way in which we instrumentalize it, forget its "poetry," remove it from the realm of symbol and memory (and human pathos, where it seemingly belongs). Siding perhaps inadvertently with the German philosopher Martin Heidegger, Colette condemns the plant as image. In this way, her writings anticipate the work of a critic like Michael Marder, who sees in time-lapse a violence done to the plant rather than a kind of mediation prefigured by and within the plant itself, always already machine.

Colette acknowledges the ability of time-lapse images of plant growth to conjure up a vegetal agency and to dissolve the affective zones in which human subjectivity takes shape. In this vision, the plant enacts its own kind of violence on the human: it is no longer primarily a vulnerable object but retains its power to mobilize humans in ways that they find painful or, at least, unpleasurable. Yet, it is also reduced in this transformation. Colette hesitates between seeing the rendering of the plant on film as a kind of violation (of its vegetal essence) and appreciating the galvanizing effects of this rendering on humans. We might say, then, that she reveals a certain contradiction within Dulac's and Epstein's more consistently joyful celebrations of the plant-machine. While these two artists optimistically keep faith in the ability of the plant to open a portal to a new world (of altered, albeit indefinite, selves), Colette highlights the open-endedness of this *"invitation au voyage."* What if the journey away from the plant as keeper of secrets—and as a steward of all-too-human affects, including our affection for place, our memory of our childhood, and our attachment to a world that technology threatens to tear asunder—is an anxious rather than a pleasurable one? Colette renders the manipulation of the plant's temporality as ultimately an exploitation (and denaturalization) of its being rather than a way into its world; Colette's "deanthropocentrism," as Amad calls it, is more cautious than Dulac's or Epstein's. Colette is more obviously the heir of a Romantic involvement in the plant as the site of a desiring yet vulnerable mutuality that may be disturbed and harmed by human intervention. In this sense, she is also in tune with later developments in popular film, which would turn to the plant, after the war, as a source of horror and alienation—yet one that nevertheless still carries furtively within it the possibility of pleasures yet to come. Here the cataclysm embraced by Dulac and Epstein is turned inward—toward the vegetable itself, which once again becomes menacing (as in Poe's fiction), and toward human society, which is revealed to be both indifferent to its subjects and vegetal in its own right. Yet, even here something of the interest of the plant as a figure for cinema itself—its pleasures and its perils—is retained. As we show in the next chapter, Colette's ambivalence is remobilized and reordered in the burgeoning postwar genre of plant horror.

CHAPTER 6

Plant Horror: Love Your Own Pod

Who Is (Still) Afraid of the Pods?

If, as Slavoj Žižek claims, films teach us what and how to desire, the plant horror genre seems to show us what happens when desire disappears.¹ Jack Finney's pulp serial *Body Snatchers*, first published in *Collier's* magazine in 1954, tells the tale of alien seedpods that take over a small California town by duplicating its citizens one by one and replacing them with unfeeling, conformist pod-people. While the short story went through multiple editions and was undeniably popular in its own right, it is perhaps best known now for having inspired the two classic films that have come to define plant horror in the United States, both titled *Invasion of the Body Snatchers* (released in 1956 and 1978, respectively).² In these film versions of the narrative, the viewer participates in the dramatic loss of the world of human experience (through the eyes of those who escape initial transformation into humanoid alien vegetables)—even as, visually, everything remains the same. Rewatched today, the films continue to confront us with the opposite of what we expect from cinema: instead of a space where our projected desires appear, we witness desire's end, as the takeover by the pods brings about the demise of human need and feeling. These films seem to ask: what if *this* world were not *our* world? Yet, the answer to this question differs in each case. The 1956 version ends with the reestablishment of familiar human authority figures, while the 1978 one concludes with the famous inarticulate cry that suggests both an affect (horror) and the absence of any human meaning. In this sense, where the 1956 version attempts to close off the threat posed by the pods,[3] the 1978 film represents an opening to a world entirely inhabited by vegetal beings.

After the period of experimentation with vegetal movement in early twentieth-century avant-garde cinema that we discuss in Chapter 5, plants in narrative film are generally relegated essentially to the background, to the role of "fillers" (to use Franco Moretti's term).[4] The function they serve is thus analogous to that of mundane passages characterized by "regularity" and "hidden rhythms."[5] As Moretti puts it, "fillers rationalize the novelistic universe, turning it into a world of few surprises, fewer adventures, and no miracles at all."[6] Critic Amitav Ghosh cites Moretti in the process of making the point that "serious fiction" does not deal with matters outside the predictable order of modern life, such as the question of climate change.[7] Yet, nonrealist genres, including the Gothic novel and, later on, science fiction and fantastic literature, have arguably long attended to ecological catastrophe and unpredictable disaster. These genres are often assigned a secondary or subordinate status as fiction or, in the case of cinema, relegated to the category of B movies. As the twentieth century wears on, we find the question of vegetal alterity most extensively taken up in the context of a sometimes "pulpy" approach to cinematic narrative that does not pretend to be realism. If cinema asserts itself as a primarily animal medium in the twentieth century (as Akira Lippit argues in *The Electric Animal*), plants appear in "unserious" genres in a way that leaves the dominant realism of most narrative cinema, based on an animal logic of movement and desire, unchallenged.

Both versions of *Invasion* play on the ambivalent status of plants as at once paradigmatic "filler" and vibrant, animate life-forms. The pastoral Southern California landscape in the first *Invasion* at first seems little more than background; later, its vegetal inhabitants upend bourgeois expectations of a predictable reality, thereby threatening the American dream of a prosperous and ordered world.[8] The second *Invasion* invites us to take a "plant's eye view" of our own transformation into pods. Insofar as both films allow us to recognize the "ordinary" reality behind (or prior to) the upheaval brought by the plants, they might be presumed to kindle a longing or nostalgia for it. Yet, in their blatant challenge of realism's basic premises, these films foreground vegetal alterity in order to show the way in which a focus on plant life transforms a human sense of what is real and what is possible. In this sense, they represent an extension of the speculative impulse so vividly highlighted in the French avant-garde cinema from earlier in the century.

In their pitting of sympathetic humans against rapacious and invading pod-people, the *Invasion* films have long been read as speaking primarily to their audience's paranoia, including fears of totalitarianism and McCarthyism, anxieties generated by the U.S. government's use of atomic power, and concerns about the creeping standardization and proliferating bureaucracy that are among the privileged symptoms of midcentury modernity.[9] With their emphasis on monstrously vegetal life-forms, these films show some affinities with the "creature feature," particularly in their reflections on the intrinsic power of cinema to give us access to modes of being that threaten and overwhelm our own. In this way, the plant horror genre shows some continuity with the rise of the monster plant that T. S. Miller has identified as emerging in sensational nineteenth-century narratives often published as journal articles in which fiction takes on the guise of reporting.[10] Miller underscores the ubiquity of the monstrous plant within modern speculative fiction but argues for a strictly Darwinian etiology underpinning this figure. In this context, monster plant fiction functions as a reaction to the implications of Charles Darwin's theory of evolution, which positions humans in dangerous proximity not just to apes and animals but also to plants. Thus, in Miller's reading, plants take on agency and, in some sense, enact their revenge on human beings for the latter's delusions of superiority.[11] In contrast, we trace the connections between the *Invasion* films and a much older tradition of foregrounding plants and giving them agency, not always monstrous.[12] The plant horror genre in cinema responds to the longer speculative tradition we outline in this book, one that aims at animating the plant—first by revealing that its mechanisms are compatible with those of the universe, then by attributing a vitality to them that cannot be fully assimilated into animal models of life, and later by uncovering the ways in which they usher humans into a new spatiotemporal reality. The *Invasion* films activate sensations of terror and delight as they move our attention toward the power of a vegetality that both invades and structures human consciousness.

The two best-known versions of *Invasion* are especially compelling entries in the category of cinematic plant horror[13]—a genre that includes twentieth-century works such as *The Thing from Another World* (1951), featuring a vampiric carrot; *Day of the Triffids* (1962), with its carnivorous plants bent on consuming blinded humans; and *Swamp Thing* (1982), in addition to twenty-first-century variants *The Ruins* (2008) and *The Happening* (2008).[14] While all of these films exploit the particular anxieties of the moments in which they appear—from Cold War anti-communism to worries over ecological disaster—the potential of their serial plant-monsters (be they pods or people) is not fully exhausted in the projection of various real or imagined fears onto the vegetable's monstrous nature. Indeed, the prospect of vegetal transformation, as envisioned by plant horror films, is not just terrifying but fascinating—and, on occasion, alluring, as the persistence of the theme indicates. If within this proliferating postwar genre we highlight two versions of *Invasion* in particular, it is because of the clear obsession these films have with processes of production and reproduction both on the individual and societal level. Each *Invasion* probes the economic and social conditions of capitalism and the aim of postwar U.S. society to foster a better, safer, healthier, and more prosperous way of life. The films present the pods not as simply interrupting this process of modernization and rationalization but as furthering it, albeit in ways that clearly underscore the forms of dehumanization internal to its workings.

Plant "striving" (to echo the Aristotelian term once again) is the antithesis of and a threat to this social project, but strangely it is also a way of embracing and implementing it with more efficacy than one could expect from the human beings replaced by their vegetal counterparts.[15] The effect of this efficacious realization of the goals of American modernity is the elimination of desire and of the predictable conflicts and disappointments that sometimes trouble the banality of modern bourgeois existence. Yet, the extinction of human "nature" within the otherworldly need of the plant holds its own visceral and spectacular appeal in these films. In a frightful augmentation of the dream of a vegetal eugenics that originates in the eighteenth century, the plant, or rather the pod, reigns supreme and carries out the ends of human existence. As we will argue here, if the *Invasions* deserve our attention today, it is not so much through the era-specific fears that they address but for the way in which they make use of the figure of the plant (and its visual and aural attributes made fully accessible by cinema) to invoke a form of being that is both emotionless and productive, both shapeless and full of lively forms, both ancient and well suited to navigate the crises that capitalist modernity appears to carry in its wake. Plants that take on human form allow us to imagine the demise of humanity itself as not just terrible but pleasurable; as in Cyrano's fictions, changes in shape enable the transmission of affects and thoughts across widely different bodies. The films present (to human cinemagoers) an opening to a world without humans, a world whose delights and fears will be more fully explored in posthumanist plant fiction, as we will discuss in Chapter 7.

The literary roots of plant horror remain visible in the extent to which so many of the monstrous film vegetables of the twentieth century find their origins in narrative fiction (including those of the *Invasion* series). While, as Marder reminds us, plants have typically taken on secondary and tertiary roles in metaphysics, they explode onto the scene in plant horror films, pushing their way to the forefront of consciousness in all their fleshiness, a quality that often accounts for the literal "pulp" in these surprisingly visually engaging B movies. While they seek to inspire terror as well as delight, these images of invasive pod-people do more than just provide another venue for the paranoia of being "taken over" by something that is "out there"; they consistently allow audiences to imagine, from within a state of delighted fear, the pleasures and pains of becoming another form of lively matter designated as vegetal.[16] Ultimately, the *Invasions* suggest that cinema is a privileged place for representing nonhuman life in general, specifically in its links to reproduction. Rendering the rapacious alien plant of fiction in visual terms, the two *Invasion* films zoom in on the specific productivity of plants. Both films share an acute preoccupation with the question of how human communities and human bonds, public and private, may be sustained at the moment of confrontation with modes of being that are strange to us even as we recognize ourselves in them, and they do this not in the mode of escapist fantasy (where no one really believes such a thing could or would happen in real life) but as an ironic commentary on a perceived reality. As Timothy Morton affirms: "Democracy is well served by irony, because irony insists that there are other points of view that we must acknowledge. Ugliness and horror are important, because they compel our compassionate coexistence to go beyond condescending pity."[17] Plant horror constructs a sense of other points of view on a world that looks like ours and is in many ways exactly the same as ours but ultimately is not ours. It is in this context that the plant, once again, has a particularly vital role to play in imagining the future, since, in plant horror, vegetal beings are figured as having found a way to navigate the contradictions of modern social relations that stymie or defeat human (or humanist) impulses. The plant threatens to transform us from within, even as it invades us from elsewhere (somewhere or nowhere), and in doing so challenges our assumptions about the continued capacity of the human to nurture and reproduce itself from within the very frameworks (economic, aesthetic, and, finally, ontological) that make it visible as such.

The Invasion *Films' Origins: Finney's* Body Snatchers

Jack Finney's short story articulates at some length what might be at stake in the notion of a plant "invasion," at the moment when the vegetal replicant Professor Budlong explains to the shocked Miles Bennell, the still-human town doctor, that the seedpods' striving to survive at the expense of other species is not so different from human behavior:

> What has the human race done except spread over this planet till it swarms the globe seven billion strong? What have you done with this very continent but expand till you fill it? And where are the buffalo who roamed this land before you? Gone. Where is the passenger pigeon, which literally darkened the skies of America in flocks of *billions*? The last one died in the Philadelphia Zoo in 1913. Doctor, the function of life is *to live if it can*, and no other motive can ever be allowed to interfere with that. There is no malice involved; did you hate the buffalo?[18]

Here the plants speak critically about unrestrained human striving, yet they do so from the position of beings whose behavior recalls and even exceeds the callous and irrational human drive for survival. The horror of the pods, as Miles points out, is that they do not care whether other species live or die.[19] The pods claim to copy the callous human drive for survival, reproduction, and dominance, only to remind us of something else supposedly human that the pods themselves cannot reproduce. The pods discard the immaterial value of humanity as a moral and political ideal in the name of species dominance and survival, but in the process they end up kindling the memory of and nostalgia for humanity, with the result of generating resistance in the human community. Finney's tale suggests that human specificity is required if we are to *care* for the extinction of species, to feel their loss, and thus the very possibility of an environmentalist argument on behalf of other life-forms becomes part and parcel of the representation of human exceptionalism.

In the story, this attribution of a cold and ruthless survivalism to the vegetal simulacra thus works not to call into question human behavior but to highlight humanity itself as in possession of a unique ethical responsibility to the members of its own species, defined in strikingly homogenous terms. The possibility of human heroism, acting both on the individual and the community, is necessary to oppose an "alien" social Darwinism.[20] Within this framework, Finney's narrative provides a nostalgic view of an almost exclusively white, small Californian town whose inhabitants mutually recognize one another and are tied by emotional bonds; racial and class differences barely come up in the story and then only to create embarrassment. The film conjures up the vision of a supposedly warmer, more livable, bucolic way of life by presenting the pod-people as the standard-bearers of a dully uniform existence in which affect no longer plays a role. Ironically, even as Finney's hero fears the conformism represented by the plants, he remains more or less oblivious to the erasure of difference that marks the small-town public sphere.

Ultimately, human life is held up in Finney's story as not simply superior to the vegetal energy of the plants but also somehow more alive. Even the pods admit that their "duplication *isn't* perfect. And can't be. It's like artificial compounds nuclear physicists are fooling with: unstable, unable to hold their form."[21] Pod mimesis, like Platonic mimesis, is declared to be secondary to natural reproduction; the pods' striving for survival, in the story, is merely the copy of life, and, as such, their mode of being remains atomic and brittle, always already crumbling and barren.[22] The true agents of social change, those with authentic vitality, are the humans, and it is their actions that eventually and almost miraculously force the pods to take off ("climbing up through the faint mist, on and on toward the space they had come from . . .") and leave earth to its own happy ending.[23] The plants' departure recalls a swarm of bees or a flock of birds; they become yet another species that the now-militant humans, ready to "fight . . . in the fields, and in the streets," have eradicated from Earth.[24] The novella thus acts as an affirmation of human existence just as its ending proclaims the (somewhat unexpected) triumph of specifically human effort. Action, the mark of true or full life, is the prerogative of humans alone, as is a genuinely ethical relation to others.

Body Snatchers promotes the idea of a heroic human individualism and shows that the alien pod creatures, as extraterrestrial plants, are excluded from the successful reproduction of a society that is idealized in human terms. Even so, the narrative is momentarily destabilized by the fact that the novella shows some men and women to be shut out from this process of idealization. In two brief episodes, juxtaposed by the narrator, Miles, racial difference and vegetal being are represented as equivalent. The first is the story of Billy, the black shoeshine man whose obsequious manner with his clients is revealed as a facade when Miles, after a night of drinking, finds himself in a "run-down section of town" and, lying in the back seat of his car, overhears Billy imitate his own speech in a "quietly hysterical parody of himself."[25] The second scene gives us the pods masquerading as the townspeople; although they *sound* like the humans whose shapes they have taken on, their true identity becomes clear when they "laugh falsely in a hideous burlesque of embarrassment" about their own behavior.[26] In the first episode, Miles's own shame does not simply stem from the fact that Billy turns out to be merely pretending to care about his patrons but also from his role as witness to the condescending treatment Billy receives from these same patrons, all white. In the second episode, the embarrassment both provoked and performed by the pods (since they cannot actually *feel*) is read by Miles as a commentary on the social consensus that accepts the exclusion of black people from the centers of small-town sociability. This embarrassment lingers even as the story's happy ending overwrites it—one blow to "our" sense of superiority in the face of the confirmation of the unique moral status supposedly shared by all humans.

The cinematic adaptations of Finney's story from 1956 and 1978 restage this threat of standardization—and, thus, the erasure of human exceptionalism—posed by the plants. In both *Invasion* films, the monstrous replicants—grown from enormous seeds—evoke a dehumanization wrought through the stripping away of affect, passion, and care, while the pods take on human shape and human activities.[27] But the vegetal is not merely a brittle figure of ruthless survivalism and soulless conformism in these filmic adaptations. Don Siegel's and Philip Kaufman's films undeniably lend the plants more vitality than does the novella. Both directors reject the depiction of the pods as lacking in life in favor of a portrayal of the alien beings as oozing, "at work," and, last but not least, visually moving for their spectators. They are also both less nostalgic about the human communities they depict (a small town in Southern California in the 1950s and San Francisco in the 1970s). As it turns out, behind the representation of plants as cold invaders, there lies another understanding of plants as spectacularly vital, material beings. Thus, both films engender more sympathy toward the plants, as well as more horror, than does the story. Siegel and Kaufman also dispense with the sped-up mortality of the pods, thus discarding the hierarchy Finney's novella sets up between being "really alive" and simply imitating life, wherein the plants function as the bad copy of a more vibrant human existence. Through these portrayals of material and vegetal vitality, the films not only reflect anxieties about the declining "energy" of human communities as the soulless plants extinguish the most passionate affections that structure human relationships in both intimate and collective contexts, but they also envision plant life as full of visual and narrative potential.

Instead of the (crudely interpreted) evolutionary fight for survival as depicted in Finney's novella, the cinematic pods struggle to express their super-reproductive potential—revealing along the way an ability to combine production and reproduction in a manner that far outstrips any human capacities. The pods thus mimic modernity and its obsession with growth and productivity, but in outpacing humans at their own game, they take on a new, positive power of their own. The *Invasion* films seep with a materiality that saturates the small-town milieu of Santa Mira (Siegel) and the urban space of San Francisco (Kaufman) with not just dramatic tension but newly fascinating sounds and sights. Siegel's rendering of the pods as frothy bodies that issue forth from uterine cavities calls into question the boundaries separating life and lifeless matter; this tension is heightened in Kaufman's remake. At the same time, the cinematic plants themselves, speaking with the voices of the former owners of their bodies, advocate on behalf of escape into a physical materiality ripe with erotic appeal.[28] The plants are not only morphologically but economically successful; they infiltrate the landscapes of these films with their bodies (often enticing) and their spectacular (re)productivity.

California Anti-Pastoral: The Invasion *of 1956*

Siegel's *Invasion* continues to exploit ideas about the defective life of plants; his pod-people are without emotions (including any concern for others), lack desires and ambitions (other than the need to survive), and possess no individuality. As Vivian Sobchack asserts of the pods in *Screening Space*: "What gives the aliens away? . . . [I]t is primarily a matter of *negative* behavior, of *not* doing something: a gasp not gasped, a kiss not returned." If "*suspense is nothing happening*," the domain of the vegetal can seem designed to elicit precisely this kind of response—a breathless, almost lifeless waiting for the void to be filled.[29] Indeed, the heroine, Becky, inadvertently reveals her humanity to the pod-creatures by expressing concern for a dog dashing out into the street. People and animals are linked by the bonds of sentiment. What is in it for plants? Precisely, it would seem, nothing.

Despite the pod-people's continued identification with an absence of affect, Siegel's cinematic adaptation, like Kaufman's, succeeds in bringing to life a form of plant-being that undermines and undercuts the assertive humanism championed in Finney's story. In short, things get increasingly vegetal in the films. The pods are depicted on-screen as giant uterine containers oozing and nursing exact replicas of their human hosts.[30] These simulacra are initially presented as incomplete—Siegel shows us a naked male body lacking fingerprints and exact features, while Kaufman's pods excrete the film's characters in miniature—but when the process of duplication is finished, the replicants immediately "take over" and impose their way of life on the humans. Even though Siegel's *Invasion* features a studio-imposed hopeful ending, in the film plants work tirelessly to highlight the vulnerability of the kind of Californian good life that the fictional small town of Santa Mira (the patron saint of the gaze?) is meant to exemplify. Prior to the invasion, the inhabitants of Santa Mira cultivate a form of mutual recognition (whose racist overtones in Finney are not overtly referenced by the film). As a community, they appear to embody respect for modern, "enlightened" forms of authority (including the policemen, doctors, and psychiatrists who function as the town's de facto voices of reason), relative economic self-sufficiency, and collective appreciation for what is eventually named by a human turned plant psychiatrist as "love, desire, ambition, faith" (a strange and somewhat contradictory list). Before it emerges as a disruptive force, the vegetal backdrop serves initially as the ambient and nourishing frame for a bucolic small-town capitalism, where prosperity and contentment reign; all too soon, however, the seemingly inert background moves to the forefront of our consciousness. When the protagonist, Dr. Miles Bennell (Kevin McCarthy), returns from a medical convention to Santa Mira and confronts the disaster unfolding before him, the first apparent sign of the terrible change that awaits him is a deserted vegetable stand—the metaphor of trouble in the social realm, which, paradoxically, suggests that the agency of cultivation in the imaginary society of Santa Mira has been wrenched from the hands of humans and taken over by plants, no longer goods to be bought and sold but fully alive in their own right. The plants of Santa Mira have abandoned their role as objects destined for human consumption and have assumed the status of producers, and superefficient ones at that. In so doing, they collapse the distinction between vegetable-as-merchandise and vegetable-as-subject (e.g., which Holberg continues to uphold), for they are the objects of their own productive activities: they are self-generating.

While the pod-beings are recognizable, initially, for that which they do not have (emotion, a "look in the eye"), they become most threatening for that which they actively undertake: a transformation of the idyllic agricultural economy of Santa Mira into a terrifically effective (and pain-free) production line—the triumph of an inhumanly efficient form of agricultural labor (that serves to bring more pods into existence) amid the destruction of the local, emotionally connected community. The plant-people of Santa Mira may, on the one hand, function as figures of a Soviet-style collectivism, where individuals fall easily into line, but they are *at one and the same time* emblems of a U.S.-style postwar capitalism, where a rationalized production system and a "heartless" drive to (re)produce threaten the capacity of the medical and political authority figures to guarantee a happy life to the inhabitants of the California town, previously "living the dream." Indeed, the plants describe their vegetal existence as better—and easier—than that of humans; it is most certainly more successful, both reproductively and, we are led to believe, ideologically as well. In fact, in the new vegetal regime, modes of production blend seamlessly with processes of reproduction: the agricultural backdrop of Southern California becomes a space of breeding and harvesting alike.

The homogenization brought about by the pods has been read many times over as the criticism of various standardizing tendencies in 1950s American life, since the imposition of uniformity is something the pods do more successfully than humans. But the vegetal pods prove themselves to be masters of crossing all sorts of boundaries: they are morphologically unstable and thus take on the characteristics both of the townspeople themselves and of their *very opposite*—the "secret" agents of routinized production, who invade the town from the inside. They also reveal within the few remaining humans "vegetal-like" needs and a fascination with a vegetal life that seems to feign being human better than humans themselves can. If humans have built themselves a social order that will eventually collapse around them, it will do so because, as it turns out, this order is a kind of expression of a vegetal drive that coexists alongside (and within) the human. The cinematic image becomes the emblem of both the strangeness of the vegetal and its fascinating-because-formless power over us.

The very "body" of the film—celluloid—suggests that vegetal life participates more intimately in our most "human" fascinations than we might otherwise expect, and that the distinction between the human and the inhuman, or for that matter between original life and duplicate, between organic life and the life of bodies without organs, is not just impossible to uphold but powerless in the face of other, more insistent forms of striving.[31] As a narrative of interpenetration of plant and human, the first *Invasion* is most concerned with the fragility and, ultimately, insignificance of any human desire in the face of a vegetal agency that works better, longer, harder—and that in its very success oozes a kind of unearthly erotic appeal, which is, in the final moments of the film, linked to the allure of cinema itself. Unlike in Finney's novella, the first *Invasion* does not work to preserve the hierarchical order separating human life-forms from their copies, as indicated by Miles's inability to resist his love interest Becky's (played by Dana Wynter) gooey duplicate, discovered in the greenhouse during an otherwise convivial barbecue scene. When he comes across

Becky's pod, instead of stabbing her vegetal copy to death, Miles turns and puts a pitchfork through the heart of his *own* replicant. The sweat on his brow as he commits this act of *Selbstmord* resonates visually with the foamy slime covering the emergent pod-Becky; in destroying the copy of himself, Miles paradoxically reaffirms his connection to his nude and vegetal beloved. This scene shows erotic attachment (and, more broadly, any sort of desire) as capable of moving across the human and nonhuman bodies presented to us, and circulating from character to spectator and back again.[32]

In a different valence, Neil Badmington gives a reading of the 1956 *Invasion* that suggests instead that the film is centrally concerned with the moment when "humanism begins to falter"[33] and "things are most certainly not what they seem."[34] Badmington carefully unpacks the scene in which Miles hesitates when given the opportunity to destroy Becky's vegetal replicant. For Badmington, Miles's hesitation is borne of his (human) desire: "Because the alien reminds him of Becky, Miles cannot avoid acting as if it/she were the true object of his desire."[35] His amorous interest in the plant thus threatens the human Becky, who will be consumed by her replica if Miles does not act. For Badmington, "[t]o be human is to desire, to possess emotions, but to desire is to trouble the sacred distinction between the human and the inhuman."[36] We are arguing here that, in crossing this boundary, the film envisions a vegetal ontology that succeeds not just in standing alone but in fulfilling human promise better than humans ever could. Siegel's *Invasion* invites us to envision, in the demise of strictly human (or rather normative) forms of desire, a vegetal striving that attaches us not just to other modes of being but to the image itself as a product of the morphological energies that undergird plants' capacity for limitless growth. As in the avant-garde French films we examined earlier, cinema itself is a vegetal medium. In the fusion of plant and human bodies, human subjectivity disappears. The mutuality at stake here is thus not or not fully an echo of Romantic fantasies about the affinities linking humans and plants; instead, it embraces the demise of the human as a sovereign or autonomous subject. This demise is framed in visual and narrative terms that are both terrifying and appealing.

At the same time, the first *Invasion* conveys its own, historically specific anxieties about reproduction, as Cindy Hendershot argues in claiming that the film exploits the fear of radiation contamination, believed to be especially detrimental to male sexual potency. In her analysis of the film, she writes: "Human reproduction is replaced by an asexual plant reproduction."[37] Transforming into a pod (as a result of the sleep that the characters

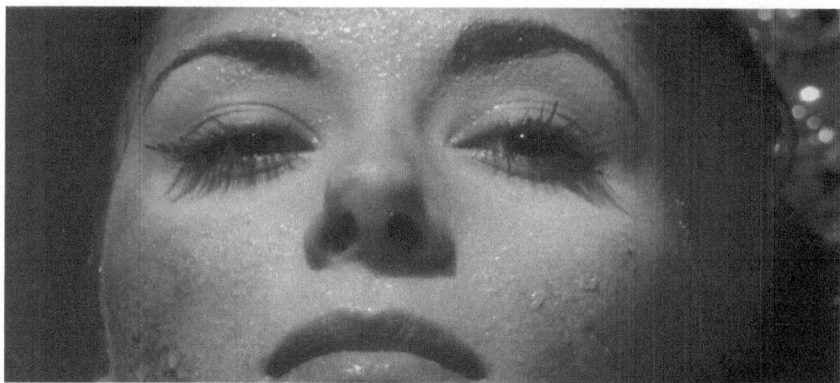

Figure 10. Becky Driscoll (Dana Wynter) emerges from the mud as a pod-person. *Invasion of the Body Snatchers* (Siegel), 1956 [1:15:11].

struggle to resist throughout the film) would mean that Miles would father no children to Becky; sexuality in this sense, as a propagation of a male line through the generation of individuated offspring, is indeed erased by the plants, just as Poe and Gilman anticipate. However, while individualized reproduction linked to masculinity is clearly under threat, images of female reproduction proliferate and intensify. In this sense, there is nothing "asexual" about the pods; instead, they help us imagine an erotic (and reproductive) life in which desire is as much a product of the images that surround us as it is a function of the bodies we embrace. Becky's attempt at quoting Shakespeare's *A Midsummer Night's Dream*—"It's summer and the moon is full and I know a bank where the wild thyme blows"—hints at both the magic transformations that occur during sleep and the erotic power of plants to contaminate the human world of reason and normative marriage.[38] Production and reproduction are reunited in an economy of startling efficiency and heightened visual allure, as we learn with the final shot of Becky, lips and eyes glistening, as she invites Miles to join her in the plant-being to which she has ultimately succumbed.

Siegel's *Invasion* initially seems oriented toward a conventional romance plot,[39] but the marriage that might be the expected outcome of Miles's renewed interest in Becky is consistently deferred by the proliferation of the pod-people (eventually including Becky herself). In their flight from the plants, Miles and Becky lower themselves into a hole in an abandoned mine, hoping to escape detection there. But, unlike the plants whom they resemble despite themselves, they fail to "implant" and are lured out of hiding by a siren song so haunting that it suggests to Becky that "we're not the only ones left to know what love is." When Miles returns to the cave in his continued search for Becky, after discovering to his horror that plants can use technology to mimic the beauties of local culture by broadcasting far and wide a seemingly human melody, he finds her half-asleep, sighing in response to his embrace. As he attempts to carry her out of the cave, he stumbles and falls upon her body, pressing his lips to hers as they lie together in the mud. In this, the most overtly erotic scene of the film, we soon discover that Becky has already become a plant; Miles's kiss transforms her—but not him—into the vegetal lover of his nightmares. Where he first destroys the plant copy of himself, here he seems somehow responsible for the production of Becky's replica through his own desire. As she emerges from the mud, lips shining, eyes wide and wet and open, we might remember her earlier lovelorn whisper—"I want your children"—as a kind of threat.

Erotic interest, in this scenario, is linked to the vegetal copy rather than to the human original—to cinema that provides and disseminates images rather than to flesh. It is not so much Miles's desire that is unusual but the *object* of this desire, the plant. For an instant, Miles is mesmerized before the simulacrum that he himself seems to have touched and kissed into an eerie vegetal life—a moment that recalls the Pygmalion myth, as the "pod" from which Becky's new body emerges is moving, pulsing, and oozing with life. In other words, Hollywood cinema has given agency to plants not unlike that bestowed upon them by Shakespeare in *A Midsummer Night's Dream*. But instead of having recourse to a premodern notion of magic, the film shows us the celluloid image partaking in an erotic economy that effectively blurs the lines between producing and reproducing.

Flower Power: The Invasion *of 1978*

Inspired by a post-1968 disillusionment with U.S. political culture, the creators of the 1978 remake of the *Invasion* aimed to highlight the increasing pressure on Americans to participate in processes of globalization. In interviews, director Kaufman underscores an intent to express disappointment with changes in American political life, including the fact that people were being forced to conform to a "standardized new mass culture, something that could work on a world scale."[40] This comment is in part an allusion to *Star Wars*, whose first installment was released the previous year and with which the *Invasion* of 1978 shares a sound editor (Ben Burtt). It also reflects the awareness that globalization, as a larger process affecting more than just filmmaking, had become increasingly inescapable. Plants operate, in this context, as figures both for the soulless working of markets, with their alienating effects on human beings, and, simultaneously, for a form of material diversity that this global standardization fails to contain.[41] They bring their promise of vibrancy to an urban environment in which many "types" of beings may, in theory, flourish, even as the cinematic San Francisco of the 1970s also bears the marks of racial segregation and discrimination, along with a (muted and problematic) racial and ethnic diversity (especially in its representations of Asian American culture). Kaufman's version, significantly, does not offer us the point of view of a person of color, even as it acknowledges the diversity of the city that it represents. Plants provide an opening or an escape from the social and political malaise that pervades the city, thereby leaving the question of racial difference unaddressed. They are agents of homogenization and global capitalism in the film even as they are also the carriers of a vitality that capitalism attempts to territorialize.

Set in San Francisco, the second *Invasion* explores the tension within a city space characterized by hybridity, difference, and multiplicity on the one hand, and intensive bureaucratic management and surveillance (paradoxically required to "cultivate" this multicultural space) on the other. The doctor, Miles Bennell, of the first *Invasion* becomes public employee for the city's health department, Matthew Bennell, in the second; where Miles embodies a certain scientific objectivity—and authoritative diagnostic powers—Matthew is distinguished less for his rationality than for his ability to care, not just for the heroine, Elizabeth (another man's girlfriend), but for the city itself. In one of the early scenes of the film, Matthew (played by Donald Sutherland) is shown inspecting a French restaurant where he identifies a piece of rat turd in the bouillon. The ensuing contentious face-off between Matthew, the French chef, and the French restaurant owner highlights the point that Matthew's job is to protect humans from dangerous forms of intrusion, including food poisoning. The figures of the rat turd, the rats, and maybe also the French chef—all bent on introducing "foreign" elements into the bouillon—foreshadow the looming invasion by the pods, but Matthew's role is not without its own ambiguity. Is he an agent of homogenization, or is he instead protecting a diversity that is inherent in the city itself? The film seems to decide in favor of the latter when we see Matthew cooking stir-fry in a wok and hanging a Chinese banner in his office; both of these acts evoke an ethnic and cultural multiplicity, in theory characteristic of San Francisco as a community. The film steers away from idealizing the smug familiarity of small-town California that dominates the first version, inviting us to be fascinated by organic matter as such, before it takes definite shape, and to acknowledge the strangeness within the familiar. Indeed, the second *Invasion* proposes biodiversity as an extension of the racial diversity that is part of city life.

The vibrant backdrop provided by the city initially represents urban space as nourishing positive and pleasure-giving modes of heterogeneity, until the plants take over in a (successful) attempt to do the humans one better. Kaufman's film adaptation thus reveals a political and social idealism that is structured around hybridity and difference, not, as in Siegel's film, around ideological stability and sameness. But, as in the first *Invasion*, we soon realize that plants are more successful than humans at precisely this new way of being. Not only does Kaufman's *Invasion* abandon the original cinematic version's suburban setting by transferring the narrative to an ethnically and racially mixed urban space, and from a sunny to a rainy landscape, but the film also makes the vegetal into the figure of the very hybridity that presumably characterizes urban communities. The second *Invasion* reintroduces the idea of difference into the narrative by reinventing Jack Finney's cosmic seeds. (The overt cosmic motif is missing in Siegel's *Invasion*, since the origins of the invasion are never shown.) In Kaufman's version, the invaders morph into identical replicas of the city's inhabitants in a process revealed to be analogous to that of a graft. The opening images of the film imply both the danger and the fascinating appeal of this kind of adaptation: alien seeds sprout with amazing speed into red and pink flowers that quickly implant themselves within the verdant, moist, and colorful urban landscape. The fertility of this space no longer stems from standardization and exclusion, as in the first *Invasion*, but from the forms of diversity and hybridity that are not invented but intensified by the plants. However, the second film's vision of racial and ethnic difference remains limited. The second *Invasion* promises to enchant us with scenes of human diversity that themselves treat the existence of Asian culture in San Francisco as a kind of background. This is a mode of multiculturalism that can be easily recuperated by the very mechanism of global capitalism that the film critiques. At the same time, Kaufman's *Invasion* confronts us with vegetal matter as an emerging image of a speculative elsewhere in which globalization does not operate, or does so otherwise.

As a result, Finney's dream of a human community reconstituting itself in reaction to the homogeneity of the pods retreats even further in the second *Invasion*, even as the vulnerability of the human becomes all the more a source of horror. Finally, in keeping with its intensification of the vegetal motif, the second *Invasion* reveals the (re)productivity of plants to be both more profoundly feminine (in a ripely physiological sense) and more disturbingly effective than ever. With its vaginal images of the replicants emerging from their vegetal shrouds (backed by fetal whooshing noises), Kaufman's film stresses the similarity between biological femininity and modes of vegetal being; the pods, like women's bodies, evoke images of nurture as a form of passivity—an inferior mode of being that is plantlike in its seeming immobility but, ultimately, awesomely successfully in its ability to captivate and transform an audience.

As the film's images embrace the ideal of a hybrid city, ethnically and culturally diverse, they simultaneously portray this hybridity as both replicated and surpassed by the colorfully beautiful flowers that invade it. The heroine, Elizabeth (played by Brooke Adams), is so taken by the reddish-pink buds of the alien species that she (unsuspectingly) takes one home at the outset of the movie. After perusing a botanical manual in a flurry of botanophilia, she manages to identify the blossom as a "grex" or "cultivar" (in a terminology that recalls orchids and other hybrid plant species). Is her interest in an unknown plant species—portrayed as a mysterious hybrid adapting to its new environment—another figure for the diversity of the city whose heterogeneity the creators endorse even as the apocalyptic narrative unfolds? If we understand the film from a realist point of view, the representation of the city and its inhabitants is disappointingly superficial. If we read the representation of plant life—in the form of the invading pod-people—as an otherworldly extension of the logic of difference into a nonhuman context, we can see vegetality as something other than a destructive force. A more vibrant and vital representation of biodiversity emerges here, even as the film fails to depict human difference adequately or even thoughtfully. Is this representation of difference recuperable for human social life or social projects? The film is ambivalent in this regard, even as it invests plants with a speculative energy that the humans themselves lack.

As this "indigenous" hybridity of the city is emblematized and heightened by the alien presence of the plants, it simultaneously engages us (and the heroine) visually and stirs up anxieties about the extinction and demise of the human species. Once again, the plants seem designed both to awaken the vegetal impulses latently present in the human characters, and to render the most intrinsically "human" qualities of these characters always already plantlike in nature. The film encourages the increasing involvement, however ambivalent, of the spectator in the urban spaces of San Francisco remade by the pods, even as it makes the pods themselves the index of an already occurring economic and social phenomenon—

Figure 11. Elizabeth Driscoll (Brooke Adams) is fascinated by the "grex." *Invasion of the Body Snatchers* (Kaufman), 1978 [4:44].

namely, the standardization of individual human life. Early on in the film, we see Elizabeth coming home to her disaffected boyfriend, Geoffrey (Art Hindle), who will shortly be transformed into a pod (but is for the moment still human). Rooted to the couch watching football and barely acknowledging her except when he cajoles her into having sex, the portrayal of Geoffrey suggests that the mutuality and reciprocal affective bonds supposedly unique to humans (as in the first *Invasion*) are already absent where this couple is concerned. We realize that some humans have already transformed themselves into plants and do not even really need the arrival of the pods, which (as the opening of the movie suggests) may or may not have taken place before the film begins. (The origin of the pods might be prehistoric or quite recent; the credits themselves do not clarify this point.)

In a similar vein, we find the character of the original *Invasion*'s psychiatrist, Dr. Danny Kaufman, transformed into a feel-good psychotherapist and author of popular self-help books, played, in an ironic twist, by actor Leonard Nimoy. Nimoy is, of course, best known for playing the role of Spock, the iconic figure from the original *Star Trek* television series and the representative of an imaginary alien species, the Vulcans, distinguished primarily by a lack of emotion. Nimoy's presence onscreen suggests, even before we learn that Dr. David Kibner (as he is known in the remake) is, in fact, a pod, that the therapist has never cared for his patients. Here, too, the invading plants seem to make visible a transformation that has already happened rather than providing the impetus for it. Finally, in yet another scene identifying humanity with plant life, we witness in the Bellicec mud baths row upon row of human beings comfortably reclining in tubs of slime; the baths' clients seem to resemble potted plants as they luxuriate in the therapeutic mud. In all of these instances, the nourishing "me-generation" attitude toward pleasure is shown to be already vegetal—in part responding to a human desire for emotional responsiveness and connection, in part exposed from within as susceptible to cold manipulation—and capable of making humans into plants, albeit with diminished vitality.

In his book titled *Gilles Deleuze and the Fabulation of Philosophy*, critic Gregory Flaxman reads Kaufman's *Invasion* as a film about simulacra. He writes, "People are so stoned, pharma-colonized, psychiatrized, and finally deadened that when the affect-less aliens eventually hatch, they seem no different than their human counterparts. The old means of judgment have become impossible and, we might say, irrelevant: the spiritual distinction has been erased. The copy now expresses the evacuation of any originality, of any fixed identity, because the quality of 'being human' is always already estranged, alienated: the copy has no model."[42] With this reading, Flaxman brings the film up to date. By arguing that the city's takeover by the pods stands for the reterritorialization of human life by the pharmaceutical and psychiatric industries, in short by late capitalism (with its attendant feel-good and self-help markets), he points to the continuing relevance of the film today. His Deleuzean approach reveals that the play of simulacra is ongoing and inescapable. In other words, there is no outside to the domain of the copy, not even when the main character, played by Donald Sutherland, breaks out in a terrifyingly inhuman scream, announcing that the last vestiges of humanity have been lost. Flaxman argues that instead we, the audience, at this point also "find ourselves among the doubles."[43]

Flaxman's reading highlights the fact, likewise emphasized by the director, that the film reveals the workings of global capitalism and its decentralizing or rhizomatic operation. The pods do not represent the sudden demise of an original human essence but are instead an extension and continuation of an ongoing process of the manipulation of life, initiated under capitalism and indeed postmodernity. With their arrival, human beings are further deterritorialized. Late capitalism does not cause alienation only through standardization, although the globalization of markets shapes tastes by offering the same products everywhere it reaches.

It also generates and encourages biological growth in order to create a surplus of life that can be reincorporated into the neoliberal economy.[44] Capitalism intervenes on the molecular level of life itself. Thus, the figure of the rhizome is itself assimilable into the logic and workings of late capitalism.

In a related context, Jeffrey T. Nealon points out that Deleuze and Guattari's rhizome may have seemed in the 1980s to evoke the liberatory undoing of the boundaries that had been imposed by the welfare state (including a bureaucratic apparatus such as the Health Department, where Matthew busies himself with protecting the city from intruders like urban rodents and pods). However, this figure loses some of its liberationist potential as neoliberal economies harness a kind of rhizomatic power in their operations. Nealon contends,

> In both theory and practice, then, the giddy philosophical thrust of Deleuze and Guattari's work on the rhizome tends to deflate when the conversation turns specifically to human political power and to capitalism—which, as they remind us, is unique as a sociopolitical organizing principle insofar as capitalism encourages and benefits from deterritorialized flows (of money, labor, flexibility) rather than constantly trying to ward them off (as the older political sovereign and state forms constantly did).... In a disciplinary world of rigid political segmentation (say, monarchy or fascism) such an ontological stance emphasizing grounding flows has an obvious progressive or resistant political valence. However, in a neoliberal world that dreams not of rigid obedience to accepted norms but of endless flows..., the 'n-1' tools of rhizomatics can seem less than revolutionary.[45]

The pods turn out to be representatives of neoliberalism and its biopolitical power, even as they suggest the existence of another world. With their ability to intervene in the elements of life itself, they prefigure the rise of an economy that successfully exploits these elements in the name of profit and the expansion of markets. The turn to speculation here can be understood in an economic sense; plants are not the figures of resistance to quantification and objectification, since in late capitalism, thinking of life as vegetal is no longer necessarily radical, and vegetal life-forms, too, have become fully biopolitical subjects. The pod-people are moreover a global force to be reckoned with, undeniably more successful than their human competitors. The greenhouses of Santa Mira have become, in the 1978 film, a giant shipping plant where the pods are grown in spaces that are at once flowerbeds, incubators, and industrial production lines.

When Matthew runs to the city's harbor in the hopes of escaping on an enormous shipping tanker, he finds out that this ship, seemingly a beacon of optimism, is carrying a massive load of seedpods. It remains unclear whether the ship is coming in or going out, but we do know that the invasion has already taken place on a global level. In the film, judging from Matthew's frightened expression, the globalization of markets stands for the closing of the social and political horizons of a world that is simultaneously celebrated and reviled in the film. Matthew's fear, however, is only in part generated by the representation of global flows. It is more clearly a reaction to the implementations of standardization that Kaufman links with globalization. The pods certainly ensure the flow of "goods" (i.e., the pods themselves), and they enable a kind of mass production, but in doing so they resemble a bit too much the very welfare state that they set out to destroy, at least to the extent that this apparatus, too, appears concerned with a kind of uniformity and erasure of difference. Kaufman's negative depiction of globalization, through the film, does not consistently expose the deterritorializing power of markets and their ability to invest in the desiring individual (rather than in the homogenous figure of the average consumer) as an object of critique. In the horror Matthew expresses at the idea of certain modes of collectivization, and in the vilification of the welfare state, we can still detect a rehearsal of a pro-capitalist agenda in which "freedom of choice" means freedom to consume. Not everyone needs a film with light sabers: let some of us love our own pod!

Thus, the seedpods reveal the ambivalent force of capitalism in the form of an organicized, frothing, oozing, whooshing vegetal *psūchē*. At the same time, they clearly hold a positive power to replicate the life of the city and place us, as spectators, inside it. But just what does it mean to find ourselves among the "doubles"? If we wish to bring the film up to date even more than we have done so far, with the help of Flaxman and Nealon, we need to underscore the film's speculative dimension, which makes us feel as if we were pods ourselves by gradually drawing us into the world of the film, then finally taking away the perspective of the human hero. This is a form of becoming-plant (a process that we discuss more fully in the next chapter). In this context, the familiar plants that we see on-screen from the beginning of the narrative, the red grex and the oozing seedpods, join forces with the sensory experience of the urban environment, and that of San Francisco in particular, to invite the viewer to become part of the fabric and fiber of the city as a site of hybridity, exposure to alterity, and a potentially engaging public life. In contrast to Flaxman, we emphasize the positive material presence of vegetal matter in the film; this matter is organic, although never fully formed, and exerts a fascination in its malleability. Kaufman inherits this interest from Siegel's earlier version, with its images of Becky's transformation and her vegetal double. Thus, the world of the replicas, or bad copies, is not just alienating or melancholic—a zone of nostalgia for an absent original—but is a fully material world capable of transforming, producing, and reproducing itself. The pods are thus not only representatives of the workings of an increasingly rhizomatic capitalism. The film preserves a materialist aspect, in which matter is not only instrumentalized but also world-making in its own right. Kaufman's *Invasion* projects the total erasure of human beings (with their human essence and their moral ideals) while maintaining the very social and economic structures—the material form—of urban life in San Francisco, which remains a source of pleasure for the spectators who can thus, by the end of the film, imagine being present in the visual and auditory experience of a city of pod-people.

The film portrays San Francisco's privileged "me-generation" as thriving but a bit thoughtless, without much autonomy, already conforming and docile in accepting the nourishment doled out to them by various services. The arrival of the pods both thrusts them into even more conformity and, on the contrary, redeems them from a drab existence. It is the latter experience that our materialist reading of the film underscores. Gradually, the images of flaccid, plantlike humans are reinjected with an excess of life, thanks to the invasion; the alien beings bring with them the promise of not only biological vitality but a vigorous efflorescence that can be substituted for the failed utopia represented by the multiethnic and multicultural but well-policed and ultimately fairly homogenous San Francisco (as well as by Elizabeth's lifeless relationship). The film revels in representing hybridity as simultaneously a source of aesthetic pleasure and of fear—the motivating principle behind a grotesque, but not always unpleasant, world whose avatars include the rat turd in the French bouillon, the invading seedpods drifting languorously toward Earth, flowering plants, a dog with a human head, and the naked body of Elizabeth, who becomes, posttransformation, a kind of alien Eve.

In a scene toward the middle of the film, Nancy Bellicec (Veronica Cartwright), wife of the poet-philosopher Jack Bellicec (Jeff Goldblum), in an attempt to make sense of the invasion, frames the mission of the aliens in the context of the extraterrestrial origin theories propagated in the 1970s. "They could start getting into our systems and screwing up our genes or, like, DNA, recombining us, changing us," she says. "Of course, this is just the same way spacemen came to mate with monkeys and create the human

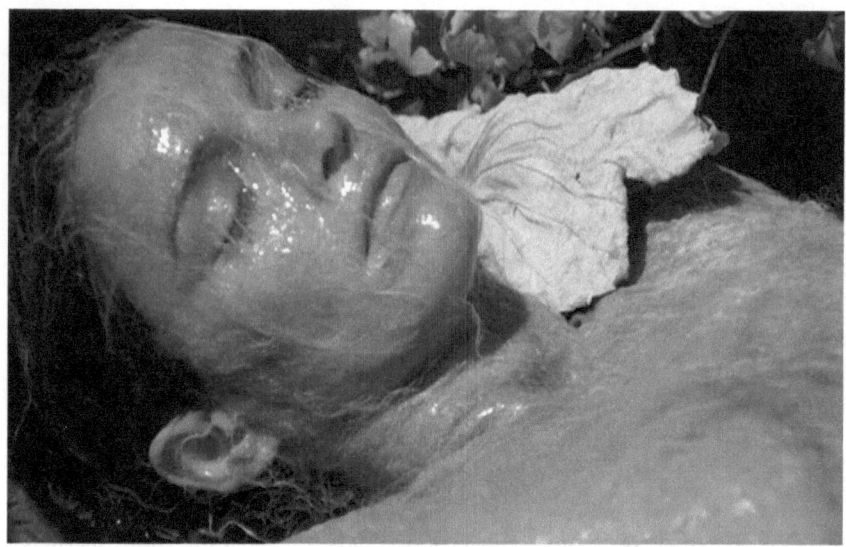

Figure 12. Matthew Bennell (Donald Sutherland) discovers Elizabeth's body covered in weblike tendrils. Later, more pods emerge to the accompaniment of a fetal heartbeat. *Invasion of the Body Snatchers* (Kaufman), 1978 [50:17].

race." This statement, dominated by the image of a vegetal other that is both alien and already intrinsic to the human, not only expresses a fear of hybridization as bringing about the end of humanity but (ambivalently) acknowledges the fundamental role played by hybridity in generating all life, including human life. We are getting ever-more plantlike, the film suggests, even as we cultivate our own human ways of doing things. Clearly, the second film dispenses with the optimism (however obligatory) of the first. Conversely, its most remarkable aspect stems from the fact that Kaufman transforms the vegetal threat of standardization posed by the pods into images and sounds that conjure vitality even as the city itself is shown to be in peril. While Siegel's *Invasion* embraces, at least initially, the prospect of heteronormative romance as the source of a potential happy ending to the narrative (even if the imagined remarriage never occurs), Kaufman's *Invasion* follows a tragic plot only to conclude with a bleak affirmation of the importance (and impossibility) of individual desire and nonconformism. Matthew is a "tragic hero" (in director Kaufman's terms) not only because he loves and loses Elizabeth but also because his focus on the care and cultivation of both public and private spaces comes to an end with his abrupt transformation into a screaming pod. One could argue that the famous final scene—featuring an openmouthed Sutherland shrieking into a void that recalls the iconic scream queen of the Hollywood B movie genre—further feminizes the already effeminate hero (busy with caring and nurturing during most of the movie's plot) as much as it exposes him as an alien.

In the scene just before the conclusion, less famous but equally significant, we see Matthew in his office in the Health Department headquarters clipping newspaper articles—possible evidence of either a strikingly human inefficiency (and rebellion against the pressures of productivity) or of a podlike compulsiveness; when he gets up from his desk along with his coworkers (presumably all already pods) at noon to go to lunch, he follows Elizabeth with his eyes, watching her through a tiny window in the elevator door as it closes in front of him. For a moment, we believe that his care for her is intact. However, it is not the fact that we are soon to be disabused of our faith in Matthew's humanity that makes this scene remarkable. It is that once we realize that he, too, is a pod, we also come to understand that the film has drawn us into a world where we may be doubled as well. But the possibility of doubling—the very absence of an original that might "correct" the copy—is what it means to *live* in a material world in which our mode of being is not stabilized by reference to a metaphysical plane transcending that of the physical. Matthew and Elizabeth may be pods now, but they are no less alive. And San Francisco, as a city inhabited by pods, is a world of material wonder—containing everything from the texture of the newspaper that Matthew is clipping to the old building in which the Health Department is housed. In fact, this city is both recognizable in and yet transfigured by the vitality of matter.

If in the film, it is Matthew who promises Elizabeth a way out of a passionless relationship with Geoffrey—not through intense romance but by cooking Chinese food and manifesting his sublimated, asexual desire as loyalty—then the final scene, paradoxically, provocatively shows that what he leads her into is not some romance warmed by impassioned or heroic affection but a richly sensory world where his asexual libido now can continue to thrive.[46] His desire subverts rather than reinforces the standardization represented in Elizabeth's relationship and her stale domestic life with Geoffrey, a standardization that is only intensified when Geoffrey becomes a pod. The scene at the elevator, when we are made to recall Matthew's genuine affection for Elizabeth, even though neither of them is human any longer, thus functions as a commentary on the moment, early in the movie, when Elizabeth returns home with the hybrid pink flower that fascinates her much more than her first relationship does. Once more, the line between our most human impulses and our most vegetal obsessions is blurred. Likewise, the full-throated inarticulate scream that closes the movie does not simply evoke the horror felt by our sudden apprehension of the lack of Matthew's humanity but also resonates with the rich sound effects that film offers us, and through which it draws us into the sensory, material, and indeterminately and incompletely organic world of the pods. The *Invasion* films render plants as both formless and alluringly shapely, both uncannily passive in their reproductive energies and highly active in their ability to "take over" systems of production that appear to have exceeded human capacities to manage or even comprehend them (including the aesthetic production of cinema itself). In doing so, the vegetal beings of the two films make a positive use of the atomic materiality of the pods as the latter is described by Finney.[47] In the films, the pods acquire more and more life; their images transform the "grey matter" that oozes out of them in the novella like slow-moving "lava" into a dynamically cellular/celluloid materiality that takes us out of the realm of (nearly) inert minerals and into an asexual vegetal vitality. The pods not only bring with them a dystopian new social order but the promise of social "life," the ability to receive and generate affects that humans themselves are in the process of losing.

Finney's novella contrasts vegetal growth with the human ability to reproduce and perpetuate (as well as to protect) the species, even as it contains an implicit commentary on the cost of that human "authenticity." The films, conversely, reimagine his scenes of diminished pod materiality as evidence of the fascinating power of plant life; the two *Invasion* films reveal to us the vegetal striving that undergirds our fantasies of a more human future. Both films investigate the possibility that there is a species that is more successful, indeed unique, in cultivating aims that might once have seemed to be intrinsically human, including a capacity for productive labor and an investment in the image as a source of erotic fulfillment. At the same time, humans come to appear more and more limited in their ability to manipulate or even justify the systems that they have put into place.

What is more, the cinematic plants of the *Invasion* films expose the fact that the human environment, instead of being richer than that of plants, is itself experienced as empty: plants fill it. In the *Invasion* of 1956, plants—in a lushly cinematic disguise as a beautiful woman—supply the erotic power that first fuels then exceeds the marriage plot. Not only are *they* always awake, but humans are all on the verge of sleep. And plants, unlike humans, work all the time. In Kaufman's remake, plants excel at both the urban cultivation of multicultural diversity and the surveillance and policing of nonendorsed otherness. Matthew, as tragic hero, may remind us of the positive impact of human affect on communities, but he is doomed to fail (at least as a human) in his efforts to nurture, while plants proliferate and, in doing so, fill in this tragic space with economically successful hybridity and life—providing the most alluring images of the vitality toward which we all tend. They are thus capable of negotiating contradictions that undo us; they stand not only for soulless forms of standardization, production, and consumption but for the kind of energy (and openness) that the second *Invasion* celebrates. In plant horror, vegetal beings generate this vitality aesthetically, thanks to their forcefulness and their oozing and unfinished organicism mixed with sensory, even libidinal appeal, just as they show the disappearance of vital force from human society. In the end, we witness with the *Invasion* films not so much desire's demise as its transferal onto the plants themselves, which usher us into a speculative (asexual or presexual) reality where we are both present (through cinema's ability to draw us into sensory worlds) and absent (insofar as our desires and ideals are concerned). The vibrancy of the image complements and supplements the morphological potency of the plants.

The Twenty-First Century: The Return of the Plant?

The cinematic pods of the *Invasion* films appear to diagnose a variety of social and political ills—from fears about creeping standardization, to worries about the effects of global capitalism on diversity, to anxieties around the negotiation of difference (sexual as well as racial) in the public and private spaces of the modern United States—but they do not posit solutions to these ills, even within the domain of the narratives themselves. Moreover, plants and humans are both susceptible to being entirely absorbed into the framework of a global capitalism that increasingly intervenes in life on the molecular level. Plants, as Nealon points out, are, in fact, at the forefront of this development; pods do not avoid it. The *Invasion* films force us to confront the knowledge that there is no dissociating the human from the vegetal, and that modern life (with its cinematic investments and its global economic ambitions) is itself plantlike to the core. This modern reformulation of an ancient interest in the plant-as-being, both powerful and formless, becomes a way of imagining and rendering visual not the superiority of the human but the end of our familiar world that continues to reproduce itself after it has ceased to be ours—the collapse into a mode of "vegetal being" that outperforms men and women on the production line as well as on the screen.

Anticipating an ecological discourse that postdates these films, we might say, then, that they gesture toward, without fully accepting, the possibility of a new mode of environmental thinking, one in which the separation between "natural object" and "human subject" no longer informs our relationships to the world around us. Moreover, insofar as it uncouples the figure of the other from the humanoid monster or automaton, the plant horror genre provides us with a kind of preview of what Timothy Morton has recently described as "the ecological thought"—a way of acting and thinking that refuses the long-standing distinctions between outside and inside, between "us" and "another," that have so often informed the human approach to nature. The *Invasion* films show us that our environment not only resists our attempts to manage and control it but is always already present within us—as a challenge to forms of human exceptionalism that present the capacity to engage with (or care about) the natural world as yet another in an array of heroically human traits. In this context, the *Invasion* films point the way to a new mode of imaginative fiction, one in which the imagined separation between human and vegetal being is consistently shown up to be both a figment of our imagination and a symptom of our own failure to acknowledge the ways in which the systems we have created to order our worlds, in fact threaten us with the fact of our own vulnerability.

In other words, the pod-people of plant horror reveal themselves to be uniquely suited to the twin milieus of global capitalism, on the one hand, and speculative fiction, on the other. In both films, the pods/plants represent an escape from the homogenizing forces of society without, for all that, standing in for an alternative form of political subjectivity. The *Invasion* films help warn us of the dangers of a political position that slides too easily into narratives of "self" and "other"—that attempts to manage an environment that already lies within. The transformations of incomplete organic matter open up horizons that also anticipate (without fully foreseeing) the powers of neoliberal economies. Contemporary writers and artists will take up this problem as a challenge to generate new modes of speculation, ones that address head-on the difficulty of representing a vegetal subjectivity that resists capture even as it comes to structure human experience.

CHAPTER 7

Becoming Plant Nonetheless

Why Become Plant Today?

Early modern radical botanists demonstrate that plants can function as technologies of animation, setting in motion human desires, ideas, and bodies, even as they recede from the values and social ideals that we may try to project onto them. Excavating this marginalized tradition allows us to rethink our relation to plants (including our "love" of plants, to cite Erasmus Darwin) in a way that is not determined by analogies to human sexuality or broader social formations. Insofar as this earlier materialist and speculative tradition, in conversation with a proto-empiricist and empiricist natural philosophy, attributes affective and animating powers to plants, it can be included in post-Romantic projects where plants once again function in concert with the technologies, such as cinema, that seize upon them. In plant horror, which has lent a pulpy but fascinating substance to the Hegelian figure of plant indifference at least since Edgar Allan Poe's intervention in the Romantic garden, plants paradoxically generate human affect, including a certain impish pleasure; they intervene in human consciousness even as they do not recognize us or ratify our sense of our own uniqueness. Long interpreted as promoting paranoia, plant horror can allow us to become affectively involved with aspects of our world that have traditionally been ignored or effaced within the broader frameworks of Western modernity. Plants not only augment and transform how we perceive but change and undo what we are. In contemporary theoretical terms, this is a posthuman world indeed. In this last chapter, we explore how vegetal forms of speculation have taken on an increasingly large scope, especially in an era marked by artificial intelligence and other technologies that represent not just enhancements of "our" reality but new ways of defining plants, as we will show. To situate ourselves in this postbotanical present, we first trace the materialist, feminist genealogy of becoming plant today and the migration of this becoming into posthumanist and ecologically oriented contexts.

In recent years, studies of how plants sense and interact with the environment have in part given way to speculative attempts to define their "intelligence"—efforts that return, in certain instances, to metaphysical questions about the essence of consciousness and the self. Thus, Stefano Mancuso and Alessandra Viola assert that recognition of plant intelligence opens up sci-fi-worthy technological possibilities while influencing human ethics and perhaps law and politics as well. They call plants a "universal" form of life, extraterrestrial par excellence: "They—or rather their most typical cellular organelles, the chloroplasts—are the link connecting the activities of the whole organic world (that is, of everything we call life) with our solar system's energy center. . . . [P]lants have a universal function for life on our planet. Animals don't." Mancuso and Viola go on to explain that specific attributes of plants allow them to "open the way" for new technologies such as "plant-inspired robots," "plant-based networks" or "Greenternet," "phytocomputers," new pharmaceuticals, clean energy sources, new artificial materials, and "incalculable unexplored possibilities in the chemical and biological world." At the same time, they call for an even more intensive regulation of our dealings with plant life and its even greater inclusion in our legal and ethical order. "[O]n this . . . moral philosophers, molecular biologists, naturalists, and ecologists . . . unanimously agreed . . . : plants cannot be treated arbitrarily. Their indiscriminate destruction is morally unjustifiable."[1]

We begin this final chapter with Mancuso and Viola's popular scientific work, because these authors urge us to shift scale, suggesting that plants have relevance in the context of climate management, advances in computing, and the human relationship to the cosmos. Mancuso and Viola effectively put an end to the botanical mode of inquiry in which a human observer examines vegetal bodies singularly or as part of a carefully delineated ecosystem. Instead, they zoom out and make of plants, with their ability to convert solar energy into starches, the portal to the cosmos imagined as a vast network. Mancuso and Viola's reevaluation of plant life takes us right into the contemporary situation of plants as *both* drivers of innovation in science and technology, with an outsize importance for the planet and beyond, *and* newly emerging ethical and biopolitical subjects. From their perspective, plants are already robots—that is, their swarm intelligence fits seamlessly with other developments in AI currently under way.[2] Yet, the vegetal model of thought that they champion also rehearses many of the classical elements of the liberal subject (especially in its universality and its abstraction). Departing from a botanical perspective, Mancuso and Viola ascribe to plants a networked notion of intelligence that is not based in organs; this shift in turn enables their assertion of the ethical and legal rights of plants. As they argue, the sky is the limit to technological and, presumably, social changes, yet the classical liberal subject is supposed to remain intact. In fact, these authors combine a cybernetic notion of posthuman vegetal intelligence with an older universalist model of the rights-bearing subject, both of which, as N. Katherine Hayles has affirmed, construe subjectivity as disembodied.[3] For Mancuso and Viola, the plant is still our double; it may even function as a way to "upgrade" liberalism for a future reserved for disembodied intelligence and the latter's worldmaking power.[4]

Indeed, contemporary science confirms the puzzling mathematical intelligence of plants. Plants have been revealed to calculate their starch use with algorithms and thus function in ways that invoke the workings of the stock market, which uses algorithms to direct the flows of capital.[5] At the same time, they remain vulnerable beings and, in their unique and species-specific existence, face the dangers of extinction and disappearance (as humans do). With our increased ability to intervene in life, plants are also more likely to find themselves on the receiving end of techniques of manipulation and exploitation. Today, plants are at the forefront of genetic modification, industrialized mass production, urban planning, studies of the climate, the "terraforming" of earth, and other forms of biopolitical control enabled by their biology; they point toward an imagined future in which all life and all genomes can and probably will be altered and augmented as part of a speculative bio-economy that Melinda Cooper has called "life as surplus."[6] This situation calls not for "raising" plants to the status of coequal liberal subjects but for making plants privileged subjects of speculation in order to challenge universalist human pretensions, in the spirit of the early modern project of radical botany.

We can now return to Cyrano's question: Do plants speculate? In late late modernity, plants once again have the potential to be treated as human surrogates, either in the demand to accord them rights or in the consideration of plants as profoundly embroiled (like humans) in regimes of quantification and mathematization.[7] Can plants help us imagine life differently with their inclusion in human economies of pleasure, agency, and speculative creation? This time the answer must engage with the status of plants as both material bodies and (potential) subjects with their own specificity and substance.

If, in this chapter, we investigate the way in which modern novelists, artists, and scholars have explored the plant as part of an attempt to animate a feminist politics and a critique of contemporary capitalism, it is because these modes of inquiry are not inevitably nostalgic for abstracted models of the self (including masculinist, cisgender, and heteronormative ones). The task of becoming woman and that of becoming plant are historically linked in ways that we should not overlook, for the plant has long been identified with the feminine body and has just as regularly been exploited, naturalized, and subjected to social and (bio)political control.[8] As we have shown in earlier chapters, identification with plants in literature and cinema can help deessentialize marginalized subject positions. Although there is a long tradition of identifying feminine, non-Western, and queer bodies with those of plants (or violently placing them into the garden of culture where they may be "cultivated"), by doubling down on this identification some feminist authors, filmmakers, and artists have revealed the nonnormative possibilities inherent in vegetal modes of being. By becoming plant, they have located themselves outside of or in opposition to the socially accepted norms of woman- or personhood. The works that we discuss here show how plants can destabilize, exceed, or bypass our limited human faculties and our efforts at world-making rather than necessarily upgrading or augmenting these efforts. Contemporary radical botany proposes a renewed and increased intimacy with plants in their specificity, encouraging us to give in to the ability of plants to solicit our fascination, love, and even sympathy at the same time as we acknowledge that plants do not recognize or respond to our desires and our models of individuated subjectivity.

Arguably the most significant philosophical attempt to center plant life within a technological and capitalist modernity occurs with Gilles Deleuze and Félix Guattari's *A Thousand Plateaus* (first published in French in 1980, with a complete English translation appearing in 1987), in which the figure of the rhizome opens out onto an effort to think life in its inorganic processes, or "flows." With the rhizome, Deleuze and Guattari allow for a rethinking of becoming plant as a process endemic in late capitalism and available to *all* bodies, including nonhuman and nonorganic ones. Indeed, the rhizome can be claimed as a radical botanical figure in the sense we have developed throughout this book, one in which an inorganic or materialist vegetality takes priority over the pastoral, organicist, or metaphysical plant, and in which plants and their modes of life are accorded primacy over those of humans. Deleuze and Guattari's inorganic vitalism, like that of the other radical botanists we have studied here, plays with and extends the analogy between plants and other life-forms while also dismantling and undercutting the distinctions that serve to categorize and define various modes of life.

At the same time, these French thinkers inaugurate a vision of late modernity as postbotanical. Some theorists of ecology have responded to late modern biopolitical regimes by intensifying the critique of the liberal subject available in continental or "French" theory, especially in Deleuze and Guattari's concept of the "rhizome," to the point of all but giving up the material histories and subject positions the liberal subject has assumed over time. In this context, plants once again give us access to large-scale events and systems beyond the here and now, such as slow violence, deep time, big data, climate crisis, the Anthropocene, and species thinking, which digital tools might allow us to partially apprehend. Here, too, the shift in scale tends to undo or negate the perspective of botany, which is often local and small-scale. For example, Jeffrey Nealon warns us that to understand Deleuze and Guattari literally—that is, to understand becoming plant as becoming like an organic plant—is to misread them, for the rhizome is not specifically botanical in nature but rather "a machinistic network of finite automata." As the site of nonorganic flows and assemblages that make individuation possible, the rhizome cannot serve as a locus of self-identification or identity formation in any classical sense. Nealon writes,

> [T]he questionable "organic" reading goes something like this: insofar as becoming-animal is becoming *an* animal or *like* an animal, then rhizomatics would or could entail becoming (like) *a* plant. . . . When D&G talk of becoming, or when they talk of animals or plants as rhizomatic, they are referring not so much to this or that privileged or

exemplary organism (the leaves of grass or the rats, the orchid or the wasp) as they are conjuring the multiple processes (the territories of becoming) that traverse any given phenomenon or organism—the swarms of white blood cells in mammals, the global winds that blow the dust from the Sahara to the rain forests of South America, the lightning that causes brush fires, the abundance of prairie life that follows a decade after such fires, the interplanetary forces of gravity, or the odd brain chemical effects coming from the ingestion of THC or poppies. These rhizomatic becomings are nonorganic bases of the organism—the swarm of verbs that literally make up the nouns of organisms, subjects, or objects: "a machinistic network of finite automata (a rhizome)."[9]

This consideration of the nonorganic bases of the organism directs our attention toward processes rather than objects—such as the death of phytoplankton in the acidifying terrestrial oceans and the genetic modification of plants—processes that we cannot reliably claim to have sovereign decision-making power over.[10] Thus, despite their distinct critical approaches, Nealon's plant theory steers us in the direction of Timothy Morton's "thing" or "hyperobject" (which resists localization and cannot be directly experienced).[11] In *Ecology without Nature*, Morton likewise gives an antibotanical definition of plants as "at bottom" algorithms.[12]

We agree that we cannot simply become a plant, in part because, as we have discussed in this book, plants are not somehow an "alternate" subjectivity: instead, they point to the dissolution of the human subject, insofar as the latter is ascribed a psychology, a consciousness, and a desiring individuality. Yet, we also underscore the idea that plants bring us back to finitude, pace Mancuso and Viola, not because they "possess" a body (this remains debatable, as Nealon argues) but because they appeal to and affect us. Trans performance artist, scholar, and poet Micha Cárdenas's question "If Guattari was serious about becoming woman, why did he not use his body as an experimental plateau?"[13] can also be applied to Nealon's reading of the rhizome. If all organisms are, deep down, a "machinistic network of finite automata," can bodies experiment with the very subject positions they inhabit? As feminist and queer new materialists thinkers have emphasized, desire, pleasure, and matter should be part of political strategizing in the era of climate emergency. Digital and algorithmic modeling of the physical and social world, including small-scale objects such as plants, can become allies to theorists and critics working to inject subjectivities, bodies, and materialities into ecological discussions. For instance, in her work on dissolving seashells in acidifying oceans—shells and botanical life-forms are similar in their smallness, their ability to provoke human curiosity and fascination, and their local yet dispersed nature—feminist ecotheorist Stacy Alaimo moves to articulate tiny beings and life-forms with massive events. As she notes in *Exposed*: "Paradoxically, while the temporal and geographic scale of the Anthropocene is vast, the scale of human responses to environmental catastrophe is often minute."[14] New materialist thought attempts to grapple with the agency of human and nonhuman, feminist, queer, and environmentalist subjects, with analyses that are oriented toward the minute and partial but situated inside large-scale events. In what follows, we explore the vegetal genealogy of this thought through literature and art, both looking back to an era of women's becoming plant that precedes Deleuze and Guattari and then moving forward into contemporary ecological art and fiction.

If we agree with Nealon's claim that in our current biopolitical situation we both cannot make decisions that are sovereign and cannot *not* make decisions, what does this portend about subjectivities to come? Speculative fiction and aesthetics, which combine an emphasis on narrative and voice with the capacity for dramatic scale-shifting, can provide responses to this question. Deleuze and Guattari's preference for the rhizome over the tree has much to do with the late capitalist context in which they write, to which they respond, and whose mechanisms they sought both to subvert and explain through a figure of a radical decentralization. We do not, however, believe that this concept does injustice to trees or, for that matter, has in itself made anyone particularly fond of rhizomatic root systems. The botanical particularity of plants can lead toward new speculative orientations, in its strangeness to the categories that organize our experience, and at the same time this particularity permits us to enter into affective contact with alien ways of organizing matter. The latter are not inevitably susceptible to abstraction or sublation into concepts; they retain their link to plant bodies and thus to botany, and they interrupt the schemata that we introduce to explain them, whether we like it or not.

Moreover, as we have argued throughout this book, while modern humans make use of plants, plants also participate in and shape modernity. Richard Doyle's "plant power" enters into human experience insofar as it produces hallucinatory experiences, new languages, or poetry, and Nealon's reminder that we share a territory with plants also encourages us to find in botanical speculation ways to render this intimacy a matter of experience. The greatest force of radical botany today may lie in its ability to help us imagine, think, and visualize ways of disassembling our socially and historically located subjectivities to open them up to forms of speculation that are both local and cosmic. Global heating, the accelerated annihilation of wildlife, and the destruction of the ecosystems, each a matter of daily experience, oblige us to contend with a profound interconnectedness among beings that likewise implies the dissolution of human subjectivity conceived as sovereign. Recognition of this entanglement is not only a philosophical proposition, or a set of ontological or aesthetic injunctions, but must be lived in concert with other beings. A key remit of ecological thought is to challenge the widespread tendency to resist and reject the interdependence of beings on one another, particularly from a state of imagined or real comfort made possible by capitalist consumerism or philosophical universalism. Can radical botany, as a politically oriented materialism that has long acted to generate speculative fictions, be operative in this large-scale paradigm, after the end of the "world," as some critics describe the end of phenomenologically stable, bounded subjective experiences?

As we saw in Chapter 5, Colette describes how affective identification with the time-lapse images of plants provokes physiological changes and a pattern of dancelike movement in spectators, particularly children. Colette's enthusiasm for this serious form of make-believe (which she partially recants as she realizes its antibotanical and antihumanist potentials) is echoed by Natasha Myers who, in her article "A Kriya for Cultivating Your Inner Plant," affirms precisely the imaginative and affective bond that links human bodies performing dance or yoga poses with plant bodies. Myers writes, "Here I invite you to cultivate your inner plant. This is not an exercise in Anthropomorphism—a rendering of plants on the model of the human. Rather, it is an opportunity to vegetalize your already more than human body. In order to awaken the latent plant in you, you will need to get interested and involved in the things that plants care about. Follow the plants. Let yourself be lured by their tropic turns and you will acquire freshly vegetalized sensory dexterities. Try this Kriya. Tree Pose will never be the same again."[15] What is the full scope of the injunction "Follow the plants!," sounded by Myers in an echo of Deleuze and Guattari?[16] Today, we can no longer hope to extricate ourselves from the double bind of the plant machine that frightened Colette.

To follow the plants effectively in the present, we need to put plant theory back into conversation with literature, art, and other media. While plant theorists productively excavate the ways in which plants act upon us and undo us in their connections to material processes (Doyle, Nealon), and examine how they can be our allies and partners in critiquing capitalist, colonial, racist, or sexist social orders (Myers), moments of outright transformation from human to plant are only fully available in literary and poetic writing, visual art, cinema, and, more recently, digital media such as virtual reality. In part, we need to acknowledge the feminist precursors of the rhizome, including women authors who both recognize and upend the association of woman and plant, to enable new alliances, political and material, to come to be. While contemporary theory has made great strides toward giving plants a specific "body" of their own—with all the implications that this move implies, including, explicitly or implicitly, granting plants political or at least ethical subjecthood—the fantasy of becoming plant retains links to a materialist, feminist, and queer tradition that prioritizes literature and art as spaces of metamorphic experimentation in which identities are in flux and marginalized subject positions may be foregrounded. Is this desire to experience a vegetal sensorium an organicist fallacy or a way of using the plant body as an experimental plateau to construct new subjectivities?

We trace here two modalities that shape the contemporary fictional engagement with becoming plant: first, the collapse of human subjectivity in(to) vegetality and, second, the dispersal of this limit-form into media that recuperate it otherwise and nonetheless. We show how fictions of plant-becoming, in literature and other media, activate the ontology of the plant as without interiority, emphasize its resistance or indifference to analogies with the animal or human, and highlight its ability to hover at the border of affective identification, thereby fueling feminist, materialist, and ecological political goals while also putting pressure on the ability of political and social structures to contain, represent, or account for these vegetal subjects. In these fictions, on the one hand, the plant preserves an alien aspect in its function as a bad copy of the human. On the other hand, the plant seems to lend itself to diverse forms of representation; it remains an amazingly flexible trope, a shape-shifter and a scale-shifter. The texts we examine oblige us to oscillate (once again) between these two possibilities. We refer to this oscillation as the speculative excess of plant fiction, wherein plant-becoming is the site of a predicament—one that is equal parts pleasurable and horrifying. Of course, the personification of plants has a long history, but what we call becoming plant in contemporary critical plant studies and plant theory is not a project of ventriloquism or prosopopoeia. The goal here is not to explore the ethical subjecthood of plants, including conjuring the world of a plant (if there is such a thing[17]), but rather to trace the material implications of our symbiotic or trans-corporeal relatedness to plants[18] and the indebtedness of our social categories to them. Twentieth- and twenty-first-century plant fictions join the critical power of plant theory to outright fantasy. If we take up the scenario of virtual transformation, seemingly against Nealon's cautioning words, it is because these attempts to become plant take us away from diagnosis and back into the otherwise messy domain of political and social speculation (replete with categories such as "woman" and "human"), which is also to say the realm of engagement—the site of radical botany today.

Before we begin, a word of caution: The feminist reinterpretation of "becoming plant" is a potentially uneasy one. The current posthumanist turn (whose roots reach back to the early modern fascination with the inorganic and nonorganic plant) allows us to begin to grasp the extent of plants' active presence within the technocratic capitalism of the present day. Nealon and Doyle suggest that we owe more to plants than we admit insofar as we participate in biopolitics, biopower, and the assemblages that make political participation possible. Still, despite our shared vulnerability to the crises of late capitalism, we cannot presume the affinity of plants for humans or for human interests.

Feminist Speculative Plant Fictions

Before Deleuze and Guattari immortalized the rhizome, and with it the line of flight, Anne Richter (1939–), a Belgian critic and author of fantastic literature and science fiction, published the short story "Un Sommeil de plante" ("The Sleep of Plants") in 1967.[19] This tale, one of a series of fantastic narratives that take as their protagonists nonhuman beings (including objects), tells the story of a young woman's transformation into first a potted plant and then a flowering tree.[20] The motif of human-plant transformation has, of course, long been present in fantastic and horror narratives—from Ovid and Cyrano de Bergerac to the pods—but with Richter human individuality is arguably fully traded for a new kind of vegetal subjectivity as the human-turned-plant protagonist generates new social assemblages, even if not without some disturbance to existing social bonds.[21] "Un Sommeil de plante" concludes with what might be called an unlikely moment of apotheosis, with the heroine, Ania, now fully transfigured as a tree and planted in the backyard of the young man who was once her fiancé, presiding over the family life that she initially rejects. Yet, Richter's story does not shy away from the potentially horrifying social effects that the heroine's transformation entails; becoming plant, for Ania, is both an act of feminist resistance to the family structures that constrain her and a withdrawal that, the narrator makes clear, is not without its ridiculous and disturbing aspects. (She plants herself in a pot that her mother dutifully vacuums around, "her face expressionless."[22]) The very first sentence of the story—"She lived like a plant"[23]—suggests more a state of pathological inactivity or complete submission then it does an act of transvaluation.

In her embrace of what initially appears to be the absolute passivity of a vegetable, the heroine succeeds in angering and terrifying those who expect her deference to patriarchal norms of conduct to be decorous and measured. In this sense, becoming plant in Richter's tale is an exploration of what it might mean to retreat fully from human social life in a radical refusal of human society. It resembles, then, madness—albeit a quiet and passive madness rather than one that demands acknowledgment or recognition. As she gradually takes on the attributes of a plant, Ania does not so much embody a new ethical relationship (to herself or to others) as she does a retreat from ethical choice or decision-making as such. She simply remains, without physical needs beyond water and sunlight, unmoored from the bonds of language and obligation. "She furled her leaves, lived on nothing. She was like a cactus, skin tender behind protecting needles, needing little water and light to live."[24] Ania transforms herself into not just any plant but a domestic plotted plant, usually contemplated (or ignored) in its mundane immobility. The large flower pot into which she plants herself is the banal object that becomes the means of her fantastic transformation. However, the potted plant that she becomes is transfigured by the end of the story, when its role in the family and the space it occupies dramatically change. Moreover, the potted plant's ability to grow into a tree and, finally, "put forth splendid blossoms"[25] is activated by Ania's own decision to withdraw from her role in her human family. In Ania's very refusal to move lies a kind of power, and not just to disturb or terrify her mother. "She decided to fall silent, and in silence, animate the world."[26] Ania emerges in her plant-form as a point of stillness in a world in motion: she is the sole "source of movement" even as she remains entirely immobile.[27] Therein lies the political and speculative significance of the story: the metamorphosis of the stubborn young woman from fiancée to tree compels a series of alterations (in her, in family life, in structures of kinship) that are as momentous as they are quiet. This transformation remains fantastic, enabled by the classical narrative trope of metamorphosis acting in concert with a willed withdrawal. Richter evokes no transcendental power (e.g., magic) outside of the operations of the story itself so that fiction is the sole medium in which the transformation occurs, thanks to the genre's specific properties and points of reference (including not just work by Ovid[28] but writing by women authors such as Jeanne-Marie

Leprince de Beaumont and Mary Shelley, who took their own interest in metamorphosis).

In "Un Sommeil de plante," Richter is not only building on but also revising a long tradition of identification of women with plants (often as passive and decorative objects)—a history that includes early entries in the plant horror genre such as Nathaniel Hawthorne's "Rappaccini's Daughter" (1844). At the same time, she sketches out what it might mean to assume not only the appearance of a plant but a vegetal subjectivity. Vegetal Ania represents a liminal consciousness or even a subject without consciousness. Richter's concern is thus not primarily with exploring the ramifications of a tradition that has used the analogy between women and plants to ratify or confirm structures of exclusion and exploitation. Instead, Richter moves into a fantastical and speculative mode in which a human might fully manifest and inhabit the position of vegetal alterity (and thus perhaps also cease to exist as a woman defined in reference to her status as daughter or bride). In doing so, Richter avoids universalist and metaphysical claims about the infinite generosity of both women and plants.[29] The heroine's apotheosis comes not at all as a form of self-realization or actualization, even though she is able, as a tree, to revitalize the family structures that she initially experiences as pathological and stifling. She presides over the marriage of her fiancé to another woman and is carried over the bridal threshold in her pot, preceding the bride herself. Here Richter's narrative retains a link to a more utopian tradition—indeed a more pastoral vision—that sees plants as restoring justice and order to a pathological human world, even as the story deploys the virtual medium of fiction to transform a woman into a plant, an effect diametrically opposed to pastoralism's nostalgic insistence on the natural.

Ania makes a choice, informed by a feminist critique of patriarchal family life, to exist as a plant rather than as a married woman. In this context, the decision to become a plant preserves some limited attachment to the dynamics of self-making, even as the feminine or indeed human self is *un*made and undercut. Ultimately, the story gestures toward the creation of virtual identities for which fiction may serve as an experimental plateau. It is only in fiction that a daughter and a bride can become a potted or garden plant, but this fantasy is not a mere escape. Rather, it inaugurates changes that serve to rip apart and open up social norms and family structures; it also prefigures recent discussions around the inclusion of plants (and nonliving things) in political thinking and political imaginaries, even as the human self dissolves or is exploded.[30] Still, at the edges of the narrative we see a kind of ambivalence around the heroine's passivity, best expressed in the scene describing what it means for her to pot herself, an act that upsets both her mother and her fiancé. Ania herself suffers from dissolution of the mother-child bond. Her existence in a pot takes her deeper into a kind of liminal consciousness that is barely recognizable to humans. After all, how exactly can political subject-building include becoming a plant (rather than, say, a emancipated woman, or a queer or trans person)?

Richter's protagonist chooses between the role of fiancée and that of potted plant, both domestic positions, even though the latter is an absurd one. It is the improbability of this choice, offered in fiction but not elsewhere, that opens up a speculative dimension within plant-human relations. Rather than cultivating an affective investment in the plant, the protagonist takes the place of a plant, thanks to the declarative power of the narrative. What this imagined becoming sets in motion is an oscillation between human subjectivity and plant-being in their joint animation, even as it imaginatively closes the gap between the two states of being. In other words, fiction is not just capable of taking us toward plants and into a form of engaged coexistence, but it also leads us away from political acts of decision-making and into the vicissitudes, contingencies, and risks that must accompany transfiguration.

Like Richter, U.S. speculative fiction author Ursula K. Le Guin (writing around the same time) explores a feminist political position that resonates with contemporary scholarship on both gender and the environment. Le Guin (1929–2018) poses the question of the human encounter with vegetal alterity—and the possibility of a human subject becoming integrated into a plant empire—in her 1971 short story "Vaster Than Empires and More Slow," where one of the main characters merges with alien plant life. Le Guin tells the tale of a group of humanoid interstellar researchers from a distant future who land on a planet inhabited only by plants, "a pure phytosphere"[31]: "Nobody here ate anybody else. All lifeforms were photosynthesizing or saprophagous, living off light or death, not off life. Plants: infinite plants, not one species known to the visitors from the house of Man. Infinite shades and intensities of green, violet, purple, brown, red. Infinite silences. Only the wind moved, swaying leaves and fronds, a warm soughing wind laden with spores and pollens, blowing the sweet pale-green dust over prairies of great grasses, heaths that bore no heather, flowerless forests where no foot had ever walked, no eye had ever looked. A warm, sad world, sad and serene."[32] The alien phytosphere seems at first strangely empty and still from the point of view of the humanoids, who are busy carrying out their scientific explorations and satisfying their curiosity. World 4470 (as it is named in bureaucratic documents) is depicted as "infinite," a mirror of the cosmos, and later, as self-maintaining, interconnected, and homeostatic. After some tests carried out in the lab on the spaceship, the scientists realize not only that all the trees on the planet are in contact with one another, thanks to nodules on their roots and pollen, but that all the plants on World 4470 are aware of and reacting to their presence. The phytosphere thus resembles the homeostatic feedback loop that was theorized by James Lovelock and Lynn Margulis and became famous as the Gaia hypothesis around the time of the story's publication. Since Gaia was conceived in terms of cybernetics and systems theory, it replaced the open epistemological systems of the sciences with a closed, autonomous model of the physical world (concretized in the Daisyworld computer simulation), a world defined by one goal: to return to its state of equilibrium. Le Guin's novella places this Gaia on an alien planet consisting entirely of plants while also taking direct issue with this closed, self-correcting model by opening it up to the vicissitudes of an affective exchange, in which plants and humans react to one another with fear.[33]

On World 4470, the humanoid crew discovers an ecosystem that is actively resistant to their efforts to plumb its depths. "Sentience without senses. Blind, deaf, nerveless, moveless. Some irritability, response to touch. Response to sun, to light, to water, and chemicals in the earth around the roots. Nothing comprehensible to an animal mind. Presence without mind. Awareness of being, without object or subject. Nirvana."[34] These plants at first seem strangely indifferent, yet powerful, and they eventually get the better of the colonizing scientific mission, even as they react to the intruders with terror. Crewmember Osden's report on World 4470 recalls Blaise Pascal's famous phrase from his *Pensées* (1670), indirectly cited by Le Guin—"The eternal silence of these infinite spaces frightens me"—in which Pascal names terror as the sole awareness of the divine available to him. The fear of a metaphysical (and mathematical) nature in Pascal turns, in Le Guin's work, into a fear of the otherwise imperceptible and unfathomable other, and it is the only connection that links the plants of World 4470 to the humanoid crew. In fact, this shared affect anthropomorphizes the plants, however slightly. It is the terror generated by and within the alien plants that gives them a world—albeit one that is vaster and slower than that of humans—and that sets in place an anthropological (and political) logic of difference and resemblance. The tale of World 4470 is not, generally speaking, a story of becoming, except in the case of one character: Osden. Yet for him, this becoming is the end of subjectivity and even of human life itself.

Osden is the only person among the crew who is willing to immerse himself in the phytosphere. He is described as "the first fully cured case of Render's Syndrome—a variety of infantile autism" of which the cause is a "supernormal empathic capacity," not restricted by species.[35] He is able to empathically intuit others' thoughts and feelings, although this extraordinary empathy is presented as a disability. Yet, Osden's connection to the sensing beings around him does not produce sympathy or affinity for them. Quite the contrary. He is instead disgusted and terrified by the emotions that swirl about him and from which he can have no respite—emotions that often have aggression, defensiveness, or anxiety as their origin, and that he cannot help but channel back to the crew. The affective feedback loop created by this exchange threatens to destroy the social existence of the humanoids on the ship, just as, on the planet, it produces reverberating waves of fear in humanoid and vegetal species alike. This fear, eventually magnified to terror, is the only dubious connection the humanoids have with the newly discovered world. When they leave behind Osden, who melts into the forest (and presumably tames the terror looping in the trees), the crew takes off, and we are left to question whether Osden's fate allows for the kind of ideal identification with the environment that eludes the other humanoids. Tomiko, one of the crewmembers, reflects that "[Osden] had taken the fear into himself and, accepting, had transcended it. He had given up his self to the alien, an unreserved surrender, that left no place for evil. He had learned the love of the Other, and thereby been given his whole self."[36] But this transcendence is at the same time a form of death. Osden, "left as a colonist," is recorded as one of two "losses" by the home planet.[37] Le Guin makes the imaginary humanoid society she describes operate according to the logic of colonization, one in which plants as she depicts them can have no active role.

The tale's title is drawn from Andrew Marvell's (1621–1678) well-known seventeenth-century poem "To His Coy Mistress" (published in 1681), a text that plays on the distinction between vegetal indifference to the passage of time—"vaster than empires and more slow"—and human desire, which propels itself energetically toward death. "Vaster Than Empires" anticipates the extended critique of twentieth-century imperialism (and of the Vietnam War in particular) that Le Guin would develop in her short novel from the same period, titled *The Word for World Is Forest* (1972). For both Marvell and Le Guin, vegetal interconnectedness—in its disregard for the constraints of time and space, constraints that humans alone seem to recognize as hemming in their efforts to dominate, seduce, and occupy alien worlds—appears in one sense as the counter to an imperialist drive that depends on conquests made and control rapidly achieved in the present. In this context, the crew's voyage represents the telos of modernity, insofar as their journey is a scientific mission with the aim of colonizing space, albeit at the price of the considerable jetlag it creates for the humanoids. Le Guin's plants appear to remain outside this modern project and to have only negative agency within it, since they exist within a temporality that renders the linear progression of modernity impossible. Similarly, in Marvell's poem the slow growth of "vegetable love" hypothetically allows for all desires to be satisfied (or left behind) by stretching out time beyond the life span of the poet and his coy mistress. In the end, "Vaster Than Empires" does not answer the question of what role humans might play as part of a vegetal world or cosmos that is atelic and not driven by desire. Le Guin's humanoid characters are left to their own finite devices to build equitable societies and, if they can, to avoid the depredations wrought by colonialism, war, sexism, and racism, all endemic to human societies.

For Richter, the choice to become plant resonates with contemporary new materialist preoccupations around establishing intimacy with plants, which her story realizes in the realm of fantasy. For Le Guin in "Vaster Than Empires," the utopian dimension of the phytosphere—its nirvana— is pushed to the outside of the human social realm, making becoming plant synonymous with disappearance or death, however blissful.[38] But there are other—sometimes downright absurd—versions of becoming plant that stress the trouble that plants bring to a politics that retains any attachment to choice or agency, which is to say any politics at all.[39] These narratives can also remind us of the way in which the plant is fully incorporated within late capitalist models of life, indeed providing a kind of model of its own for *human* experience, so that "reaching out" to the plant reminds us of our own contingency and the ineffectiveness and vulnerability of the modes of agency we cultivate. In her 2007 novel *The Vegetarian*, South Korean author Han Kang (1970–) also explores the alien, atelic existence of plants and the brutal effect of such an existence on people. Also suggesting an affinity with feminist new materialism (and perhaps with Michael Marder's insistence on a material and immanent plant soul), the young woman protagonist, Yeong-hye, withdraws from her family and the world, seeking redemption from a series of structural and individual acts of violence (including her own desire for meat) in the immanence of her body. Her first act of rebellion (at least as understood by her husband) is not to wear a bra. Soon, she decides to refrain from eating meat, seeking to stop the cascading effects of trauma. Rather than functioning as a political identity or a form of alliance-building, these decisions are part of the heroine's retreat into the "last resort" of the body (Kang's term), and they lead to or are accompanied by more violence. Eventually, Yeong-hye reacts to this violence by becoming a tree—a transfiguration that results in her institutionalization in a psychiatric hospital. Unlike Richter's tale, with its joyful concluding image of a tree presiding over the human family, *The Vegetarian* ends tragically.

Kang's novel thus uses the feminist figure of becoming plant as a point of departure but disengages this figure from any clear political program. Instead, *The Vegetarian* extends the effects of trauma across the heroine's immediate family. In this sense, Kang's work takes a dystopian perspective on the dynamics that also inform Anne Richter's narrative of human-plant metamorphosis.[40] The novel portrays the heroine's transformation in the form of three narratives told from the point of view of the members of her family: first her husband, then her video artist brother-in-law, and, finally, her sister. (The first narrative is in the first person; the second two remain in the third person.) Like Yeong-hye, the other narrators seek escape from the suffering inflicted by modern capitalism (as described by the brother-in-law) and within the family life the two sisters shared under the thumb of an authoritarian and patriarchal father, and, later, dominated by uncaring husbands (as depicted by the heroine's sister, In-hye). Unlike "Un Sommeil de plante," *The Vegetarian* does not inhabit the realm of the fantastic; the metamorphosis of the heroine is described by her family, society, and the narrators of the novel as a psychological illness. In the mental hospital to which Yeong-hye is eventually committed, she continues her effort to inhabit the body and subjectivity of a plant: standing on her head, refusing all food, consuming only water, and developing a flat and indifferent affect.

Yeong-hye's sister experiences these attempts at transformation not as a joyous affirmation of enmeshment but as a horrific loss, which she attributes to the violence caused by patriarchy, capitalist society, and even her own care for family members. This loss resonates with In-hye's portrayal not just of her sister but of the landscapes she inhabits or travels through:

> There's no way for In-hye to know what on earth those waves are saying. Or what those trees she'd seen at the end of the narrow mountain path, clustered together like green flames in the early-morning half-light, had been saying.
> Whatever it was, there had been no warmth in it. Whatever the words were, they hadn't been words of comfort, words that would help

her pick herself up. Instead, they were merciless, and the trees that had spoken them were a frighteningly chill form of life. . . . They'd just stood there, stubborn and solemn yet alive as animals, bearing up the weight of their own massive bodies.[41]

The novel conjures up the plant simultaneously as the object toward which desire, control, and concern are directed even in the absence of understanding—a silent victim—and as a mute but sensual place of embodiment. Yeong-hye's desire to become a plant appears as the last resort of the sentient being in a world structured primarily by anomic capitalist consumption and interpersonal violence. Yeong-hye experiences her own desire to eat meat as one instance among many of the traumas saturating modernity. In the depiction of these acts of violence and suffering, the novel generates its own sensorium in the form of dreams, art, and sexual encounters that cut across the characters.

The affirmative aspects of becoming plant highlighted by Richter are entirely absent here. The heroine of *The Vegetarian* instead terrifyingly evokes Michael Marder's vision of the plant as the fully exposed and vulnerable subject (as we discussed in the introduction) but without the possibility for ethical action that is opened up by this figure in Marder's thought. The feminine human body, like Marder's plant body, is singularly determined and bound to be violated by the symbolic meaning-making or social values imposed on it. Kang's novel shows that becoming plant is not a position that humans can assume and from which they can advocate. Instead of the plant as a moral guide, something like the powerful and insistent presence of vegetality arises in the novel, which abounds in hallucinatory and visionary effects, from Yeong-hye's dreams about her desire to eat meat to her brother-in-law's obsessive erotic fantasies (which culminate in painting her body with flowers and filming her), and her sister's memories of trauma on a forest path. Becoming plant here represents a terrifying disappearance into a sensory realm that is cold and unlivable, where human subjectivity falls apart, even as "plant power" seems to permeate the brother-in-law's psychedelic plant-inspired pornographic video art and the sister's cosmetics business that sustains her. Yeong-hye gives herself over to the mere sensation of the elements in what could be called a retreat into vegetality: "The dark lines of rain drill into Yeong-hye's body like spears, her skinny bare feet are covered in mud."[42] At the same time, plants' cold indifference, "stubborn and solemn yet alive as animals," makes their "merciless" unresponsiveness to human expressions of pain and pleasure particularly palpable. Becoming plant allows Yeong-hye to escape from a world of human experiences that has become too traumatic to bear. But this transformation carries with it its own violence both as a reminder of past trauma (that In-hye also begins to understand with her walk through the forest, where she attempts to hear "what the cold moisture had been trying to say") and as a mode of physical suffering in its own right.[43] Kang's novel explores the psychological effects on other humans of the embrace of vegetality by one woman (and perhaps also, more gradually, by her brother-in-law and sister), even as the speculative dimension of this embrace remains closed both to In-hye's family and to the reader of the novel. It is impossible to know if becoming plant, here, functions as a positive escape from an increasingly meaningless, monotone, and exhausting existence as a housewife under late capitalism or as a total submersion into this very meaninglessness, monotony, and exhaustion. Perhaps it is both.

Kang treats the silent traumas of modernity by exploring the limits of realism. Her novel remains largely in a realist mode even as it gestures toward plant horror through the narration of visions and fantasies that can either be seen as manifestations of plant power or as downright schizophrenia. In *The Vegetarian*, vegetal sentience is given a pulsating and powerful but also terrifying reality, thereby extending and enriching the legacy inaugurated by Poe's depiction of the horror of a human consciousness contaminated by vegetality. Kang's novel is not simply about the consequences of one woman pushed into a schizophrenic break with reality; it also addresses the consciousness-altering consequences of modernity itself. The reader is obliged to ask in what way modern existence transforms human experience generally into a vegetal one. The closing scene of the trees by the road, "green fire undulating like rippling flanks of a massive animal,"[44] evokes the image of a human transfigured by what the novel identifies as "dreams": hallucinations, affects, art, novels, and acts of consumption, all offering a subjective and deeply sensory reality.

Conversely, Yeong-hye's withdrawal may also be considered a failure to inhabit a subjectivity or to use her body as an "experimental plateau" by becoming plant; her transformation entails a complete loss of human identity that is approached with a sharp but poetic realism.[45] *The Vegetarian* blocks the affective identification with the plant that plant horror—from Poe to the *Invasion* films—has often made possible for the audience, gesturing toward a becoming plant that, as the novel shows, remains empty, not because it is merely imaginary, rather than organic and real, but because becoming plant does not on its own do away with the violence that riddles social life. The novel thus straddles realism and fantasy by revealing that "virtual reality" in a broad sense is not an escape from the body in pain. In the end, *The Vegetarian* collapses schizophrenic illness and becoming plant under late modernity. This insight will serve us in the last part of this chapter as we examine other recent turns to the virtual plant, where the use of visual media and "weird" fiction sustains and enables vegetal modes of becoming.[46]

Before and After Botany

Philip Kaufman creates his version of *The Invasion of the Body Snatchers* in part to show that globalized mass cinema could turn us all into consumers who find cultural homogeneity normal and even desirable. Of course, there is much irony inherent in Kaufman's critique, since post-1980s capitalism has shown itself to be very apt at incorporating (and calling into being) every form of individual desire, including even acts of revolt against capitalism, and Kaufman himself was participating in this new cinematic market. What remains noteworthy, nonetheless, is that the body-snatching pods instill desire in us even as they horrify us. That capitalism is itself consciousness-altering was one of the insights of *A Thousand Plateaus*, which later critics, writers, and artists have continued to explore, often with specific reference to the very powerful effects of vegetal agents on human perception and engagement with the world. Plants both respond to our desires and initiate them, as artist Jessica Rath stresses in her series *Ripe* (2013–2014), which investigates the relationship between human patterns of consumption and the evolution of fruit. In her *Paragon* sculptures of one of the first-known tomato cultivars bred for uniformity of shape and color, Rath layers her luscious-looking fruits with custom urethane auto paint finish to evoke the surface of a very different object of consumption: a Ferrari. Rath reveals the ways in which the tomato directly engenders human desires—including erotic ones, since the tomato blossom-ends suggest human orifices. These desires are themselves amplified and reshaped within a capitalist economy that prioritizes "surface" appeal through color and shape, attributes that themselves structure the genetic makeup of the cultivar. (Supermarket tomatoes tend to be less sweet because by selecting for color, breeders deemphasize sweetness, Rath notes.) When we view Rath's work, especially in the gallery where her sculptures and images appear in their larger-than-life physicality, we come face-to-face with the pleasures and perversions of consumption, as she allows us to recognize the extent to which our very desire for the tomato is in a basic sense not our own (and invariably goes awry). Most importantly, we confront the force of markets

Figure 13. Jessica Rath, *Paragon*, from Ripe 2013–2014. Custom urethane on ceramic.

and the animating power of the vegetal simultaneously. Rath reveals the vegetal agency existing, inextricably, within the powerful operations of capitalism and moves away from a representation of passive consumption to a focus on the animating capacities of plant matter for humans.

Jeff VanderMeer's 2014 Southern Reach trilogy likewise takes up the project of examining the transformative potential of the plant for humans, this time in the context of a new, "weird" speculative fiction that presents vegetality as a kind of prosthetic device that succeeds in reshaping our awareness. In his novels, literary narrative crosses over into the territory of virtual reality, as not only the characters but also their perceptions and experiences of self and world become augmented and altered by a process that has no regard for them and is only partially explained. Thus, VanderMeer updates several popular or "pulp" genres (his books draw on sci-fi and gritty detective fiction alike) for our contemporary moment, defined not only by environmental crisis but by technologies that shape reality and our perception of it. "Weird fiction,"[47] the generic term VanderMeer prefers, might be the literary equivalent of the various augmented realities and computer-generated images that technology offers. The trilogy describes how a mysterious "Area X" emerges as a result of an unknown event that took place about three decades before the inception of the story, without anyone, including the byzantine government agency called the Southern Reach, being able to account for it. The official explanation is that an environmental disaster produced Area X, but the "nature strikes back" plot centering on ecological apocalypse is quickly invalidated as the first volume of the trilogy unfolds: the landscape of Area X is both pristine compared to the corrupt agency tasked with investigating and containing it, and reveals itself as powerful and vigorously alive, able to infiltrate, transform, and deactivate the corrupt human world. What seems like nature quickly becomes something else, something ungraspable, in a manner reminiscent of Timothy Morton's hyperobjects, as critic David Tompkins has pointed out.[48] VanderMeer has given an ecological function to Area X, which is capable of invading and rendering unfamiliar or alien our world, thereby effectively ending it. The novels suggest that ecological thought can only proceed if we give up those deep connections we feel to the natural and social world. VanderMeer has been called "Weird Thoreau,"[49] but he is perhaps no Thoreau at all. Yet, the power of this ecological invasion of the human world, the ending of nature, relies on the plant as our entry point into the transformation. Despite its startling metamorphoses, Area X has the features of a coastal ecosystem (partially inspired by St. Marks National Wildlife Refuge on the northern coast of Florida and the rain forests of the Pacific Northwest).[50] It is packed full of fleshy and pulpy, vegetal or fungal matter.

With the trilogy, VanderMeer here and elsewhere has been committed to revising and enlarging the genealogy of speculative fiction (often in partnership with Ann VanderMeer) by studying its variants in diverse times and places, and by exploring the new potential of the genre in the twenty-first century. In search of the trilogy's literary forebears, we should consider, rather than Henry David Thoreau's *Walden* (1854), a tradition of speculative writing that includes not only Anglophone authors such as Poe but Francophone writers such as Anne Richter and Michel Bernanos (1923–1964). (The latter's work is cited by VanderMeer in a 2014 interview with Buzzfeed critic Lincoln Michel.) Bernanos's short tale *La Montagne morte de la vie* (written shortly before the author's death and translated into English as *The Other Side of the Mountain*) tells the story of two men shipwrecked on a mysterious island devoid of human inhabitants and populated in part by monstrous carnivorous plants. Through this reference, VanderMeer rejoins a Francophone tradition of speculative literature that activates the plant as a material (and materialist) figure to destabilize the assumptions of metaphysics and theology, and to question concepts of space and time as universal structures defining consciousness. Bernanos's story evokes Poe's tales of shipwrecks that drag their victims into a world whose inhabitants are all either mineral or vegetal and where the categories that shape human experience no longer apply; the protagonists of *The Other Side of the Mountain* explore a strange red island in which plants appear to genuflect before a physical (rather than metaphysical) divinity, a mountain with an eye set deep into one of its crevasses. The humans in his story are themselves gradually mineralized as they attempt to make their way off the island, in the end becoming statues still inhabited by the material memory of their suffering.[51]

VanderMeer takes up this and other experiments in altered consciousness that emerge from the dismantling of the *scala natura* that gradually reveals itself to have alien—and specifically vegetal—origins. The first plant that we encounter in the trilogy is a scrawl of words in English that has a vegetal form but turns out to be a luminescent insect-fungal symbiosis in the shape of vines and flowers. Upon closer examination, the vines reveal themselves as fungi "or other eukaryotic organism," "curling filaments" that resemble a "miniature forest."[52] They spell out words written by the Crawler, the gelatinous and deadly monster that is perhaps the reincarnation of the lighthouse keeper Saul Evans; the Gothic scrawl contains a sermon about the "seeds of the dead," which Saul used to preach before his move to the lighthouse (and prior to coming out as a gay man). Of course, these seeds take on a biological significance as both references to fungi and plants, and as living beings in their own right. Here vegetality actually reveals itself as a camouflage for a fungal organism, one that enters the biologist, producing a mysterious "shining" in her, as well as the Southern Reach itself, filling it with a telltale "rotting honey" smell. This organism is botanical only as a copy or a form of mimicry, and from this point on, we have reason to doubt the identity of everything that looks like a plant. The plant-in-appearance-only also reminds the biologist of the floral wallpaper in the house she shared with her husband. It is an aesthetic object, and draws the biologist to it, even as it reveals itself to be material and actively transformational.

In an article on weird fiction, VanderMeer describes his fascination with plants and explains it through a reference to contemporary microbiology and quantum mechanics. According to VanderMeer, "There are so many contradictions in who we are now as human beings—immersed in a culture of modern technology and 'progress' that still rates as primitive in the context of, for example, the way plants use quantum mechanics during photosynthesis."[53] The motif of a vegetal quantum mechanics recurs in the trilogy. In *Acceptance*, the third novel in the series, a mysterious plant turns up on the lawn of the lighthouse and, perhaps functioning as an energy-transfer device, becomes the catalyst for the lighthouse keeper Saul Evans's transformation:

> Only to see something glittering from the lawn—half hidden by a
> plant rising from a tuft of weeds near where he'd found a dead squirrel

> a couple of days ago. Glass? A key? The dark green leaves formed a rough circle, obscuring whatever lay at its base. He knelt, shielded his gaze, but the glinting thing was still hidden by the leaves of the plant, or was it part of a leaf? Whatever it was, it was delicate beyond measure, yet perversely reminded him of the four-ton lens far above his head. The sun was a whispering corona at his back. . . . Nothing existed in that moment except for the plant and the gleam he could not identify. He had gloves on still, so he knelt beside the plant and reached for the glittering thing, brushing up against the leaves. Was it a tiny shifting spiral of light? It reminded him of what you might see staring into a kaleidoscope, except an intense white. But whatever it was swirled and glinted and eluded his rough grasp, and he began to feel faint. Alarmed, he started to pull back. But it was too late. He felt a sliver enter his thumb.[54]

The "glinting thing"—perhaps part of the plant—functions like a wormhole, never fully explained, which either brings the aliens to Saul or, perhaps, carries Saul away from Earth into another world, where he becomes the Crawler. The plant, somehow linked to the powerful lens of the lighthouse, is a mechanism for moving light and energy. Its sharp glass or metallic texture suggests this thinglike quality, a mechanism of unfathomable scale that nonetheless draws us in, inspires human curiosity and desire.

The plant found by Saul might also remind us of the specimen brought back by the director as a "field sample" from Area X. Although it resembles a "normal" plant, it will not die and, as one character explains, "is not a plant," even though it behaves like one, looks like one, and engages in photosynthesis:

> "I don't think we're looking at a plant," Whitby says, tentative, at one status meeting, risking his new relationship with the science division, which he has embraced as a kind of sanctuary. "Then why are we seeing a plant, Whitby?" Cheney, managing to convey an all-consuming exasperation. "Why are we seeing a plant that looks like a plant being a plant. Doing plant things, like photosynthesis and drawing water up through its roots. Why? That's not a tough question, is it, really? Or is it? Maybe it is a tough question, I don't know, for reasons beyond me. But that's going to be a problem, don't you think? Having to reassert that things we think are the things they are actually are in fact the things they are and not some other thing entirely. Just think of all the fucking things we will have to reevaluate if you're right, Whitby—starting with you!" . . .

Later Whitby will regale you with information on how quantum mechanics impacts photosynthesis, which is all about "antenna receiving light and antenna can be hacked," about how "one organism might peer out from another organism but not live there," how plants "talk" to one another, how communication can occur in chemical form and through processes so invisible to human beings that the sudden visibility of it would be "an irreparable shock to the system."[55]

Whitby's definition of the plant as a device for energy transfer and camouflage is based on a set of scientific hypotheses.[56] Thus, plants in the trilogy become "things" that do other "things," and life dissolves into processes. If plants communicate, as Whitby seems to suggest, this does not make them more like us but deals an "irreparable shock to the system" and to our belief in a human (or animal) subjectivity.

All members of each mission that has been sent into Area X by the government have undergone hypnosis, supposedly because crossing the largely invisible boundary between worlds would otherwise be unbearable. They are thus unaware of crossing over, and at first everything seems normal to them, until Area X itself starts altering their bodies and minds. More generally, hypnosis functions as a disguise or mask by means of which the "normal" world covers up its own operations; it is also a metamorphosis in itself, and a numbing one. There is thus a chiasmic relation linking the authorities in the "normal" world that alter and manipulate the consciousness of their subjects to the transformations brought about by Area X. When the biologist inhales the spores in the tunnel, she realizes not only that hypnosis no longer works on her but that she perceives and experiences what others cannot. (Tellingly, the "tunnel" does not figure on any map, and, likewise, for those viewing the sky from Area X, the constellations are not recognizable, causing disorientation and a sense of being somewhere other than Earth.) On the one hand, characters become part of a hyperobject in which categories of human experience expire and give place to an ontology of things; on the other hand, marking VanderMeer's indebtedness to a longer speculative literary tradition, human consciousness is invaded by matter and textures that bring about open-ended transformations. The biologist surmises that any "hidden meaning" of Area X could only be "activated" "by the eye of the beholder," and indeed her new perceptive faculties function as such an activation device, one that mimics VanderMeer's prose in aiming to create new meaning or acceptance (the title of the last volume) of an ecological kind. In the trilogy, it is the descriptions of Area X as perceived by the characters, abounding in rich and strange details that are difficult for the reader to visualize, that constitute its most striking narrative realization and lead us away from the objectifying processes of our normal world and toward an awareness that we are part of something larger that changes us—an ecological experience par excellence.

As in Bernanos's story, in the trilogy organic or creaturely shapes tend to become disassembled and reassembled. Area X is a living or at least dynamically changing thing capable of powerful acts of mimicry; strange life-forms crop up in it, such as the dolphin whose human eye gives away its identity as something other than itself (perhaps a former expedition member); a tuft of grass shaped like a human being (and, upon closer examination, containing "human cells"); an owl, possibly once the biologist's estranged husband; monstrous shapes such as that of the Crawler; a living mountain with many eyes (the biologist's avatar); and Ghost Bird, a near-identical copy of the biologist, among others. There is *something* human in Ghost Bird—she carries memories and a compassion for humans even as she no longer is one—without this something making her fully human. The human statues in Bernanos and the human copies in VanderMeer both point toward the breaking down of organic life, yet in their materiality both remain alive, even if haltingly and hesitantly so. Subjectivity here is not only transformed but enters into a state of passivity—a "death that would not mean being dead," as the biologist puts it. This passivity is what makes new states of active being possible.

On the one hand, the biologist is the figure of an ecological awareness that enriches the self, thanks to her childhood encounter with a "complete" ecosystem growing in an overgrown pool in their backyard. On the other, as she puts it, she sees the Crawler's scrawl: "As we descended into the tower, I felt again, for the first time, the flush of discovery I had experienced as a child. But I also kept waiting for the snap." This "snap," when deep connections are severed, is an experience constitutive of the biologist's character. She grows up amid experiences of the failure of the family, including the loss of her beloved pool, and later persists in a marital life in which she is barely present. (Ghost Bird is initially the nickname given to her by her husband.) At the beginning of the trilogy, she goes off to look for her husband, but she is in many ways as disaffected a wife as she was a daughter. Her avatar Ghost Bird is totally severed from any family, albeit not entirely from the biologist herself, or from Control, the new director of the Southern Reach (and another character estranged from his mother and his job), who develops a fascination for her.[57] These moments of deep links being broken come to a head when the biologist finds herself profoundly drawn to the vegetal-fungal scrawls in the tunnel and is waiting for the snap to occur. The writing itself mimics a plant in its function as a copy of life that exerts a fascination (as would an arabesque line in dance or the motion of a plant in a time-lapse image) but is itself a place where the bonds, marital or familial, that seem to sustain human subjectivity in a patriarchal order are broken. One might be reminded of Charlotte Perkins Gilman's giant wisteria's deadly grip on mother and child as it simultaneously cradles their bodies; here, too, the values of a patriarchal society, upheld by the mother who tries to impose them on the daughter, can only be undone by the radical passivity of the plant. (The biologist, when viewing her mother's paintings as a child, thinks that they resemble wallpaper, perhaps indicating that in this case as well mother-daughter identification has come to a grinding halt.) While Gilman marks the passive agency of the plant as both a copy of and a challenge to patriarchal authority that provides a starting point for feminist critique, VanderMeer's scrawl will transform human subjectivity itself.

Defining the human, including our engagement in science and social and technological world-building, here takes place by way of the plant, in its quantum mechanical thingliness. This defamiliarization of the human is brought about in the trilogy by a plant device that operates to transfer energy—the "brightness" in the novel that enters, takes up residence in, and transforms the biologist and others. By confronting us with this device, the trilogy does not become antitechnological, for the novels want us to accept the unfamiliarity of the human, its transformation into something that we only partially recognize. Instead, VanderMeer uses the plant as an energy transfer device to mimic (and transform) the universalizing force of technologically oriented modernity. Plants then become prosthetic devices producing the changes and transfigurations charted in the novel, gesturing toward the cosmos as a giant computation that also withdraws from our efforts to construct knowledge about it.

The quantum mechanical theory of photosynthesis, inspired by VanderMeer's mining of scientific literature for fantastical ends,[58] organizes the narrative threads of the three novels. This particular mode of "plant power" loses the residual squishiness of the rhizome and moves a little closer to speculative realism's mathematical "outdoors"—until its disembodying power is enmeshed in narrative. VanderMeer's plant devices resonate with the notions of plant intelligence envisioned by Mancuso and Viola (whose ideas we discussed at the beginning of this chapter), and with Morton's "at bottom" algorithmic plants as modes of apprehension that are at odds with human ways of experiencing and knowing the world, but, in the story, contact with these devices does not make available to us an augmented version of our idealized selves, nor does it leave us caught in the chilly web of quantum physics. In the trilogy, the plant transfigures the human, and in this way it gestures toward the methods of feminist authors who have turned to becoming plant as a form both of galvanizing women and of allowing them to productively withdraw from a normative identity and thus from a political field that is dominated by patriarchal and heteronormative structures.

VanderMeer links "intelligence," a matter of science, technology, and philosophy, to the ability to make sense of or gather evidence, as we do in inhabiting a world and in the classic mode of detective fiction (inaugurated again by Poe). Taking up the conventional tropes of plant horror, the trilogy makes repeated reference to an alien landing, perhaps by a species whose planet has been destroyed by meteors. These aliens are technologically sophisticated, adept at camouflage, and capable of concentrating and moving energy (possibly by using plants or devices that look like plants) in ways that far surpass human capacities. Indeed, Area X may no longer be on Earth. Yet, the many clues offered in the story, each the result of detective work and scientific research conducted alongside each other, make up a puzzle that is never completed: Area X remains an unsolved or "inexplicable case." Indebted as VanderMeer may be to postmodernism, detective fiction is not simply dealt the blow of postmodern metacritique here. We never wrap up the investigation, not only because of the epistemological uncertainties presented by Area X but also because the novel brings to a halt identifications of a social and natural kind (e.g., with mothers and with plants) and uses this "snap" to gesture toward the possibility of new subjectivities and new worlds that do not assume the certainty and authority of old ones.

Thus, plants in the trilogy combine the cold objectivity of a device and the squishiness of biological matter engaging in forms of camouflage. VanderMeer activates a notion of the plant in which it retreats from our understanding and becomes a thing that we can barely conceive of, no longer anything we can "simply" experience as a plant. He also highlights how plants exert a passive power in their withdrawal from human social and ethical concerns, a withdrawal visible in the arabesque shape that appeals to us on a wallpaper, the fascinating fungal scrawl in the shape of vines, and the glinting plant in a garden. These plants disconnect the characters from their families and the ecosystems they inhabit, even as they connect them in other ways to one another.

VanderMeer tackles universalizing and cosmic themes (including the mathematical modeling of photosynthesis in quantum physics) while also tracing the effects of seemingly abstract processes in a local world of embodied subjects that are never fully available to being mapped and known. Although systems are "in shock" from the large-scale transformations at work in the exploded ecologies of Area X, lives go on in a surreal yet plotted way. VanderMeer uses the narrative devices of weird fiction to reveal the unfolding in individual lives of processes of energy transfer on a cosmic scale. We can thus detect in VanderMeer's work a strain of radical botany that resonates with the work of Guy de La Brosse (with whom our book begins): both authors represent the plant as one of the creatures or beings that sets us in contact with the universe by virtue of its ability to solicit our attention, affect, and desire at the same time as plants help us to acknowledge our finitude and the limitations of our perception and knowledge. Despite VanderMeer's preoccupation with plants as postbotanical quantum mechanical machines, the novels keep returning to the botanical images of fungal-vegetal scrawl that fascinate the biologist, the strange flower in the lighthouse keeper's yard, and the alien plant kept in the director's office. In all of these figures, the plant is a messenger of the shared intimacy of material beings but not in the ways we might expect or be comforted by. For VanderMeer, as for La Brosse, we are led by plants to discover a cosmos that lies beyond the boundaries of a properly (and exclusively) human mind or rationality, even as we often encounter these plants in seemingly humble and quotidian contexts.

In VanderMeer's work, the words on the wall of the "topographical anomaly," made up of "dimly sparkling green vines progressing down into the darkness" and forming a cursive scrawl, become the new sermon for the posthuman era.[59] When the biologist first reads the sermon and finds herself contaminated by the spores, the ability of language to signal, its referential quality, becomes a "conduit" for another kind of material "meaning"; this meaning passes across bodies and species, and it acts against our will and without our consent. Like the sermon, VanderMeer's poetic novels make out of "living matter"—including plants, fungi, rabbits, humans, and cats—those simulacra that give meaning to our existence. As the linguist Hsyu suggests, reversing the conventional hierarchy, there are means of communication in which language does not carry the sense but is only "the method of communication . . . the pipeline, the highway," while "the real meaning would be conveyed by the combinations of living matter that composed the words, as if the 'ink' itself was the message."[60] This strong materialist reading of the sign allows VanderMeer to steer clear of French philosopher Jean Baudrillard's rather Manichean approach to communication (devoid not only of authenticity but also of being).[61] Here the proliferation of copies, "bad" and "good," is where being happens, as becoming weird and, perhaps, becoming plant, but with the botanical plant poised on the brink of disappearing into a fast-changing ecosystem, morphing into a psychedelic vision, a machine, or a technology—a medium for experiences of the posthuman kind.

As the novels progress, Area X becomes a zone in which categories of space and time are fully destabilized, yet Ghost Bird and Grace, the center's African American assistant director (and maybe the only extant human character), nonetheless continue to navigate their environment without maps or clocks to guide them. In what is perhaps an allusion to Bernanos, they throw stones in front of them to define the parameters of their surroundings, and to register the invisible and perhaps no longer available boundary of Area X. Area X remains replete with perceptions, lives, characters, and evolving topographies whose contours do not take us back to a familiar or even brave new world but which can nonetheless be affirmed or, in the novel's terms, accepted. Changes happen not just to bodies but also in affects and perceptions.[62] VanderMeer thus leads us to a vision of hybridity that can be affirmed for an ecologically committed, pro-feminist, and anti-racist political project. His novels recall the emphasis that structures the *Invasion* films, with their focus on the "bad copy" that is nonetheless both alluring and transfiguring, but without the films' ambivalence around social hybridity or cultural difference. While most copies of former expedition members seem emptied of memories and affect, the character of Ghost Bird allows for the reader's affective participation in the transformations that the environment undergoes and that permeate the human protagonists themselves. (She is also both a human-fungal symbiosis and an exact replica of the biologist's cisgender Asian American human body.) Like a latter-day Matthew (Donald Sutherland) from the second *Invasion*, Ghost Bird and Grace guide us into a world of doubles, this time "so rich and full."[63] In this sense, the trilogy brings the plant horror genre up to date, situating it as part of a posthuman project.

Our reading has shown how VanderMeer makes plants and their avatars the mediators of the kind of becoming that is predicated upon the dissolution of the self as we conventionally recognize it. At the same time, these plants are not some mechanism for escaping our limitations but matter that has volatile and changeable organic qualities and relies on shape and mimicry. VanderMeer does not suggest, unlike some of the other authors and filmmakers we have discussed, that plants have been in control all along; nor does he posit the search for a future in a world of intense biopolitical vulnerability as a matter of somehow getting along with or even fully merging with plants. Instead, he stresses the way in which plants function like a language that, in the alien fullness of its materiality, works through us to transfigure us. While in the texts we examined earlier in the chapter, becoming plant was a way of unbecoming bride, colonizer, or individual in a modern capitalist, colonialist, and patriarchal society, here plants draw us in (in their strangeness) and exceed our social and ecological categories; they undo us as individuals and as part of an ecosystem.

This is a radical botany that is no longer strictly speaking on the botanical scale: it is a turn to the plant as our guide to the end of the world, moving us toward new political possibilities and responsibilities that remain unmapped. If Nealon's diagnosis of vegetal life today suggests that we are in the postbotanical realm of late capitalism, then VanderMeer's plants both mimic our blocked access to epistemological categories, to our "own" human world, and reveal the continued life of the plant and of speculative botany, accompanying us despite the transformations of scale we mutually undergo. Here our undoing via the plant is also the possibility of our engagement, as subjects emerging in its prosthetic grip, with a process that disassembles and reassembles us, an involuntary but accepted embrace of the vegetal modernity explored in the early modern texts with which we began. Will plants outlive us? Perhaps they have already done so.

ACKNOWLEDGMENTS

Over the course of our work on this project, we have accumulated many debts of gratitude. We thank the USC-Huntington Early Modern Studies Institute (EMSI) for funding our 2009 symposium titled "The Spiritual Life of Plants," which allowed us to initiate a generative and galvanizing conversation about plant life with prominent scholars of botany and the vegetal world, including Dominique Brancher, whose work on botany continues to inspire us; Tom Conley; François Delaporte; Eleanor Kaufman, whose remarks on plant horror sparked the initial idea for this book; and Pierre Saint-Amand. Funding from the USC College Commons initiative, led by Hilary Schor, helped us initiate productive and freewheeling cross-disciplinary discussions with Monique Allewaert, Sarah Feakins, and Timothy Morton. In his role as director of EMSI and divisional dean for the humanities at USC-Dornsife, Peter C. Mancall has offered us intellectual, moral, and institutional support; we are grateful for all three. Brooke Holmes and Jeff Dolven, organizers of "The Secret Life of Plants" symposium at Princeton in 2013 (with funding from the Interdisciplinary Doctoral Program in Humanistic Studies), made possible a whole host of intellectually sustaining connections and discoveries.

We have been lucky to benefit from a wonderful local community of colleagues and mentors who have been generous enough to read, comment on, and encourage our work together. They include Emily Hodgson Anderson, Arne de Boever, Olivia Harrison, Edwin Hill, Peggy Kamuf, Eleanor Kaufman, Akira Lippit, Béatrice Mousli, Panivong Norindr, Hector Reyes, Margaret (Tita) Rosenthal, and Sherry Velasco. As the project developed, this community expanded to become global. We will remain thankful for the support and guidance extended to us and to our work by Robert Barrett, James Cahill, Tom Conley, Timothy Holland, Timothy Morton, Vin Nardizzi, Jeffrey T. Nealon, and Caroline Trotot. Conversations with Stacy Alaimo, Sarah Benharrech, Amanda Jo Goldstein, Louisa Mackenzie, Blanca Missé, Anna Rosensweig, Helen Thompson, and Phillip John Usher have also immeasurably enriched our project. Jessica

Rath has been a source of inspiration, solidarity, and brilliant creative invention since we first met her in 2013. With her artistry and joy, Cati Jean has helped make sustained intellectual work possible. Anne Magruder has been a beacon of light and good humor. May, Leon, Annette, and Louis, Amanda and Caroline, thank you for being family.

We are most grateful to Tom Lay at Fordham University Press for his support of the project, to the anonymous reviewers of the manuscript for their thoughtful comments and engaged readings of our work, and to Nicole Wayland for her meticulous and efficient copyediting. We would also like to thank Wayne State University Press and the editorial team at *Discourse: Journal for Theoretical Studies in Media and Culture* for allowing us to publish as Chapter 5 a version of our article "From the Century of the Pods to the Century of the Plants: Plant Horror, Politics, and Vegetal Ontology," which first appeared in *Discourse* 34, no. 1 (2012): 32–58.

Without the intellectual contributions and labor of many wonderful graduate students, this book would not have seen the light of day. We would like to thank Alvin Chuan, Émilie Garrigou-Kempton, Brieuc Gérard, Katie Hammitt, Ennuri Jo, Jayson Lantz, Laurel Schmuck, Michaela Telfer, Lucille Toth, and Mary Traester for their hard work and excellent ideas. Undergraduates Ryan Green, Aidan Moravec, and Luna White lent their excitement and thoughtfulness to us in conversation and in the classroom. Colin Conwell helped us think through the linkage between plant and machine.

Of course, it is our partners and families who have carried much of the weight of this endeavor, for many years. Thanks are not enough for Alice Flather, Szabari Vera, Szabó Mária Éva (*köszönöm, tudjátok mit*), the late Szabari István (who knew his classificatory botany), Kate and Newell Flather (best in-laws), and Michael and Gesine Meeker, Elena Meeker, and Dave Tomkins.

We hope that Félix and Linnaea will enjoy this book one day, too, which was born, in a sense, with them.

NOTES

PREFACE

1. Qtd. in François Dosse, *Gilles Deleuze and Félix Guattari: Intersecting Lives*, trans. Deborah Glassman (New York: Columbia University Press, 2010), 9. From Gilles Deleuze, qtd. by Robert Maggiori in *Libération*, September 12, 1991.

2. Qtd. in Dosse, *Gilles Deleuze and Félix Guattari*, 10. From Gilles Deleuze, interviewed by Raymond Bellour and François Ewald in *Le Magazine Littéraire* 257 (September 1988).

3. However, since Deleuze was the one who molded the book into shape, inspired by and freely editing Guattari's letters, this sentence may have come entirely out of Deleuze's mind (and hands). Guattari, as attested by his journal, was less idealistic about the collaboration and felt hemmed in by the orderliness of Deleuze's academic writing style.

4. Adam Shatz, "Desire Was Everywhere," review essay of Dosse, *Gilles Deleuze and Felix Guattari: Intersecting Lives*, in *London Review of Books* 32, no. 24 (December 2010): 12.

1. RADICAL BOTANY: AN INTRODUCTION

1. The term "plant blindness" was coined by James H. Wandersee and Elisabeth E. Schussler in 1998 to describe the tendency of humans to overlook the life of plants; this tendency has effects on education as well as on many other dimensions of human culture and social life. See "Toward a Theory of Plant Blindness," *Plant Science Bulletin* 47, no. 1 (Spring 2001): 2–8.

2. The scholarly literature on botany is vast. Important historical studies of the emergence of modern botany include, notably, François Delaporte's *Nature's Second Kingdom: Explorations of Vegetality in the Eighteenth Century*, trans. Arthur Goldhammer (Cambridge, Mass.: MIT Press, 1982); Londa L. Schiebinger's *Nature's Body: Gender in the Making of Science* (New Brunswick, N.J.: Rutgers University Press, 2004) and *Plants and Empire: Colonial Bioprospecting in the Atlantic World* (Cambridge, Mass.:

Harvard University Press, 2007); and, recently, Lincoln Taiz and Lee Taiz's *Flora Unveiled: The Discovery and Denial of Sex in Plants* (New York: Oxford University Press, 2017).

3. In this book, we toggle back and forth between two senses of "affect" as the term is used in contemporary critical discourse. On the one hand, we invoke affect to refer to the new kinds of intimacies and feelings that encounters with plant life enable—forms of sensation and perception that have often been marginalized or overlooked. In this sense, we are indebted to affect theory as developed by and in conversation with the works of Eve Kosofsky Sedgwick, including her essay with Adam Frank, "Shame in the Cybernetic Fold: Reading Silvan Tomkins," in *Shame and Its Sisters: A Silvan Tomkins Reader* (Durham, N.C.: Duke University Press, 1995), 1–28. On the other hand, we also use affect to refer to the forces that a body exerts in its contact with another body, even one that remains unknowable to or ungraspable by it. Plants in this sense have an affective hold on humans. Here we are calling upon a Deleuzean and Spinozist strain in affect theory as developed in the works of thinkers such as Brian Massumi in *Politics of Affect* and John Protevi in *Political Affect*. Our use of affect thus reflects once again the profound oscillation of plant being between diverse categories, forms, and modes.

4. Timothy Morton, *Ecology without Nature: Rethinking Environmental Aesthetics* (Cambridge, Mass.: Harvard University Press, 2007), 185–186. For example, Amitav Ghosh, in his endorsement of nonhuman and non-Western agencies, reads ecological discourse through the lens of Romanticism. See Amitav Ghosh, *The Great Derangement: Climate Change and the Unthinkable* (Chicago: University of Chicago Press, 2016).

5. Robert Mitchell's reading of a "mutual atmosphere" in Shelley's poetry underscores and extends this Romantic idea into contemporary critical thought. See *Experimental Life: Vitalism in Romantic Science and Literature* (Baltimore: Johns Hopkins University Press, 2013).

6. Such claims are made in *The Language of Plants: Science, Philosophy, Literature* (Minneapolis: University of Minnesota Press, 2017), which stresses the idea that plants have something to tell us. We read in the introduction by Monica Gagliano, John C. Ryan, and Patrícia Vieira: "The language of plants has implications for ethics, politics, and sustainability" (xxii).

7. "Hence the epistemological precedence enjoyed by botany: the area common to words and things constituted a much more accommodating, a much less 'black' grid for plants than for animals; insofar as there are a great many constituent organs visible in a plant that are not so in animals, taxonomic knowledge based upon immediately perceptible variables was

richer and more coherent in the botanical order than in the zoological." Michel Foucault, *The Order of Things: An Archeology of the Human Sciences*, trans. Alan Sheridan (London: Routledge, 1970), 149. Originally published in French under the title *Les mots et les choses* (Paris: Gallimard, 1966).

8. In our use of this term, we are inspired by Mel Y. Chen's book *Animacies: Biopolitics, Racial Mattering and Queer Affect* (Durham, N.C.: Duke University Press, 2012), to which we will return.

9. Timothy S. Miller, "Lives of the Monster Plants: The Revenge of the Vegetable in the Age of Animal Studies," *Journal of the Fantastic in the Arts* 23, no. 3 (2012): 460–479. We see the Darwinian investment in plants as part of a much longer history that gives a vegetal foundation to modernity itself.

10. Stacy Alaimo deploys the concept of transcorporeality in *Bodily Natures: Science, Environment, and the Material Self* (Bloomington: Indiana University Press, 2010), and *Exposed: Environmental Politics and Pleasures in Posthuman Times* (Minneapolis: University of Minnesota Press, 2016).

11. We are thus writing a narrative of the emergence of modernity as not indebted solely to the instrumentalization of matter—the disenchantment model of which the limitations have been eloquently formulated by Jane Bennett (among others). See Jane Bennett, *The Enchantment of Modern Life: Attachments, Crossings, Ethics* (Princeton, N.J.: Princeton University Press, 2001).

12. Dominique Brancher, *Quand l'esprit vient aux plantes: Botanique sensible et subversion libertine (XVIe–XVIIe siècles)* (Geneva: Droz, 2015), 243.

13. Hallé explains, "Fundamentally a volume, an animal easily accommodates the effects of growth; little change in form is required. In terms of geometry, we can say that animals are homotropic during their development.... Essentially a surface, a plant would become too voluminous by remaining homotropic. Compromised in such a way, plants would not have enough photosynthetic surface and could not survive." As he points out, the ancient question of whether plants are motile is difficult to answer, since their relationship to space (fixed but capable of movement through growth and other means) is different from that of animals, as is their relation to time (since their lives can span longer periods). Plants not only move, despite our very limited ability to perceive this movement, but conquer space by means that are unavailable to animals. Francis Hallé, *In Praise of Plants*, trans. and foreword by David Lee (Portland, Ore.: Timber Press, 2002), 50. Originally published in French under the title *Éloge de la plante, pour une nouvelle biologie* (Paris: Seuil, 1999).

14. Hallé, *In Praise of Plants*, 33.

15. Jahren calls attention to the needs of plants, and while she occasionally individualizes and anthropomorphizes them, she also shows how the scientist moves between an objective practice of research and empathetic

care for the objects of this research. Take, for instance, her description of the treatment of "C6," a test plant that *"acted* differently from others while it grew." "C-6 was not part of a formal study, but it changed everything. I had journeyed over some kind of intellectual hill and I could see new territory. We instinctively claimed it using a new language, one that flouted the old rules. Not content with referring to C-6 as 'him,' we gave him a real name, 'Twist and Shout' (which later reverted to 'TS-C-6'). We got used to greeting him first thing in the morning and took a kind of sick satisfaction in his ability to endure the torments to which we subjected him. He didn't live for all that long, eventually becoming one of the casualties of Bill's horrible migraine headaches." Hope Jahren, *Lab Girl* (New York: Knopf, 2016), 261; emphasis original.

16. Daston and Mitman warn us that it is a mistake to anthropomorphize plants, in either of the two senses that Daston and Mitman identify: one that attributes "human" capacities to animals (e.g., the ability to suffer pain, plan for the future, and recognize familial ties) and another that amounts to "a form of self-centered narcissism" in which human beings see themselves in the natural world as if in a fateful mirror. Daston and Mitman suggest, like Brancher, that plants evade our attempts to recognize ourselves in them, but, unlike Brancher, they do not see this vegetal illusiveness as epistemologically productive. See Lorraine Daston and Gregg Mitman, *Thinking with Animals: New Perspectives on Anthropomorphism* (New York: Columbia University Press, 2005), 12–13.

17. Ibid.

18. See Stefano Mancuso and Alessandra Viola, *Brilliant Green: The Surprising History and Science of Plant Intelligence*, trans. Joan Benham, foreword by Michael Pollan (Washington, D.C.: Island Press, 2015). In his introduction to the English translation of *Brilliant Green* as well as in an article reviewing the controversial emergent field of "plant neuroscience," Michael Pollan emphasizes the imaginative leap necessary to formulate a theory of plant intelligence, which, because it cannot be linked to an empirically observable organ, remains marginal to scholarly research. Plants are thus at the forefront of questioning not only core "human" concepts such as intelligence and consciousness but also the value of positing an empirical locus for such entities. Michael Pollan, "The Intelligent Plant: Scientists Debate a New Way of Understanding Flora" *New Yorker*, December 15, 2013, https://www.newyorker.com/magazine/2013/12/23/the-intelligent-plant. For a nuanced discussion of plant faculties for nonspecialists, which does not embrace the idea of a "thinking plant" but argues instead on behalf of a "plant awareness," see Daniel Chamovitz, *What a Plant Knows: A Field Guide to the Senses* (New York: Scientific American/Farrar, Straus and Giroux, 2012).

19. See Antonio Damasio, *Self Comes to Mind: Constructing the Conscious Brain* (New York: Pantheon, 2010).

20. N. Katherine Hayles, *How We Became Posthuman: Virtual Bodies in Cybernetics, Literature, and Informatics* (Chicago: University of Chicago Press, 1999), 42.

21. Our reflections on the emergent vegetal subjects of posthumanism resonate with Maureen N. McLane's remark in her brilliant essay "Compositionism: Plants, Poetics, Possibilities; or, Two Cheers for Fallacies, Especially Pathetic Ones!": "Yet now that we seem to have arrived at a postnatural, posthuman/ist, posthistorical moment, it is worth wondering: are we postplant? I would say that in many ways I am preplant" (102).

22. Michael Marder, *Plant-Thinking: A Philosophy of Vegetal Life* (New York: Columbia University Press, 2013), 117 et passim.

23. Tondeur's herbarium contains not dry plants as a traditional herbarium would but the impressions of plants on a photosensitive surface. Michael Marder and Anaïs Tondeur, *The Chernobyl Herbarium: Fragments of an Exploded Consciousness* (London: Open Humanities Press, 2016).

24. The glow of Anaïs Tondeur's photographs takes us back to the 1980s and British filmmaker Derek Jarman's Dungeness Garden, which, located next to a nuclear power plant, works to "'queer'" natural spaces, to emphasize human agency vis-à-vis a precarious landscape that has been excluded from mainstream practices of "nature going," and to attest to a libidinal freedom located in the exclusion from normative society by embracing the wasteland. See Catriona Mortimer-Sandilands, "Melancholy Natures, Queer Ecologies," in *Queer Ecologies: Sex, Nature, Politics, Desire*, edited by Catriona Mortimer-Sandilands and Bruce Erickson (Bloomington: Indiana University Press, 2010), 331–358. Jarman's films, especially *The Tempest* (1979) and *The Garden* (1990), weave together images of plants and gardens with botanical metaphors to create queer natural-cultural spaces.

25. Marder and Tondeur, *Chernobyl Herbarium*, 44.

26. A similar argument is adopted, for example, in Matthew Hall's *Plants as Persons: A Philosophical Botany* (Albany: State University of New York Press, 2011), and the recent volume *The Language of Plants*.

27. Marder, *Plant-Thinking*, 27.

28. For an excellent comprehensive reading of Rousseau's botany, see Alexandra Cook, *Jean-Jacques Rousseau and Botany: The Salutary Science* (Oxford: Voltaire Foundation, University of Oxford, 2012).

29. See Nealon's review of *Plant-Thinking* in *Notre Dame Philosophical Reviews*, April 10, 2013, http://ndpr.nd.edu/news/39002-plant-thinking-a-philosophy-of-vegetal-life/.

30. Nealon is a great reader of subterranean currents in canonical literary and philosophical texts or, for that matter, rock music.

31. Jeffrey T. Nealon, *Plant Theory: Biopower and Vegetable Life* (Stanford, Calif.: Stanford University Press, 2016), 32. Citing *De Anima* in *The Complete Works of Aristotle: The Revised Oxford Translation*, ed. Jonathan Barnes (Princeton, N.J.: Princeton University Press, 1984), 424a30–35.

32. Nealon, *Plant Theory*, 33. Other examples of potentially positive (or at least productive) assessments of vegetal attributes that have no animal analogy include Derrida's tacit claim that plants are not alive and have no world, and, most importantly, Deleuze and Guattari's account of the rhizome, which we will discuss later on in this book.

33. The "mesh" is Timothy Morton's term for "the interconnectedness of all living and non-living things" in *The Ecological Thought* (Cambridge, Mass.: Harvard University Press, 2010), 28. For Doyle, plant superpower designates plant's "dense interconnection." Richard Doyle, *Darwin's Pharmacy: Sex, Plants, and the Evolution of the Noösphere* (Seattle: University of Washington Press, 2011), 8–9.

34. Nealon, *Plant Theory*, 14. For further discussion of Brian Massumi's use of this expression, see, for example, his *Politics of Affect* (London: Polity, 2015), 25.

35. Nealon, *Plant Theory*, xiv.

36. For Nealon, "the untainted moral high ground is impossible when it comes to thinking about meshes of life." Yet, he continues, "[u]ndecidability complicates decision; it doesn't make decision impossible" (*Plant Theory*, 117).

37. The term may also be used in a narrower sense to denote fiction with more serious, less "trashy" or "pulpy" ambitions that avoids easy recourse to fantasy worlds and escapism. This is how Margaret Atwood, for example, invokes the category. Science fiction "has monsters and spaceships," while speculative fiction "could really happen," suggests Atwood, although the distinction as she makes it has been questioned by critics. See Cecilia Mancuso, "Speculative or Science Fiction? As Margaret Atwood Shows, There Isn't Much Distinction," *The Guardian*, August 10, 2016, https://www.theguardian.com/books/2016/aug/10/speculative-or-science-fiction-as-margaret-atwood-shows-there-isnt-much-distinction.

38. Lucretius, *On the Nature of the Universe* [*De rerum natura*], book 1, line 73. Trans. R. E. Latham (New York: Penguin Books, 1951), 11–12.

39. Here the Latin "fabula" (fable, tale, story) replaces "speculation." See Gregory Flaxman, *Gilles Deleuze and the Fabulation of Philosophy* (Minneapolis: University of Minnesota Press, 2012).

40. On Haraway's critique of "corporeal fetishism," see McKenzie Wark, *Molecular Red: Theory for the Anthropocene* (London: Verso, 2016).

41. Bruno Latour, *Aramis or the Love of Technology*, trans. Catherine Porter (Cambridge, Mass.: Harvard University Press, 1996), ix. The term "scientifiction" was first proposed by Hugo Gernsback in 1916.

42. Donna Haraway explores "speculative fabulation" in her "Camille stories" about sympoiesis in *Staying with the Trouble: Making Kin in the Chthulucene* (Durham, N.C.: Duke University Press, 2016), 134–168. The narrative of Camille grew out of a writing workshop at Cerisy called "Narration spéculative" organized by Belgian philosopher of science Isabelle Stengers; Haraway emphasizes the shared authorship of the stories with filmmaker Fabrizio Terranova and psychologist, philosopher, and ethnologist Vinciane Despret. Terranova has since made a film titled *Donna Haraway: Story Telling for Earthly Survival* (2016). Haraway's Camille stories are decidedly utopian. They respond to crises engendered under the "Anthropocene, Capitalocene and Plantationocene" in order to offer remedies through a hands-on empirical making that is nonetheless bound to involve "terrible political and ecological mistakes" (136).

43. See, in this context, Ursula K. Le Guin's story "The Author of the Acacia Seeds and Other Extracts from the Journal of the Association of Therolinguistics," in *The Unreal and the Real: The Selected Short Stories of Ursula K. Le Guin* (New York: Saga Press, 2016), 617–625. Haraway underscores that Le Guin's story evokes "the art of the redwood or the zucchini" and the "transient lyrics of the lichen" (*Staying with the Trouble*, 213n3).

44. Jane Bennett, *Vibrant Matter: A Political Ecology of Things* (Durham, N.C.: Duke University Press, 2010).

45. This call is also present in work by ethnobotanists and anthropologists such as Eduardo Kohn and Debbora Battaglia. See Eduardo Kohn, *How Forests Think: Toward an Anthropology beyond the Human* (Berkeley: University of California Press, 2013).

46. Natasha Myers, "Photosynthesis: Theorizing the Contemporary," *Cultural Anthropology*, January 21, 2016. https://culanth.org/fieldsights/photosynthesis.

47. See, for example, Natasha Myers and Carla Hustak, "Involuntary Momentum: Affective Ecologies and the Sciences of Plant/Insect Encounters," *Differences: A Journal of Feminist Cultural Studies* 23, no. 3 (2012): 74–118.

48. https://culanth.org/fieldsights/photosynthesis. Emphasis original.

49. Natasha Myers, "Photosynthetic Mattering: Rooting into the Planthropocene," in *Moving Plants*, ed. Line Marie Thorsen, catalogue of

exhibition *Moving Plants*, July 1–September 25, 2017 (Naestved, Denmark: Roennebaeksholm, 2017), 123–127, see esp. 124.

50. With this phrase, we acknowledge our debt to the work of Donna Haraway's *Staying with the Trouble*.

51. Marder, *Plant-Thinking*, 35.

52. See Hallé's *In Praise of Plants*, 27–29, for an example of this view.

2. LIBERTINE BOTANY AND VEGETAL MODERNITY

1. For a scientifically informed overview of early modern cosmologies, see Marcelo Gleiser, *The Island of Knowledge: The Limits of Science and the Search for Meaning* (New York: Basic Books, 2014), 35–54. Copernicus's astronomical observations were limited in scope and number, as Geiser argues. At the same time, Copernicus not only resolutely propagated a sun-centered universe (albeit using mostly the knowledge inherited from Ptolemaic astronomy and its Islamic successors) but also "the attitude toward the reality of his vision: to Copernicus the Sun-centered cosmos was not simply a computing device but the true arrangement of the world. Astronomy was not a mere description of the cosmos but a mirror of physical reality as perceived by the human mind" (36).

2. Dominique Brancher, *Quand l'esprit vient aux plantes: Botanique sensible et subversion libertine (XVIe–XVIIe siècles)* (Geneva: Droz, 2015), 24.

3. Cyrano and La Brosse both participated in the intellectual communities that formed around Pierre Gassendi and the other *libertins érudits* of the famous Tétrade (Elié Diodati, Gassendi, Gabriel Naudé, and François de La Mothe le Vayer). Yet despite their noble titles and elite connections, they both worked in some sense at the margins of established philosophical, scientific, and (in the case of La Brosse) medical discourse. Rio Howard describes Guy de La Brosse as a "hybrid" thinker who left behind no intellectual progeny. Rio Howard, "Guy de La Brosse: Botanique et chimie au début de la révolution scientifique," *Revue d'histoire des sciences* 31, no. 4 (1978): 325.

4. The Aristotelian definition deprives plants in general of the attributes comprised by the animal and rational souls. However, Philip Ritterbush argues that Aristotle did not make a radical distinction between life-forms, and that he admitted the existence of zoophytes, intermediate categories of organic life (between animals and plants) that later, in the eighteenth century, became objects of great interest in the natural sciences. See Philip C. Ritterbush, *Overtures to Biology: The Speculations of Eighteenth-Century Naturalists* (New Haven, Conn.: Yale University Press, 1964), 58.

5. Theophrastus calls this way of being plant "striving."

6. Aristotle, *On the Soul, Parva Naturalia, On Breath* (Loeb Classical Library no. 288), trans. W. S. Hett (Cambridge, Mass.: Harvard University Press, 1957), II.iv.165.

7. It is this "privative" definition of the Aristotelian vegetative soul upon which Michael Marder bases his critique of metaphysics. As part of this critique, Marder deemphasizes the material vigor of Aristotle's plant as well as a long tradition of materialist botanical thought. See Michael Marder, *Plant-Thinking: A Philosophy of Vegetal Life* (New York: Columbia University Press, 2013).

8. As Aristotle explains, "And in animals the soul is naturally such, all natural bodies being the soul's instruments, those of plants in just the same way as those of animals, and existing, then, for the sake of the soul" (*On the Soul*, II.iv.166).

9. Brancher, *Quand l'esprit vient aux plantes*, 29–48.

10. Mel Y. Chen, *Animacies: Biopolitics, Racial Mattering, and Queer Affect* (Durham, N.C.: Duke University Press, 2012), 4.

11. We are inspired in this reading by Eleanor Kaufman's talk, given on Friday, April 10, 2009, as part of a symposium titled "The Spiritual Life of Plants." In her presentation, Kaufman stressed the proximity of vegetal and mineral forms of life in ancient philosophy.

12. Chen, *Animacies*, 2.

13. René Pintard, *Le libertinage érudit dans la première moitié du XVIIe siècle* (Geneva: Slatkine, 2000 [1943]), 196.

14. Ibid., 197. Pintard remains relatively unconcerned with the details of La Brosse's botanical work.

15. La Brosse's reputation for libertine behavior seems moreover to have been the stuff of considerable legend, and he is thought to have given libertine poet Théophile de Viau a narcotic prior to his death, in a sort of assisted suicide (according to Pintard). Still, relatively little is known about him.

16. Howard writes that *De la Nature . . . des plantes* is thus the "apologétique de la philosophie botanique que De la Brosse voulait appliquer en fondant le Jardin des Plantes" (308). He cautions against viewing La Brosse as a systematizer, however, since La Brosse insists strongly on the specificity and variability of plant life.

17. Edmond Rostand, *Cyrano de Bergerac* (1897) (Paris: Flammarion, 2013).

18. Pintard, *Le libertinage érudit dans la première moitié du XVIIe siècle*, 330.

19. The medieval world of herbals identifies the feral growth of plants with the ability of matter to take shape and considers plants as "indices" of

raw matter. In alchemy, visual representations depict the uncreated world as undulating, "foliate" vegetal matter. In the sixteenth century, Michel de Montaigne, who was not only an essayist and a bureaucrat but, together with his wife, also a rural estate owner and manager, makes use of an amalgam of Aristotelian and Epicurean notions to depict plants as earthly beings and infinitely mobile instantiations of matter. For the first insight, we are indebted to Lara Farina's essay "Vegetal Continuity and the Naming of Species," in *Postmedieval: A Journal of Medieval Cultural Studies* 9, no. 4 (2018): 420–431. For a more extensive analysis of Montaigne and vegetality, see Antónia Szabari, "Montaigne's Plants in Movement," in *Early Modern Ecologies*, ed. Pauline Goul and Phillip John Usher (Amsterdam: Amsterdam University Press, forthcoming 2019).

20. Guy de La Brosse, *De la nature, vertu, et utilité des plantes: Divisé en cinq Livres* (Paris: Rollin Baragnes, 1678).

21. The opening inscription of *De la nature* gives as the work's motto: "Truth, not authority" ("La vérité et non l'autorité"). La Brosse clearly prioritizes the use of individual reason and practices of experimentation over the application of principles received from earlier generations.

22. La Brosse, *De la nature, vertu, et utilité des plantes*, Book I. "Chap. VI: Si l'ame des Plantes est incorruptible," 43.

23. Didier Kahn, "Plantes et médecine, (al)chimie et libertinisme chez Guy de la Brosse," Bibliothèque numérique Medic@, April 2007. http://www.biusante.parisdescartes.fr/histoire/medica/brosse.php

24. La Brosse, *De la nature, vertu, et utilité des plantes*, "Au Liseur," n.p.

25. Ibid., Book I. "Chap. I: De l'excellence des plantes," 1–2.

26. Ibid., 7.

27. We thus argue that La Brosse diverges from the simple mirroring relation between the sub- and the supralunar realms that Michel Foucault identifies with early modern alchemy and the paradigm of preclassical botany. See *The Order of Things: An Archeology of the Human Sciences* (London: Routledge, 1970), 22–23.

28. La Brosse, *De la nature, vertu, et utilité des plantes*, Book II. "Chap. I: Definition de la plante," 161–162.

29. Ibid., Book I. "Chap. III: Queles plantes sont animees," 20.

30. Ibid., 21.

31. Francis Bacon, *Sylva Sylvarum, or a Natural History, in Ten Centuries* (1626/7), Cent. VII. Cap. 607 (London, printed by J. R. for William Lee: William Rawley, 1670), 126.

32. While Brancher is right to point out the animal qualities La Brosse attributes to plants, his plants, which are suspended somewhere between mineral things and animals, never quite emancipate themselves from the soil

and never quite become animals; they convey the affective life and animation of all matter. As Brancher suggests, La Brosse's vision of the emotional faculties of the plant brings the marvelous, even the extraterrestrial, close to home and, inversely, renders what seems to be the familiar events of the domestic garden a source of wonder, curiosity, and abiding fascination—the portal to another world in which matter is animated.

33. La Brosse, *De la nature, vertu, et utilité des plantes*, Book I. "Chap. I: Definition de la plante," 11.

34. Ibid., Book I. "Chap. XII: Du sexe des Plantes," 79.

35. Ibid., Book I. "Chap. VIII: Si les Plantes ont quelque sens," 53.

36. Ibid.

37. Ibid., Book V. "Dessin d'un Jardin Royal pour la culture des Plantes Medicinales à Paris: A Monseigneur le Tres-illustre et le Tres-reverend Cardinal, Monseigneur le Cardinal de Richelieu," 712.

38. Brancher, *Quand l'esprit vient aux plantes*, 63.

39. La Brosse, *De la nature, vertu, et utilité des plantes*, Book I. "Chap. VI: Si l'Ame des Plantes est incorruptible," 44.

40. The text La Brosse references is Joseph du Chesne's (Josephus Quercetanus), *Ad veritatem hermeticae medicinae ex Hippocratis veterumque decretis ac therapeusi . . . adversus cuiusdam Anonymi phantasmata responsio* (Frankfurt: Conrad Neben, 1605).

41. Citations in French may be found in Cyrano de Bergerac, *Les États et Empires de la Lune; Les États et Empires du Soleil*, ed. Jacques Prévot (Paris: Folio, 2004). The work is divided into two parts. The first one, *Les États de la Lune*, has been translated by Andrew Brown as *Journey to the Moon* (London: Hesperus Classics, 2007). We will provide our own translations for the second part, *Les États et Empires du Soleil*.

42. As defined by Jacques Prévot in *Cyrano de Bergerac romancier* (Paris: Belot, 1977), 59–67. Sylvie Romanowski similarly suggests that Cyrano's narratives might usefully be read as "savoir fiction" ("knowledge fiction"), capable of exploring and incorporating competing epistemological paradigms. See her essay "Cyrano de Bergerac's Epistemological Bodies: 'Pregnant with a Thousand Definitions,'" *Science Fiction Studies* 25, no. 3 (1998), 415.

43. Brown, *Journey to the Moon*, 34–36; Cyrano de Bergerac, *La Lune*, 77–80.

44. Didier Kahn has shown that among the contemporary trends of thought, mystical alchemy has no place in Cyrano's fiction (or only an ornamental one). Kahn, "Quelques notes d'alchimie et d'histoire des sciences à propos des romans de Cyrano de Bergerac," in *Lectures de Cyrano de Bergerac, Les États et Empires de la Lune et du Soleil*, ed. Bérengère Parmentier. (Rennes: Presses Universitaires de Rennes, 2004), 59–76.

45. Cyrano de Bergerac, *Œuvres comiques, galantes et littéraires de Cyrano de Bergerac*, comp. P. L. Jacob (Paris: Adolphe Delahays, 1858), 30. Translation our own.

46. Jean-Charles Darmon, *Philosophie épicurienne et literature au XVIIe siècle: Études sur Gassendi, Cyrano de Bergerac, La Fontaine, Saint-Évremond* (Paris: Presses universitaires de France, 1998), 214.

47. Ibid., 211–262.

48. Alexandra Torero-Ibad, "Les representations de la nature chez Cyrano de Bergerac," in *Libertinage et philosophie au XVIIe siècle: Les libertins et la science*, ed. Antony McKenna, Pierre-François Moreau, and Frédéric Tinguely (Saint-Étienne: Publications de l'Université de Saint-Étienne, 2005), 163–193. Elsewhere, Torero-Ibad writes: "Cyrano se propose d'appréhender tout ce qui est comme entièrement matériel, c'est-à-dire de concevoir le monde, la nature et les hommes qui en font partie à partir de la seule matière et de ses transformations." This materialism is pluralist, as Torero-Ibad points out. *Libertinage, science et philosophie dans le matérialisme de Cyrano de Bergerac* (Paris: Honoré Champion, 2009), 23.

49. Torero-Ibad explains, "Je considère pour ma part que la démarche de Cyrano est à la fois cohérente et pluraliste. Son unité consiste dans sa capacité à appréhender tout ce qui est comme entièrement matériel. Son pluralisme réside dans le fait que Cyrano ne propose pas de système alternatif" (*Libertinage*, 29).

50. *Semina* in the Latin does not refer exclusively to the seeds of plants; it can designate the germinal elements of all kinds of bodies, including inorganic ones, such as fire. As Hirai discusses, the term *semina* is also not specific to Lucretius; *semina* is an important term in Paracelsus and the Paracelsian tradition more generally. Hiro Hirai, *Le concept de sémence dans les théories de la matière à la Renaissance: De Marsile Ficin à Pierre Gassendi* (Turnhout: Brepols, 2005). The Lucretian deployment of the expression "seeds of things"—*semina rerum*—suggests an analogy between the atomic particles that make up the universe, in the Epicurean account, and the seeds of plants. The metaphoric centrality of the seed to the Lucretian rendition of Epicurean philosophy does not correspond to a particular interest in plant life on the part of Lucretius, although the Roman philosopher does make use of the agricultural resonance of the metaphor in his discussion of the generation of things on earth. Lucretius also uses other terms to refer to atomic particles, including "corpora," "figura," and "materia," but never uses the Greek word—*atom*—as Duncan Kennedy reminds us in *Rethinking Reality: Lucretius and the Textualization of Nature* (Ann Arbor: University of Michigan Press, 2002).

51. The very first steps toward a newly mechanist physiology of plants were made by Francis Bacon, Kenelm Digby, Descartes, and others in the seventeenth century, but Cyrano ignores these kinds of inquiries into the hidden life of plants.

52. While Cyrano's narratives are not sexual in the modern sense of rendering the permutations of human sexuality for the reader's delectation or edification, Cyrano plays on the connection, already present in Lucretius, between vegetal seeds and human "seed." Jonathan Goldberg points out, in *The Seeds of Things: Theorizing Sexuality and Materiality in Renaissance Representations* (New York: Fordham University Press, 2009), that "Lucretius's figuring of the atoms as bodies and seeds fills his poem with a sexual figuration of the atoms, which are, technically, not bodies at all" (3). Cyrano's plants are heavily libidinally invested.

53. Frédéric Tinguely shows that Cyrano treats scientific information with great liberty, as there could be no doubt in the scientific discussions of the time that an object thrown up into space vertically lands at the same place as the one from which it was launched, for it revolves with the revolving earth, rather than staying in one location while the earth revolves around it. See "Un libertin dans la Lune? De la distraction scientifique chez Cyrano de Bergerac," in *Libertinage et philosophie au XVIIe siècle: Les libertins et la science*, 73–84.

54. Brown, *Journey to the Moon*, 8; Cyrano de Bergerac, *La Lune*, 50.

55. Sexual reproductive power, in Cyrano, is a significant form of energy—a crucial force that brings bodies together and pulls them apart. In attributing the rotation of the earth to the force of the rays of the sun, the analogy dictates that seeds also set the plant body in motion—just as sexual longing can set the human body on a quest for satisfaction. As we will show later in this chapter, when the narrator Dyrcona eventually makes his way to the sun, he discovers plants that are constantly at work not only reproducing themselves and moving in space but stimulating human libido in all of its variability and (potential) eclecticism.

56. Brown, *Journey to the Moon*, 90; Cyrano de Bergerac, *La Lune*, 133–134.

57. Brown, *Journey to the Moon*, 106; Cyrano de Bergerac, *La Lune*, 150.

58. Brown, *Journey to the Moon*, 92; Cyrano de Bergerac, *La Lune*, 135. Although, in a somewhat self-contradictory fashion, the philosopher also affirms the specificity of each "fire" enlivening each kind of matter. The fire of cinnamon is different from the fire of sugar in its shape and number of angles. Brown, *Journey to the Moon*, 90; Cyrano de Bergerac, *La Lune*, 133.

59. Brown, *Journey to the Moon*, 18; Cyrano de Bergerac, *La Lune*, 60.

60. This drive to use fiction as a site of experimentation represents another inheritance from the Epicurean/Lucretian tradition, wherein atoms

are invisible and thus never simply given for observation but may be made visible and palpable in the effects of the poem on the reader.

61. Brown, *Journey to the Moon*, 78–79; Cyrano de Bergerac, *La Lune*, 122.

62. As Jean-Joseph Goux has discussed, Cyrano's moon is a place where the legitimacy of paternal authority, so carefully preserved on Earth, may be overturned, where the young discipline the old, and where "the father is no more than an animal of the male sex who serves his mate." Jean-Joseph Goux, "Language, Money, Father, Phallus in Cyrano de Bergerac's Utopia," *Representations* 23, no. 1 (Summer 1988), 108.

63. Bruno Roche, "Lucrèce et Cyrano: Stratégies libertines pour l'approche du Chant III du *De Rerum natura*," in *Libertinage et philosophie au XVIIe siècle: Les libertins et la science*, 211–223.

64. Brown, *Journey to the Moon*, 80; Cyrano de Bergerac, *La Lune*, 124.

65. This sort of indirect questioning of religious tenets was typical of seventeenth-century libertines, who were often crypto-atheists. On Cyrano's atheism, see Jean-Pièrre Cavaillé, *Postures libertines: La culture des esprits forts* (Paris: Anacharsis, 2011), 129–144.

66. On the symbolic rise of the French garden within discourses of national and domestic order in the second half of the sixteenth century, see Tom Conley, "Civil War and French Better Homes and Gardens," *South Atlantic Quarterly* 98, no. 4 (1999): 725–759.

67. It is unclear whether Cyrano is parodying Stoic-Christian ideas of human reason through the concession by the demon that plants lack immortality, or if he is anticipating mechanistic accounts of plants that, while inspired by atomism, ultimately postulated an immaterial spirit for human beings but not for plants. The English natural philosopher Kenelm Digby, for example, denied that plants were, strictly speaking, alive as they lacked their own principle of motion. See Digby, *Discourse Concerning the Vegetation of Plants* (London, 1661). See also Wilson, *Epicureanism at the Origins of Modernity* (New York: Oxford UP, 2008), 61.

68. Brown, *Journey to the Moon*, 81; Cyrano de Bergerac, *La Lune*, 124.

69. Ibid.

70. Similarly, La Brosse's desire to place the Jardin du Roi outside the walls of Paris for fear that the gases of the city would hurt the plants signals a worry that plants' needs are incompatible with those of the society (which uses them to generate heat for homes, forges, and glass manufactories) and expresses a desire to create an alternative, utopian space for both human and plant life. Brancher, *Quand l'esprit vient aux plantes*, 50.

71. Another instance of eroticization of the vegetal appears in the work of the seventeenth-century English poet Andrew Marvell. See Marjorie

Swann's "Vegetable Love: Botany and Sexuality in Seventeenth-Century England," in *The Indistinct Human in the Renaissance*, ed. Jean E. Feerick and Vin Nardizzi (New York: Palgrave Macmillan, 2012), 139–159. Unlike Cyrano, Marvell remains fully committed to an Aristotelian notion of the vegetal, and it is the nonsexual quality of plants that he (unconventionally) revalues as queerly erotic and alluring.

72. See our article titled "Libertine Botany: Vegetal Sexuality, Vegetal Form," *Postmedieval: A Journal of Medieval Cultural Studies* 9, no. 4 (2018): 478–489, for an analysis that emphasizes the libidinal aspects of vegetality in La Brosse and Cyrano, as well as the implications of a libertine model of vegetal sexuality for queer theory and gender studies.

73. Cyrano de Bergerac, *La Lune*, 218.

74. Ibid., 218.

75. Ibid., 219–221.

76. We note that in Jeffrey Jerome Cohen and Lowell Duckert's collaborative work the vortex becomes the very shape of ecocritique. See Cohen and Duckert, eds., *Elemental Ecocriticism: Thinking with Earth, Air, Water, and Fire* (Minneapolis: University of Minnesota Press, 2015), and Cohen and Duckert, eds., *Veer Ecology: A Companion for Environmental Thinking* (Minneapolis: University of Minnesota Press, 2017).

77. Cyrano de Bergerac, *La Lune*, 274.

78. Ibid., 218.

79. Ibid., 222.

80. We thus disagree with Michael Marder's argument that the shapelessness of plants, their lack of definite and fixed organs, can only be meaningful as a kind of bad infinity. See his *Plant-Thinking*. Cyrano inaugurates a materialist tradition that attributes positive, albeit fictional, powers to the metamorphoses of plant morphology. This legacy will eventually be revised in the form of Gilles Deleuze and Félix Guattari's rhizome, another materialist figure of dynamic vegetality.

81. Jane Bennett's reading of Walt Whitman's "shapes of sympathy" inspires this line of argumentation. See her article "Whitman's Sympathies," *Political Research Quarterly* 69, no. 3 (2016): 608.

82. Gassendi proposes that everything that occurs in the physical world is also produced, in no less material ways, in the imagination, thus making it hard to distinguish between real and virtual modes of being. Cyrano's fiction takes full advantage of the possibility of such confusion. See Darmon, *Philosophie épicurienne et littérature au XVIIe siècle*, 90–91.

83. In a recent article, Ann Delehanty and Tyler Blakeney discuss the progression in Cyrano's use of images of trees and fruit. They describe how Cyrano moves toward "a breakdown in categorical thinking" through his

deployment of the talking trees in the second narrative. We link up this use of trees to a more general investment in the plant as a figure of epistemological generativity. See Delehanty and Blakeney, "Textual Engagement with the Other in Cyrano de Bergerac's *L'Autre Monde*," *French Studies* 68, no. 3 (July 2014): 313–327. Erica Harth, in *Cyrano de Bergerac and the Polemics of Modernity* (New York: Columbia University Press, 1970), sees Cyrano's corpus as prefiguring (albeit not inspiring) the debates that marked the Quarrel of the Ancients and the Moderns that took place a generation after Cyrano's death.

84. Cyrano Bergerac, *La Lune*, 256.
85. Ibid., 257.
86. Ibid, 261.
87. La Brosse, *De la nature, vertu, et utilité des plantes*, Book I. "Chap. XV: De la generation des plantes," 101–113.
88. Cyrano de Bergerac, *La Lune*, 268.
89. We analyze the deployment of the plant as a human cultural archive in our review essay "Who Will Remember Us? Plants and the Archive: Dornith Doherty, 'Archiving Eden: The Vaults,' 2008–present; Jessica Rath, 'Take Me to the Apple Breeder,' Pasadena Museum of California Art, 2012," *Oxford Literary Review* 36, no. 1 (2014): 151–154.

3. PLANT SOCIETIES AND ENLIGHTENED VEGETALITY

1. "Objet de savoir et de poésie," as Emmanuelle Sempère calls it in "Le végétal chez Tiphaigne, image(s) ou modèle(s)?," in *Imagination scientifique et littérature merveilleuse: Charles Tiphaigne de La Roche*, ed. Yves Citton, Marinne Dubacq, and Philippe Vincent (Pessac: Presses universitaires de Bordeaux, 2014), 229.

2. For instance, Emmanuelle Sempère argues that, in the work of Tiphaigne de La Roche, vegetality becomes the "incarnation d'un monde vivant autonome, aux voies de reproduction non seulement mystérieuses mais visiblement variées, à la vitalité étonnante—admirable au point qu'on puisse le jalouser pour l'homme, l'égaler, l'imiter peut-être." Sempère, "Le végétal chez Tiphaigne, image(s) ou modèle(s)?," 212.

3. François Delaporte, *Nature's Second Kingdom: Explorations of Vegetality in the Eighteenth Century*, trans. Arthur Goldhammer (Cambridge, Mass.: MIT Press, 1982), 23.

4. Bernard de Jussieu was the uncle of Antoine Laurent de Jussieu (1748–1836); Bernard's unpublished work became the basis for Antoine Laurent's natural classification system, a counter to that of Linnaeus (and in certain regards more successful than the latter's).

5. Delaporte, *Nature's Second Kingdom*, 189.

6. Christophe Bonneuil and Jean-Baptiste Fressoz, *L'Évènement Anthropocène: La Terre, l'histoire et nous* (Paris: Seuil, 2016, 2nd revised and augmented edition), 224–226.

7. *Encyclopédie, ou dictionnaire raisonné des sciences, des arts et des métiers, etc.*, ed. Denis Diderot and Jean le Rond D'Alembert, article "Animal" (vol. 1, 468–474), Denis Diderot and Louis-Jean-Marie Daubenton, University of Chicago: ARTFL Encyclopédie Project (Autumn 2017 Edition), ed. Robert Morrissey and Glenn Roe, http://encyclopedie.uchicago.edu/, vol. 1, 472.

8. Ibid. Buffon describes these forms of plant movement in his *Histoire naturelle générale*, "Histoire des animaux," in *Œuvres*, ed. Stéphane Schmitt and Cédric Crémière (Paris: Gallimard, 2007), 137.

9. For a fuller and more speculative expression of this leveling as a form of interconnectedness, see the famous passages on "humus" and the block of marble from *Le Rêve de d'Alembert* (1769). See Diderot, *Le Rêve de d'Alembert*, ed. Colas Duflo (Paris: Garnier-Flammarion, 2002).

10. For discussions of the polyp and its significance, see Aram Vartanian's classic article titled "Trembley's Polyp, La Mettrie, and Eighteenth-Century Materialism," *Journal of the History of Ideas* 11, no. 2 (June 1950): 259–286, and, more recently, Nathalie Vuillemin's reconsideration of the polyp, with a focus on the reaction of the great naturalist René Antoine Ferchault de Réaumur to its discovery, in "Hydres de Lerne et arbres animés: Fantasmagories savantes autour du polype," *Dix-huitième siècle* 42, no. 1 (2010): 321–338.

11. Abraham Tremblay, *Mémoires pour servir à l'histoire d'un genre de polypes d'eau douce, à bras en forme de cornes* (Leiden: Jean et Herman Verbeek, 1744).

12. *L'Homme-plante*, with its focus on vegetal sexuality, has a kinship with part II of Erasmus Darwin's *The Botanic Garden* (1791), *The Loves of the Plants*, with its insistent rendering of plant marriages. In both cases, humanized or animalized sexuality is taken as the master term in the analogy.

13. Julien Offray de La Mettrie, *Man a Machine* and *Man a Plant*, trans. Richard A. Watson and Maya Rybalka (Indianapolis: Hackett Publishing Company, 1994), 85. Citations in French may be found in La Mettrie, *L'Homme-plante*, in *Œuvres philosophiques*, vol. 1, ed. Francine Markovits (Paris: Fayard, 1987), 293.

14. La Mettrie, *Man a Plant*, 79; La Mettrie, *L'Homme-plante*, 286.

15. La Mettrie relegates plants to the status of fully dependent bodies, thereby returning to the Aristotelian image of the adult plant as resembling an embryo in its dependence on the earth.

16. La Mettrie, *Man a Plant*, 91; La Mettrie, *L'Homme-plante*, 301.

17. La Mettrie, *Man a Plant*, 89; La Mettrie, *L'Homme-plante*, 299.

18. La Mettrie, *Man a Plant*, 83; La Mettrie, *L'Homme-plante*, 291. La Mettrie found refuge for a time in Frederick's court.

19. La Mettrie, *Man a Plant*, 83; La Mettrie, *L'Homme-plante*, 291.

20. Michel Foucault, *The Birth of Biopolitics: Lectures at the Collège de France 1978–1979*, ed. Michel Senellart and trans. Graham Burchell (New York: Picador, 2008).

21. Poe's narrator in "The Fall of the House of Usher," which we will discuss in Chapter 4, makes a reference to Holberg's novel. See Peter Fitting's "Buried Treasures: Reconsidering Holberg's *Niels Klim in the World Underground*," *Utopian Studies* 7, no. 2 (1996): 93–112, for a thoughtful discussion of Holberg's influence and predecessors, including Swift, whose *Gulliver's Travels* remains the much better-known work.

22. Calvino's novel is set on the eve of the Napoleonic conquest of Northern Italy, which ushers in both the demise of old aristocratic society and large-scale deforestation. The biopolitical regimes of both the aristocracy and the new Napoleonic state order are being resisted by the young baron, who moves up into the high branches of the trees that cover the region in a vast forest. From this perch, he organizes an alternative society of renegades, thieves, and peasants, and reads botanical treatises of the French Enlightenment. In the second half of the twentieth century, at a time when industrialization was reshaping post–World War II Italy, Calvino thus returns to the Enlightenment's vision of vegetal life as serving the anthropocentric goal of providing utopian or alternative social models for humans. Italo Calvino, *The Baron in the Trees*, trans. Archibald Colquhoun (Orlando, Fla.: Harcourt, 1959 [originally published in Italian in 1957]).

23. Although the Crakers are not plant-people in the strict sense of the term, we mention them here because Atwood endows them with some plantlike characteristics, including the chlorophyll their bodies contain (from their grazing diet) and the light citrus smell (a natural insect repellent) that they emit. Their innocent, nonpredatory behavior (avoiding even the cultivation of plants and thus also any form of trade) renders them both descendants of the tree people of Enlightenment fiction and absurd (to the point of being laughable) to the rugged human survivors who become their chaperones. With this trilogy, Atwood reinterprets, under late modernity and in a satirical key, the Enlightenment narrative of rationally built social utopias. See Atwood's *Oryx and Crake: A Novel* (London: Bloomsbury, 2003); *The Year of the Flood* (London: Bloomsbury, 2009); and *MaddAddam* (London: Bloomsbury, 2013).

24. Baron Ludvig Holberg, *The Journey of Niels Klim to the World Underground*, ed. and intro. James I. McNelis Jr. (Lincoln: University of Nebraska Press, 1960), 7. Originally published as *Nicolai Klimii iter subterraneum: Novam*

telluris theoriam ac historiam quintae monarchiae adhuc nobis incognitae exhibens e bibliotheca B. Abelini (Hafniae; Lipsiae: Sumptibus Iacobi Preussii, 1741).

25. Ibid., 7.
26. Ibid., 12.
27. Ibid., 17.
28. Ibid., 19.
29. Ibid., 26.
30. Ibid., 121.
31. Ibid., 7.
32. Ibid., 214.
33. Ibid., 222.
34. Ibid., 223.
35. Ibid., 33.
36. Ibid., 35.
37. As we see in Atwood's trilogy, mentioned earlier, for example. For a discussion of the notion of activation, see Yves Citton's *Lire, interpréter, actualiser: Pourquoi les études littéraires?* (Paris: Éditions Amsterdam, 2007). Citton advocates for interpretations that "activate" modern concepts and problems in older literary works.
38. Holberg, *The Journey of Niels Klim to the World Underground*, 78. See Heather Keenleyside's analysis of Lockean theories of movement, and their relationship to the action of the will, for a discussion of the capacity to stand still as connected to the capacity for thought itself. See Keenleyside, "The Rise of the Novel and the Fall of Personification," in *Eighteenth-Century Poetry and the Rise of the Novel Reconsidered*, ed. Kate Parker and Courtney Weiss Smith (Lewisburg, Pa.: Bucknell University Press, 2014), 105–133.
39. Holberg, *The Journey of Niels Klim to the World Underground*, 60.
40. Ibid., 60.
41. Ibid., 69.
42. Ibid., 73.
43. Ibid., 78.
44. Ibid., 36.
45. For a wide-ranging reflection on the connection between plants and divinity in western European philosophy, alchemy, and literature—along with a return to a vegetal utopics based at least in part on the notion of the angelic plant—see Emanuele Coccia's *La vie des plantes: Une métaphysique du mélange* (Paris: Rivages, 2016).
46. Holberg, *The Journey of Niels Klim to the World Underground*, 81.
47. Ibid., 83.
48. Ibid., 104.
49. Ibid., 104.

50. Ibid., 104–105.
51. Ibid., 104.
52. Ibid., 105.
53. Ibid., 105.
54. Klim is eventually banished from Nazar to "the Firmament," where he is carried by a giant bird, and where he finds lands populated by monkeys, musical instruments, and, ultimately, other humans.
55. We might see here the latent influence of Buffon, whose analogical model of the "moule intérieur" is, according to Thierry Hoquet, a means of thinking all generation (including that of animal life) in vegetal terms. See Hoquet, *Buffon: Histoire naturelle et philosophie* (Paris: Honoré Champion, 2005), 413. For a discussion of Buffon's influence on Tiphaigne (and of Tiphaigne's botanical and scientific intertexts more generally), see Sarah Benharrech's eloquent presentation of Tiphaigne in her critical edition of his *Questions relatives à l'agriculture et à la nature des plantes*, in Charles-François Tiphaigne de La Roche, *Œuvres complètes*, vol. 1, ed. Jacques Marx (Paris: Éditions Classiques Garnier, 2018), 593–633.
56. Tiphaigne de La Roche, *Questions relatives à l'agriculture et à la nature des plantes* (The Hague: Jean Neaulme, 1759), 89. Translation our own. Benharrech points out that in this treatise, Tiphaigne returns to the arguments made by seventeenth-century libertines around plant life, including those of Guy de La Brosse.
57. Ibid., 101.
58. Ibid., 102.
59. Ibid., 102.
60. Ibid., 62–64.
61. Ibid., 91–92.
62. Ibid., n.p. While the preface refers to Tiphaigne in the third person, it is unattributed. Benharrech affirms that certain similarities between the preface and the body of the text suggest that Tiphaigne is the author of both. (He repeated this gesture in other works.) Little is known about the exact circumstances in which the preface was composed, although an abridged version of the text was read in 1758 to the members of the Académie de Caen by Noël-Sébastien Blot, Tiphaigne's friend, an esteemed botanist in his own right, and the student of Bernard de Jussieu.
63. Ibid., n.p.
64. Here we might note Tiphaigne's interest in a medium that resembles a kind of proto-photography, as described in his novel *Giphantie* (1760), in which a civilization of superior beings invents a technology reminiscent of the first *héliographie* or photographic imaging (and communicates by means of a device that resembles a kind of television).

65. Tiphaigne de La Roche, *Amilec and Other Satirical Fantasies*, trans. Brian Stableford (Tarzana: Black Coat Press, 2011), 17. For the French original, henceforth we will be referring to Tiphaigne de La Roche, *Amilec ou la graine d'hommes qui sert à peupler les planètes*, Troisième édition, augmentée très considèrablement, À Lunéville, aux dépens de Chr. Hugene, à l'enseigne de Fontenelle, n.d. [1754], 4. The second part of this work is titled *Zamar, député à la Lune par Amilec, Grand Maître de la Manufacture des Graines d'Hommes* and appears as part of the same 1754 edition. We have also consulted Philippe Vincent's excellent and comprehensive modern critical edition: Tiphaigne de La Roche, *Amilec: Ou la graine d'hommes qui sert à peupler les planètes*, ed. Philippe Vincent, foreword Yves Citton (Mont-Saint-Aignan: Presses universitaires de Rouen et du Havre, 2012).

66. Stableford, *Amilec*, 17; Tiphaigne de La Roche, *Amilec*, part 1, 3.

67. Stableford, *Amilec*, 18; Tiphaigne de La Roche, *Amilec*, part 1, 5.

68. Stableford, *Amilec*, 18; Tiphaigne de La Roche, *Amilec*, part 1, 6.

69. Henceforth, we will stop using quotation marks around this term, whose history is, of course, likewise mined by Cyrano.

70. Satire is never entirely absent from the narrative and takes aim, for example, at debauched women whose seeds are drawn to those of fops.

71. Stableford, *Amilec*, 19; Tiphaigne de La Roche, *Amilec*, part 1, 9.

72. Stableford, *Amilec*, 19; Tiphaigne de La Roche, *Amilec*, part 1, 9.

73. Stableford, *Amilec*, 20; Tiphaigne de La Roche, *Amilec*, part 1, 14.

74. His notion of reproduction corresponds to the agamist theory, according to which the seed contains the preformed plantelet. Tiphaigne applies this idea to humans as well. François Delaporte points out that in the eighteenth century, it was the plant seed to which animal seeds (male or female) were compared (Delaporte, *Nature's Second Kingdom*, 114–115). This was thus one area in which the plant-animal analogy prioritized the plant.

75. Tiphaigne de La Roche, *Questions*, 50.

76. Ibid., 50.

77. Stableford, *Amilec*, 20; Tiphaigne de La Roche, *Amilec*, part 1, 14.

78. As Philippe Vincent has pointed out, at various moments in the text, Tiphaigne engages with both preformationist and epigenetic theories of reproduction. "Dans *Amilec* . . . ," he writes, "se retrouvent à la fois épars et mélangés comme dans un pot-pourri—la *satura* latine—tous les discours de savoir et les modèles scientifiques trainant de la génération" (108). Philippe Vincent, "Charles Tiphaigne et la génération dans *Amilec, ou la graine d'hommes* (1754)," *Féeries* 6 (2009): 107–115.

79. Stableford, *Amilec*, 24; Tiphaigne de La Roche, *Amilec*, part 1, 27–28.

80. Stableford, *Amilec*, 23; Tiphaigne de La Roche, *Amilec*, part 1, 14.

81. Stableford, *Amilec*, 23; Tiphaigne de La Roche, *Amilec*, part 1, 12.

82. Stableford, *Amilec*, 23; Tiphaigne de La Roche, *Amilec*, part 1, 13.
83. Stableford, *Amilec*, 54; Tiphaigne de La Roche, *Amilec*, part 2, 10.
84. Stableford, *Amilec*, 55; Tiphaigne de La Roche, *Amilec*, part 2, 12.
85. Stableford, *Amilec*, 33; Tiphaigne de La Roche, *Amilec*, part 1, 56–57.
86. Yves Citton, foreword to Charles-François Tiphaigne de La Roche, *Amilec ou la graine d'hommes qui sert à peupler les planètes*, ed. Philippe Vincent, 9–17, 11.
87. Yves Citton underscores the presence of a Foucauldian biopolitics in *Amilec*: "Depuis les Zaziris jusqu'à la plante, en passant par l'homme et le singe, ce que l'époque se représentait comme une 'grande chaîne des êtres' apparaît chez Tiphaigne comme une vaste hierarchie de niveaux d'exploitation, comme une vaste circulation d'influences, de manipulations et de contrôles." Ibid., 12.
88. Stableford, *Amilec*, 34; Tiphaigne de La Roche, *Amilec*, part 1, 60.
89. Stableford, *Amilec*, 35; Tiphaigne de La Roche, *Amilec*, part 1, 62.
90. Stableford, *Amilec*, 36–37; Tiphaigne de La Roche, *Amilec*, part 1, 68–69.
91. Stableford, *Amilec*, 37; Tiphaigne de La Roche, *Amilec*, part 1, 69–70.
92. Stableford, *Amilec*, 45; Tiphaigne de La Roche, *Amilec*, part 1, 97–98.
93. Gilles Deleuze and Félix Guattari, *What Is Philosophy?*, trans. Hugh Tomlinson and Graham Burchell (New York: Columbia University Press, 1994), 213.
94. Christopher S. Nealon, *The Matter of Capital: Poetry and Crisis in the American Century* (Cambridge, Mass.: Harvard University Press, 2011).
95. Margaret Atwood's MaddAddam trilogy shows clearly the paradoxes of social improvement where the restarting of society is only possible using biological weapons and genetic engineering, with results that are ambivalent if not horrifying substitutes for a social utopia.

4. THE INORGANIC PLANT IN THE ROMANTIC GARDEN

1. We will discuss this turn at more length in Chapter 7.
2. Deleuze and Guattari famously take up the question of inorganic life in *A Thousand Plateaus*: "This streaming, spiraling, zigzagging, snaking, feverish line of variation liberates a power of life that human beings had rectified and organisms had confined, and which matter now expresses as the trait, flow or impulse traversing it. If everything is alive, it is not because everything is organic or organized, but, on the contrary, because the organism is a diversion of life. In short the life in question is inorganic, germinal, and intensive, a powerful life without organs, a body that is all the more alive for having no organs." Gilles Deleuze and Félix Guattari, *A Thousand Plateaus: Capitalism and Schizophrenia*, trans. Brian Massumi

(Minneapolis: University of Minnesota Press, 1987), 499. Originally published in French under the title *Mille Plateaux: Capitalisme et Schizophrénie 2* (Paris: Minuit, 1980), 623.

3. As Joshua Dittrich argues, Deleuze and Guattari develop the concept of "inorganic life," of which the rhizome is one instantiation, from the "vegetal ornament" as analyzed by Wilhelm Worringer (1881–1965), a German art historian whose anti-Hegelian thought was a frequent reference point for them. Dittrich explores the fascinating genealogy of the concept of "inorganic life" and its origins in the *Lebensphilosophie* of the nineteenth and twentieth centuries. He reminds us that Georg Lukács critiqued Worringer's notion of inorganic life as an inappropriate flickering or shimmer (*Schillern*) between experience and life, subjectivity and objectivity. See Joshua Dittrich's "A Matter of Life and Death: Inorganic Life in Worringer, Deleuze, and Guattari," *Discourse* 32, no. 2 (Spring 2011): 256.

4. See, for example, Elaine P. Miller, *The Vegetative Soul: From Philosophy of Nature to Subjectivity in the Feminine* (Albany: State University of New York Press, 2002); Theresa M. Kelley, *Clandestine Marriage: Botany and Romantic Culture* (Baltimore: Johns Hopkins University Press, 2012); and Robert Mitchell's *Experimental Life: Vitalism in Romantic Science and Literature* (Baltimore: Johns Hopkins University Press, 2013).

5. For a nuanced analysis of Rousseau's and Bernardin's investment in botanical description, see Joanna Stalnaker's *The Unfinished Enlightenment: Description in the Age of the Encyclopedia* (Ithaca, N.Y.: Cornell University Press, 2010). As Stalnaker shows, Bernardin's conception of natural harmonies linking diverse categories of beings to one another and to their surroundings accords fantastic attention to even the most minute (and seemingly banal) forms of plant life. Ultimately, though, Bernardin views animal life as representing an even richer field of inquiry, even as he dreams of the study of the humble strawberry plant as opening a perspective onto its own marvelous world. For a broad, historical overview of a botany that regards human and plant sexuality as analogous and another, "queer" botany that breaks down this analogy, see Natania Meeker and Antónia Szabari, "Gender and Sexuality in Botanical Contexts," in *Macmillan Interdisciplinary Handbooks: Gender*, ed. Renée C. Hoogland (New York: Palgrave Macmillan, 2017), 159–169. See also our "Libertine Botany: Vegetal Sexuality, Vegetal Form," *Postmedieval: A Journal of Medieval Cultural Studies* 9, no. 4 (2018): 478–489.

6. For an important and engaging analysis of Rousseau's botanical investments, see Alexandra Cook, *Jean-Jacques Rousseau and Botany: The Salutary Science* (Oxford: Voltaire Foundation, University of Oxford, 2012).

7. Jean-Jacques Rousseau, *Rêveries du promeneur solitaire* (Vanves: Librairie Générale Française, 2001), 149. Translation our own.

8. Ibid., 142.

9. In a dialogue that he inserts in the first edition of his *Voyage à l'Isle de France*, published in 1773, Bernardin plays with the hypothesis that plants are, in fact, made of miniscule animal bodies—"animalcules"—that display their own collective interests, rationality, and even wisdom. Here, too, plant life (which takes on an explicitly animal form) represents a corrective to the viciousness of humans (and to the forms of violence propagated under colonialism in particular). Bernardin distanced himself from this piece—which he describes as a "libertinage de mon esprit" (cited in Vuillemin, 289)—but, as Nathalie Vuillemin has convincingly argued, its preoccupations return elsewhere in his corpus. See Vuillemin, "Les 'Entretiens entre un voyageur et une dame sur les arbres, les fleurs, et les fruits' de Bernardin de Saint-Pierre: Libertinage d'esprit ou naissance du propos critique?" *Studies on Voltaire and the Eighteenth Century* 7 (2005): 281–293.

10. Amanda Jo Goldstein brilliantly rereads Romanticism as itself taking up a Lucretian materialism in *Sweet Science: Romantic Materialism and the New Logics of Life* (Chicago: University of Chicago Press, 2017). If we follow Goldstein's reading, Poe's critique of the assumptions undergirding plant-human mutualism could be understood as a (pessimistic) expression of the Epicurean strand within Romanticism.

11. As Devin Griffiths shows in a recent article, Erasmus Darwin moves in his corpus from a male-dominated concept of generation to a mutualist one of "double affinity" in which vegetal and animal particles "embrace" each other. See Griffiths, "The Distribution of Romantic Life in Erasmus Darwin's Later Works," *European Romantic Review* 29, no. 3 (2018): 309–319.

12. In emphasizing the intimate connection between women and botany, Erasmus Darwin participates in a broader historical trend that cuts across Europe in the eighteenth century and extends into the nineteenth. While many women make significant contributions to botanical science during this period (and beyond), their work was not always or even regularly acknowledged. See our article "Une artiste en résidence dans le monde des fleurs: L'art botanique de Madeleine Françoise Basseporte," in *Autoportraits, autofictions de femmes à l'époque moderne: Savoirs et fabrique d'identité*, ed. Caroline Trotot (Paris: Classiques Garnier, 2018), 157–188, for a study of the French botanical illustrator Madeleine Basseporte, who experienced the paradoxes and contradictions of being a highly accomplished woman in a field dominated by men.

13. "Darwin . . . imagined a selective pornographic paradise. All sorts of female stereotypes—the virtuous virgin, the timorous beauty, the laughing belle, the dangerous siren—reflect the desires and prejudices of Georgian gentlemen. . . . In Darwin's fantasy garden, gods and goddesses might seem

to cavort freely, but in reality their amorous exploits are strictly controlled." Patricia Para, *Erasmus Darwin: Sex, Science, and Serendipity* (Oxford: Oxford University Press, 2012), 95.

14. Yet, in the speculative plant fiction of the seventeenth and eighteenth centuries, plants manage to instantiate both a proto-vitalist *and* a mechanist conception of materiality, often at the same time.

15. Thus, we diverge from the genealogy of early modern botany outlined by Francois Delaporte (in *Nature's Second Kingdom*), who argues that the eighteenth century relies most heavily on an analogical model between plants and animals, and that this model, retained from the classical period, remains epistemically distinct from the development of a plant physiology. In Delaporte's schema, with the arrival of physiology and biology, the analogy falls away. We argue that the eighteenth century, while indeed preoccupied with analogy, also resorted, in significant ways, to mechanistic and inorganicist models. Moreover, the plant-animal analogy does not always work to the advantage of the animal, as Poe clearly recognizes. The late eighteenth- and early nineteenth-century vitalisms that coexisted with an interest in plant physiology and, later, nascent biology retained a connection between the plant and the animal (and human) in the general understanding of life, even as they saw the mechanics of plant functions and structures as increasingly specific and even alien.

16. Poe, in asserting the power of vegetal sentience, rejects outright the aesthetics of the garden in favor of a terrifying and human-destroying tarn that cannot be reified and has no clear boundaries.

17. See Monique Allewaert, *Ariel's Ecology: Plantations, Personhood, and Colonialism in the American Tropics* (Minneapolis: University of Minnesota Press, 2013), 173–181.

18. Ibid., 180.

19. Lazzaro Spallanzani, *Opuscules de physique animale et végétale*, trans. and introduction by Jean Senebier (Geneva: Chez Pierre J. Duplain, 1787), 1:xix.

20. Hegel describes the "innocent indifference of plant life" in his analysis of flower religions. See Georg Wilhelm Friedrich Hegel, *Phenomenology of Spirit*, trans. A. V. Miller (Oxford: Clarendon Press, 1977), 420. On Hegel, see Miller, *The Vegetative Soul*, 119–147.

21. Hegel's contemporary Goethe disagreed and argued that plants contain their own principles of life—or metamorphosis—thereby lifting them up into the realm of poetry. Johann Wolfgang von Goethe, *The Metamorphosis of Plants*, trans. Douglas Miller, introduction by Gordon L. Miller (Boston, Mass.: MIT Press, 2009 [originally published in German in 1790]).

22. Some of these assumptions return today, albeit in the form of an admiration echoing the Romantic sentiment that celebrates and welcomes the otherness of the plant and its transformational power over human beings, in plant biologist Francis Hallé's statement that plants are "more completely immersed in their immediate modes of life" than animals and are independent of humanity for their survival on the planet (while humanity remains absolutely dependent on plants). Francis Hallé, *In Praise of Plants* (Portland, Ore.: Timber Press, 2002 [originally published in French in 1999]), 288.

23. Percy Bysshe Shelley, *Shelley's Poetry and Prose*. Norton Critical Edition, 2nd Edition, ed. Neil Fraistat and Donald H. Reiman (London: W. W. Norton, 2002), 288.

24. Ibid.

25. Ibid., 290.

26. Ibid., 291.

27. Ibid., 292.

28. Ibid., 294.

29. Ibid., 295.

30. "This haunting and haunted life of vegetation is often identified . . . as a slow torque or twining: the fond twisting of living ivy around its ruins; the bindweed that surrounds and drags the rose down to earth in *The Ruined Cottage*; or the 'serpentine/Upcoiling, and invertedly convoluted' trunks of Wordsworth's yew trees, which upcoil precisely by drawing an animal image ('serpentine') down into the deep time of trees." Mitchell, *Experimental Life*, 195.

31. Ibid., 201.

32. Ibid., 201.

33. Ibid., 202.

34. Shelley, *Shelley's Poetry and Prose*, 293.

35. It is significant that weeds are "classed" together with smaller, invasive forms of life; their vitality is contaminating and destructive rather than simply "innocent," as Hegel's vegetal indifference is, which suggests Shelley's greater investment in thinking difference at the core of life as such.

36. Edgar Allan Poe, "Marginalia," *Southern Literary Messenger* 15, no. 5 (May 1849): 292–296.

37. See Chapter 3, "Poe's Methodology," in John Limon, *The Place of Fiction in the Time of Science: A Disciplinary History of American Writing* (Cambridge: Cambridge University Press, 2009), 75.

38. For example, in *Ariel's Ecology*, Allewaert reads Poe's short stories as evincing a persistent fascination with what she calls "animism," an imbuing of nonorganic matter with spirit or mind that gives rise, in the *Narrative of Arthur Gordon Pym of Nantucket* (1838), to a "diversifying materialism." Allewaert, *Ariel's Ecology*, 119.

39. See Amanda Jo Goldstein's chapter titled "Growing Old Together: Lucretian Materialism in Shelley's *The Triumph of Life*," in *Sweet Science*, 136–165. For more on Poe's vitalism and the breakdown of a subject/object distinction, see Branca Arsić, "Materialist Vitalism or Pathetic Fallacy: The Case of the House of Usher," *Representations* 140, Fallacies Special Issue (Fall 2017): 121–136. Arsić discusses Poe's relationship to Richard Watson, with a special emphasis on the sensuousness and vitality of the mineral world—a vitality that Watson himself often frames in vegetal terms. She also affirms that "in Usher's world everything is a form of sensuous vegetal life" (133) but does not accord any particular prominence to vegetality as such in her general analysis of Poe's vitalism.

40. Limon, "Poe's Methodology," 79.

41. This exploration has political effects. For Allewaert, "Poe will play out his most radical possibilities by converting recognizably political concerns into natural historical and materialist ones." Allewaert, *Ariel's Ecology*, 178.

42. Limon, "Poe's Methodology," 76.

43. The arabesque is a recurring figure in Poe's writing. His *Tales of the Grotesque and Arabesque*, a collection of short stories, was first published in 1840, a year after "Usher" appeared. The arabesque style, present in Islamic art (and often used as orientalist ornament in the nineteenth century), is a form of vegetal ornamentation evoking the shapes of flowers and leaves. Patricia Smith, in her article "Poe's Arabesque," cites the *Encyclopaedia Americana* from 1831, which defines arabesque under the entry "grotesque": "Arabesques are flower-pieces, consisting of all kinds of leaves and flowers, real and imaginary." Deleuze and Guattari refer to the arabesque as the "nomadic line" or "gothic line" toward the end of *Thousand Plateaus*, citing Worringer, whom we mention early in this chapter. More recently, Laura Marks has explored the Deleuzean resonances of the arabesque in her book *Enfoldment and Infinity: An Islamic Genealogy of New Media Art* (Cambridge, Mass.: MIT Press, 2010).

44. In describing the invasion of the House of Usher by vegetal sentience, Poe may also, implicitly, be drawing on the descriptions of vital matter in the German scientist and explorer Alexander Humboldt's description of tropical vegetation and atmosphere and American botanical treatises, including William Bartram's, that describe the vitality of plants in the Americas as outsized and threatening in contrast with tamer European flora. Allewaert traces this genealogy of vitalist botany and suggests that these treatises grasp the significance of an ecology, made up of a diversity of life-forms, that does not privilege the human and could also destroy it. Allewaert, *Ariel's Ecology*, 51–82.

45. Herbert F. Smith, "Usher's Madness and Poe's Organicism: A Source," *American Literature* 39, no. 3 (November 1967): 379–389.

46. Sara Crosby, "Beyond Ecophilia: Edgar Allan Poe and the American Tradition of Ecohorror," *Interdisciplinary Studies in Literature and the Environment* 21, no. 3 (Summer 2014): 515.

47. Matthew A. Taylor, "The Nature of Fear: Edgar Allan Poe and Posthuman Ecology," *American Literature* 84, no. 2 (2012): 370. See also Matthew A. Taylor, *Universes without Us: Posthuman Cosmologies in American Literature* (Minneapolis: University of Minnesota Press, 2013).

48. Taylor, "The Nature of Fear," 369.

49. Edgar Allan Poe, *The Selected Writings of Edgar Allan Poe*, ed. Gary Richard Thompson. Norton Critical Edition (New York: W. W. Norton, 2004), 199.

50. Poe, *Selected Writings*, 200.

51. Ibid., 208–209.

52. Deleuze and Guattari, *Thousand Plateaus*, 239; Deleuze and Guattari, *Milles plateaux*, 292.

53. The latter is not the American poet James Gates Percival, as Harry R. Warfel shows in a short essay, but the English doctor Thomas Percival, who produced a brief treatise on the sensitivity of plants titled "Speculations on the Perceptive Power of Vegetables," dated 1785. Harry R. Warfel, "Poe's Percival: A Note on the Fall of the House of Usher," *Modern Language Notes* 54, no. 2 (February 1939): 129–131.

54. We find here an echo of Cyrano's portrayal of the angelic cabbage as infinitely generous with its "head."

55. Richard Watson, *Chemical Essays*, Vol. 5 (London: Merrill, 1789), 129–130.

56. Ibid., 116–117.

57. Smith, "Usher's Madness."

58. Poe, *Selected Writings*, 202.

59. Ibid., 209.

60. Ibid., 201.

61. As Arsić likewise affirms.

62. This is a move that has particular consequences, as Monique Allewaert argues, in the Americas, where new species were being discovered on an almost daily basis and vegetal life seemed to possess a force that it lacked in the European context. Poe's corpus reopens the question of the relationship between the colonial agency of plants—one in which the vegetal takes over other forms of being—and the American colonial enterprise. Allewaert, *Ariel's Ecology*, 54–63.

63. Poe, *Selected Writings*, 209.

64. Ibid., 113; emphasis original.
65. Ibid.
66. Taylor, *Universes without Us*, 15.
67. This interpenetration of plant and human consciousness evokes the arguments of Richard Doyle's *Darwin's Pharmacy: Sex, Plants, and the Evolution of Noösphere* (Seattle: University of Washington Press, 2011). Doyle argues that rhetoric and poetry are the products of contamination by "plant power," the profound interconnectedness of plants with everything.
68. Poe, *Selected Writings*, 204.
69. Cited in James June Schneider, dir., *Jean Epstein, Young Oceans of Cinema* (France: Bathysphère Productions, 2011), film.
70. Jeffrey Nealon, *Plant Theory: Biopower of Vegetal Life* (Stanford, Calif.: Stanford University Press, 2016), 95.
71. Poe, *Selected Writings*, 200.
72. Dennis R. Perry and Carl H. Sederholm, *Poe, "The House of Usher," and the American Gothic* (New York: Palgrave Macmillan, 2009), 19–32.
73. Charlotte Perkins Stetson Gilman, "The Giant Wisteria," in *New England Magazine* 4 (June 1891): 482.

5. THE END OF THE WORLD BY OTHER MEANS

1. *La Fin du monde*. Directed by Abel Gance (1931; Neuilly-Sur-Seine: Gaumont Vidéo, 2015).
2. For a comprehensive study of Gance's utopianism, with an in-depth discussion of *La Fin du monde*, see Paul Cuff's *Abel Gance and the End of Silent Cinema: Sounding Out Utopia* (Basingstoke: Palgrave Macmillan, 2016).
3. Flammarion's work is a source of inspiration for other authors of apocalyptic science fiction, including H. G. Wells and Olaf Stapledon, whose 1930 epic *Last and First Men: A Story of the Near and Far Future* (London: Methuen, 1930) owes much to *Omega* (New York: Cosmopolitan Publishing Company, 1894). The original French title of *Omega* was *La Fin du monde* (Paris: Ernest Flammarion, 1894).
4. Gance adopted Flammarion's *Omega* without much regard for the author's real agenda; the filmmaker simply borrows the plotline of the sudden appearance and impending impact of a comet along with the ultimate (and last-minute) failure to collide. In *Omega*, scientists confirm well before the impact that the comet will avoid the planet. This discovery allows the Chicago stock exchange to reopen as well as the calamity itself to be rethought in somewhat different terms. It is no longer an imminent disaster but one that unfolds into a futurity that can both be predicted (to some extent) through scientific research and cannot be measured in human lifetimes—a kind of deep time. In Flammarion's work, scientists are given

an opportunity with this missed cataclysm to present their theories of other ongoing catastrophes that will eventually destroy life on the planet, albeit in millions of years. (These include the slow erosion of dry land, a universal drought through the gradual loss of water, and planetary cooling.) These alternative disastrous visions reflect the central preoccupation of Flammarion, here and in other narratives (including *Lumen*), with an eschatology that eludes the grasp of human history. At the same time, Flammarion also invents a vantage point that allows for the narration of a very distant future by insisting on the reality of metempsychosis, in which the immortality of the soul provides continuity in a physical world of constant change, one in which no life-form endures.

5. Gilles Deleuze, *Cinéma 1: L'image mouvement* (Paris: Minuit, 1983), 88. He cites the first chapter of Henri Bergson's *Matière et Mémoire* (Paris: Félix Alvan, 1896).

6. With Gance, Dulac served as vice president of the first official ciné-club, *le Club des amis du septième art*. Jean Epstein and Abel Gance were friends, and Gance's wife, Marguerite, starred in *La Chute de la maison Usher*, directed by Jean Epstein (France: Films Jean Epstein, 1928). We will discuss this *long-métrage* at length later.

7. This image consciously evokes Akira Lippit's "electric animal" of early cinema, a figure that he investigates in his *Electric Animal: Toward a Rhetoric of Wildlife* (Minneapolis: University of Minnesota, 2008). We are inspired as well by Oliver Gaycken's "The Secret Life of Plants: Visualizing Vegetative Movement, 1880–1903," *Early Popular Visual Culture* 10, no. 1 (2012): 51–69. In this article, Gaycken remarks, in reference to Lippit's discussion of the relationship between animals and technologies of representation, that "the similarity of the relation of plants to imaging technologies suggests a possible extension of Lippit's argument, from electric animal to electric vegetable" (65). Gaycken discusses the development of time-lapse techniques for imaging plant movement and the application of these techniques in both scientific and popular contexts. Gaycken's focus is mainly on English and German sources; in this chapter, we emphasize the migration of these techniques into both philosophy and film in French contexts.

8. The tales of Flammarion and Poe are both important sources of inspiration for the filmmakers we will discuss. Although it will not be a central concern to us in this chapter, another book written by Flammarion, *Récits de l'infini: Lumen, histoire d'une âme; Histoire d'une comète; La Vie universelle et éternelle* (Paris: Marpon et E. Flammarion, 1892 [first published in 1872]), presents an imaginary plant society as part of its tour of the cosmos and the beings that inhabit it. This society echoes some of the concerns of the vegetal utopias of the eighteenth century.

9. The scientific photography and films of Jean Comandon are crucial sources for time-lapse images of plants and for the Albert Kahn archive more generally. French critics and writers Antonin Artaud, Blaise Cendrars, Colette, Louis Delluc, and Emile Vuillermoz all discuss time-lapse images of flowers and other plants in their writing. For a fascinating study of this period with a focus on the Albert Kahn archive, see Paula Amad's *Counter-Archive: Film, the Everyday, and Albert Kahn's Archives de la Planète* (New York: Columbia University Press, 2010). Amad explores the "rediscovery of the everyday" that occurred in French film theory and criticism of this period. Gaycken's article also presents an excellent overview of some of these developments. See also James Cahill's discussion of animal photogénie in "Animal Photogénie: The Wild Side of French Film Theory's First Wave," in *Animal Life and the Moving Image*, ed. Michael Lawrence and Laura McMahon (London: British Film Institute, 2015), 23–41, for a nuanced perspective on the debates around anthropomorphism and science film during this period.

10. Inga Pollman has described filmmakers and film theories on "the path of alienation" who "gave in to the temptation—and to its aesthetic and political potential—to cross-breed human, animal, and technological perceptions." Inga Pollman, "Invisible Worlds, Visible: Uexküll's Umwelt, Film, Theory," *Critical Inquiry* 39, no. 4 (2013): 782.

11. Time-lapse photography of plants provoked criticism at the time, as it does today. Philosopher Michael Marder writes of time-lapse: "[A] filmic alteration of the plant's temporal rhythms, made to coincide with that of human temporality, is not free of the residual violence that takes place whenever alien frames of reference are imposed on a given form of life. If we are to believe Heidegger's thesis that the meaning of being is time, then denying the plant its own time amounts to robbing it of its being." Marder, "The Place of Plants: Spatiality, Movement, Growth," *Performance Philosophy* 1, no. 1 (2015): 185–194. See also his *Plant-Thinking*, 103–104.

12. Gregory Flaxman interprets Gilles Deleuze's concept of philosophical science fiction or sci-phi as an embrace of the fact that there is no end of the world because the now has become too "volatile" (to use a word Flaxman borrows from sci-fi author William Gibson), and the future is in the now. Gregory Flaxman, *Gilles Deleuze and the Fabulation of Philosophy* (Minneapolis: University of Minnesota Press, 2012), 315.

13. The other two parts, never completed, were titled *Ecce homo* and *Le Royaume de la Terre*. About three hours of footage from *Ecce homo* survives. Cuff, *Abel Gance and the End of Silent Cinema*, 7.

14. Ibid., 106–108.

15. Ibid., 113.

16. Jean Epstein, *Jean Epstein: Critical Essays and New Translations*, ed. Sarah Keller and Jason N. Paul (Amsterdam: Amsterdam University Press, 2012), 294.

17. Jean Epstein, *Le Cinématographe vu de l'Etna* (Paris: Les Écrivains Réunis, 1926). Cited in Epstein, *Jean Epstein*, 289.

18. Epstein, *Jean Epstein*, 289–290.

19. Ibid., 292.

20. Ibid., 288.

21. Similarly, in another famous example, Epstein compares the mirror-covered stairwell of his Sicilian hotel to a device analogous to the camera.

22. Epstein calls the camera "this most beloved living machine." Epstein, *Jean Epstein*, 290. Vitality pervades the camera; it, too, is alive.

23. Oliver Gaycken, *Devices of Curiosity: Early Cinema and Popular Science* (Oxford: Oxford University Press, 2015), 53.

24. Francis Darwin, "The Movements of Plants," *Nature* 65, no. 1672 (1901): 43–44, cited by Gaycken in *Devices of Curiosity*, 55.

25. See Lippit, *Electric Animal*, 23 and 186.

26. Comandon made a series of instructional films focused on plants, including his 1929 *Mouvements des végétaux* (with Pierre de Fonbrune, produced by the Laboratoire de biologie du centre de documentation Albert Kahn and distributed by the Institut Pasteur under the title *La Croissance des végétaux*), which we will discuss at more length here. The precise date of *La germination d'un grain de blé*, possibly the film described by Epstein, is unclear. The Centre national du cinéma et de l'image animée (CNC) has a copy of Comandon's "Essais de prises du vues de végétaux en accéléré: Germination de graines de blé," tentatively dated 1924.

27. See Thierry Lefebvre's introduction to *Filmer la science, comprendre la vie: Le cinéma de Jean Comandon* (Paris: Édition Centre national du cinéma et de l'image animée, 2012), 40.

28. In this context, we can view Comandon's work as part of a French tradition of instructional science films with close affinities with surrealism. Moreover, Comandon's films were an influence on the work of Jean Painlevé (1902–1989), who collaborated with surrealists and mines the surreal elements of nonhuman life-forms to great effect in his own science films.

29. Philippe-Alain Michaud, "*Croissance des végétaux* (1929): La melancolia de Jean Comandon," *Association française de recherche sur l'histoire du cinéma*, no. 14 (October 1995): 266.

30. Michaud compares the movement of these plants to the gestures of women in Florentine Renaissance painting as analyzed by art historian and theorist Aby Warburg. This reading confirms the "ghostly" zoomorphism

and anthropomorphism that time-lapse imaging of plants is capable of producing. Ibid., 270.

31. Michaud does not mention the links between Comandon and the contemporary experimental filmmakers and theorists discussed by Lefebvre.

32. Jean Epstein, *Poésie d'aujourd'hui: Un nouvel état d'intelligence* (Paris: Éditions de la sirène, 1921).

33. Christophe Wall-Romana, *Jean Epstein: Corporeal Cinema and Film Philosophy* (Manchester: Manchester University Press, 2016), 19–20.

34. Epstein, *Poésie d'aujourd'hui*, 153; and Wall-Romana, *Jean Epstein*, 20.

35. Lippit, *Electric Animal*, 174. Berger explains that, insofar as the animal's expression prompts a recognition of our resemblance to it, we see ourselves, but insofar as the animal is silent and beyond understanding, we are confronted with the limits of subjectivity itself. Jean Berger, *About Looking* (New York: Vintage, 1980), 4–5.

36. Lippit, *Electric Animal*, 162–197.

37. Jean Epstein, *The Intelligence of a Machine*, trans. Christophe Wall-Romana (Minneapolis: University of Minnesota Press, 2014), 29.

38. Epstein, *Le Cinématographe vu de l'Etna*, 289.

39. Epstein, *The Intelligence*, 16.

40. Wall-Romana argues that, while a speculative realist inspired by early quantum theory, Epstein does not share the premise of contemporary speculative realists, according to which relations—always understood as human-centered—conceal the metahuman singularity of objects. In fact, Epstein is a wonderful thinker and liberator of objects and body parts, which are not simply isolated in close-ups as part of a dramatic plot but more importantly serve to disclose a new epistemology of affects crossing between human and nonhuman worlds. See Wall-Romana's introduction to *The Intelligence*, vii.

41. Wall-Romana, *Jean Epstein*, 74.

42. Epstein, *The Intelligence*, 23.

43. Ibid., 18.

44. Ibid., 23.

45. Ibid.

46. Jean Epstein, "Le monde fluide de l'écran," in *Écrits sur le cinema 1921–1953*, vol. 2: *1946–1953* (Paris: Seghers, 1975), 149, 401.

47. Ibid., 57.

48. Epstein, *The Intelligence*, 28.

49. Epstein, dir., *La Chute de la maison Usher* (France: Films Jean Epstein, 1928), 18:22.

50. Darragh O'Donoghue, "On Some Motifs in Poe: Jean Epstein's *La chute de la maison Usher*," *Senses of Cinema*, February 2004, http://sensesofcinema.com/2004/feature-articles/la_chute_de_la_maison_usher.

51. Malcolm Turvey glosses this process in a Bergonian vein, writing that *"The Fall of the House of Usher* . . . uses these techniques to escape the limitations of human vision and consciousness and penetrate behind the surface appearance of objects in order to reveal a Bergsonian, mobile reality that the characters in the film are unable to see. Indeed, the film can be interpreted as an allegory of Bergson's claim that 'to perceive is to immobilize' as well as immobilization's pernicious consequences" Malcolm Turvey, *Doubting Vision: Film and the Revelationist Tradition* (Oxford: Oxford University Press, 2008), 98.

52. Wall-Romana, *Jean Epstein*, 45.

53. Jean Epstein, dir., *Finis terrae* (Paris: Société générale des Films, 1929).

54. Flaxman, *Gilles Deleuze and the Fabulation of Philosophy*, 84–85. Flaxman references Deleuze's essay *L'île déserte: Textes et Entretiens, 1953–1974* (Paris: Minuit, 2002).

55. Tami Williams, *Germaine Dulac: A Cinema of Sensations* (Champaign: University of Illinois Press, 2014).

56. Germaine Dulac, "Conférence: Le cinéma est un art nouveau," Fonds Germaine Dulac 306-B20, La Cinémathèque française, Paris, 12. Translations of Dulac's texts all our own.

57. The term was first used by George Sadoul to identify the work of filmmakers Dulac, Louis Delluc, Epstein, and Marcel L'Herbier. Dulac herself uses the term in 1921 in reference to her own films. Williams, *Germaine Dulac*, 91.

58. Williams, *Germaine Dulac*, 154.

59. Germaine Dulac, dir., *L'invitation au voyage* (France, 1927).

60. Williams, *Germaine Dulac*, 148.

61. Germaine Dulac, dir., *Étude cinématographique sur une arabesque* (Paris: La cinémathèque française, 1929). Dulac's film, an intertext inspired by Debussy's "Two Arabesques," underlines the affiliation of the arabesque or arabesque style, also invoked by Poe, with vegetal patterns.

62. Germaine Dulac, dir., *Thèmes et variations* (1928) (Paris: Light Cone, 2016).

63. In an undated satirical poem that appears among her archival papers, Dulac reflects on the commodification of cinema and the genre's relationship to older forms of vaudeville, music hall, and even Rabelais's gaulois humor. Dulac does not appear to have developed a concept of lesbian libertinage—unlike Colette, whom she knew, who came closer to doing so—which is not entirely surprising given the appropriation of *libertinage* and *gauloiseries* into a heterosexual and nationalist framework. But the poem suggests Dulac's interest in "liberating" "notre vieux Cinéma" for a more joyous future: "Puisqu'enfin, libre, il va nous ouvrir des fenêtres/Sur un

monde trop gai qui nous attend pour naître." "Dans ce mot 'libertin,'" Fonds Germaine Dulac 272-B17, La Cinémathèque française, Paris.

64. Dulac, "Conférence," 10.
65. Ibid.
66. Germaine Dulac, "Le sens du cinéma," in *Écrits sur le cinéma (1919–1937)*, introduction by Prosper Hillairet (Paris: Paris expérimental, 1994), 162.
67. Dulac, "Conférence," 3.
68. Ibid., 8.
69. Ibid., 8–9.
70. Paula Amad suggests that Dulac made her own film of plant germination, *Germination d'un haricot* (1928), which she projected during her lectures. While this film is listed in multiple filmographies for Dulac and referenced by many critics, including Sandy Flitterman-Lewis in the magisterial *To Desire Differently: Feminism and the French Cinema* (New York: Columbia University Press, 1996), we have not been able to locate an actual copy. Images of beans germinating that were inserted into *Thème et variations* bear a striking similarity to sequences from Jean Comandon's film, a fact that in no way diminishes Dulac's accomplishment in this and other experimental works that use time-lapse images of plants.
71. Prosper Hillairet, "Un Cinéma sans entrave," in Dulac, *Écrits sur le cinéma*, 18.
72. Dulac, "Conférence," 16.
73. Ibid., 14.
74. Ibid., 12–13.
75. Ibid., 15.
76. Dulac, "Du sentiment à la ligne," in *Écrits sur le cinéma*, 88.
77. Dulac, "Correspondance générale," Fonds Germaine Dulac 433-B43, La Cinémathèque française, Paris. We were unable to acquire authorization to reproduce the sketches here, although we consulted them in the Fonds Germaine Dulac. Tami Williams eloquently discusses the correspondence with Napierkowska, and Dulac's relationship with her, in *Germaine Dulac*, 51–54.
78. Ibid.; Dulac, "Le sens du cinéma," in *Écrits sur le cinéma*, 164.
79. Dulac and Colette knew each other and apparently planned to collaborate at one point, although this plan was never realized. See Paula Amad, "'These Spectacles Are Never Forgotten': Memory and Reception in Colette's Film Criticism," *Camera Obscura* 20, no 2 (2015): 137.
80. Ibid.
81. Sidonie-Gabrielle Colette, "Cinema," in *Colette at the Movies: Criticism and Screenplays*, ed. Alain Brunet and Odette Virmaux, and trans.

Sarah W. R. Smith (New York: Ungar, 1975), 61. French citations may be found in Colette, Œuvres, vol. 3, ed. Claude Pichois (Paris: Gallimard, 1991), 101–104.

82. Amad, "'These Spectacles Are Never Forgotten,'" 137.

83. Dulac, "Conférence," 14.

84. Sidonie-Gabrielle Colette, "Secrets," in *Flowers and Fruit*, ed. Robert Phelps and trans. Matthew Ward (New York: Farrar, Straus and Giroux, 1986), 95–96. French citations may be found in Colette, Œuvres, 3:697.

85. Colette, "Secrets," in Phelps and Ward, *Flowers and Fruit*, 96–97. Colette, Œuvres, 3:698.

6. PLANT HORROR: LOVE YOUR OWN POD

1. Slavoj Žižek, "Part One," *The Pervert's Guide to Cinema*, directed by Sophie Fiennes (2006; London: P. Guide Ltd., 2006), DVD.

2. In this chapter, we will concentrate on the earlier versions of *Invasion*, in part because they follow Finney's narrative quite closely and in part because later iterations tend to move away from the vegetal theme. For a helpful discussion of the adaptation of Finney's work into the first *Invasion*, see Barry Keith Grant's *Invasion of the Body Snatchers* (London: British Film Institute, 2010). According to Grant, Finney wrote the story with filmic adaptation in mind. Plant horror is, in fact, a global phenomenon, as works such as *The Day of the Triffids* (a British film released in 1962 and based on the 1951 novel by John Wyndham), *Les Raisins de la mort* (made in France in 1978 by cult director Jean Rollin), and *Matango: Attack of the Mushroom People* (filmed in Japan in 1963 and directed by Ishiro Honda) suggest.

3. The original ending of the 1956 version was more pessimistic, with a shot of the hero screaming his warning at passing cars, whose occupants fail to hear him. The studio demanded a revision of the ending to a more optimistic conclusion in which the Federal Bureau of Investigation is notified of the threat.

4. Franco Moretti, *The Bourgeois: Between History and Literature* (London: Verso, 2013), 74–78.

5. We have seen in the previous chapters that plants had an earlier cinematic life in which they were the focus of both narrative interest and the camera's "eye." If Epstein and Dulac, as experimental filmmakers, were interested in time-lapse images of plants, it was precisely because they reveal to us that reality is not predictable or rational.

6. Moretti, *The Bourgeois*, 82.

7. Amitav Ghosh, *The Great Derangement: Climate Change and the Unthinkable* (Chicago: University of Chicago Press, 2016), 9. Ghosh cites Moretti on page 17.

8. This holds true, even as plant horror does not significantly challenge the racial ordering or segregation of society, a point that we will discuss in the fourth section of this chapter.

9. On paranoia and 1950s science fiction, see Vivian Sobchack's by-now classic study *Screening Space: The American Science Fiction Film* (New Brunswick, N.J.: Rutgers University Press, 1987); Cyndy Hendershot's *Paranoia, the Bomb, and 1950s Science Fiction Films* (Bowling Green, Ky.: Bowling Green State University Popular Press, 1999); Ray Pratt's *Projecting Paranoia: Conspiratorial Visions in American Film* (Lawrence: University Press of Kansas, 2001); and Grant's *Invasion of the Body Snatchers*. Don Siegel has suggested that the film includes a critique of U.S. totalitarian tendencies, particularly as embodied in the figure of Senator Joseph McCarthy. Alan Lovell, *Don Siegel. American Cinema* (London: British Film Institute, 1975), 46–48.

10. Timothy S. Miller, "Lives of the Monster Plants: The Revenge of the Vegetable in the Age of Animal Studies," *Journal of the Fantastic in the Arts* 23, no. 3 (2012): 460–479.

11. Miller rightly points to this fiction as ultimately reestablishing the hierarchy of being, called into question by Charles Darwin's theory of evolution, by firmly placing human beings back on top. Moreover, he stresses that the monster plant genre does this by reestablishing many other hierarchies, including racial, gendered, and social ones.

12. This earlier genealogy might help explain the fact that, as Miller notes, the first examples of monster plant fiction actually predate the publication of *On the Origin of Species* in 1859.

13. We first proposed this generic term in an earlier article version of this chapter. Since then, the notion of "plant horror" has been taken up by an edited volume titled *Plant Horror: Approaches to the Monstrous Vegetal in Fiction and Film*, ed. Dawn Keetley and Angela Tenga (New York: Palgrave Macmillan, 2016).

14. *The Thing from Another World*, *Day of the Triffids*, *Swamp Thing*, and *The Ruins* are all drawn from print sources and have been remade in various media.

15. The new vitality of the pods recalls the notion of "entelechy" as it was revived by early twentieth-century vitalist thinkers such as the French philosopher Henri Bergson and the embryologist Hans Driesch. The pods might serve in a sense as representatives of the kind of "vibrant" materialism discussed by Jane Bennett in her book *Vibrant Matter*. Jane Bennett explains that while entelechy in Aristotle is almost synonymous with the idea of actualization or completion—as in the actualization of a piece of marble as a statue, or of the human being in the act of thinking—later vitalist notions of

entelechy ("*élan vital*," in Bergson's case) carried with them connotations of freedom and political possibility. "Perhaps one of the reasons they enjoyed great popularity in America . . . was because they were received as defenders of freedom, of a certain open-endedness to life, in the face of modern science whose pragmatic successes were threatening to confirm the picture of the universe as a godless machine." Jane Bennett, *Vibrant Matter: A Political Ecology of Things* (Durham, N.C.: Duke University Press, 2010), 64.

16. Both writer Jack Finney and director Philip Kaufman admit to having been inspired by stories circulating in the press in the 1950s and the 1970s, respectively, about alien sources of life on Earth. They also both turn to the plant (primarily in the form of spores, seeds, and seedpods) to provide the figure of a vegetal being that reveals to us something fundamental about who we are rather than focusing on humanoid aliens arriving in spaceships. ("Why do we expect them to arrive in metal ships?" asks one of the protagonists of Kaufman's *Invasion*.) The vegetal dimension of these creatures forces audiences to formulate an image of a being that is both nonhuman and vital. Finney mentions an unspecified newspaper article as a source, while producer Robert Solo of the 1978 version refers to an article from *New Scientist* (November 1977). See Charles Freund, "Pods over San Francisco," *Film Comment* 15, no. 1 (January/February 1979): 25.

17. Timothy Morton, *The Ecological Thought* (Cambridge, Mass.: Harvard University Press, 2010), 17.

18. Jack Finney, *Invasion of the Body Snatchers*, 1st Scribner Paperback Fiction edition (New York: Simon and Schuster, 1998), 184–185; emphasis original.

19. "There is no real joy, fear, hope, or excitement in you, not any more. You live in the same kind of grayness as the filthy stuff that formed you," Miles exclaims to the pod replica of Budlong. Finney, *Invasion of the Body Snatchers*, 182.

20. Miller's argument about the function of monster plant narratives similarly underscores their power to reestablish the belief in human exceptionality.

21. Finney, *Invasion of the Body Snatchers*, 183; emphasis original.

22. Finney's seedpods, described in great detail, emit a "grey substance" that exudes from the pods "slowly as lava." Their opening resembles a "brittle leaf snapping in two"; they are composed of dry, lifeless or no-longer-living matter, bearing the stamp of inauthenticity. Finney, *Invasion of the Body Snatchers*, 98.

23. Ibid., 214.

24. Ibid.

25. Ibid., 134–135.

26. Ibid., 136.

27. See Neil Badmington's *Alien Chic: Posthumanism and the Other Within* (London: Routledge, 2004) for a reading of this "defining lack" as the marker of the boundary between human and inhuman.

28. As we shall explain later, the films focus in on images of vegetal matter as uncannily alive—from the rendering of "moving lava" to the uterine depiction of the pods.

29. Sobchack, *Screening Space*, 125; emphasis original.

30. Kaufman's version also makes ample use of sound effects that, as the makers of the film explain in their commentary, were in part created by squishing vegetables, in part by slowing down the recording of a fetal heartbeat obtained from the director's pregnant wife.

31. In a banal sense, plants are everywhere; they function as the material support for a whole variety of media, including the printed word. In plant horror, the ubiquity of plants themselves becomes an object of fascination, forcing us to reflect on the monstrous urgency of our need of them by focusing in on their monstrous need of us. Film gives them substance, even as they provide the very substance of the film itself.

32. Thus, we disagree with Jennifer Jenkins's claim that "[u]nlike the automata of E.T.A. Hoffman's stories—and films from *Metropolis* onward—Becky's double is neither seductive nor appealing" (488). The pods are attractive not as humanoid automata but as vegetal others. We agree with Jenkins as she contends that "pods ooze goo and a foamy web-like substance reminiscent of the moss that covers the House of Usher" (490); here we see the influence of a speculative tradition originating with Poe, who himself chronicles the fascination of humans for their own vegetalized selves. Although Jenkins argues that the *Invasion* of 1956 engages in a critique of marriage as a powerful tool of social normativization, she only identifies this subversive potential in the early scenes where Miles and Becky both act as transgressors (in that they are flirtatious and sexual as opposed to asexual and married); however, she does not see the pods as subversive but only as agents of homogeneity. See Jennifer L. Jenkins, "Lovelier the Second Time Around: Divorce, Desire, and Gothic Domesticity in *Invasion of the Body Snatchers*," *Journal of Popular Culture* 45, no. 3 (2012): 478–496.

33. Badmington, *Alien Chic*, 137.

34. Ibid., 139.

35. Ibid., 138–139.

36. Ibid., 139.

37. See Cindy Hendershot, "The Invaded Body: Paranoia and Radiation Anxiety in *The Invaders from Mars*, *It Came from Outer Space*, and *Invasion of the Body Snatchers*," *Extrapolation* 39, no. 1 (1991): 30.

38. In Shakespeare's comedy *A Midsummer Night's Dream* (1595/1596), the transformation that Titania (and others) are subjected to by the potion (drawn from a "little flower") is revealed to be love itself, while in *Invasion*, it is sleep that threatens to make the characters over as pods.

39. Miles and Becky are both divorcées on their way to a romance that could potentially end in a second marriage. This particular romance narrative is thus a *second* romance plot, another copy of a sort.

40. See Philip Kaufman's statement, "Commentaries," Disc 2, *Invasion of the Body Snatchers*, DVD.

41. Bennett suggests that political slogans such as "Flower power, or Black power, or Girl power" be abandoned in favor of the more capacious standard of "Thing-Power." There is a tension within vibrant materialist models of life between a valorization of specific bodies and experiences (as instantiated in these political slogans) and the distribution of value across *all* bodies. While Bennett's version aims at greater inclusion, thus opening the way for an ecological politics, it also risks occulting political subjects who are already marginalized and disempowered. We see a similar tension emerge in Kaufman's *Invasion*, which prioritizes plant life but turns away from a diversity conceived in strictly human terms; Kaufman's San Francisco is a largely white and middle-class city. In Chapter 7, we explore other possibilities for deploying plant-becoming as a model of political transformation. Bennett, *Vibrant Matter*, 6.

42. Gregory Flaxman, *Gilles Deleuze and the Fabulation of Philosophy* (Minneapolis: University of Minnesota Press, 2012), 312.

43. Even as Flaxman also suggests that the simulacrum always indirectly invokes the model, which still resonates in the end of the film. Ibid., 314.

44. See Melinda Cooper, *Life as Surplus: Biotechnology and Capitalism in the Neoliberal Era* (Seattle: University of Washington Press, 2008).

45. Jeffrey T. Nealon, *Plant Theory: Biopower and Vegetable Life*. Stanford, Calif.: Stanford University Press, 2016), 100–101.

46. In an interview that appeared in French two decades after the making of *Invasion*, Philip Kaufman describes himself as a director of films about rebellion and sexuality. Kaufman's conversation with Michael Henry focuses on his film *Quills* (2000), loosely based on the life of Marquis de Sade, in which the French libertine writer is devoured by a chocolate crucifix—a commentary on the artist's role as rebel. "La joie du cinéaste, c'est d'entrer dans le rêve," interview with Philip Kaufman by Michael Henry, *Positif: Revue mensuelle de cinéma* 482 (April 2001): 25–29.

47. Even professor-turned-pod Budlong acknowledges in *Invasion* that the reproduction of matter atom by atom, mere materiality, has an element of unpredictability and openness: "Life takes whatever form it must: a

monster forty feet high, with an immense neck, and weighing tons—call it a dinosaur. When conditions change, and the dinosaur is no longer possible, it is gone. But life isn't; it's still there, in a new form. Any form necessary." Finney, *Invasion of the Body Snatchers*, 174.

7. BECOMING PLANT NONETHELESS

1. Stefano Mancuso and Alessandra Viola, *Brilliant Green: The Surprising History and Science of Plant Intelligence*, trans. Joan Benham, foreword by Michael Pollan (Washington, D.C.: Island Press, 2015), 156–159.

2. This swarm mentality is depicted as "brittle" materiality in Jack Finney's *The Body Snatchers* (first published in serial form in 1954), discussed in the previous chapter.

3. See in particular N. Katherine Hayles, *How We Became Posthuman: Virtual Bodies in Cybernetics, Literature, and Informatics* (Chicago: University of Chicago Press, 1999).

4. See Mancuso's acknowledgment of the power of time-lapse imaging on the thinking process of the scientist in Michael Pollan, "The Intelligent Plant: Scientists Debate a New Way of Understanding Flora," *New Yorker*, December 15, 2013, https://www.newyorker.com/magazine/2013/12/23/the-intelligent-plant. The algorithmic modeling of plant growth, the Lindenmayer system or L-system, developed in the 1960s by theoretical botanist and biologist Aristid Lindenmayer, first enabled viewing plants as a form of AI. See Przemyslaw Prusinkiewicz and Aristid Lindenmayer, with James S. Hanan, F. David Fracchia, Deborah R. Fowler, Martin J. M. de Boer, and Lynn Mercer, *The Algorithmic Beauty of Plants* (New York: Springer, 1996).

5. Plants also operate not just in late capitalist speculative economies but also in early proto-capitalist ones, as the tulip bubble of the 1630s reminds us.

6. Melinda Cooper, *Life as Surplus: Biotechnology and Capitalism in the Neoliberal Era* (Seattle: University of Washington Press, 2008).

7. This applies not just to the idea of plant-based robots or genetically modified organisms but also to the problem of quantifying the value of forests for the earth's climate, a calculation critiqued by Natasha Myers. She thus argues against trying to accurately measure the benefits or disadvantages to the atmosphere and the earth's climate derived from the photosynthesizing activity of forests and plants in "Photosynthesis: Theorizing the Contemporary," Cultural Anthropology, January 21, 2016, https://culanth.org/fieldsights/photosynthesis.

8. Luce Irigaray and Michael Marder discuss this imbrication of feminine and vegetal modes of being in *Through Vegetal Being: Two Philosophical Perspectives* (New York: Columbia University Press, 2016).

9. Nealon, *Plant Theory: Biopower and Vegetable Life* (Stanford, Calif.: Stanford University Press, 2016), 94; emphasis original. Gilles Deleuze and Félix Guattari, *A Thousand Plateaus: Capitalism and Schizophrenia*, trans. Brian Massumi (Minneapolis: University of Minnesota Press, 1987), 18.

10. This scale-shifting away from botany into a universalist concept of the plant has even led to a plant-inspired metaphysics as recently envisioned by Emanuele Coccia in *La vie des plantes: Une métaphysique du mélange* (Paris: Rivages, 2016).

11. Timothy Morton, *Hyperobjects: Philosophy and Ecology after the End of the World* (Minneapolis: University of Minnesota Press, 2013).

12. Timothy Morton, *The Ecological Thought* (Cambridge, Mass.: Harvard University Press, 2010), 68.

13. Micha Cárdenas et al., *The Transreal: Political Aesthetics of Crossing Realities*, ed. Zach Blas and Wolfgang Schirmacher (New York: Atropos Press, 2011), 122.

14. Stacy Alaimo, *Exposed: Environmental Politics and Pleasure in Posthuman Times* (Minneapolis: University of Minnepolis Press, 2016), 2.

15. Natasha Myers, "Sensing Botanical Sensoria: A Kriya for Cultivating Your Inner Plant," Centre for Imaginative Ethnography, 2014, http://imaginativeethnography.org/imaginings/affect/sensing-botanical-sensoria/. Myers writes movingly about "dancing with" plants in addition to making them "allies."

16. Deleuze and Guattari, *A Thousand Plateaus*, 11.

17. A recent volume of essay seeks in part to include the plant in a study of "how beings bring forth their lifeworlds." The editors write, "This book is based upon the premise that we should continue trying to listen to what plants tell us in their own modes of expression." *The Language of Plants: Science, Philosophy, Literature*, ed. Monica Gagliano, John C. Ryan, and Patricia Vieira (Minneapolis: University of Minnesota Press, 2017), xix, xviii.

18. Stacy Alaimo, *Bodily Natures: Science, Environment, and the Material Self* (Bloomington: Indiana University Press, 2010).

19. The story was first published in 1967. It was reprinted in *Le Fantastique féminin d'Ann Radcliffe à Patricia Highsmith*, ed. Anne Richter (Brussels: Editions Complexe, 1995), 525–534. It was recently published in English, translated by Edward Gauvin, in *Sisters of the Revolution: A Feminist Speculative Fiction Anthology* (Oakland, Calif.: PM Press, 2015), edited by Ann and Jeff VanderMeer, whose trilogy we will discuss later on in this chapter. Ann VanderMeer, a publisher and editor, has herself been instrumental in the rise of "weird fiction" as well as in the development of experimental and avant-garde fantasy genres.

20. See also Kathe Koja's "The Neglected Garden," first published in 1991, for another variation on the theme of women becoming plants. Kathe Koja, "The Neglected Garden," in *Extremities* (New York: Four Walls Eight Windows, 1998), 11–20.

21. In her writing as in her critical work, Richter insists on the investment of what she calls "the female fantastic" in the theme of metamorphosis more generally. As she puts it, "In writings of female authors, metamorphosis into an animal or a plant very often becomes an accomplishment, or a broader, royal way, an apotheosis of sorts." Interview with Christopher Gérard published in *La Cause littéraire*. http://www.lacauselitteraire.fr/anne-richter-ecrivain-pantheiste. We aim to investigate what sort of accomplishment recent vegetal metamorphoses in feminist fiction—by Richter, Le Guin, and Han Kang—represent.

22. Anne Richter, "The Sleep of Plants," in VanderMeer and VanderMeer, eds., *Sisters of the Revolution*, 134.

23. VanderMeer and VanderMeer, eds., *Sisters of the Revolution*, 131.

24. Ibid., 133.

25. Ibid., 136.

26. Ibid., 133.

27. Ibid.

28. We could imagine Richter's story as in some sense a reversal of the Daphne/Apollo narrative, in which Daphne becomes a tree in an effort to avoid rape by the god.

29. Cyrano both parodies and materializes the idea of an infinitely hospitable and abundant vegetable.

30. Still, as Alaimo cautions, we need to be attentive to the tensions animating feminist and environmentalist movements, and acknowledge the ways in which their goals can and do diverge, sometimes problematically. She writes, "Feminist organizations, which aim for gender mainstreaming within climate science and policy, may inadvertently be mainstreaming gendered heteronormativity and homophobia, as well as rigid, essentialized notions of what 'men' and 'women' are. In a world of diverse, multiple, and exuberant genders and sexuality, the dualism of man and woman cannot serve as ballast against the rapid, even catastrophic alterations of climate change. There is no safe haven—not in the domestic sphere, not in the family, and not in the invocation of the complementary creatures 'man' and 'woman.'" Alaimo, *Exposed*, 108.

31. Ursula Le Guin, "Vaster Than Empires and More Slow," in *The Found and the Lost: The Collected Novellas of Ursula Le Guin* (New York: Saga Press, 2016), 1–36.

32. Le Guin, *The Found and the Lost*, 10.

33. As Heise suggests, Le Guin's phytosphere may resonate with the interconnectedness of the 1970s Gaia hypothesis, but it does not ensure a reassuring return to Mother Earth; instead, "the biosphere's total connectedness is what makes it even more strange than its remoteness or its unfamiliar species." Ursula K. Heise, *Sense of Place and Sense of Planet: The Environmental Imagination of the Global* (Oxford: Oxford University Press, 2008), 20.

34. Le Guin, *The Found and the Lost*, 27.

35. Ibid., 3–4.

36. Ibid., 35.

37. Ibid., 36.

38. Le Guin's short story "Direction of the Road: A Story" (originally published in 1973), narrated from the point of view of an oak tree, also ends with the death of a human, although here the narrative encourages the reader to view the oak as a being with perspective, awareness, and language, unlike the plants in "Vaster Than Empires." Le Guin, "Direction of the Road: A Story," in *The Wind's Twelve Quarters and the Compass Rose*, introduction by Graham Sleigh (London: Orion Publishing Group, 2015), 247–253.

39. Here we are inspired once again by Donna J. Haraway's resonant injunction to "stay with the trouble." Haraway writes, "There is a fine line between acknowledging the extent and seriousness of the troubles and succumbing to abstract futurism and its affects of sublime despair and its politics of sublime indifference." Vegetal indifference may cause trouble for us, especially in a time of crisis, but it does not imply an indifferent response on our part. See Haraway, *Staying with the Trouble: Making Kin in the Chthulucene* (Durham, N.C.: Duke University Press, 2016), 4.

40. On Kang and writing as a process of "unearthing" a traumatic past, see Jiayang Fan, "Han Kang and the Complexity of Translation," *New Yorker*, January 15, 2018, https://www.newyorker.com/magazine/2018/01/15/han-kang-and-the-complexity-of-translation.

41. Han Kang, *The Vegetarian*, trans. Deborah Smith (London: Hogarth, 2015), 174–175.

42. Ibid., 174.

43. Ibid., 187.

44. Ibid., 188.

45. We have read the novel in Deborah Smith's translation (approved by the author). Charse Yun, in an article published in the *Los Angeles Times* (September 22, 2017), argues that Smith's translation "amplifies Han's spare, quiet style and embellishes it with adverbs, superlatives, and other emphatic word choices" in a way that risks covering over the specific South Korean

cultural references. One of the images where the legibility of South Korean literary tradition disappears for English-speaking readers is that of Yeonghye as a tree, a reference to early twentieth-century Korean poet Yi Sang, who described "catatonic withdrawal" in the face of the oppressive Japanese colonial regime as becoming plant.

46. For an example of a virtual reality film that allows humans to inhabit the simulated "body" of a plant, see *Tree*, directed by Milica Zec and Winslow Porter (Brooklyn: Chicken and Egg Pictures, 2016). The film incites us to become tree by donning a VR set complete with growth and heat sensors that simulate for us the sensations of a tree growing in the Amazonian rain forest. We "feel" not the raindrops or warmth but digitally produced stimuli. Our body is a tree body in a virtual environment, and, even though the creators make certain decisions that allow this experience to remain anthropocentric and zoocentric, this film also makes use of the allure of a "tree perspective" on life that older cinema, notably time-lapse imaging, has also promoted. We are not so much in a fusion with the natural world here, as Romantic visions of nature projected. Instead, we become the tree and are thus presented with a transformed experience of our own embodiment. At the end of the film, the tree is cut down.

47. Weird fiction is a genre that is usually identified with the work of early twentieth-century American writer Howard Phillips Lovecraft (1890–1937). VanderMeer avoids images of invasion that imply a fear of impurity and even miscegenation, as in Lovecraft's work, to present instead ecosystems in rapid change, symbiotic relationships, and shared territories. In the end, it is not the fear of invasion or miscegenation that drives the plot of the trilogy but an increasing acceptance of hybridity in lieu of purity, transformation in lieu of essence, artifice in lieu of nature. Joyce Carol Oates notes Lovecraft's "paranoid fantasies of miscegenation" in her review essay "The King of Weird," in *New York Review of Books* (October 31, 1996): http://www.nybooks.com/articles/1996/10/31/the-king-of-weird/. See also Nnedi Okorafor's blog post "Lovecraft's Racism and the World Fantasy Award Statuette, with Comments from China Miéville," December 14, 2011, http://nnedi.blogspot.com/2011/12/lovecrafts-racism-world-fantasy-award.html.

48. Tompkins describes the trilogy as an "ecologically minded" piece of weird fiction that embraces miscegenation rather than being horrified by it. See David Tompkins, "Weird Ecology: On the Southern Reach Trilogy," *LA Review of Books* (September 30, 2014): https://www.lareviewofbooks.org/article/weird-ecology-southern-reach-trilogy/.

49. Joshua Rothman, "The Weird Thoreau," *New Yorker*, January 14, 2015, http://www.newyorker.com/culture/cultural-comment/weird-thoreau-jeff-vandermeer-southern-reach.

50. As Tompkins argues, Area X is a transitional ecosystem (the field of specialization of the taciturn but persistent biologist, one of the main characters), and its unaccountable strangeness is a quality that applies to all ecosystems, even those we think of as more familiar. In this transitional state, we cannot be sure if anything exists as a concrete, knowable individual entity, including the plant as object of botany or classification.

51. We note the symbolist resonance of Bernanos's work, which begins with a quote from Baudelaire. Michel Bernanos, *La Montagne morte de la vie* (1964) (Bordeaux: L'Arbre vengeur, 2017).

52. Jeff VanderMeer, *Annihilation* (New York: Farrar, Straus and Giroux, 2014), 24.

53. Jeff VanderMeer, "The Uncanny Power of Weird Fiction," *The Atlantic*, October 30, 2014, https://www.theatlantic.com/entertainment/archive/2014/10/uncanny-fiction-beautiful-and-bizarre/381794/.

54. VanderMeer, *Acceptance* (New York: Farrar, Straus and Giroux, 2014), 24–25.

55. VanderMeer, *Acceptance*, 218–219.

56. VanderMeer has read Mancuso's *Brilliant Green*, which he refers to as "mind-expanding." See VanderMeer's "Epic List of Favorite Books Read in 2015," *Electric Lit*, https://electricliterature.com/jeff-vandermeers-epic-list-of-favorite-books-read-in-2015-2e9370a71ebf.

57. This unbecoming is abandoned in Alex Garland's 2018 adaptation of the first volume of the trilogy, *Annihilation*, under the same title. An intentionally loose adaptation, Garland's evocative and thoughtful sci-fi movie recreates a human social frame largely undone in the novels (e.g., by giving characters names, strengthening the marriage plot, and simplifying the epistemological uncertainty), from within which biological transformation is to be understood. The film is structured around the couple of Lena (the cinematic avatar of the biologist) and her husband (later his own avatar), who face what we could call an alien invasion that accelerates and refracts the genetic processes of cell division. The film holds on to the theme of mutation but, perhaps because of the constraints imposed by the film industry, represents it in terms of human perceptions and experiences.

58. According to which molecules in plants are able to transfer energy in ways that have no explanation in classical physics but correspond to quantum mechanical principles.

59. VanderMeer, *Annihilation*, 23.

60. VanderMeer, *Authority* (New York: Farrar, Straus and Giroux, 2014), 106.

61. See in particular Jean Baudrillard, *The Ecstasy of Communication*, trans. Bernard Schutze and Carline Schutze (New York: Semiotext[e], 1988).

62. Rothman writes, "But there's not much that's post-apocalyptic about VanderMeer's novels. They're not interested in how life ends, but in how it changes, and they are fascinated by the question of persistence through change." "The Weird Thoreau."

63. VanderMeer, *Acceptance*, 331.

Works Cited

PRIMARY SOURCES

Aristotle. *The Complete Works of Aristotle: The Revised Oxford Translation*. Edited by Jonathan Barnes. Princeton, N.J.: Princeton University Press, 1984.

———. *On the Soul, Parva Naturalia, On Breath* (Loeb Classical Library no. 288). Translated by W. S. Hett. Cambridge, Mass.: Harvard University Press, 1957.

Atwood, Margaret. *MaddAddam*. London: Bloomsbury, 2013.

———. *Oryx and Crake: A Novel*. London: Bloomsbury, 2003.

———. *The Year of the Flood*. London: Bloomsbury, 2009.

Bacon, Francis. *Sylva Sylvarum, or a Natural History, in Ten Centuries* (1626/7), Cent. VII. Cap. 607. London, printed by J. R. for William Lee: William Rawley, 1670.

Bernardin de Saint-Pierre, Jacques. *Voyage à l'Isle de France*. Amsterdam: Merlin, 1773.

Bernanos, Michel. *La Montagne morte de la vie* (1964). Bordeaux: L'Arbre vengeur, 2017.

Buffon, Georges-Louis Leclerc, comte de. "Histoire des animaux." *Histoire naturelle, générale et particulière* (1749–1788). In *Œuvres*, edited by Stéphane Schmitt and Cédric Crémière, 133–178. Paris: Gallimard, 2007.

Calvino, Italo. *The Baron in the Trees*. 1957. Translated by Archibald Colquhoun. Orlando, Fla.: Harcourt, 1959.

Colette, Sidonie-Gabrielle. "Cinema." In *Colette at the Movies: Criticism and Screenplays*, edited by Alain and Odette Virmaux, and translated by Sarah W. R. Smith, 59–61. New York: Ungar, 1975.

———. *Œuvres*. Vol. 3. Edited by Claude Pichois. Paris: Gallimard, 1991.

———. "Secrets." In *Flowers and Fruit*, edited by Robert Phelps and translated by Matthew Ward, 95–100. New York: Farrar, Straus and Giroux, 1986.

Cyrano de Bergerac, Savinien De. *Les États et Empires de la Lune; Les États et Empires du Soleil*. Edited by Jacques Prévot. Paris: Folio, 2004.

———. *Journey to the Moon*. Translated by Andrew Brown. London: Hesperus Classics, 2007.

———. *Œuvres comiques, galantes et littéraires de Cyrano de Bergerac*. Compiled by P. L. Jacob. Paris: Adolphe Delahays, 1858.

Darwin, Erasmus. *The Botanic Garden* (1791). London: Jones and Company, 1825.

Darwin, Francis. "The Movements of Plants." *Nature* 65, no. 1672 (1901): 43–44.

Deleuze, Gilles, and Félix Guattari. *Mille Plateaux: Captalisme et Schizophrénie 2*. Paris: Minuit, 1980.

———. *A Thousand Plateaus: Capitalism and Schizophrenia*. Translated by Brian Massumi. Minneapolis: University of Minnesota Press, 1987.

Digby, Kenelm, Sir. *A Discourse Concerning the Vegetation of Plants*. London, printed by J. C. for John Dakins, 1661.

Dulac, Germaine. "Conférence: Le cinéma est un art nouveau." Fonds Germaine Dulac 306-B20, La Cinémathèque française, Paris.

———. "Correspondance générale." Fonds Germaine Dulac 433-B43, La Cinémathèque française, Paris.

———. "Dans ce mot 'libertin.'" Fonds Germaine Dulac 272-B17, La Cinémathèque française, Paris.

———. *Écrits sur le cinéma (1919–1937)*. Introduction by Prosper Hillairet. Paris: Paris Expérimental, 1994.

Encyclopédie, ou dictionnaire raisonné des sciences, des arts et des métiers, etc. Denis Diderot and Jean le Rond D'Alembert, eds. Article "Animal," Denis Diderot and Louis-Jean-Marie Daubenton. University of Chicago: ARTFL Encyclopédie Project (Autumn 2017 Edition), Robert Morrissey and Glenn Roe, eds. http://encyclopedie.uchicago.edu/.

Epstein, Jean. *Le Cinématographe vu de l'Etna*. Paris: Les Écrivains Réunis, 1926.

———. *Écrits sur le cinema 1921–1953*. Vol. 2: *1946–1953*. Paris: Seghers, 1975.

———. *L'Intelligence d'une machine*. Paris: Jacques Melot, 1946.

———. *The Intelligence of a Machine*. Translated by Christophe Wall-Romana. Minneapolis: University of Minnesota Press, 2014.

———. *Jean Epstein: Critical Essays and New Translations*. Edited by Sarah Keller and Jason N. Paul. Amsterdam: Amsterdam University Press, 2012.

———. *Poésie d'aujourd'hui: Un nouvel état d'intelligence*. Paris: Éditions de la sirène, 1921.

Finney, Jack. *Invasion of the Body Snatchers* (1954). 1st Scribner Paperback Fiction edition. New York: Simon and Schuster, 1998.

Flammarion, Camille. *La Fin du monde*. Paris: Ernest Flammarion, 1894.

———. *Omega*. New York: Cosmopolitan Publishing Company, 1894.
———. *Récits de l'infini: Lumen, histoire d'une âme; Histoire d'une comète; La Vie universelle et éternelle*. 1872. Paris: Marpon et E. Flammarion, 1892.
Gilman, Charlotte Perkins. "The Giant Wistaria." *New England Magazine* 4 (June 1891): 480–485.
Goethe, Johann Wolfgang von. *The Metamorphosis of Plants*. 1790. Translated by Douglas Miller. Introduction by Gordon L. Miller. Boston, Mass.: MIT Press, 2009.
Hallé, Francis. *Éloge de la plante, pour une nouvelle biologie*. Paris: Seuil, 1999.
———. *In Praise of Plants*. Translated and with a foreword by David Lee. Portland, Ore.: Timber Press, 2002.
Holberg, Ludvig, Baron. *The Journey of Niels Klim to the World Underground*. Edited and introduction by James I. McNelis Jr. Lincoln: University of Nebraska Press, 1960.
———. *Nicolai Klimii iter subterraneum: Novam telluris theoriam ac historiam quintae monarchiae adhuc nobis incognitae exhibens e bibliotheca B. Abelin*. Hafniaae, Lipsiae: Sumptibus Iacobi Preussii, 1741.
———. *Niels Klims underjordiske reise, oversat efter den latinske original af Jens Baggesen*. Illustrated by Johan Frederik Clemens. Kiöbenhavn [Copenhagen]: Johan Frederik Schultz, 1789. Cotsen Children's Library, Department of Rare Books and Special Collections, Princeton University Library.
Jahren, Hope. *Lab Girl*. New York: Knopf, 2016.
Kang, Han. *The Vegetarian*. Translated by Deborah Smith. London: Hogarth, 2015.
Koja, Kathe. *Extremities*. New York: Four Walls Eight Windows, 1998.
La Brosse, Guy de. *De la nature, vertu, et utilité des plantes: Divisé en cinq Livres* (1631). Paris: Rollin Baragnes, 1678.
La Mettrie, Julien Offray de. *L'Homme-plante* (1748). *Œuvres philosophiques*. Vol. 1. Edited by Francine Markovits. Paris: Fayard, 1987.
———. *Man a Machine* and *Man a Plant*. Translated by Richard A. Watson and Maya Rybalka. Indianapolis: Hackett Publishing Company, 1994.
Le Guin, Ursula K. "The Author of the Acacia Seeds and Other Extracts from the *Journal of the Association of Therolinguistics*." In *The Unreal and the Real: The Selected Short Stories of Ursula K. Le Guin*, 617–625. New York: Saga Press, 2016.
———. "Direction of the Road: A Story" (1973). In *The Wind's Twelve Quarters and the Compass Rose*, introduction by Graham Sleight, 247–253. London: Orion Publishing Group, 2015.
———. "Vaster Than Empires and More Slow" (1971). In *The Found and the Lost: The Collected Novellas of Ursula Le Guin*, 1–36. New York: Saga Press, 2016.

Lucretius. *On the Nature of the Universe* [*De rerum natura*] (first century BCE). Translated by R. E. Latham. New York: Penguin Books, 1951.
Mancuso, Stefano, and Alessandra Viola. *Brilliant Green: The Surprising History and Science of Plant Intelligence.* Translated by Joan Benham and foreword by Michael Pollan. Washington, D.C.: Island Press, 2015.
Poe, Edgar Allan. "Marginalia." *Southern Literary Messenger* 15, no. 5 (May 1849): 292–296.
———. *Narrative of Arthur Gordon Pym of Nantucket.* New York: Harper and Row, 1838.
———. *The Selected Writings of Edgar Allan Poe.* Edited by Gary Richard Thompson. Norton Critical Edition. New York: W. W. Norton, 2004.
Quercetanus, Josephus. *Ad veritatem hermeticae medicinae ex Hippocratis veterumque decretis ac therapeusi . . . adversus cuiusdam Anonymi phantasmata responsio.* Frankfurt: Conrad Neben, 1605.
Richter, Anne. "The Sleep of Plants." Translated by Edward Gauvin. In *Sisters of the Revolution: A Feminist Speculative Fiction Anthology,* edited by Ann and Jeff VanderMeer, 131–136. Oakland, Calif.: PM Press, 2015.
———. "Un sommeil de plante." In *Le Fantastique féminin d'Ann Radcliffe à Patricia Highsmith,* edited by Anne Richter, 525–534. Brussels: Editions Complexe, 1995.
Rostand, Edmond. *Cyrano de Bergerac* (1897). Paris: Flammarion, 2013.
Rousseau, Jean-Jacques. *Rêveries du promeneur solitaire* (1776–1778). Vanves: Librairie Générale Française, 2001.
Senebier, Jean. "Introduction." In Lazzaro Spallanzani, *Opuscules de physique animale et végétale,* Vol. 1. Geneva: Chez Pierre J. Duplain, 1787.
Shakespeare, William. *A Midsummer Night's Dream* (1595/1596). Edited by Barbara A. Mowat and Paul Werstine. New York: Folger Shakespeare Library (Simon and Schuster), 2016.
Shelley, Mary. *Frankenstein, or the Modern Prometheus.* London: G. and W. Whittaker, 1823.
Shelley, Percy Bysshe. *Shelley's Poetry and Prose.* Norton Critical Edition, 2nd Edition. Edited by Neil Fraistat and Donald H. Reiman, 286–295. London: W. W. Norton, 2002.
Stapledon, Olaf. *Last and First Men: A Story of the Near and Far Future.* London: Methuen, 1930.
Theophrastus. *Enquiry into Plants* (fourth to third century BCE). Vols. 1–5 (Loeb Classical Library no. 70). Translated by Arthur F. Hort. Cambridge, Mass.: Harvard University Press, 1916.
Tiphaigne de La Roche, Charles-François. *Amilec and Other Satirical Fantasies.* Translated by Brian Stableford. Tarzana: Black Coat Press, 2011.

---. *Amilec, Ou la graine d'hommes qui sert à peupler les planètes* (1753). Edited by Philippe Vincent with foreword by Yves Citton. Mont-Saint-Aignan: Presses universitaires de Rouen et du Havre, 2012.

---. *Amilec ou la graine d'hommes qui sert à peupler les planètes*. Troisième édition, augmentée très considèrablement, À Lunéville, aux dépens de Chr. Hugene, à l'enseigne de Fontenelle, n.d. [1754].

---. *Questions relatives à l'agriculture et à la nature des plantes*. The Hague: Jean Neaulme, 1759.

Tremblay, Abraham. *Mémoires pour servir à l'histore d'un genre de polypes d'eau douce, à bras en forme de cornes*. Leiden: Jean et Herman Verbeek, 1744.

VanderMeer, Jeff. *Southern Reach Trilogy: Annihilation*. New York: Farrar, Straus and Giroux, 2014.

---. *Authority*. New York: Farrar, Straus and Giroux, 2014.

---. *Acceptance*. New York: Farrar, Straus and Giroux, 2014.

Watson, Richard. *Chemical Essays, Vol. 5*. London: Merrill, 1789.

SECONDARY SOURCES

Print

Alaimo, Stacy. *Bodily Natures: Science, Environment, and the Material Self*. Bloomington: Indiana University Press, 2010.

---. *Exposed: Environmental Politics and Pleasures in Posthuman Times*. Minneapolis: University of Minnesota Press, 2016.

Allewaert, Monique. *Ariel's Ecology: Plantations, Personhood, and Colonialism in the American Tropics*. Minneapolis: University of Minnesota Press, 2013.

Amad, Paula. *Counter-Archive: Film, the Everyday, and Albert Kahn's Archives de la Planète*. New York: Columbia University Press, 2010.

---. "'These Spectacles Are Never Forgotten': Memory and Reception in Colette's Film Criticism." *Camera Obscura* 20, no. 2 (2005): 119–163.

Arsić, Branca. "Materialist Vitalism or Pathetic Fallacy: The Case of the House of Usher." *Representations* 140, Fallacies Special Issue (Fall 2007): 121–136.

Atwood, Margaret. *Speculative or Science Fiction? As Margaret Atwood Shows, There Isn't Much Distinction*, August 10, 2016. https://www.theguardian.com/books/2016/aug/10/speculative-or-science-fiction-as-margaret-atwood-shows-there-isnt-much-distinction.

Badmington, Neil. *Alien Chic: Posthumanism and the Other Within*. London: Routledge, 2004.

Baudrillard, Jean. *The Ecstasy of Communication*. Translated by Bernard Schutze and Carline Schutze. New York: Semiotext(e), 1988.

Benharrech, Sarah. "Presentation." In Charles-François Tiphaigne de La Roche, *Œuvres complètes*, edited by Jacques Marx, Vol. 1, 593–633. Paris: Éditions Classiques Garnier, 2019.

Bennett, Jane. *The Enchantment of Modern Life: Attachments, Crossings, Ethics.* Princeton, N.J.: Princeton University Press, 2001.

———. *Vibrant Matter: A Political Ecology of Things.* Durham, N.C.: Duke University Press, 2010.

———. "Whitman's Sympathies." *Political Research Quarterly* 69, no. 3 (2016): 607–620.

Berger, Jean. *About Looking.* New York: Vintage, 1980.

Bergson, Henri. *Matière et Mémoire.* Paris: Félix Alvan, 1896.

Bonneuil, Christophe, and Jean-Baptiste Fressoz. *L'Événement Anthropocène: La Terre, l'histoire et nous.* 2nd revised and augmented edition. Paris: Seuil, 2016.

Brancher, Dominique. *Quand l'esprit vient aux plantes: Botanique sensible et subversion libertine (XVIe–XVIIe siècles).* Geneva: Droz, 2015.

Cahill, James. "Animal Photogénie: The Wild Side of French Film Theory's First Wave." In *Animal Life and the Moving Image*, edited by Michael Lawrence and Laura McMahon, 23–41. London: British Film Institute, 2015.

Cárdenas, Micha, et al. *The Transreal: Political Aesthetics of Crossing Realities.* Edited by Zach Blas and Wolfgang Schirmacher. New York: Atropos Press, 2011.

Cavaillé, Jean-Pierre. *Postures libertines: La culture des esprits forts.* Paris: Anacharsis, 2011.

Chamovitz, Daniel. *What a Plant Knows: A Field Guide to the Senses.* New York: Scientific American/Farrar, Straus and Giroux, 2012.

Chen, Mel Y. *Animacies: Biopolitics, Racial Mattering, and Queer Affect.* Durham, N.C.: Duke University Press, 2012.

Citton, Yves. *Lire, interpréter, actualiser: Pourquoi les études littéraires?* Paris: Éditions Amsterdam, 2007.

Citton, Yves, Marinne Dubacq, and Philippe Vincent, eds. *Imagination scientifique et littérature merveilleuse: Charles Tiphaigne de La Roche.* Pessac: Presses universitaires de Bordeaux, 2014.

Coccia, Emanuele. *La vie des plantes: Une métaphysique du mélange.* Paris: Rivages, 2016.

Cohen, J. J., and L. Duckert, eds. *Elemental Ecocriticism: Thinking with Earth, Air, Water, and Fire.* Minneapolis: University of Minnesota Press, 2015.

———. *Veer Ecology: A Companion for Environmental Thinking.* Minneapolis: University of Minnesota Press, 2017.

Conley, Tom. "Civil War and French Better Homes and Gardens." *South Atlantic Quarterly* 98, no. 4 (1999): 725–759.

Cook, Alexandra. *Jean-Jacques Rousseau and Botany: The Salutary Science.* Oxford: Voltaire Foundation, University of Oxford, 2012.

Cooper, Melinda. *Life as Surplus: Biotechnology and Capitalism in the Neoliberal Era*. Seattle: University of Washington Press, 2008.

Crosby, Sara. "Beyond Ecophilia: Edgar Allan Poe and the American Tradition of Ecohorror." *Interdisciplinary Studies in Literature and the Environment* 21, no. 3 (Summer 2014): 513–525.

Cuff, Paul. *Abel Gance and the End of Silent Cinema: Sounding Out Utopia*. Basingstoke: Palgrave Macmillan, 2016.

Damasio, Antonio. *Self Comes to Mind: Constructing the Conscious Brain*. New York: Pantheon, 2010.

Darmon, Jean-Charles. *Philosophie épicurienne et littérature au XVIIe siècle: Études sur Gassendi, Cyrano de Bergerac, La Fontaine, Saint-Évremond*. Paris: Presses universitaires de France, 1998.

Daston, Lorraine, and Gregg Mitman, eds. *Thinking with Animals: New Perspectives on Anthropomorphism*. New York: Columbia University Press, 2005.

Delaporte, François. *Nature's Second Kingdom: Explorations of Vegetality in the Eighteenth Century*. Translated by Arthur Goldhammer. Cambridge, Mass.: MIT Press, 1982.

Delehanty, Ann, and Tyler Blakeney. "Textual Engagement with the Other in Cyrano de Bergerac's *L'Autre Monde*." *French Studies* 68, no. 3 (July 2014): 313–327.

Deleuze, Gilles. *Cinéma 1: L'image mouvement*. Paris: Minuit, 1983.

———. *L'île déserte: Textes et Entretiens, 1953–1974*. Paris: Minuit, 2002.

Deleuze, Gilles, and Félix Guattari. *What Is Philosophy?* Translated by Hugh Tomlinson and Graham Burchell. New York: Columbia University Press, 1994.

Diderot, Denis. *Le Rêve de d'Alembert*. Edited by Colas Duflo. Paris: Garnier-Flammarion, 2002.

Dittrich, Joshua. "A Matter of Life and Death: Inorganic Life in Worringer, Deleuze, and Guattari." *Discourse* 32, no. 2 (Spring 2011): 242–262.

Dosse, François. *Gilles Deleuze and Félix Guattari: Intersecting Lives*. Translated by Deborah Glassman. New York: Columbia University Press, 2010.

Doyle, Richard. *Darwin's Pharmacy: Sex, Plants, and the Evolution of Noösphere*. Seattle: University of Washington Press, 2011.

Fan, Jiayang. "Han Kang and the Complexity of Translation." *The New Yorker*. January 15, 2018. https://www.newyorker.com/magazine/2018/01/15/han-kang-and-the-complexity-of-translation.

Farina, Lara. "Vegetal Continuity and the Naming of Species." *Postmedieval: A Journal of Medieval Cultural Studies* 9, no. 4 (2018): 420–431.

Finney, Jack. *Invasion of the Body Snatchers*. New York: Simon and Schuster, 1998.
Fitting, Peter. "Buried Treasures: Reconsidering Holberg's *Niels Klim in the World Underground*." *Utopian Studies* 7, no. 2 (1996): 93–112.
Flaxman, Gregory. *Gilles Deleuze and the Fabulation of Philosophy*. Minneapolis: University of Minnesota Press, 2012.
Flitterman-Lewis, Sandy. *To Desire Differently: Feminism and the French Cinema*. New York: Columbia University Press, 1996.
Foucault, Michel. *The Birth of Biopolitics: Lectures at the Collège de France, 1978–1979*. Edited by Michel Senellart and translated by Graham Burchell. New York: Picador, 2008.
———. *Les mots et les choses*. Paris: Gallimard, 1966.
———. *The Order of Things: An Archeology of the Human Sciences*. Translated by Alan Sheridan. London: Routledge, 1970.
Frank, Adam, and Eve Kosofsky Sedgwick. "Shame in the Cybernetic Fold: Reading Silvan Tomkins." In *Shame and Its Sisters: A Silvan Tomkins Reader*, 1–28. Durham, N.C.: Duke University Press, 1995.
Freund, Charles. "Pods over San Francisco." *Film Comment* 15, no. 1 (1979): 22–25.
Gagliano, Monica, John C. Ryan, and Patrícia Vieira, eds. *The Language of Plants: Science, Philosophy, Literature*. Minneapolis: University of Minnesota Press, 2017.
Gaycken, Oliver. *Devices of Curiosity: Early Cinema and Popular Science*. Oxford: Oxford University Press, 2015.
———. "The Secret Life of Plants: Visualizing Vegetative Movement, 1880–1903." *Early Popular Visual Culture* 10, no. 1 (2012): 51–69.
Gérard, Christopher. "Interview with Anne Richter." *La Cause littéraire*. May 21, 2011. http://www.lacauselitteraire.fr/anne-richter-ecrivain-pantheiste.
Ghosh, Amitav. *The Great Derangement: Climate Change and the Unthinkable*. Chicago: University of Chicago Press, 2016.
Gleiser, Marcelo. *The Island of Knowledge: The Limits of Science and the Search for Meaning*. New York: Basic Books, 2014.
Goldberg, Jonathan. *The Seeds of Things: Theorizing Sexuality and Materiality in Renaissance Representations*. New York: Fordham University Press, 2009.
Goldstein, Amanda Jo. "Growing Old Together: Lucretian Materialism in Shelley's 'Poetry of Life.'" *Representations* 1, no. 1 (Fall 2014): 60–92.
———. *Sweet Science: Romantic Materialism and the New Logics of Life*. Chicago: University of Chicago Press, 2017.
Goux, Jean-Joseph. "Language, Money, Father, Phallus in Cyrano de Bergerac's Utopia." *Representations* 23, no. 1 (Summer 1988): 105–117.

Grant, Barry Keith. *Invasion of the Body Snatchers*. London: British Film Institute, 2010.
Griffiths, Devin. "The Distribution of Romantic Life in Erasmus Darwin's Later Works." *European Romantic Review* 29, no. 3 (2018): 309–319.
Hall, Matthew. *Plants as Persons: A Philosophical Botany*. Albany: State University of New York Press, 2011.
Haraway, Donna. *Staying with the Trouble: Making Kin in the Chthulucene*. Durham, N.C.: Duke University Press, 2016.
Harth, Erica. *Cyrano de Bergerac and the Polemics of Modernity*. New York: Columbia University Press, 1970.
Hayles, N. Katherine. *How We Became Posthuman: Virtual Bodies in Cybernetics, Literature, and Informatics*. Chicago: University of Chicago Press, 1999.
Hegel, Georg Wilhelm Friedrich. *Phenomenology of Spirit*. Translated by A. V. Miller. Oxford: Clarendon Press, 1977.
Heise, Ursula K. *Sense of Place and Sense of Planet: The Environmental Imagination of the Global*. Oxford: Oxford University Press, 2008.
Hendershot, Cyndy. "The Invaded Body: Paranoia and Radiation Anxiety in *The Invaders from Mars, It Came from Outer Space*, and *Invasion of the Body Snatchers*." *Extrapolation* 39, no. 1 (1991): 26–39.
———. *Paranoia, the Bomb, and 1950s Science Fiction Films*. Bowling Green, Ky.: Bowling Green State University Popular Press, 1999.
Henry, Michael. "Interview with Philip Kaufman." *Positif: Revue mensuelle de cinéma* 482 (April 2001): 25–29.
Hirai, Hiro. *Le concept de sémence dans les théories de la matière à la Renaissance: De Marsile Ficin à Pierre Gassendi*. Turnhout: Brepols, 2005.
Hoquet, Thierry. *Buffon: Histoire naturelle et philosophie*. Paris: Honoré Champion, 2005.
Howard, Rio. "Guy de La Brosse: Botanique et chimie au début de la révolution scientifique." *Revue d'histoire des sciences* 31, no. 4 (1978): 301–326.
Irigaray, Luce, and Michael Marder. *Through Vegetal Being: Two Philosophical Perspectives*. New York: Columbia University Press, 2016.
Jenkins, Jennifer L. "Lovelier the Second Time Around: Divorce, Desire, and Gothic Domesticity in *Invasion of the Body Snatchers*." *Journal of Popular Culture* 45, no. 3 (2012): 478–496.
Kahn, Didier. "Plantes et médecine, (al)chimie et libertinisme chez Guy de la Brosse." Bibliothèque numérique Medic@, April 2007. http://www.biusante.parisdescartes.fr/histoire/medica/brosse.php.
———. "Quelques notes d'alchimie et d'histoire des sciences à propos des romans de Cyrano de Bergerac." In *Lectures de Cyrano de Bergerac, Les*

États et Empires de la Lune et du Soleil, edited by Bérengère Parmentier, 59–76. Rennes: Presses Universitaires de Rennes, 2004.

Keenleyside, Heather. "The Rise of the Novel and the Fall of Personification." In *Eighteenth-Century Poetry and the Rise of the Novel Reconsidered*, edited by Kate Parker and Courtney Weiss Smith, 105–133. Lewisburg, Pa.: Bucknell University Press, 2014.

Keetley, Dawn, and Angela Tenga, eds. *Plant Horror: Approaches to the Monstrous Vegetal in Fiction and Film*. New York: Palgrave Macmillan, 2016.

Kelley, Theresa M. *Clandestine Marriage: Botany and Romantic Culture*. Baltimore: Johns Hopkins University Press, 2012.

Kennedy, Duncan. *Rethinking Reality: Lucretius and the Textualization of Nature*. Ann Arbor: University of Michigan Press, 2002.

Kohn, Eduardo. *How Forests Think: Toward an Anthropology beyond the Human*. Berkeley: University of California Press, 2013.

Latour, Bruno. *Aramis or the Love of Technology*. Translated by Catherine Porter. Cambridge, Mass.: Harvard University Press, 1996.

Lefebvre, Thierry. "Introduction." In *Filmer la science, comprendre la vie: Le cinéma de Jean Comandon*. Paris: Édition Centre national du cinéma et de l'image animée, 2012.

Limon, John. "Poe's Methodology." In *The Place of Fiction in the Time of Science: A Disciplinary History of American Writing*, 70–120. Cambridge: Cambridge University Press, 2009.

Lippit, Akira. *Electric Animal: Toward a Rhetoric of Wildlife*. Minneapolis: University of Minnesota Press, 2008.

Lovell, Alan. *Don Siegel: American Cinema*. London: British Film Institute, 1975.

Mancuso, Cecilia. "Speculative or Science Fiction? As Margaret Atwood Shows, There Isn't Much Distinction." *The Guardian*, August 10, 2016, https://www.theguardian.com/books/2016/aug/10/speculative-or-science-fiction-as-margaret-atwood-shows-there-isnt-much-distinction.

Marder, Michael. *Plant-Thinking: A Philosophy of Vegetal Life*. New York: Columbia University Press, 2013.

———. "The Place of Plants: Spatiality, Movement, Growth." *Performance Philosophy* 1, no. 1 (2015): 185–194.

Marder, Michael, and Anaïs Tondeur. *The Chernobyl Herbarium: Fragments of an Exploded Consciousness*. London: Open Humanities Press, 2016.

Marks, Laura. *Enfoldment and Infinity: An Islamic Genealogy of New Media Art*. Cambridge, Mass.: MIT Press, 2010.

Massumi, Brian. *Politics of Affect*. London: Polity, 2015.

McLane, Maureen N. "Compositionism: Plants, Poetics, Possibilities; or, Two Cheers for Fallacies, Especially Pathetic Ones!" *Representations* 140, no. 1 (2017): 101–120.

Meeker, Natania, and Antónia Szabari. "Une artiste en résidence dans le monde des fleurs: L'art botanique de Madeleine Françoise Basseporte." In *Autoportraits, autofictions de femmes à l'époque moderne: Savoirs et fabrique d'identité*. Edited by Caroline Trotot, 157–188. Paris: Classiques Garnier, 2018.

———. "From the Century of the Pods to the Century of the Plants: Plant Horror, Politics, and Vegetal Ontology." *Discourse* 34, no. 1 (Winter 2012): 32–58.

———. "Gender and Sexuality in Botanical Contexts." In *Macmillan Interdisciplinary Handbooks: Gender*. Edited by Renée C. Hoogland, 153–169. New York: Palgrave Macmillan, 2017.

———. "Libertine Botany: Vegetal Sexuality, Vegetal Form." *Postmedieval: A Journal of Medieval Cultural Studies* 9, no. 4 (2018): 478–489.

———. "Who Will Remember Us? Plants and the Archive: Dornith Doherty, 'Archiving Eden: The Vaults,' 2008–present; Jessica Rath, 'Take Me to the Apple Breeder,' Pasadena Museum of California Art, 2012." *Oxford Literary Review* 36, no. 1 (2014): 151–154.

Michaud, Philippe-Alain. "*Croissance des végétaux* (1929): La melancolia de Jean Comandon." *Association française de recherche sur l'histoire du cinéma* no. 14 (October 1995): 265–283.

Michel, Lincoln. "An Interview With Jeff VanderMeer: 'Full Disclosure, I'm Really A Komodo Dragon.'" *Buzzfeed*, March 15, 2014. https://www.buzzfeed.com/lincolnmichel/jeff-vandermeer.

Miller, Elaine P. *The Vegetative Soul: From Philosophy of Nature to Subjectivity in the Feminine*. Albany: State University of New York Press, 2002.

Miller, Timothy S. "Lives of the Monster Plants: The Revenge of the Vegetable in the Age of Animal Studies." *Journal of the Fantastic in the Arts* 23, no. 3 (2012): 460–479.

Mitchell, Robert. *Experimental Life: Vitalism in Romantic Science and Literature*. Baltimore: Johns Hopkins University Press, 2013.

Moretti, Franco. *The Bourgeois: Between History and Literature*. London: Verso, 2013.

Mortimer-Sandilands, Catriona. "Melancholy Natures, Queer Ecologies." In *Queer Ecologies: Sex, Nature, Politics, Desire*, edited by Catriona Mortimer-Sandilands and Bruce Erickson, 331–358. Bloomington: Indiana University Press, 2010.

Morton, Timothy. *The Ecological Thought*. Cambridge, Mass.: Harvard University Press, 2010.

---. *Ecology without Nature: Rethinking Environmental Aesthetics.* Cambridge, Mass.: Harvard University Press, 2007.
---. *Hyperobjects: Philosophy and Ecology After the End of the World.* Minneapolis: University of Minnesota Press, 2013.
Myers, Natasha. "Photosynthesis: Theorizing the Contemporary." *Cultural Anthropology*, January 21, 2016. https://culanth.org/fieldsights/photosynthesis.
---. "Photosynthetic Mattering: Rooting into the Planthropocene." In *Moving Plants.* Edited by Line Marie Thorsen, 123–127. Naestved, Denmark: Roennebaeksholm, 2017.
---. "Sensing Botanical Sensoria: A Kriya for Cultivating Your Inner Plant." Centre for Imaginative Ethnography. 2014. http://imaginativeethnography.org/imaginings/affect/sensing-botanical-sensoria/.
Myers, Natasha, and Carla Hustak. "Involuntary Momentum: Affective Ecologies and the Sciences of Plant/Insect Encounters." *Differences: A Journal of Feminist Cultural Studies* 23, no. 2 (2012): 74–118.
Nealon, Christopher S. *The Matter of Capital: Poetry and Crisis in the American Century.* Cambridge, Mass.: Harvard University Press, 2011.
Nealon, Jeffrey T. *Plant Theory: Biopower and Vegetable Life.* Stanford, Calif.: Stanford University Press, 2016.
---. Review of "Plant-Thinking: A Philosophy of Vegetal Life." *Notre Dame Philosophical Reviews*, April 10, 2013. http://ndpr.nd.edu/news/plant-thinking-a-philosophy-of-vegetal-life/.
Oates, Joyce Carol. "The King of Weird." *New York Review of Books*, October 31, 1996. http://www.nybooks.com/articles/1996/10/31/the-king-of-weird/.
O'Donoghue, Darragh. "On Some Motifs in Poe: Jean Epstein's *La Chute de la maison Usher*." February 2004. http://sensesofcinema.com/2004/feature-articles/la_chute_de_la_maison_usher/.
Okorafor, Nnedi. "Lovecraft's Racism and the World Fantasy Award Statuette, with Comments from China Miéville." December 14, 2011. Nnedi's Wahala Zone Blog. http://nnedi.blogspot.com/2011/12/lovecrafts-racism-world-fantasy-award.html.
Para, Patricia. *Erasmus Darwin: Sex, Science, and Serendipity.* Oxford: Oxford University Press, 2012.
Perry, Dennis R., and Carl H. Sederholm. *Poe, "The House of Usher," and the American Gothic.* New York: Palgrave Macmillan, 2009.
Pintard, René. *Le libertinage érudit dans la première moitié du XVIIe siècle.* Geneva: Slatkin, 2000 [1943].
Pollman, Inga. "Invisible Worlds, Visible: Uexküll's Umwelt, Film, Theory." *Critical Inquiry* 39, no. 4 (2013): 777–816.

Pollan, Michael. "The Intelligent Plant: Scientists Debate a New Way of Understanding Flora." *New Yorker*, December 15, 2013. https://www.newyorker.com/magazine/2013/12/23/the-intelligent-plant.

Pratt, Ray. *Projecting Paranoia: Conspiratorial Visions in American Film*. Lawrence: University Press of Kansas, 2001.

Prévot, Jacques. *Cyrano de Bergerac romancier*. Paris: Belot, 1977.

Protevi, John. *Political Affect: Connecting the Social and the Somatic*. Minneapolis: University of Minnesota Press, 2009.

Prusinkiewicz, Przemyslaw, and Aristid Lindenmayer, with James S. Hanan, F. David Fracchia, Deborah R. Fowler, Martin J. M. de Boer, and Lynn Mercer. *The Algorithmic Beauty of Plants*. New York: Springer, 1996.

Ritterbush, Philip C. *Overtures to Biology: The Speculations of Eighteenth-Century Naturalists*. New Haven, Conn.: Yale University Press, 1964.

Roche, Bruno. "Lucrèce et Cyrano: Stratégies libertines pour l'approche du Chant III du *De Rerum natura*." In *Libertinage et philosophie au XVIIe siècle: Les libertins et la science*, edited by Antony McKenna, Pierre-François Moreau, and Frédéric Tinguely, 211–223. Saint-Étienne: Publications de l'Université de Saint-Étienne, 2005.

Romanowski, Sylvie. "Cyrano de Bergerac's Epistemological Bodies: 'Pregnant with a Thousand Definitions.'" *Science Fiction Studies* 25, no. 3 (1998): 414–432.

Rothman, Joshua. "The Weird Thoreau." *New Yorker*, January 14, 2015. http://www.newyorker.com/culture/cultural-comment/weird-thoreau-jeff-vandermeer-southern-reach.

Schiebinger, Londa L. *Nature's Body: Gender in the Making of Science*. New Brunswick, N.J.: Rutgers University Press, 2004.

———. *Plants and Empire: Colonial Bioprospecting in the Atlantic World*. Cambridge, Mass.: Harvard University Press, 2007.

Sempère, Emmanuelle. "Le végétal chez Tiphaigne, image(s) ou modèle(s)?" In *Imagination scientifique et littérature merveilleuse: Charles Tiphaigne de La Roche*, edited by Yves Citton, Marinne Dubacq, and Philippe Vincent, 211–230. Pessac: Presses universitaires de Bordeaux, 2014.

Shatz, Adam. "Desire Was Everywhere." Review essay of *Gilles Deleuze and Félix Guattari: Intersecting Lives* by François Dosse, trans. Deborah Glassman (New York: Columbia University Press, 2010) in *London Review of Books* 32, no. 24 (December 2010): 9–12.

Smith, Herbert F. "Usher's Madness and Poe's Organicism: A Source." *American Literature* 39, no. 3 (November 1967): 379–389.

Smith, Patricia. "Poe's Arabesque." *Poe Studies* 7, no. 2 (December 1974): 42–45.

Sobchack, Vivian. *Screening Space: The American Science Fiction Film.* New Brunswick, N.J.: Rutgers University Press, 1987.

Stalnaker, Joanna. *The Unfinished Enlightenment: Description in the Age of the Encyclopedia.* Ithaca, N.Y.: Cornell University Press, 2010.

Swann, Marjorie. "Vegetable Love: Botany and Sexuality in Seventeenth-Century England." In *The Indistinct Human in the Renaissance.* Edited by Jean E. Feerick and Vin Nardizzi, 139–159. New York: Palgrave Macmillan, 2012.

Szabari, Antónia. "Montaigne's Plants in Movement." In *Early Modern Ecologies.* Edited by Pauline Goul and Phillip John Usher, Amsterdam: Amsterdam University Press, Forthcoming 2019.

Taiz, Lincoln, and Lee Taiz. *Flora Unveiled: The Discovery and Denial of Sex in Plants.* New York: Oxford University Press, 2017.

Taylor, Matthew A. "The Nature of Fear: Edgar Allan Poe and Posthuman Ecology." *American Literature* 84, no. 2 (2012): 353–379.

———. *Universes without Us: Posthuman Cosmologies in American Literature.* Minneapolis: University of Minnesota Press, 2013.

Tinguely, Frédéric. "Un libertin dans la Lune? De la distraction scientifique chez Cyrano de Bergerac." In *Libertinage et philosophie au XVIIe siècle: Les libertins et la science,* edited by Antony McKenna, Pierre-François Moreau, and Frédéric Tinguely, 73–84. Saint-Étienne: Publications de l'Université de Saint-Étienne, 2005.

Tompkins, David. "Weird Ecology: On the Southern Reach Trilogy." *LA Review of Books.* September 30, 2014. https://www.lareviewofbooks.org/article/weird-ecology-southern-reach-trilogy/.

Torero-Ibad, Alexandra. *Libertinage, science et philosophie dans le matérialisme de Cyrano de Bergerac.* Paris: Honoré Champion, 2009.

———. "Les representations de la nature chez Cyrano de Bergerac." In *Libertinage et philosophie au XVIIe siècle: Les libertins et la science,* edited by Antony McKenna, Pierre-François Moreau, and Frédéric Tinguely, 163–193. Saint-Étienne: Publications de l'Université de Saint-Étienne, 2005.

Turvey, Malcolm. *Doubting Vision: Film and the Revelationist Tradition.* Oxford: Oxford University Press, 2008.

VanderMeer, Jeff. "Epic List of Favorite Books Read in 2015." *Electric Lit,* December 18, 2015. https://electricliterature.com/jeff-vandermeers-epic-list-of-favorite-books-read-in-2015-2e9370a71ebf.

———. "The Uncanny Power of Weird Fiction." *The Atlantic.* October 30, 2014. https://www.theatlantic.com/entertainment/archive/2014/10/uncanny-fiction-beautiful-and-bizarre/381794/.

Vartanian, Aram. "Trembley's Polyp, La Mettrie, and Eighteenth-Century Materialism." *Journal of the History of Ideas* 11, no. 3 (June 1950): 259–286.

Vincent, Phillippe. "Charles Tiphaigne et la génération dans *Amilec, ou la graine d'hommes* (1754)." *Féeries* 6 (2009): 107–115.

Vuillemin, Nathalie. "Les 'Entretiens entre un voyageur et une dame sur les arbres, les fleurs, et les fruits' de Bernardin de Saint-Pierre: Libertinage d'esprit ou naissance du propos critique?" *Studies on Voltaire and the Eighteenth Century* 7 (2005): 281–293.

———. "Hydres de Lerne et arbres animés: Fantasmagories savantes autour du polype." *Dix-huitième siècle* 42, no. 1 (2010): 321–338.

Wall-Romana, Christophe. *Jean Epstein: Corporeal Cinema and Film Philosophy*. Manchester: Manchester University Press, 2016.

Wandersee, James H., and Elisabeth E. Schussler. "Toward a Theory of Plant Blindness." *Plant Science Bulletin* 47, no. 1 (Spring 2001): 2–8.

Warfel, Harry R. "Poe's Percival: A Note on the Fall of the House of Usher." *Modern Language Notes* 54, no. 2 (February 1939): 129–131.

Wark, McKenzie. *Molecular Red: Theory for the Anthropocene*. London: Verso, 2016.

Williams, Tami. *Germaine Dulac: A Cinema of Sensations*. Champaign: University of Illinois Press, 2014.

Wilson, Catherine. *Epicureanism at the Origins of Modernity*. Oxford: Oxford University Press, 2008.

Yun, Charse. "How the Bestseller 'The Vegetarian,' Translated from Han Kang's Original, Caused an Uproar in South Korea." *Los Angeles Times*, September 22, 2017. https://www.latimes.com/books/jacketcopy/la-ca-jc-korean-translation-20170922-story.html.

AUDIOVISUAL

Comandon, Jean, dir. *Essais de prises de vues de végétaux en accéléré: Germination de graines de blé*. France: Office national des recherches scientifiques et industrielles et des inventions, 1924[?]. Film.

Comandon, Jean, and Pierre de Fonbrune, dirs. *Mouvements des végétaux: Éclosion des fleurs, plantes grimpantes, le mécanisme des vrilles, les plantes qui dorment*. France: Laboratoire de biologie du centre de documentation Albert Kahn, 1929. Film.

Craven, Wes, dir. *Swamp Thing*. Hollywood, Calif.: Shout Factory, 1982. Film.

Dulac, Germaine, dir. *Étude Cinématographique sur une arabesque*. Paris: La Cinématèque française, 1929. Film.

———. *L'invitation au voyage*. France, 1927. Film.

———. *Thèmes et variations*. 1928. Paris: Light Cone, 2016. Film.

Epstein, Jean, dir. *La Chute de la maison Usher*. France: Films Jean Epstein, 1928. Film.

———. *Finis terrae*. Paris: Société générale de Films, 1929. Film.
———. *La Roue*. Paris: Films Abel Gance, 1923. Film.
Gance, Abel, dir. *La Fin du monde*. 1931. Neuilly-Sur-Seine: Gaumont Vidéo, 2015. Film.
Garland, Alex, dir. *Annihilation*. Hollywood, Calif.: Paramount Pictures, 2018. Film.
Honda, Ishiro, dir. *Matango: Attack of the Mushroom People*. Tokyo: Tokyo Shock, 1963. Film.
Jarman, Derek, dir. *The Garden*. London: Basilisk Communications, 1990. Film.
———. *The Tempest*. UK: Boyd's Company, 1979. Film.
Kaufman, Philip, dir. *Invasion of the Body Snatchers*. Hollywood, Calif.: Shout Factory, 1978. Film.
———. *Quills*. Hollywood, Calif.: Twentieth Century Fox, 2000. Film.
Nyby, Christian, dir. *The Thing from Another World*. Hollywood, Calif.: Warner Bros., 1951. Film.
Rollin, Jean, dir. *Les Raisins de la mort*. France: Redemption Films, 1978. Film.
Schneider, James June, dir. *Jean Epstein, Young Oceans of Cinema*. France: Bathysphère Productions, 2011. Film.
Seigel, Don, dir. *Invasion of the Body Snatchers*. Hollywood, Calif.: Olive Films, 1956. Film.
Sekely, Steve, dir. *Day of the Triffids*. Hollywood, Calif.: Allied Arts Entertainment, 1962. Film.
Shyamalan, M. Night, dir. *The Happening*. Beverly Hills, Calif.: Twentieth Century Fox, 2008. Film.
Smith, Carter, dir. *The Ruins*. Hollywood, Calif.: DreamWorks, 2008. Film.
Terranova, Fabrizio, dir. *Donna Haraway: Story Telling for Earthly Survival*. Brussels: Atelier Graphoui, 2016. Film.
Zec, Milica, and Winslow Porter, dirs. *Tree*. Brooklyn: Chicken and Egg Pictures, 2016. Virtual Reality Film.
Žižek, Slavoj. "Part One." *The Pervert's Guide to Cinema*, directed by Sophie Fiennes. London: P. Guide Ltd., 2006, DVD.

INDEX

Abildgrad, Nicolai Abraham, 65, 72
Acceptance (VanderMeer), 193–194
acculturation, 83
affect, 145; absence of, 152; desire and, 199; humans, affective possibilities for, 137; positive impact of, 169; transmitting, 136
affective identification, 179
affect theory, 206n3
agency, 5, 7, 13, 35, 59, 79, 109, 112, 153, 174, 177, 209n24; inorganic, 88; rhizomatic, 14; vegetal, 4, 15, 53, 98–99, 143, 154, 157, 186, 191, 197, 232n62
agriculture, 71, 117
Alaimo, Stacy, 7, 19, 177, 247n30
alchemy, 2, 24, 38–40, 41, 213–214n19, 214n27, 215n44, 223n45
alienation, 21, 141, 158, 146
alien seeds, 159
Allewaert, Monique, 91, 230n38, 231nn41,44, 232n62
Amad, Paula, 139, 140, 143, 239n70
Ambroise (fictional character), 130, 131
Amilec (fictional character), 77–79, 80, 81, 82, 83
Amilec ou la graine d'hommes (Tiphaigne de La Roche), 77–83
amnios, 60
analogies, 4, 87, 93, 95–96, 99–101, 224n55, 229n15; plants and, 56–63, 116, 120, 171
ancien régime bureaucracy, 79
Ania (fictional character), 180–183
De anima (Aristotle), 30
animals, 14, 23, 35, 58, 67; humans and, 208n16; nonanimal animacy, 54; plants turned into, 26; *psūchē* and, 29; souls of, 36; vegetative life and, 124
animated plants, 37, 141
Annihilation (2018), 250n57

Annihilation (VanderMeer), 250n57
anthropocentrism, 97, 207n15
anthropogenic global heating, 23
anthropomorphism, 4, 21
anti-communism, 147
Anti-Oedipus (Deleuze and Guattari), vii
arabesque, 87, 92, 96, 97, 104, 107, 108, 109, 111, 112, 128, 132–139, 197, 198, 231n43; *Cinematographic Study of an Arabesque* (1929), 134–135
Aramis, or the Love of Technology (Latour), 19
Area X (fictional place), 191–192, 194, 195, 198–200, 250n50
Ariel's Ecology (Allewaert), 91
Aristotelian ontology, 48
Aristotelian tripartite system of ensoulment, 29–30
Aristotle, 13, 28, 30–31, 212n4; minerality, 108, 213n11; on plants, 37, 48; vegetative soul and, 213nn7,8
artistic liberation, 136
assemblage, filmmaking of, 139; of human and vegetal elements, 107, 175; of inorganic elements, 99; of life, 17, 19, 21; of literary and cinematic narratives, 5, 19, 27; social, 180
atmosphere, 20, 94, 98, 104–105, 106–107, 110, 206n5, 231n44, 245n7
atomism, 41, 44, 218n67; Epicurean, 2, 24, 42; vegetal, 83
Atwood, Margaret, 63, 210n37, 222n23, 223n37, 226n95
autonomy, 84
L'Autre monde (*The Other World*) (Cyrano de Bergerac), 41–54, 63
avant-garde, 18; cinema discourse, 141; filmmakers, 116, 121; French cinema, 26, 87, 132, 146; vegetal cinema, 115
Avatar (2009), 63

269

Bacon, Francis, 34, 36, 217n51
Badmington, Neil, 155
Bannec, 130
The Baron in the Trees (Calvino), 63
Basseporte, Madeleine Françoise, ix
Baudelaire, Charles, 109–110, 133
Baudrillard, Jean, 200
Becky Driscoll (fictional character), 154–155, 156, *156*
becoming plant, 6, 22, 106, 125, 171–180, 190–201; feminist reinterpretation of, 180–190
Belfagor (Machiavelli), 105
Benharrech, Sarah, 224nn55,56,62
Benjamin, Walter, 124
Bennett, Jane, 19, 207n11, 219n81, 241n15, 244n41
Berger, John, 124
Bergson, Henri, 115, 241n15
Bernanos, Michel, 192, 196
Billy (fictional character), 150–151
biodiversity, 159
bio-economy, 173
biologist (fictional character), 193, 195, 196, 197, 199, 200
biopolitics, 163, 174, 226n87
birth, 46, 140; of biopolitical control, 62; in "The Giant Wistaria," 111; human, 60–61
Blakeney, Tyler, 219n83
Body Snatchers (Finney), 144, 149–152
botanical observation, 16
The Botanic Garden (Darwin, E.), 89
botanophilia, 93, 97
botanophobia, 93, 97, 103
Brancher, Dominique, 8, 15, 29, 30, 37; Aristotle and, 30; La Brosse and, 37, 214n32; on plant resurrection, 38
Buffon, Comte de, 58, 59–60, 224n55

cabbage, rational or angelic, 43, 46–49, 51, 52, 53, 63, 71, 232n54
Calvino, Italo, 63, 222n22
cameras: Dulac and, 118; Epstein and, 118; human-camera hybrid, 127; human perception and, 108; obscura, 90; plant motion and, 116, 125; reality and, 119; "sleep" of mimosa plants captured by, 122; temporality and, 124, 126; vitality and, 120
Cameron, James, 63
Campanella (fictional character), 50–51

Campanella, Tommaso, 41, 42, 105
capitalism, 14, 26, 153, 162, 169, 190; ambivalent force of, 164; decentralizing mechanisms of, 17; feminist critique of, 174; late, 18, 201; pod-people and, 170; rhizome and, 163; social conditions of, 147; suffering inflicted by, 187; techno-capitalist modes of identity formation, 88; unbound, 63
capitalist exploitation, 9
Cárdenas, Micha, 176
CGI. *See* computer-generated imagery
Chemical Essays (Watson), 99–103, 105
Chen, Mel, 31, 207n8
The Chernobyl Herbarium (Marder and Tondeur), 11, 22
children, 53, 80–81, 131, 140, 141, 156–157, 178
chorion, 60
La Chute de la maison Usher (1928), 127–128
cinema, 6, 118, 136, 144, 168, 238n63; allegory of, 127; avant-garde, discourse, 141; avant-garde French, 26, 87, 132, 146; avant-garde vegetal, 115; contemporary, 142; discontinuity of cinematic images, 125; Dulac and, 132–139, 141; Epstein and, 124; experimental, 120; globalized mass, 190; interwar French, 115, 123, 132; invention of, 120; metacinema, 115; plants and, 116, 130; "pure," 132, 135, 140, 142
"Cinema" ("Cinéma") (Colette), 140–141
"Cinema is a New Art Form" ("Le Cinéma est un art nouveau") (Dulac), 135–136
The Cinema Seen from Etna (*La Cinématographe vu de l'Etna*) (Epstein), 119, 125
Cinémathèque française, 127
La Cinématographe vu de l'Etna (*The Cinema Seen from Etna*) (Epstein), 119–120, 125
Cinematographic Study of an Arabesque (*Étude cinématographique sur une arabesque*) (1929), 134
Citton, Yves, 81
The City of the Sun (Campanella), 105
class, 112

Index

classification, 1, 2, 5, 18
Clemens, Johan Frederik, 65, 72
climate crisis, ix, 14, 21,175
climate emergency, 15, 176
clovers, 122–123
Colette, Sidonie-Gabrielle, 115, 139–140, 178; deanthropocentrism and, 143; flowers, symbol of, and, 141; instructional science short films and, 142
collaboration, vii–x, 11, 19, 133, 205n3, 236n28, 239n79
collectivism, 153
Collier's (magazine), 144
Comandon, Jean, 121, 122, 123, 235n9, 236n26; Epstein and, 123; time-lapse photography and, 122, 129
companionship, 7
computer-generated imagery (CGI), 7
"Contemporary Poetry" ("Poésie d'aujourd'hui") (Epstein), 123
Control (fictional character), 196
Cooper, Melinda, 173
Copernican turn, 28
La Coquille et le clergyman (1928), 132
corruption, 71, 82
cosmologies, 106, 212n1
Country of Innocence (fictional country), 70–71
critical plant studies, ix
Crosby, Sara, 97
crucifixion, 117
Cuff, Paul, 116
cultivation, 83
cultural multiplicity, 158
curiosity, 194
Cyrano de Bergerac, Savinien, 3, 24–25, 29–33, 42, 77, 218n67; Goux and, 218n62; La Brosse and, 60; materialism and, 51, 54; materiality and, 39; plants and, 48; rationality and, 71; seeds and, 43, 81; sexuality and, 217n52; vegetal modernity and, 85; works of, 41, 56, 63, 147

daisies, 122, 131, 132
Damasio, Antonio, 10
dance, 16, 49–51, 81, 133–135, 138, 178, 197
Danny Kaufman (fictional character), 161
Darmon, Jean-Charles, 42
Darwin, Charles, 120, 146, 149

Darwin, Erasmus, 88–90, 95, 228n12
Darwin, Francis, 120
Darwinism, 7
Daston, Lorraine, 9, 208n16
David Kibner (fictional character), 161
Day of the Triffids (1962), 146
deanthropocentrism, 143
deforestation, 7, 58, 222n22
degeneration, 45
dehumanization, 151
De la nature, vertu et utilité des plantes (La Brosse), 34–41, 53
Delaporte, François, 57–58, 205n2, 225n74, 229n15
Delehanty, Ann, 219n83
Deleuze, Gilles, vii–viii, x, 13, 86, 99, 163, 174–175, 190, 226n2; arabesque and, 231n43; Bergson and, 115; collaboration and, 205n3; Flaxman and, 235n12; on islands, 130; line of flight and, 180; materialism, Deleuzean, 19; minerality and, 108; Nealon and, 21; trees and, 177; vitalism and, 83
deliberation, 4
denaturalization, 30
De rerum natura (Lucretius), 17
Derrida, Jacques, 13, 210n32
Descartes, René, 41, 125, 217n51; Aristotelianism and, 29; break with Scholasticism and, 242; cosmography and, 106; mechanism of, 4
"A Descent into the Maelström" (Poe), 105
desire, 4, 8, 9, 16, 24, 25, 51, 54, 75, 93, 132, 133, 218n70; absence of, 62, 73; adapting, 21; affect and, 199; agency and, 13, 154; asexual, 167; for companionship, 7; curiosity and, 194; elimination of, 147; Epstein and, 113; erotic, 90; feminine, 94–95, 134; function of, 156; hidden, 125; human economies of, 24, 31; human paradigms of, 103; indifference to, 107; individual, 166, 190; interiorized, 91; internally generated, 79; Myers, 20; objects of, 157; plants and, 26, 49, 60, 89, 169, 171; pleasure and, 48, 176; proto, 113; queer, 2; for recognition, 6, 23; satisfaction of, 186; sexual, 138; subjectivity and, 174; transpecial atmospherics of, 92; universality of, 104; world-making, 15; Žižek and, 144

deterritorialization, x, 21, 162–164
Diderot, Denis, 10, 58–60
Digby, Kenelm, 217n51, 218n67
disembodied intelligence, 173
Dittrich, Joshua, 227n3
Doyle, Richard, 13, 177
Driesch, Hans, 241n15
Dulac, Germaine, 115, 117, 135–136, 140, 238n63, 239n70; cameras and, 118; cinema and, 132, 137–138, 141; Dulacian images, 133; Epstein and, 139, 143; experimental lms of, 116; melodrama and, 137
Dyrcona (fictional character), 41, 49–53

Earth, 34, 81, 165
ecological breakdown, 23
Ecology without Nature (Morton), 176
ecosystems, 178
electric plant, 6, 18, 26, 39, 103, 121–124, 135
electric vegetable, 120, 137; electric vegetable as monster, 139 (*see also* electric plant)
Elizabeth Driscoll (fictional character), 158, 160, *161*, 165, *166*, 167
Emerson, Ralph Waldo, 92, 102
empiricism, 34, 35
The End of the World (*La Fin du monde*) (1930), 114–115, 116, 118
Enlightenment, 5, 25, 57, 58, 70; natural history and, 76, 99; plants and, 68, 84; universalism of, 114; utopia and, 86, 222n22
ensoulment, 24, 29–30, 32, 36–37, 234n4
Epicurus, 2, 41, 43, 73, 214n19, 216n50, 217n60
Epstein, Jean, 107, 109, 115, 117, 121, 129–130; cameras and, 118; cinema and, 124; Comandon and, 123; desire and, 113; Dulac and, 139, 143; experimental films of, 116; melodrama and, 137; plants and, 127; science film and, 142; vegetal movement and, 126
erotic interest, 157
erotic power, 168
Esau, Katherine, ix
Les États et Empires de la Lune (*The States and Empires of the Moon*) (Cyrano de Bergerac), 41–49

Les États et Empires du Soleil (*The States and Empires of the Sun*) (Cyrano de Bergerac), 41, 45, 49–55
ethics, 1, 5, 14, 179, 198
Étude cinématographique sur une arabesque (*Cinematographic Study of an Arabesque*) (1929), 134
eugenics, 147
Eureka (Poe), 96
Europe, 5, 28
evolution, 7, 146
exceptionalism, 151
experimental fiction, 22, 42
Experimental Life (Mitchell), 94
Exposed (Alaimo), 177
extinction, 173
extraterrestrial origin theories, 165

fabulation, 17, 19, 20, 210n39
Faculté de médecine de Paris, 31
"The Fall of the House of Usher" (Poe), 25, 87, 95, 96, 98, 101; adaptation of, 127; inhuman forms of perception, 104; narrator of, 106; vegetal hypersensibility and, 107; vitalism and, 97
feminism, 2, 11, 87, 110–113, 172, 182, 247n30; becoming plant, feminist reinterpretation of, 26–27, 180–190; capitalism, feminist critique of, 174; new materialism, feminist, 6, 186; rhizome, feminist precursors of, 179
"Les femmes et le cinéma" ("Women and Cinema") (conference), 135–137
fiction, 6, 27, 33, 43, 45; botanical, 23; in eighteenth-century, 56; experience of plants through, 22; experimental, 22, 42; genre, 122; Gothic, 103–105, 107, 109, 110, 111, 122, 129; literary, 15; materiality and, 39; philosophical, 41; plant, 24; plant surrogates in, 16; pleasurable communication, 51; Romantic aesthetics and, 25; weird, 190, 191, 193, 249n46; world-making and, 86. *See also* science fiction; speculative fiction
film documentaire, 140
La Fin du monde (*The End of the World*) (1930), 114–115, 116, 118
Finis terrae (1929), 127, 129–130, *131*
Finney, Jack, 144, 149–151, 154, 159, 242n16; humanism and, 152; reproduction and, 168

fire, 29, 35, 42–45, 128–129, 189, 216n50
Flammarion, Camille, 114, 233n4
Flaxman, Gregory, 162, 164, 235n12
flowers, symbol of, 133–135, *134*, 137, 141
food poisoning, 158
Foucault, Michel, 5, 13, 62, 214n27
Frank, Adam, 206n3
Frederick the Great, 61
freedom, 164
fruits, 190
fungi, 95, 98, 99, 103, 193, 199
Fuseli, Henry, 104

Gaia hypothesis, 184
Gance, Abel, 114–115, 117–118, 233n4
garden, 3, 21, 31–33, 49, 112, 198, 215n32; cosmic, 35, 47; Epicurean, 73; Romantic, 86, 87, 91, 93–95, 171; self-animating, 34, 45–46, 48
Gassendi, Pierre, 33, 42
Gaycken, Oliver, 120, 234n7, 235n9
gender, viii, 6, 94, 110, 183; gender equality, 64; gender studies, 219n72, 241n11, 247n30
genetically modified organisms, 7, 245n7
Geneviève d'Arc (fictional character), 116
genre fiction, 122
Geoffrey (fictional character), 161, 167
germination, 138, 239n70
Ghosh, Amitav, 145
"The Giant Wistaria" (Gilman), 111–113
Gilles Deleuze and the Fabulation of Philosophy (Flaxman), 162
Gilman, Charlotte Perkins, 25, 87, 92, 108–113, 197
global heating, 178
globalization, 157, 162, 164
Goethe, Johann Wolfgang von, 88, 90, 95, 229n21
Goldstein, Amanda Jo, 96, 228n10, 231n39
Gothic fiction, 103–105, 107, 109, 110, 111, 122, 129
Goux, Jean-Joseph, 218n62
Greek language, 54
Guattari, Félix, vii–viii, x, 13, 86, 99, 163, 174–175, 190, 226n2; arabesque and, 231n43; collaboration and, 205n3; line of flight and, 180; trees and, 177; vitalism and, 83

Hagopian, Bill, viii
Hallé, Francis, 9, 230n22
Han Kang, 186–187, 188, 189
The Happening (2008), 147
Haraway, Donna, ix, 19, 21, 211n42, 212n50, 248n39
"The Haunted Palace" (Poe), 99
Hawthorne, Nathaniel, 182
Hayles, N. Katherine, 11, 173
"Héautontimorouménos" (Baudelaire), 110
Hegel, Georg W. F., 93, 95, 103–104, 105, 107, 108, 171, 230n35
Heidegger, Martin, 142, 235n11
Hendershot, Cindy, 155
herbs, 213n19
hermeticism, 34
heteronormativity, 90, 133, 174, 247n30; heteronormative romance, 166
heterosexuality, 95
hierarchy of beings, 42, 54
Hillairet, Prosper, 137
Hirai, Hiro, 43
Histoire naturelle, générale et particulière (Buffon), 58
Hoffman, E. T. A., 243n32
Holberg, Ludvig, 25, 57, 58, 62–74, 84, 100, 105; materialism and, 73; seeds, 82; trees and, 68; vegetal life and, 67
L'Homme-plante (*Man a Plant*) (La Mettrie), 59–60, 74, 78
Hoquet, Thierry, 224n55
Howard, Rio, 34
human body, 3, 45, 71, 138, 178, 217n55; feminine, 188; living matter of, 106; machines and, 139; maternal, 112; vegetal structures and, 61
human-camera hybrid, 127
human consciousness, 5
human contingency, 21
human culture, 22
human experience, 177
humanism, 152, 155
human nature, 147
human perception, 108
human-plant transformation, 180
humans, 75; affective possibilities for, 137; animals and, 208n16; dehumanization, 151; delusions of superiority of, 146; hierarchy of beings and, 42; plant-human mutuality, 95; plants, imagined allegiances with, vii; Poe, human life and, 98; smallness of human life, 82
human society, 47, 55, 62, 66

human subject positions, 22
Hustak, Carla, ix
hyperobjects, 192

imagination, 7, 9, 15, 30, 41, 49, 52–53, 57, 81, *105*, 140–141, 170, 219n82
immobility, 75
immortality, 39, 218n67, 233n4
impassivity, 5, 6
individualism, 150
inhuman form of perception, 104, 235n10; camera as, 125–126, 129; ecological experience as, 195–196; queered perception as, 115; plant sensorium as, 29, 75–76, 100–101, 105
In-hye (fictional character), 187
inorganic life, 13, 96, 99, 103, 104, 119, 125, 227n3; in Deleuze and Guattari, 83, 175, 226n2; of machines, 118; vegetality as, 26, 57, 83–84, 88, 113, 137, 229n15
inorganic matter, 108
intelligence, 10, 172, 173
The Intelligence of a Machine (*L'Intelligence d'une machine*) (1946), 124, 125
interconnectedness, 91
interwar French cinema, 115, 123, 132
Invasion of the Body Snatchers (1956), 144–146, 147, 156, *156*, 200; Badmington and, 155; dehumanization and, 151; fragility and, 154; heteronormative romance and, 166; hopeful ending of, 153; materiality of, 152; plants, productivity of and, 148
Invasion of the Body Snatchers (1978), 144–146, 147, 165, *166*, 169, 200; biodiversity and, 159; dehumanization and, 151; globalization and, 157; globalized mass cinema and, 190; individual desire and, 166; materiality of, 152; plants, productivity of, 148; simulacra and, 162
Invitation to the Voyage (*L'Invitation au voyage*) (1927), 132–135
Irigaray, Luce, ix, 245n8
irony, 148
irrationality, 71
islands, 130
Ivanoff, Vassili, 116

Jack Bellicec (fictional character), 165
Jahren, Hope, viii–ix, 9

Jardin du roy pour la culture des plantes médicinales (Scalberge), *32*
Jean-Marie (fictional character), 130–131, *131*
Jean Novalic (fictional character), 116, 117
Jenkins, Jennifer, 243n32
The Journey of Niels Klim to the World Underground (Holberg), 63–74, 105
Jussieu, Bernard de, 57

Kahn, Didier, 34, 215n44
Kant, Immanuel, 17
Kaufman, Philip, 151–152, 157, 160, 162, 164, 242n16, 244n46; globalized mass cinema and, 190; race and, 158; Siegel and, 165
Keenleyside, Heather, 223n38
kelp, 130–131, *131*, 132
"A Kriya for Cultivating Your Inner Plant" (Myers), 178

Lab Girl (Jahren), viii, 9
La Brosse, Guy de, 3, 24–25, 29, 30–34, 38, 52, 53, 199, 224n56; Brancher and, 37, 214n32; divine rationality and, 36; individualized plants and, 49; on plants, faculties of, 35; plants and, 54, 76; spectral plant and, 39; vegetal modernity and, 85
La Mettrie, Julien Offray de, 59–60, 61, 70, 74, 78, 84
Langlois, Henri, 127
Latour, Bruno, 19
League of Nations, 117
Leclerc, Georges-Louis, 58
Le Guin, Ursula K., 63, 88, 183–186, 211n43, 247n21
liberalism, 173
libertine botany, 3, 18, 24, 28–29, 31–34, 48, 51, 60, 73, 89, 213n15, 219n72
libertine materialism, 33, 41, 89
libertines, 3, 24, 29, 41, 47, 213n15, 218n65, 224n56
light, 76
liminal consciousness, 182, 183
Limon, John, 96–97
limpid object of knowledge, 5
line of flight, 180
literary fiction, 15
literary production, 16
logging, 7

Index

Louis XIII (king), 31
Lovecraft, Howard Phillips, 249n46
Lovelock, James, 184
Lucretius, 17, 43, 216n50, 217nn52,60
Lukács, Georg, 227n3

Machiavelli, Niccolò, 105
machines, 139, 143
MaddAddam trilogy (Atwood), 63, 226n95
Madeline Usher (fictional character), 98, 103, 108, 109, 110, *130*; violence and, 128–129
Man a Plant (*L'Homme-plante*) (La Mettrie), 59–60, 74, 78
Mancuso, Stefano, 10, 172–173, 176, 197
Marder, Michael, ix, 11–12, 13, 14, 22, 108, 188, 213n7; time-lapse photography and, 142–143
Marey Institute, 120
Margulis, Lynn, 184
Marvell, Andrew, 185, 218n71
Marx, Jacques, 79, 80
masculinity, 156
materialism, 2, 8, 58–59, 241n15; Cyrano de Bergerac and, 51, 54; Deleuzean, 19; eighteenth-century, 60; feminist new, 186; French materialist thought, 3; Holberg and, 73; La Brosse and, 34–35; libertine, 33–34, 41; new materialist thought, 177; new and old, 8; scientific, 60; Tiphaigne de La Roche and, 75; politically oriented, 178; vital, 131
materiality, 32, 152; fiction and, 39; nature of, 74; plants and, 38; Poe and, 97; poetics of, 33
maternal human body, 112
mathematization, 174
Mather, Cotton, 96
Matthew Bennell (fictional character), 158, 164, *166*, 167–168
McCarthyism, 146
McClintock, Barbara, ix
melodrama, 137
Mémoires pour servir à l'histoire d'un genre de polypes d'eau douce, à bras en forme de cornes (Trembley), 59–60
Merian, Maria Sibylla, ix
mesh, 13, 210n33
metacinema, 115; plants as metacinema, 118, 127, 129, 137, 139

metamorphosis, 52, 181–182, 187, 229n21, 247n21
metaphysics, 11, 100; Marder and, 213n7
Michaud, Philippe-Alain, 122, 236n30
A Midsummer Night's Dream (Shakespeare), 156, 157
mildew, 95
Miles Bennell (fictional character), 149, 150–151, 153, 154–155, 157
Miller, T. S., 7, 146
mimesis, 150
mimosa plants, 122, 126–127
minerality, 108, 213n11
minerals, 35, 124
Mitchell, Robert, 94
Mitman, Gregg, 9, 208n16
modernity, 2, 62, 117, 174; early, 8, 54; early modern cosmologies, 212n1; Han and, 189; imperatives of, 12; life under, 6; plants and, 4; rise of, 23; vegetal, 6, 85
mold, 95
monism, 100
monsters: humanoid, 170; monster plants, 146, 147
La Montagne morte de la vie (*The Other Side of the Mountain*) (Bernanos), 192, 196, 200
Montaigne, Michel de, 10, 37, 213n19
Moretti, Franco, 145
mortality, 9, 15, 47, 151
Morton, Timothy, 4, 13, 148, 170, 210n33
mothers, 46, 60–61, 111–113, 180–181, 183, 196–197, 198
motion, of plants, 116, 123, 125
"MS. Found in a Bottle" (Poe), 105
Myers, Natasha, ix, 19–20, 178; anthropomorphism and, 21

Nancy Bellicec (fictional character), 165
Napierkowska, Stasia de, 138–139
narrative, 19; conventional, 136; speculative narratives, 128; structures, 138
natural history, 10, 69, 76, 96–108
natural philosophy, 30, 76, 91, 171
Nealon, Jeffrey T., 13–14, 18, 23, 163, 169, 177; Deleuze and, 21; rhizome and, 175, 176; on vegetal life, 201
neoliberalism, 163, 170
neo-Platonism, vii

New France, 43, 44
Niels Klim (fictional character), 62–63, 64, 66–67, 68–71
Nimoy, Leonard, 161
nonrealist writing, 16, 18, 145

Omega (Flammarion), 114, 233n4
ontology, 178; Aristotelian ontology, 48; divisions, ontological, 59; dominant ontological paradigm, 57; Poe, ontological vision of, 100; vegetal, 35
organicism, 19, 87, 88, 96, 103, 135–136, 169, 175, 179
origins of life, 79
Osden (fictional character), 184–185
The Other Side of the Mountain (La Montagne morte de la vie) (Bernanos), 192, 196, 200
The Other World (L'Autre monde) (Cyrano de Bergerac), 41–54, 63
Ouessant, 130, 131
"The Oval Portrait" (Poe), 127
Ovid, 52, 53, 180

pain, 75
painting, 128
palingenesis, 39, *40*
Paracelsianism, 34, 41, 43
Paragon (Rath), 190–191, *191*
paranoia, 172
Pascal, Blaise, 184
passivity, xi, 61, 77, 83, 133, 160, 181, 196; apparent passivity of the plant, 4, 7; radical passivity of the plant, 197
patriarchy, 90, 111, 182, 201; structures of, 133; violence of, 187
Pensées (Pascal), 184
Perry, Denis R., 110
Pfeffer, Wilhelm, 120
pharmaceutical industry, 162
Phenomenology of Spirit (Hegel), 93
philosophy, 16; Aristotelian philosophy, 28; natural, 30, 76, 91, 171; philosophical fictions, 41
photography. *See* time-lapse photography
photosynthesis, 93, 194, 197
"Photosynthesis" (Myers), 20
Phytocene, 20
Phytologia (Darwin, E.), 90
phytosphere, 186, 248n33
Pintard, René, 31, 32

plant biologists, viii, 8, 9, 10, 172, 130n22; plant biologist as fictional character, 193–197
plant blindness, 1, 205n1
plant body, 3, 135
plant fiction, 24; speculative, 8, 18, 57–58, 229n14
plant horror, 6, 7, 18, 26, 87, 88, 98, 139–143, 144–169, 189, 241n8; literary roots of, 148; paranoia and, 172; plant indifference and, 171
planthropology, 20
plant-human mutuality, 95
plant indifference, 171
plant intelligence, 10, 172
plant-machine, 143
plant-made geology, 20
plant matter, 15
plant perception, 100, 102
plant power, ix, 1, 4, 5, 6, 7, 11, 19, 26, 30, 32, 33, 38, 43, 46–47, 48, 49, 54, 58, 62–74, 80–84, 90, 97–98, 104, 110, 113, 118, 157, 167, 164, 168, 169, 177, 190, 191, 197, 229n16, 230n22, 244n41
plants, xi, 35, 84; alienation and, 158; ambiguous status of, 14; animals, turned into, 26; animated, 37, 141; Aristotelian philosophy and, 28; Aristotle on, 37; becoming, 27; cinema and, 116, 130; Cyrano de Bergerac and, 41–54; denaturalizing, 139; desire and, 26, 49, 60, 89, 169, 171; Enlightenment and, 56–63, 84; Epstein and, 127; ethical subjecthood of, 179; experience of, x, 22; extinction of, 173; fiction, plant surrogates in, 16; human-plant transformation, 180; humans, imagined allegiances with, vii; immortality of, 39; La Brosse and, 34–41, 49, 54, 76; liminal movement of, 123; liveliness of, 16; materiality and, 38; modernity and, 4; monster, 146, 147; motion of, 119, 123, 125; nonsexual quality of, 218n71; passivity and, 7; personification of, 179. *See also specific plants*
plant "striving," 147, 150, 154, 155, 168, 212n5
plant studies, 8–15, 179
plant theory, 23, 176, 179, 180
Plant Theory (Nealon), 13, 23, 175–177
Plant-Thinking (Marder), 11, 13

Plato, 29, 31
pleasure, 75; desire and, 48, 176; new experiences of, 132; pleasurable communication, 51
pod-people (fictional people), 150, 151, 161–162; capitalism and, 170; without emotion, 152; homogenization brought about by, 154; mortality of, 151
Poe, Edgar Allan, 5, 25, 26, 63, 87, 95, 106, 110, 112; adaptation of stories by, 127; arabesque and, 87, 92, 96, 97, 104, 107, 108, 109, 231n43; Comandon and, 122; Epstein on, 107; Hegel and, 105; human life and, 98; materiality and, 97; ontological vision of, 100; Romanticism and, 171; vegetality and, 96; works cited by, 99, 101–102
"Poésie d'aujourd'hui" ("Contemporary Poetry") (Epstein), 123
poetry, 90
Pollan, Michael, 208n18
polyps, 59–60
popular science books, 8
posthumanism, 6, 11, 27, 88, 106, 148, 172–173, 180, 199–201
Potuans, 66–71, 73–74
Potuan society, 64, 67, 68, 69
power, 68, 81
productivity, 148
Professor Budlong (fictional character), 149
psūchē, 13, 24, 29, 48, 121, 164
Pygmalion myth, 157

Quand l'esprit vient aux plantes (Brancher), 29
quantification, 174
quantum theory, 197, 199, 237n40
queer, 133, 135, 138, 174, 176, 179, 183, 227n5; desire, 2, 131; ecology, 11, 209n24; fiction, 87; public, 133; sexuality, 49; subject, 27, 177
Questions relatives à l'agriculture et à la nature des plantes (Tiphaigne de La Roche), 74–77

race, 112, 150, 158, 169, 241n8; racial diversity, 159
"Rappaccini's Daughter" (Hawthorne), 182
Rath, Jessica, 190–191, *191*, 220n89

rationality, 29, 67, 69; Cyrano de Bergerac and, 71; divine rationality, La Brosse and, 36
rats, 158
reality, 119
reason, 5, 13, 29, 48, 58, 62, 64, 67–74, 77, 79, 83, 84, 156
recognition: desire for, 6, 23; mutual, 153
religion, 117
reproduction, 29, 30, 48, 54, 60, 62, 74, 77–78, 103, 147–150, 152, 154–156, 157, 225n74; Finney and, 168; masculinity and, 156; mimesis and, 150
resurrection, 38–39
reterritorialization, 14, 21, 162
rhizome, x, 13, 86, 99, 219n80; capitalism and, 163; feminist precursors of, 179; Nealon and, 175–177; residual squishiness of, 197
rhythm, 122, 123, 132, 134–135, 137
Richter, Anne, 88, 180–183, 186, 187, 192, 247n21
Ripe (Rath), 190–191, 220n89
Ritterbush, Philip, 212n4
Roche, Bruno, 47, 218n63
rocks, 132
Roderick Usher (fictional character), 98, 103, 108, 109, 110, 127, 128, *130*
Roi, Jardin du, 31–32, 38
Romanticism, 4, 25, 87, 88–96, 97, 103, 228n10; classical understanding of, 90; Poe and, 97–99, 171; Romantic vitalism, 88; vegetal life and, 6
Romantic plant, the, 88, 91, 92, 96
roots, 59
Rostand, Edmond, 32
Rothman, Joshua, 251n62
Rousseau, Jean-Jacques, 12–13, 88–89
The Ruins (2008), 147

Saint-Pierre, Jacques-Henri Bernardin de, 88, 89, 228n9
San Francisco, 152, 158, 160, 165
Saul Evans (fictional character), 193–194
Scalberge, Federic, 32
Schussler, Elisabeth E., 205n1
science fiction, 19, 24, 63, 145, 180, 233n3, 235n12, 241n9; Atwood on, 210n37
science film, 132, 140, 142, 235n9
scientific objectivity, 9

sci-phi, 19
Screening Space (Sobchack), 152
Secrets of Nature (film series), 121
Sederholm, Carl H., 110
Sedgwick, Eve Kosofsky, 206n3
seeds, 6, 43–45, 79–82, 95, 126, 193, 216n50; alien, 151, 159; types of, 77
segregation, 241n8
self-animating, 129
self-realization, 182
self-sufficiency, 70, 76
Senebier, Jean, 92–93
sensations, 75
"The Sensitive-Plant" (Shelley), 93–96, 104, 107
sensorium, 123
sexual difference, 90, 110
sexuality, 53, 110, 156; asexual desire in, 167; Cyrano de Bergerac and, 217n52; heterosexuality and, 95; nonsexual quality of plants, 218n71; sexual desire and, 138; sexual potency and, 155; sexual reproductive power in, 217n55; vegetal, 47
Shakespeare, William, 156, 157
shapelessness, 219n80
Shatz, Adam, x
Shelley, Percy Bysshe, 90, 93–96, 99, 102, 104, 107
Siegel, Don, 151–152, 153, 156; Kaufman, P., and, 165
simulacra, 149, 162
"The Sleep of Plants" ("Un Sommeil de plante") (Richter), 180–183
slow-motion photography, 125
Smith, F. Percy, 121, 138
Smith, Herbert F., 96, 103
Sobchack, Vivian, 152
sociability, 73
social Darwinism, 149
social order, 73
Socrates, demon of, 41, 46, 47
"Sonnet—To Science" (Poe), 96
souls, 30, 46; of animals, 36; fire and, 44; Platonic immaterial, 31; vegetative soul, 24, 29, 31, 48, 121, 213n7
Southern Reach trilogy (VanderMeer), 191–201
sovereignty, 14, 61–62, 64, 69, 74, 81, 83–84, 178
Spalank (fictional country), 70–74
Spallanzani, Lazzaro, 92, 99, 100

spectacle, 115, 117
spectral plant, 39
speculation, 1, 15, 34; inspiring, 82; realm of, 55; turn to, 163; utopian, 54
speculative fiction, 7, 11, 16; hierarchy of beings and, 42; new traction gained by, 19; Poe and, 26
speculative narratives, 128
speculative plant fiction, 8, 18, 57–58, 229n14
spontaneous generation, 30
standardization, 151, 164, 169
Star Trek (television series), 161
Star Wars (1977), 157
The States and Empires of the Moon (*Les États et Empires de la Lune*) (Cyrano de Bergerac), 41–49
The States and Empires of the Sun (*Les États et Empires du Soleil*) (Cyrano de Bergerac), 41, 45, 49–55
Staying with the Trouble (Haraway), 19, 21, 211n42, 212n50, 248n39
storytelling, 19, 21
structural inequality, viii
subjectivity, 14, 99, 178, 196, 197; collapse of, 179, 184, 188; desire and, 174; vegetal, 170
surveillance, 158
Sutherland, Donald, 162
Swamp Thing (1982), 147
Sylva sylvarum (Bacon), 36
Symmes, John Cleves, 105

taxonomy, 18, 105
Taylor, Matthew, 97, 106
technology, 48, 157
temporality, 125; cameras and, 124, 126; nonhuman temporal register, 120. See also time-lapse photography
Terranova, Fabrizio, 211n42
Themes and Variations (*Thèmes et variations*) (1929), 134
Theophrastus, 30
The Thing from Another World (1951), 146
Thinking with Animals (Daston and Mitman), 9
Thoreau, Henry David, 92, 102, 192
A Thousand Plateaus (Deleuze and Guattari), 174–175, 190, 226n2, 231n43
time-lapse photography, 16, 22, 26, 235n9; Comandon and, 122, 129; interest in, 115; Marder and, 142–143

Tinguely, Frédéric, 217n53
Tiphaigne de La Roche, Charles-François, 25, 51, 57, 58, 62, 74–85, 102; imaginary worlds of, 81; materialism and, 75; seeds, 82; vegetality and, 77
"To His Coy Mistress" (Marvell), 185–186
Tolkien, J. R. R., 63
Tondeur, Anaïs, 11, 22, 209n24
Torero-Ibad, Alexandra, 42, 44
totalitarianism, 146
transcendental empiricism, 17
transcendentalist authors, 92
transcorporeality, 7
trees, 20, 64, 66, 67, 73, 119, 177; erotic life of, 53; Holberg and, 68; images of, 128
Trembley, Abraham, 59–60
Tsing, Anna, 19
Turvey, Malcolm, 238n51

umbilical cord, 60
universalism, 114
"Un Sommeil de plante" ("The Sleep of Plants") (Richter), 180–183
Urban, Charles, 121
Urban Sciences (film series), 121
utopia: Earth as anti-, 81; Enlightenment and, 86; human society and, 66; speculation, 54; vegetal, 62, 63–74

VanderMeer, Jeff, 191–201, 249n47, 250n57
"Vaster Than Empires and More Slow" (Le Guin), 63, 183–186
vegetal alterity, 103, 182
vegetal atomism, 83
vegetal bodies, 3
vegetal communication, 53
vegetal cylinders, 74, 77, 82–83
vegetal dimension, vii
vegetal dystopias, 62, 63, 83–84, 168, 187
vegetal eugenics, 147
vegetal generation, 48
vegetal growth, 168
vegetal horror, 26
vegetal hypersensibility, 107
vegetal immobility, 127
vegetal interconnectedness, 185
vegetality, 2, 16, 91; Brancher and, 8; inorganic function of, 26; mediation performed by, 3, 6, 38, 90, 103, 107, 127, 142–143, 200; notions of, 83; Poe and, 96; speculative narratives and, 128; Tiphaigne de La Roche and, 77; violence and, 111
vegetalization, 108
vegetal life, 102, 126, 154, 201; Epicurean logic of, 73; Holberg and, 67; Romanticism and, 6; sovereignty and, 69; theorists of, 90
vegetal modernity, 6, 85
vegetal movement, 59, 126, 145
vegetal ontology, 35
vegetal ornament, 227n3
vegetal physiology, 61
vegetal postures, 51
vegetal potential, 21
vegetal *psūchē*, 24, 29, 30–31, 164, 213n7
vegetal reason, 74
vegetal rhythms, 137
vegetal sentience, 25, 26, 96–108, 109, 113, 189, 229n16
vegetal sexuality, 47, 53, 89, 156, 221n12, 227n5
vegetal simulacra, 149
vegetal sociability, 25, 55
vegetal society, 63–74
vegetal soul. *See* vegetal *psūchē*
vegetal subjectivity, 11, 36, 62, 153, 170, 174, 179, 180, 182–183, 187, 188; as biopolitical, 17–18, 163, 173
vegetal utopias, 25, 26, 53–54, 56–57, 62–74
vegetal vitality, 57
The Vegetarian (Han), 186–190
vegetative life, 124
vegetative soul. *See* vegetal *psūchē*
Vibrant Matter (Bennett), 241n15
Vincent, Philippe, 80
Viola, Alessandra, 10, 172–173, 176, 197
violence, 107, 143, 189; alienation and, 21; capacity for, 105; forms of, 74, 84; La Brosse and, 35; Madeline Usher and, 128–129; of modern economic systems, 4; natural world and, 101; of patriarchy, 187; of spirit, 93; vegetality and, 111
Virgil, 52
virtual reality, 190, 249n46
visual imaging, 22
vitalism, 5, 25, 83; "The Fall of the House of Usher" and, 96–108; inorganic, 102, 175; Romantic vitalism, 86–88; scientific theories of, 108

vitality, 5, 54, 77, 169; authentic, 150; cameras and, 120; indifferent, of vegetal life, 113; vegetal, 57
vital materialism, 131, 231n39, 241n15
vortexes, 49–50, 81, 219n76
vulnerability, 2, 4, 11, 14, 15, 23, 61, 67, 79, 82, 95, 106, 143, 153, 159, 170, 173, 186, 201

Die Wahlverwandtschaften (Goethe), 90
Walden (Thoreau), 192
Wall-Romana, Christophe, 124, 126, 129, 131
Wandersee, James H., 205n1
Warburg, Aby, 236n30
Watson, Richard, 99–103, 105; plant perception and, 102; vegetality and, 103
weeds, 95, 230n35, 231n29
weird fiction, 190, 191, 193, 249n46
Whitby (fictional character), 195
wildlife, 178
Williams, Tami, 132–133
wisteria plants, 111–112, 197
womb, 60

women, 52, 160, 177; domestic existence of, 133; feminine desire, 94–95, 134; feminine human body, 188; norms of, 174
"Women and Cinema" ("Les femmes et le cinéma") (conference), 135–137
The Word for World Is Forest (Le Guin), 185
Wordsworth, William, 90
workplace, 123
World 4470 (fictional world), 183–186
worldless plants, 13–14
world-making, 15, 86, 165, 174
World War II, 115, 118, 222n22
Worringer, Wilhelm, 227n3

xenophobia, 111

"The Yellow Wallpaper" (Gilman), 110–111
Yeong-hye (fictional character), 186–188, 189

Zamar (fictional character), 81
Žižek, Slavoj, 144
zoomorphic qualities, 4
zoophyte, 59, 212n4

NATANIA MEEKER is an associate professor of French and comparative literature at the University of Southern California. She published *Voluptuous Philosophy: Literary Materialism in the French Enlightenment* with Fordham University Press in 2006. Her research and teaching interests include animated and animating plants, vegetal ontologies, plant art and media, materialisms old and new, feminist theory and thought, and the Enlightenment, broadly conceived. She was named Chevalier de l'Ordre des Palmes Académiques in 2017.

ANTÓNIA SZABARI is an associate professor of French and comparative literature at the University of Southern California. Her scholarly interests include early modern literature and political thought, plant studies, history of botany, and speculative fiction. She is the author of *Less Rightly Said: Scandals and Readers in Sixteenth-Century France* (Stanford University Press, 2009).

www.ingramcontent.com/pod-product-compliance
Lightning Source LLC
Chambersburg PA
CBHW030436300426
44112CB00009B/1022